The

CRISIS *in*

CRITICISM

The

CRISIS *in* CRITICISM

Theory,

Literature,

and Reform

in English Studies

William E. Cain

The Johns Hopkins University Press
BALTIMORE AND LONDON

Originally published, 1984
Johns Hopkins Paperbacks edition, 1987

The Johns Hopkins University Press
701 West 40th Street
Baltimore, Maryland 21211
The Johns Hopkins Press Ltd., London

Library of Congress Cataloging-in-Publication Data

Cain, William E., 1952–
  The crisis in criticism.

  Includes index.
  1. Criticism—United States—History—20th century.
2. English literature—History and criticism—Theory, etc.
I. Title.
PN94.C3 1984 820'.9   83–24400
ISBN 0–8018–3191–1
ISBN 0–8018–3472–4 (paperback)

TO MY PARENTS
Francis W. Cain and Mary T. Cain

What aims, claims, and conceptions justify the importance we ascribe to "English"? We need to be able to answer.

F. R. Leavis, *Nor Shall My Sword: Discourses on Pluralism, Compassion, and Social Hope*

Contents

Preface

A book has to be an experiment . . . on yourself. I think that a book is part of your own life, of your own transformation, and of course a book is addressed to other people, it's supposed to be read by other people. But the fact that you write the book has its effect on you. It's hard work to write a book. Why do you do that? I think the reason is that, first, there is pleasure in discovering new things, and also there is the fact that you work on yourself, you metamorphose, you transform yourself by writing. And that's the reason it's worthwhile to do such a strange thing as writing a book.

Michel Foucault

This book is a statement of my views on a number of problems in literary theory and contemporary criticism. But it is also—as any theoretical study must be—a progress report, a record of inquiry that has not yet concluded. In a sense, a book on "theory" cannot really end. At a certain point, work on it ceases, even though one continues to think critically and skeptically about the problems—and the solutions—that the book contains.

One of the depressing facts about literary theory as it is now being written is that it is becoming increasingly *less* critical, less skeptical, about itself and its reason for being. The theory industry grinds along, and books, articles, and symposia multiply, but much of the material seems arid and unreal, out of phase with concrete issues in critical practice and pedagogy, and out of touch with human needs and interests. There are so many theorists, all of whom are devotedly pursuing the latest fads and processing the most current methodologies, that questions of value and significance are rarely asked. To ask such questions would, one feels, disrupt the marketplace, where reputations are established and inertly accepted, and where there is little time for reflection upon the point and purpose of theoretical labor.

In writing this book, I have often found myself growing impatient with theory—though I know it must continue—and with the self-imposed isolation of most theorists. But I do not mean to suggest that since theory has come close to exhausting itself, we should now return to the old ways, to "close readings" of the "great tradition" coupled with a distaste for any form of literary theory whatsoever. Such a return to "basics," as it is sometimes called, would be mistaken, and would only perpetuate the confusion and disorder that have plagued the curriculum for decades. "Close reading" is essential; we cannot do without it. But it should not be taken as the ground for the discipline, because it excludes too much and devalues too many other kinds of skills— skills in historical analysis and research, for example—that students clearly need.

But to urge that we should not "return" to the basics is somewhat misleading. It is not really a question of returning to a job we have left behind, for the the boom in literary theory has influenced and altered the curriculum only in marginal ways. Our discipline remains fundamentally intact, with minor adjustments and shifts in emphasis. Deconstruction helps to supplement techniques of close reading; Derrida, Barthes, Foucault, and others are added to the list of figures examined in "theory and criticism" courses; a few inter-disciplinary programs have emerged—this is about all we can point to. The basic shape of English studies is unchanged, and its shortcomings and deficiencies remain unexplored and unarticulated.

There is a woeful lack of system, order, and coherence in English studies, a lack that usually proves shocking to those who teach in other departments. In our discipline, a student can jump from contemporary fiction to Shakespeare's comedies to American realism and then to other areas equally disconnected from one another. We do not give our students basic tools or compelling guidelines for understanding and assessing the history of literary study. Nor do we provide students with a real feeling for continuities and relationships among writers, periods, texts, and interpretive procedures. All too often, students do not succeed in grasping a structural coherence to their work in literature and criticism; in its own right, each course seems stimulating and enjoyable, but it does not appear to help bind together the courses that preceded it, nor does it lead, in a logical way, to those that will follow. Despite all the work that has been undertaken in theory, we do not have much intelligent planning in the structure of the discipline. Our thinking stays basically "New Critical" in its orientation, and most courses remain keyed to explicating some part of the canon. We train students to be adept and sensitive "close readers"—an important task, to be sure, and one that should never be discounted—without enabling them to make the crucial transition to more general types of judgment and discrimination, and to difficult problems in both historical research and abstract thought.

Of course nearly everyone agrees that reforms must be instituted, and we have many recommendations for repairing our damaged state. But these recommendations are often superficial, or else they jar against (and are defeated by) political and economic realities—the fear, for instance, of jeopardizing enrollments. We still need, even in the face of hard political and economic facts, to look critically at the discipline and consider how it can and should be revised. As recently as several years ago, it seemed that such a revaluation was about to occur, as the traditionalists battled with the theorists, and as advocates of determinate meaning such as E. D. Hirsch confronted post-structuralists such as J. Hillis Miller. But it quickly became evident that while these debates were heated, they did not unsettle the discipline or provoke a sustained critique: the antagonists shared too much common ground. And the commodification of criticism proceeds so rapidly that the issues were no sooner defined than the various theorists and critics themselves became objects of study, each with a group of explicators and celebrants.

This largely explains the proliferation of pseudo-projects—the elaborate and glowing expositions of Derrida, the earnest if misguided attempts to make literary study "Marxist" in its bearing, the jargon-filled inquiries into the densest meditations of Lacan. I hesitate to press this point, because it threatens to smack of the intellectual intolerance that I criticize in segments of the academic world elsewhere in this book. But what I am trying to call attention to is the way in which literary theory and criticism tend to move *laterally*. There is not a steady concentration on a central set of critical and pedagogical concerns, but rather a constant movement away from the center, as commentaries on commentaries multiply.

A major task for theory at the present time is to initiate and encourage the re-examination of English studies. We need to use and draw upon theory to specify the aims of work in English, the purposes of teaching, the skills and values that we seek to transmit in pedagogy and research. When an English teacher/critic is asked to "justify" what he or she does, he or she generally fares badly. The mixture of anger, perplexity, and embarrassment, one that conceals both arrogance and uncertainty, is painful to witness. Theory should force us to undertake acts of self-scrutiny and justification and should enable us to say precisely what we do, why it is important, and what makes it cohere.

Theory can accomplish a great deal when it is properly undertaken, but it also has its dangers, as I have already begun to indicate. In writing a book on theory, one can be enticed into giving careless approval to what's new and thus easily sanction theorists or doctrines that appear at first sight to answer all the troubling problems. One also risks, I think, a lack of perspective; in focusing on theory and criticism, it is important to weigh one's enthusiasms—Derrida or Foucault, for example—in the balance with Blackmur or Leavis, or, even better, with Emerson or William James. I believe that contemporary theorists and critics have much to teach us, but I have also tried to be critical of them when criticism is warranted, and to place and judge them. I would never deny how much Derrida and, even more, Foucault have taught me or seek to diminish the challenge they pose to prevailing customs and interpretive rituals. But I also believe it is necessary to retain a sense of proportion and to avoid the temptation to allow one's admiration for these theorists (and their many disciples and commentators) to skew one's vision of what truly matters in criticism and pedagogy.

There are two more pressing dangers in writing about "theory." The first is stylistic, the second is political. A disturbing trend in literary theory has been the emphasis on "creative" style. Geoffrey Hartman, Harold Bloom, and others are right to contend that criticism and theory are "creative" forms, involving an exploratory and meditative relation to the subject at hand. But "creativity" should not mean writing for a coterie. Theorists who write in a so-called "creative" style nearly always write ineptly and obscurely, and unfortunately they are not obliged to do better. As academic celebrities, they have gotten "beyond" serious criticism and standards, and so the army of explicators rushes to admire and unravel their knotted prose even though it does not merit such close attention. Theoretical writing of this kind exhibits a failure of self-consciousness (despite advertising itself as self-conscious in the extreme), and it also reflects a fear of making statements that someone might actually absorb and evaluate.

Theorists should of course work "creatively," but they should do so in a style that readers can engage. This seems to me the best way to speak to theoretical, professional, and institutional issues and to try to stimulate intelligent discussion of them, and I have therefore attempted to write in a style that is accessible. I am less confident, however, that I have discovered the best way of dealing with "politics" and stimulating discussion of that. The relation between politics and academic work (teaching, research, curriculum planning, and so forth) is, for me, essential to ponder and act upon yet very hard to understand and resolve satisfactorily. As Fredric Jameson, Terry Eagleton, Richard Ohmann, and others have argued, there is a "politics of interpretation," and it is evident in matters that range from one's choice of a reading list to one's willingness to accept government funding for research. Politics cannot be avoided in literary study, and we should not pretend otherwise. All of us need to be aware of authority, power, institutional constraints, and the other political facts of life that shape our behavior.

But it is difficult to know just how to incorporate "politics" in teaching and research in an intelligent fashion. At times one wishes one could omit the word and keep the meaning, in part because labeling an issue "political" is often a sign in contemporary theory that thoughtful analysis has been abandoned. The political debates in contemporary theory are intense, even frenzied, but not very productive or precise, and they often appear to be generated by academics who believe they are on the front lines of ideological warfare. Like F. R. Leavis, I believe that politics is crucial for the teacher and critic, and that

> the tendency of our civilization that is in question must be of the utmost concern to everyone who thinks literature really matters. That anyone seriously preoccupied with the problems of education, and of literary criticism as a function that can enlist the powers of a responsible mind, can *not* see the given tendency as a major fact, exacting attention every day, seems to me impossible.[1]

But again like Leavis, I want to add that such a concern should not require that the teacher/critic enlist in a particular party or uphold a political platform. "What is immediately in place," he states, "is to insist that one does not take one's social and political responsibilities the less seriously because one is not quick to see salvation in a formula or in any simple creed."[2]

I cannot say that this view always satisfies me, and it is certainly open to the charge of being vague and elusive. But what it accomplishes is turning our emphasis away from political rhetoric and towards concrete work. Our politics of interpretation needs to be made more tactical, situational, pragmatic, and attentive to the tasks we are equipped to perform well. We can best make political differences, and keep teaching and criticism in contact with political concerns, through vigilant practice, not theory alone. I have profited from recent Marxist theory and deconstruction, but the desire for political change will not be satisfied by embracing these or any other "radical" positions that literary critics and theorists have advanced. Change can occur, and it is our responsibility to strive for it, but it is a slow and steady process and demands real dedication to the small but significant problems encountered in daily work, work that "theory" at the present time all too rarely affects. Slogans and position-taking are gratifying, but the basic tasks of political reformation lie elsewhere.

In our books on theory, in criticism, and in teaching our classes, we might well attend to one of the central "rules" that Foucault has outlined for the intellectual and philosopher. This is "to interpolate, to intervene and ask people: What are you doing? What are you thinking? Why do you think that? Why do you behave that way?"[3] These are questions that bear inescapably on politics, but their analytical edge is not blunted by misapplied political terms. It is this group of questions that I try to keep in mind in my study of contemporary theory and criticism, and to which I feel teachers and students should commit themselves.

In this book I focus on the critical, theoretical, and pedagogical concerns of the present—the influence of new "continental" terms and models, the question of the discipline's "authority" and "objectivity," the relation between theory and practice, and the continuing efforts to move "beyond" New Critical formalism. This emphasis on the contemporary state of English studies is evident in part one, where I examine the work of E. D. Hirsch, J. Hillis Miller, and Stanley Fish, all of whom have proposed theories—determinate meaning, deconstruction, and reader-response—that have won many supporters and modified current practice. What makes these theorists compelling for my purposes is the relation between their theoretical views and their attitudes towards the discipline and classroom practice. Hirsch seeks to stabilize English studies and re-locate it on more authoritative (and defensible) ground. Miller and Fish, on the other hand, claim to overturn the very assumptions upon which the discipline is founded—an "objective" text, an author who shapes meaning and thereby controls our response, a reader subservient to the text and mindful of New Critical decorum. Yet these theorists are closer to one another than this account implies. Hirsch strives to protect the discipline (and particularly the "authority" of the teacher) against threats—structuralism, post-structuralism, deconstruction—that impinge from "the outside"; but the major threat to the discipline, and to the stability Hirsch desires, comes instead, I shall argue, from the subversive insights Hirsch continually registers and then attempts to regulate and fend off. Miller and Fish seem to welcome those things that Hirsch sees and labors to curb, but neither is much of an interpretive radical. They accept English studies more or less as it is constituted; they simply impose a new theory on its basic structure, thereby giving us a different set of techniques to apply to traditional tasks.

My concern for the present is also apparent in part three, in which I survey major books of theory and criticism that were published or reprinted in the 1970s and 1980s. This section is also intended to remedy the problem of "choice" that anyone who writes on "theory" is certain to face. Even though this is a long book, it does not include discussion of (or reference to) all the important theorists on the current scene; I am aware that some readers will judge that I should have also treated this or that other theorist, but no book can achieve this kind of inclusiveness. I do hope that in part three I deal with a wide enough range of theorists and texts to validate, develop, and extend the themes that I trace in parts one and two and highlight in my Conclusion. I have taken the tactical liberty of examining specific texts, in part because this suits my needs in this study effectively and economically. But I have also chosen to deal with specific texts in order to delineate—especially for the "general" reader who still needs to get his or her bearings in theory—the major trends, issues, confusions, and difficulties in this crowded and contentious area. An unfortunate fact of academic life today is that books are published, positions staked out, and new projects undertaken at such a brisk pace that we are rarely able to absorb and reflect upon what passes quickly before our eyes. Nor are we always able to make clear that standards exist by which we can measure new work, standards that are firm and that are not lost in the play of politics or personality. In part three I seek to consider and make judgments upon a large number of books. I explain why these books succeed or fail, and I chart the future for English studies to which they direct us. These are not "book reviews" as much as they are "re-views," "re-examinations," of work in the field.

My book bears, then, on the contemporary scene in obvious ways. But I have also attempted to make my analysis "historical" so that my reader can see the continuities between past and present in the discipline of English. This historical orientation is evident throughout the book but is most clearly displayed in part two, which bridges the parts of my study that focus on the current situation. Here I describe the vexed matter of "subjectivity," discuss the emergence of the New Criticism, and define the process by which the New Criticism became "institutionalized." Though the New Criticism has been declared "dead" many times, it continues to inform our understanding of our "job of work." It still exerts a tight hold upon teaching, research, and theory, and it provides the terms we invoke to defend the discipline when it comes under social, economic, and political pressure.

We have gained much from the innovations that John Crowe Ransom, Allen Tate, Cleanth Brooks, and others brought to English studies, but the cost has been severe. The New Criticism—which now enjoys the status of "criticism" in general—defines the critic/teacher's duty and responsibility: he or she explicates major literary texts, reading them "closely" for significant patterns and themes and affirming the "canon" in which these texts are located. But this definition omits too much and disfigures the power that English studies should manifest. Instead of viewing ourselves as primarily "literary critics" who interpret the masterpieces, we might more profitably regard ourselves—and encourage students to regard themselves—as "intellectual workers" who draw on many disciplines, dispute the barriers between the literary and non-literary, contest the opposition between the canonical and non-canonical, and exhibit critical skills in a variety of culturally oriented ways.

This leads me to the major theme of my Introduction, but a final point is in order here. In arguing for the lingering influence of the New Criticism, I am not denying the amount and range of "new" work in literary theory that has been published during the 1970s and 1980s. At times it does seem that the New Critical era has ended and that the discipline has truly revised and renovated itself. But the basic structure of the discipline has not altered. Theory has shifted practice somewhat, but today it is primarily a field in its own right—large, lucrative, and self-contained. Theorists either supplement the strategies of the New Criticism or else (and more often) they labor in an enclosed domain that is divorced from pedagogy, curriculum planning, and canon formation. One group gives us more explications, whereas the other forsakes explication altogether in favor of ventures into the labyrinth of "pure" theory.

The most valuable direction for those in English studies to take is to relate theory and practice, resist compartmentalization of work, and see theory as a source of new terms and tools for teaching as well as for research. We should not regard theory as a means to rejuvenate "close reading" of the canon, nor should we allow it to blind us to the need for directly engaging and recasting the discipline—its curriculum, forms of teaching, understanding of its values and objectives. Compared both to the familiar duty of "close reading" and to the exultation of pure theory, these practical and pedagogical tasks may seem to constitute a tough and tedious chore. But if English studies is to acquire new life, these are the tasks we must undertake.

Acknowledgments

I began this book when I was a graduate student at Johns Hopkins. Stanley Fish was my adviser, and I am indebted to him for his inspirational teaching, rigorous criticism, and boundless generosity. I also owe a longstanding intellectual debt to George Dardess, whom I first met when I was an undergraduate. He was, and is, a superb teacher, and he has been a friend for many years.

For their support and encouragement, I wish to thank Richard Poirier, Edward W. Said, Patricia Meyer Spacks, and Gerald Graff. I have especially benefited from Professor Graff's shrewd analyses of my arguments. Eric J. Sundquist has also been a valuable critic of my work, and I am grateful for his friendship and intellectual example.

A number of other friends and colleagues have helped me with this book, either by reading (and often re-reading) parts of the manuscript, or by discussing its most difficult questions with me. I cannot say for certain that I have remembered everyone, but at least I do know that I must thank Michael McKeon, Marcia Ian, Peggy Rosenthal, Ross Posnock, Steve Mailloux, Jacqueline T. Miller, David Leyenson, Evan Carton, Jane Tompkins, Sharon Cameron, Arthur Gold, Arnold Stein, and the late Laurence B. Holland. Steve Dawley did not read the manuscript, but I have always counted on his friendship.

I am indebted to William P. Sisler, my editor at the Johns Hopkins University Press, for his advice and editorial wisdom. I have also profited from the copyediting skills of Jackie Wehmueller and the expertise in book production of Jim Johnston and Mary Lou Kenney. I was fortunate to receive an extremely detailed and tough-minded report on my manuscript when I submitted it to the Press, and I wish to thank the reader (name unknown) for helping me to clarify my thinking on several important matters.

I also want to thank the American Council of Learned Societies for awarding me a fellowship for 1982-83. In addition, I am grateful to the trustees of Wellesley College for granting me a sabbatical, and to many people on the College staff who helped me with research and word processing. In particular I should mention the reference librarians at Clapp Library, Joan Stockard and Sally Linden, and two key staff members of the College Computer Center, Hsaio-ti Falcone and Dick Schofield. Linda Conti, my tireless research assistant and typist, also gave me much practical help and regularly boosted my morale.

Portions of this book originally appeared in *College English, Bucknell Review, Modern Language Notes, Virginia Quarterly Review, Novel, Review, South Carolina Review, Western Humanities Review, Minnesota Review, Georgia Review,* and *Comparative Literature.* Most of this material has been extensively revised, but I am nevertheless grateful to the editors of these journals for permission to reprint. I am even more grateful, however, for their editorial scrutiny and generous response to my work.

Finally, I owe my greatest debt—both intellectual and personal—to Barbara Leah Harman. Her presence is in every line I write.

The

CRISIS *in*

CRITICISM

Introduction

Both the eighteenth and the nineteenth centuries have been called "the age of criticism"; surely the twentieth century deserves this title with a vengeance.
René Wellek, "The Main Trends of Twentieth Century Criticism"

An important aspect of intellectual life in the twentieth century has been the "institutionalization" of literature and criticism in colleges and universities. During the first three decades of the century, nearly all of the major critics were journalists, men-of-letters, or what one might term "general critics." Some had academic affiliations and loyalties and were involved in institutional disputes; Randolph Bourne, for instance, fought for academic freedom at Columbia and protested against the influence of corporate power on the university. But these critics—Bourne, H. L. Mencken, Edmund Wilson, and the others—made their living outside the academy, and they did most of their writing for newspapers and magazines. The "professors" were often viewed scornfully, seen as detached from contemporary life and literature and trapped in the trivialities of Germanic scholarship or lost in the mists of impressionism.

"Criticism" began to enter the colleges and universities during the 1930s, but the signs of change appeared even earlier. In England, the reform of the Tripos placed the emphasis on "practical criticism," and the pioneering work of I. A. Richards made available a new vocabulary for verbal analysis, the intensive "close reading" of poetry and prose. In America, as I explain in detail in chapter five, the calls for "criticism," for a focused study of particular texts, began to sound during the late teens and 1920s. The resistances to the "new critical" approach were marked, but by then many powerful voices were advocating and instituting "criticism." The Fugitive poets, led by John Crowe Ransom at Vanderbilt, were developing an aesthetic based on the "organic" quality of the poem and refining terms that enabled them to speak about the formal structure of texts. Even many of the major scholars, including Albert Feuillerat, E. E. Stoll, J. M. Manly, and John Livingston Lowes, noted the dulling routine of "scholarship" and argued for revisions in methods of teaching. They recognized that academic work, though needing to remain disciplined and rigorous, had to be brought up to date, centered in the literary text and connected to modern life and culture.

The drive for new critical techniques and standards was formidable, and it made an impact very quickly. Serious criticism, a criticism attuned to the poetry and essays of Eliot, Pound, Yeats, and the other great modernists, could occur, it seemed, only within an academic context. Ransom, Cleanth Brooks, Robert Penn Warren, and other leaders of New Criticism taught in a college or university; Allen Tate and R. P. Blackmur, though dubious about "professorial" life, eventually also took posts in the academy. The New Critics were not only shaping a "new criticism," but also reforming pedagogy, winning converts among students, and recasting the curriculum. These men understood themselves to be teachers as well as critics, and it became crucial for them to hone methods that would make the modernist texts available to a mass audience. Few people today read Brooks's and Warren's *Understanding Poetry* (1938), and when it is mentioned at all, it is usually dismissed. But this book is surely one of the monuments of twentieth-century criticism, a book that succeeded, whatever its gaps and shortcomings, in creating an audience for major poetry.

We cannot deny the New Critics' achievement, and it is disturbing to see frequent slaps at "well-wrought urnism" in recent studies of the movement, as though the New Criticism could be mocked and labeled in a phrase. But the effects of the New Criticism have been unfortunate, and all the more so because these are the result of methods that at first seemed beneficial. The New Critical stress on "close reading" of the text managed, as Gerald Graff suggests, to "democratize" the "literary transaction."[1] Students did not require "background" information about the poet's life and times in order to respond to and be articulate about the text. For many students, literary work became vivid and immediate as they engaged "the words on the page," usually the words of a lyric poem or a short passage from a novel or play. But localizing the "literary transaction," making it a matter of the "close reader" and the text, led to a confining and narrowing of the aims of criticism. The New Critics, Brooks in particular, maintained that historical, political, and social materials, though not primary, were relevant to critical understanding. Inevitably, however, as "close reading" lodged itself in the academy, knowledge about what was "outside" or "external" to the text faded from view altogether. As Graff observes, the New Critics "stripped down" criticism to the essentials, and this was valuable for those who had been immersed in scholarly data or dismayed by journalistic impressionism. But once history was de-emphasized, it could not help but become devalued or, at best, transformed into the "history" of poetic styles such as paradox and ambiguity.

Democratization also tended to subvert norms in interpretation and judgment. When Ransom argued for "criticism" in his essays of the 1930s, he highlighted the ways in which it displayed "scientific" precision. Though he and the other New Critics lamented the impact of science and technology on contemporary culture and society, they wanted to give English studies the prestige and exacting sense of method that the scientific disciplines enjoyed. The New Critics sought a cogent and supple speech about texts; making the poem accessible did not mean allowing the reader to indulge in personal opinion or random commentary. New Critical procedure was intended to be an orderly inquiry, as *Understanding Poetry*, with its lists of questions and sample interpretations, makes evident.

But the standards for judgment in the New Criticism were loose and invited the play of subjectivity right from the start. Whatever its provisions for "standards," the New Criticism appeared to say that each reader could interpret the poem as he or she chose; any sincere response to "the words on the page" was valid or at least hard to discredit, even if historical evidence seemed to demonstrate otherwise. The problem this created for classroom practice was obvious: if the literary transaction engaged just the reader and the text, and if other material for interpretation was not required, then how was the teacher to declare that one reading was more correct than others? What began as a scientific procedure lapsed very soon into the opposite of science, or so it seemed to many opponents of the New Criticism. Far from becoming a streamlined, modern discipline, English studies appeared to be falling back into impressionism and incoherence, its authority subverted from within by the very method that was designed to renew and revitalize it. When the teacher confronted recalcitrant students, he or she could either introduce "external" information—which struck students as breaking the rules of the game—or could invoke the authority of "the teacher," which, as the MLA revolt of the 1960s graphically demonstrated, seemed to professors as well as students to be unfair and arbitrary.

The New Critical momentum, however, was impossible to stop. The New Criticism was teachable, as other methods were not. And its methodological claims and canon ministered to our professional self-image (and means of justifying our labor) as teachers of reading and caretakers of literary art. In addition, the New Criticism opened up possibilities for publication that the expanding ranks of faculty welcomed; "publication" was needed for professional advancement, and the critical essay on a single text was relatively easy to produce. Such an essay, which might explore the unity of "The Wasteland" or the imagery of *The Golden Bowl*, did not oblige the critic to know much about history, social and political contexts, or even the writer's other works, but merely took as a "given" that the critic would be a man or woman of sensitivity and discrimination able to reveal something "new" in the text.

By the late 1940s, a number of the New Critics, especially Ransom and Brooks, were dismayed by the direction of academic criticism. They argued against the proliferation of "close readings" and appealed for a re-examination of New Critical techniques. But by this time the "New Criticism" was no longer something that the original New Critics could control; as Malcolm Cowley has stated, by the 1950s "New Critic" did not mean Ransom, Tate, or Brooks, but rather meant the "Professor X" who had read their books, digested their doctrines, and deployed their methods in the classroom and in critical essays. Indeed, by the 1950s, New Criticism was the basic form for teaching and critical writing, and it seemed so eminently suited to both activities that few could imagine doing anything else.

One suspects also—though such matters are hard to generalize about—that the politics of the late 1940s and 1950s encouraged the spread of the New Criticism and ingrained it all the more deeply in daily academic practice. The Soviet Union detonated its first atomic bomb in August, 1949; in this same month, Mao Tse-Tung's Communist forces triumphed in China. Less than a year later, North Korea invaded South Korea, entangling the United States in a conflict with communism in Asia. And throughout the early fifties, Joseph McCarthy and his associates were holding hearings that warned of the Communist menace at home and that ruined the lives of many people who once harbored (or who perhaps did not harbor at all) left-wing or Communist sympathies. These events led to extreme pressures on academic freedom and intellectual life; many, inside and outside the academy, kept silent, and those who did speak felt angry and bitter about their inability to influence public debate.[2]

I am not able to state that the New Criticism and the anti-Communist thrust of the Cold War were part of the same ideological network. Certain scholars and critics (H. Bruce Franklin, for example) have made this argument, and it seems persuasive enough in a general way: one can readily see the advantages of an apolitical method during a painful, intimidating political era. But it is difficult to prove this connection concretely (at least no one has done so yet), and it seems misleading to brand the New Critics as servants of the capitalist state when nearly all of them, in their Agrarian phase, assailed capitalism in the most severe terms. Still, one can understand how the intensities of the Cold War period might make the close reading of texts—a method that did not require commerce with politics and history—seem to be a desirable mission to pursue. Academics were pressured to stick to their work, and they were criticized when they appeared to trespass on political territory. Focusing on the text gave teachers a well-defined area of expertise, trained students in useful skills, and thus made English seem important yet marginal, necessary for the attainment of certain social goals—a literate public, for instance—but not likely to interfere with the workings of the social order.

This point—that English is important yet marginal—may seem paradoxical, but it was always part of the New Critical stance. The critic, so the New Critics affirm, should be both inside and outside culture, should serve the public good yet not comment in explicit ways on non-literary issues. Brooks states this point lucidly in an essay published in 1950 on "the role of the humanities." He urges scholars and critics to remain faithful to literary values and not to see themselves as dependent on other disciplines for the defense of humanistic studies. "Some scholars and critics," Brooks explains,

> have attempted to import values from ethics, or economics, or politics. The muse is to become a rewrite girl—in the 1920's for the values of the new humanists, in the thirties for the Marxists, in the forties for a program of liberal-democratic values. I sympathize with such scholars. Our civilization is in a bad way. I share their sense of the urgency to *do* something about it.

But, Brooks insists,

> I reflect that we can do *our most* about it by doing well our specific job: by keeping open the lines of communication with the realm of value; by re-establishing, in a language which is fast breaking down into gobbledy-gook, the capacity to communicate values; by exercising to health the now half-atrophied faculties by which man apprehends value. This is not the least important of tasks. It will seem unimportant only to the man who has made a superficial diagnosis of the sickness of our culture. A more profound diagnosis will see this as one of the essential tasks. Somebody had better undertake it. I submit that it is the task for which we who teach the humanities are peculiarly responsible.[3]

This is a principled and dignified position, and we ought not to under-rate Brooks's words. But while Brooks does gesture towards a specific "task" for the teacher/critic, he does not define it in detail or clarify the "values" literary work embodies and cultivates. True, he does suggest that English studies sharpens linguistic tools and opens the lines of communication. But while these goals are commendable, they are also very general. Brooks is right to emphasize that the tasks he outlines are "essential," yet they come to feel hollow, whatever their initial ring of truth, without a further accounting of how English studies specifically contributes to culture, social welfare, and political life. Brooks's explanation is admirable as far as it goes, but it is formal, cautious, and surprisingly modest: it does not disclose whether English studies has real content, something concrete and forceful to say.

Brooks would doubtless agree that he fails to tell us what should be the "content" of English studies, but he would add that this is a deliberate omission. He wants to avoid turning the study of literature into an occasion for promoting values drawn from other disciplines, from outside "art." The problem, however, is that such a defense of English makes English marginal; even as Brooks is marking off a specific realm within which teachers and critics can practice, he is implying that a great deal that makes our lives meaningful—ethics, economics, politics—exists elsewhere. Such a statement of the critic's role comes to feel meager, oddly limited in its scope, unfaithful to (even a devaluation of) the intellectual and imaginative gifts that a man like Brooks possesses: it is as though "criticism" *must* restrict itself to the interpretation of literary texts in purely literary contexts. With so much located outside English, it is not surprising that such a defense strikes many as an admission that English has a role only on the boundaries of culture, not at the center.

Brooks and his fellow New Critics, in arguments like this one, are striving to protect art and criticism from control by a civilization that "is in a bad way." In certain respects this task has been accomplished, but the price has been high, as Mary Pratt has observed:

> The point of the move into the university was to insulate both criticism and elite art from the direct control of the marketplace, and thus to create a point of resistance to commercialization and commodification of culture. This strategy has in some measure succeeded, but not without contradiction. Within the university, the establishment of published criticism as the measure determining job security, salary, and professional worth has commodified criticism anyway.[4]

The New Critics assigned an honorable mission to English studies, but this mission was guaranteed to prove frustrating and inadequate before too long. It is satisfying to define oneself as the spokesman for art and the opponent of "commercialization and commodification," but this will hold true only if one feels actually engaged—as critic, as antagonist—in the public and social world. The New Criticism did not empower (or entitle) the teacher/critic to experience this kind of engagement, and the results have been disturbing. Far from being "outside" the commercialized world, the men and women who work in literature and criticism have found themselves duplicating the processes of that world. English studies hence becomes another site within which commodity-culture can operate and fads and fashions can go unchecked, and teachers and critics have discovered themselves without any expertise or justification for speaking about what has happened. What has occurred within their discipline was something—the intense push and pull of commercialism and capitalism—that they were not supposed to teach, explore, or assess.

This seems to me to be an accurate diagnosis of the peculiar status of English studies. But I do not mean to imply that as critics and teachers we are powerless, without significant effect or authority. We are still groping for a vocabulary that will affirm our right to criticize culture and address the world's realities coherently and precisely; we are still, that is, searching for a means to get beyond the disciplinary definitions that the New Critics proposed and that remain extremely influential. But the power of the discipline as it now stands is extensive, and we would do well to remind ourselves of this fact. In *The Imaginary Library*, Alvin B. Kernan summarizes the situation well:

> By now serious literary activity, as well as most of the audience for litera-
> ture, is concentrated in the universities. Courses in literature provide al-
> most the only markets for literary works, old and new; university presses,
> and a few small art presses, are the primary publishers of literary history
> and criticism, poetry, and perhaps soon, it seems likely, of "serious" nov-
> els. The writers of literature have increasingly found that academic ap-
> pointments, a new form of patronage, are their principal means of sup-
> port, and with the great increase of creative writing programs, the
> university has become the place where writers are trained.

"Critical discussions of literature," Kernan adds,

> have by now almost entirely passed from the hands of public critics and
> men of letters to the scholars who teach in universities. Economic control
> has inevitably conferred control of the literary canon as well on the acade-
> mies, and the staffs of literature departments now really decide through
> criticism and textbook selection which works are to be considered litera-
> ture, or only a part of "popular culture"— that vast bin of literary apoc-
> rypha.[5]

The power exerted by English departments, even as the teachers and critics within them feel powerless and in many ways are powerless, is self-evident and impossible to ignore. We possess the power to nom-inate certain texts as more serious and urgently relevant than others; to evaluate texts and the life-choices they embody; to define "literary thinking" and its relation (or lack of relation) to other kinds of thinking; to circumscribe or bear witness to the constructive energies of the in-dividual agent, character, or author; to stay within (or transgress) dis-ciplinary and departmental boundaries; and to encourage or limit in-quiry into areas—political, social, historical—that lie "outside" literature and criticism.

Yet many in the profession do seem to ignore this power, or deny it, or else seem unable to recognize its impact and speak about it. Most of us still labor under the illusions that we are custodians of literary culture and that our primary job is to teach canonical works. In saying this, I know that I risk over-statement and may seem to libel a task that I do in fact take very seriously. But I think the reaction I may provoke is due not only to the cast of my phrasing. When confronted by the suggestion that we might do something "other" than what we do now, many academics immediately become defensive, prickly, and angrily judgmental. This is a sure sign that vested interests are perceived to be in danger, and is a further sign that the people who see themselves as the protectors of these interests do not feel wholly confident about their ability to articulate the reasons for their beliefs and behavior. Too many of us are not open to the idea that we can and should scrutinize the customary practices of the discipline, even though nearly all of us agree that the discipline is in trouble and in need of renovation. We cannot imagine that we might do something else—or something in addition—and draw on our power in different ways; and we often end up seeking to reform the discipline by re-invoking and further entrenching the practices (and the problems that accompany them) which are already in place. There is thus a great disparity between the potential of English studies and the form in which it is currently manifested. Oddly, we seem often to disparage the discipline in the attempt to defend it, and do not even appear able to acknowledge the types of power that we now wield. We proceed along our customary grooves, destined to perform a task that does us a disservice and whose effects dissatisfy us.

We need to reclaim the role that has been lost, changing our self-conception from academic teacher/critic to man or woman of letters or, better still, "intellectual worker." I cannot claim to long for another Mencken, though it would be good to hear the tones of an agitating voice; but I do believe that we should strive to emulate the diversity of interests, feeling for the present, and immersion in cultural and social life that we witness in Bourne and Wilson. This will be difficult, in part because what gave Bourne and Wilson much of their freedom was that they were not academics. We, on the other hand, work within the institution, both for idealistic reasons—we believe in teaching as a privilege and responsibility—and out of practical necessity—we cannot, as writers and teachers in the 1980s, earn a living outside the academy. But while it is hard to envision ourselves as intellectual workers, as opposed to "academic" critics and scholars, we should commit ourselves to making the attempt. If we want to defend the authority of the discipline, we must be willing to extend its boundaries; if we want to make claims for the "power" of literature and criticism, we must acknowledge both the magnitude of this power now and the new powers that the discipline might additionally display; and if we wish to affirm our "critical" role and function to the world, then we have to be willing to impose upon it, encounter it, speak to its concerns and cruelties, feel that our capacities for generalization and judgment extend beyond "academic" fields of expertise.

By "intellectual worker," I mean to suggest several specific things. Such an intellectual should, first of all, give voice to "the powerful language of resistance."[6] We are prone to take established practices for granted, leaving them unexamined and, even worse, defending them as if they were natural and inescapable. Yet it is established practice that the intellectual should seek to question and replace with something better: it is precisely the intellectual's work to "resist" and challenge what is habitually accepted. This is not an argument for endless acts of demystification, though there is a good deal of demystifying work at present to be done and many ideas, attitudes, and reputations that are blindly exalted and in need of criticism. But intellectual work should also connote the effort to locate critical and pedagogical activity on new, more defensible ground. We need positive terms and standards, for otherwise we will merely leave open a space for commodity-culture to occupy.

Such a positive account will not of course be written in stone; it will change as the historical situation changes and obliges us to craft new analytical instruments, methods of teaching, and curricula. Here, theory has a crucial part to play, as it inspects, undermines, and aims to re-locate practice. The danger—one that is all too evident today—is that "theory" will content itself with being purely theoretical, never making contact with society and culture because its own fascinations prove so arresting. For this reason we should, I think, follow Edward W. Said in distinguishing "theory" from "critical consciousness." "Critical consciousness" is

> a sort of spatial sense, a sort of measuring faculty for locating or situating theory, and this means that theory has to be grasped in the place and (of course) the time out of which it emerges as a part of that time, working in and for it, responding to it; then, consequently, that first place can be measured against subsequent places where the theory turns up for use. The critical consciousness is awareness of the differences between situations, awareness too of the fact that no system or theory exhausts (or covers or dominates) the situation out of which it emerges or to which it is transported. And above all, critical consciousness is awareness of the resistances to theory, reactions to it elicited by those concrete experiences or interpretations with which it is in conflict. . . . It is the critic's job to provide *resistances* to theory, to open it up toward historical reality, toward society, toward human needs and interests, to point up those concrete instances drawn from everyday reality that lie outside or just beyond the interpretive area necessarily designated in advance and thereafter circumscribed by every theory.[7]

"Theory" is meaningful when it is oriented towards "worldliness" and geared towards practice. It is the duty of the intellectual worker, the man or woman who displays "critical consciousness," to *resist* theory when theory loses touch with the reality of "human needs and interests." This is difficult, complex work, because it requires that we adjust and adapt our pedagogy and research according to the requirements of the historical moment. As all teachers know, it is tempting to fall into comfortable habits and rest securely with the bare minimum; many of us begin idealistically but then are gradually worn down by the chores of the classroom and burdens of the institution. "Critical consciousness," "intellectual work"—these may well appear to be noble phrases, but phrases whose meaning is elusive and whose enactment is hard to envision and sustain.

This book is intended to give substantive meaning to these phrases, and I hope in particular that my Conclusion will provide at least the beginnings of a concrete alternative to current procedures in criticism and pedagogy. But I do feel that it is inevitable here that I concede the obvious point: it is indeed a laborious task to keep the intellect, in Bourne's words, "supple and pliable." The intellectual, as Bourne perceived, is not naturally a questioner and skeptic, is not necessarily responsive to or interested in change, but rather "craves certitude" and is prone to accept half-truths. As intellectual workers, as men and women who strive to keep consciousness truly "critical," we should fear most the hazard of "premature crystallization," a stiffening of our ideas, an indulgence in either global explanations or in narrow "specializations" that fulfill our urge for certainty and lay out the exact course we should follow and never deviate from.[8]

If social and institutional change is to occur, it will take place through specific acts of intellectual work, and it will doubtless happen slowly. In recent years, we have seen a steady procession of critics and theorists announcing themselves, with great fanfare, to be deconstructionists, Marxists, or members of some other sect or cell, as if to make such an assertion were to do something revolutionary. Many of these men and women have done valuable work, but one feels often that they are speaking *at* the world rather than to it. Their language is bold, but they misunderstand the ways in which change occurs. It does not occur through rhetoric, denunciation of the academy, passionate statements on behalf of the latest variety of Marxism, or private battles among high-ranking theorists. For us to foster "change," we must initiate concrete historical research, alter the curriculum, and devise means to join all members of our profession in an intellectual bond: we must work well within the world that we know best, even as we always remember (and subject to scrutiny) the relation between this "world" and the larger one that contains it. Nothing could be less helpful than the rarified theorizing and exercises in political right-mindedness that are underway in many literary circles these days; and nothing could be more destructive than the alienating language that these men and women employ.

"Change," however, is a highly contested term, and a large segment of the theoretical vanguard believes that in expressing hope for change, we give ourselves over to illusions. These theorists, prompted by an over-zealous reading of Foucault, argue that "institutions" possess such overwhelming force that they cannot be directed or controlled. Everything about the college or university is "outside" human agency, and the practices of this institutional world are uniformly pernicious. But while it is true that there is a logic to institutional life—institutions do encourage conformity to their rituals and values—this does not mean that change is ruled out in advance, nor does it imply that all we can show for our efforts are the forms by which we inevitably dominate and discipline others into submission. The college or university constrains action but also *enables* it, makes it possible, provides opportunities that we can seize, offers us particular situations for significant new work in planning courses and building a curriculum.

The answer to institutional determinism is clear: we need to recognize that such a vision of institutions is finally self-serving. It allows us to do whatever we want without attending to the consequences, for we have said in advance that these consequences cannot really matter and have devalued the significance of critical thought. There is no reason— other than a self-excusing one—to confine our disciplinary terms to those that Foucault appears to authorize. Nor is there any reason to feel hopeless—again, such defeatism finally serves our selfish interests alone—about the possibility for constructive change that individuals can help to bring about. "Because they are historical products of human activity," Peter L. Berger and Thomas Luckmann point out,

> all socially constructed universes change, and the change is brought about by the concrete actions of human beings. If one gets absorbed in the intricacies of the conceptual machineries by which any specific universe is maintained, one may forget this fundamental sociological fact. Reality is socially defined. But the definitions are always *embodied*, that is, concrete individuals and groups of individuals serve as definers of reality.

"To understand the state of the socially constructed universe at any given time, or its change over time," Berger and Luckmann add, "one must understand the social organization that permits the definers to do their defining. Put a little crudely, it is essential to keep pushing questions about the historically available conceptualizations of reality from the abstract 'What?' to the sociologically concrete 'Says who?' "[9] This gives us something to which we can aspire and also provides us with an attitude towards (and understanding of) intellectual life that we can teach. There is much work to be done and no reason to feel defeated by our institutional situation or doubtful about our real opportunities to take initiatives that can produce a general effect.

Our institutional context is fluid and flexible, "open" to the possibility of constructive change, and thus significant human action—action whose consequences are creative and meaningful—is both possible and necessary. Many teachers and critics, however, those at the other extreme from the neo-Foucauldians, feel that literary study today is all *too* prone to change, is indeed on the verge of a mad fall into chaos. The problem, they contend, is not the absence or impossibility of change, but is rather the absurd ease with which English studies changes constantly, uncritically accepting the intellectual fashions that are in season. In the view of those opposed to still more change, criticism needs to be tightened up, its traditional techniques and values restored. Teaching and literary criticism, it is said, have lost authority, and the discipline's objective—concrete knowledge about literary texts—has dissolved in the face of structuralist and post-structuralist methods. In order to protect and promote the discipline, we need to reject the "cognitive atheists" and accept "principles."

E. D. Hirsch, to whose work I now turn, is the most effective spokesman for "authority" in interpretation. In his books and essays, he has argued against Derrida, Foucault, and other theorists who seem, in his judgment, to subvert authority, undermine determinate meaning, and sabotage the humanistic goals of English studies. Hirsch misperceives the import of these theorists, and his proposals for restructuring the scholarly and pedagogical routines of English are seriously flawed. But his work has nevertheless been very influential, and he has won many supporters to his side. Many agree with Hirsch that the time to abandon fashionable theories has arrived, and they believe that we ought to devote ourselves to "authoritative" tenets around which the profession can rally. Yet it is precisely because Hirsch has received such a favorable hearing for his advocacy of "authority" that his views demand careful scrutiny. Though Hirsch's theory is attractive, his arguments for it are highly questionable, and his own perceptions about meaning, literature, and interpretation bring him much closer to those expressed by Derrida and the others than he suspects.

PART
ONE

1.

Authority, "Cognitive Atheism," and the Aims of Interpretation: The Literary Theory of E. D. Hirsch

A text's meaning is what it is and not a hundred other things.
E. D. Hirsch, *Validity in Interpretation*

In *Validity in Interpretation* and *The Aims of Interpretation*,[1] E. D. Hirsch insists on the need for authority, order, and discipline in literary studies, and he directly challenges "relativist" attitudes towards textual interpretation that have been fostered by the New Criticism and, more recently, by structuralist and post-structuralist theory. "Relativism" defines a state of affairs where, in Hirsch's view, subjectivity thrives without constraints, thereby ruling out the possibility for a common and determinate object of knowledge. When subjectivity is allowed free reign in scholarship and teaching, every person can legitimately claim authority for his or her own interpretation. There is no central authority, no firm and consistent set of principles to rely upon to arbitrate disagreements about what a text truly means. We require, Hirsch argues, an authoritative center around which to organize the discipline, and upon which we can construct judgments about valid and invalid interpretations.

For Hirsch, this principle of authority should be based upon the distinction between "meaning" and "significance": "Meaning is that which is represented by a text; it is what the author meant by his use of a particular sign sequence; it is what the signs represent. Significance,

15

on the other hand, names a relationship between that meaning and a person, or a conception, or a situation, or indeed anything imaginable" (*Validity*, p. 8). A work's "significance" may change from one generation to the next, but its "meaning" (the "verbal meaning" willed by the author) does not. Though we often speak of changes in "meaning," we are in fact referring to changes in "significance"—how a particular "meaning" is (re)criticized during different historical periods. When Hirsch says "interpretation," he is speaking of our attempt to understand the author's "meaning," and when he discusses the function of "criticism," he is referring to efforts to locate the "significance" attached to that "meaning." Because we possess this category of "meaning," which is changeless, determinate, and reproducible, we are able to judge textual interpretation and its practice in the classroom as a "discipline" rather than a "playground" (p. 163).

I

In *Aims*, his important collection of essays, Hirsch maintains that his theoretical stance has changed little since *Validity* was published in 1967. His major themes in this book are outlined in its opening chapter: the "futility" of "relativism," the "possibility of humanistic knowledge," and the urgency of protecting the "stable determinacy of meaning"— the "object of knowledge" described in detail in *Validity*. The relativists, who deny our moral duty to advocate objective standards of interpretation and who ignore the pressures of "ordinary experience" on teachers of literature, are treated with contempt. Literary study now suffers, Hirsch contends, from a post-structuralist threat to its stability that is far more serious than that posed by the New Criticism. The proponents of "anti-rationalism, faddism, and extreme relativism," inspired by Heidegger, Derrida, and their "disciples" (p. 13), mount a frontal assault on the concept of centralized authority in interpretation and threaten to undermine the foundation for rule and discipline in the profession. These writers are the "cognitive atheists" (pp. 13, 49); they refuse allegiance to any common authority and shared principles, degrade knowledge and value, and disguise their self-indulgent "works of fiction" as "serious criticism." According to Hirsch, Derrida and his followers subvert the goal of objective knowledge that should structure our interpretations, and hence they encourage an interpretive solipsism that undercuts belief in research and teaching as a communal enterprise.

In *Aims*, as in *Validity*, Hirsch adheres to "principles" with which to combat the decadent "subjectivism" that the Derridean group promotes. He argues his positions forcefully, and his stand on behalf of "validity" is admirable in its clarity and vigor. Yet it is striking to note in both *Validity* and *Aims* the potential radicalism of the "principles" that Hirsch deploys to counter "relativistic" dogma. He is often represented as a literary "conservative," a naive advocate of the "intentional fallacy," or a supporter of crudely-defined generic categories. But many of his beliefs would prove difficult for intentionalists and neo-Aristotelians to accept, and Hirsch belongs in the "conservative" camp less for his theoretical insights than for his retreat from their implications. Frequently he makes radical literary statements—some of which even resemble Derrida's and the relativists'—only to pull back to establish a line of defense against them. He sticks to his distinction between "meaning" and "significance," along with its promise of an authoritative object of knowledge, even when it seems not to be well served by specific points in his arguments.

In *Aims* some venerable dichotomies lose their prestige. Hirsch favors, for example, a "general" rather than a "local" hermeneutics, which means that he does not recommend the study of a "poetic" language divorced from other "ordinary" uses of language. For Hirsch, there is no distinction between "poetic" and "prosaic" or "everyday" properties of language: "General hermeneutics lays claim to principles that hold true all of the time in textual interpretation" (p.18). Later references to "literature" and generic classification are equally straightforward:

> No literary theorist from Coleridge to the present has succeeded in formulating a viable distinction between the nature of ordinary written speech and the nature of literary written speech. (P. 90)

> Literature has no independent essence, aesthetic or otherwise. It is an arbitrary classification of linguistic works which do not exhibit common distinctive traits, and which cannot be defined as an Aristotelian species. (P. 135)

> A true class requires a set of distinguishing features which are inclusive within the class and exclusive outside it; it requires a differentia specifica. That, according to Aristotle, is the key to definition and to essence. But, in fact, nobody has ever so defined literature or any important genre within it. (P. 121)

Although Hirsch challenges our usual understanding of "literature" and "genre," he preserves them in his theoretical system. He does not wish to grant privileged status to these terms, but neither does he want to deny the value of literary study and the knowledge to be acquired from it. "Many modern defenders of literature," he explains in the afterword to *Aims*, "rightly claim for literature a kind of truth not usually found in other modes of discourse—vivid truths about human nature and emotion, about the forms of human desire and resistance to human desire. Literature instructs still by being true" (p. 157). Hirsch testifies eloquently to the value of the knowledge to be attained through literature, but his position is curious. His local observations about "literature" and "genre" seem to conflict with his larger goal of defending the special place of literary studies, for he calls into question the very terms he judges to be central to the discipline. Many people endorse Hirsch's appeal for "authority" in English studies, but they may feel disturbed when he concedes that important terms—terms upon which the discipline has relied—ought not to be granted privilege.

We also should not make the mistake of too quickly including Hirsch among those critics who find meaning to rest exclusively "in the text" rather than in codes and conventions of reading. He argues against theorists who claim that the text somehow projects messages that the reader then understands. "Meaning has existence only in consciousness," Hirsch states. "Apart from the categories through which it is construed, meaning can have no existence at all" (*Aims*, p. 48). But Hirsch's stand on the reader-text debate—where does the responsibility lie for generating meaning?—is again intriguing. While he refuses to locate meaning in the text, he also refuses to allow textual interpretation "from a perspective different from the original author's" (p. 49)—as though there is a particular meaning to be extracted from the text, one that may be verified by referring both to the text and to other kinds of "relevant knowledge" (the biography of the author, historical information about the period, and so forth). This argument finally inclines towards locating meaning "in the text"—the author's intention, which the interpreter must understand, is represented by the sequence of verbal marks. But Hirsch's text-centered position is not so much the product of his statements about "meaning" (which can exist "only in consciousness") as it is the sign of his desire for one special category of "meaning" to serve as an authoritative norm.

Several passages in *Validity* help to clarify this point. While Hirsch does not deny that there may be disparate interpretations of "meaning," he does argue for strict controls. If the meaning proposed by the interpreter is not "verified in some way," then it "will simply be the interpreter's own meaning, exhibiting the connotations and emphases which he himself imposes" (p. 236). The interpreter should not "exhibit" "his own subjective acts," but should instead be ruled by the single authorial intention that the text represents. Otherwise we will be confronted by complete subjectivity in interpretation: "As soon as the reader's outlook is permitted to determine what a text means, we have not simply a changing meaning but quite possibly as many meanings as readers" (p. 213). The "text," like "literature," is emptied of its usual weight, since it does not produce meaning itself. But the authority of the text remains in place, whatever Hirsch's concessions to the reader's "consciousness," since the text can represent only the "meaning" that the author intends.

When Hirsch discusses "form" and "content" in his chapter in *Aims* on stylistics and synonymity, he performs a similiar move. He stresses that "synonymity" does exist—that an "absolutely identical meaning" can be expressed "through different linguistic forms" (p. 50). Undoubtedly many critics and teachers—particularly those who teach composition—would like to share this belief in the availability of different "forms" to express the same content. But it is questionable whether they would endorse other statements in this chapter. Hirsch goes on to assert, for example, that "meaning" and "form" stand in an essentially indeterminate relationship (cf. p. 51). In fact, he points out, "the relation of form to meaning is so very flexible, even to the point of indeterminacy, that a word, or even a whole written text, is not necessarily synonymous with itself" (p. 63). This admission, however, allows room for the claims of relativist critics who argue that because understanding is a historical phenomenon, no two meanings can ever be spoken of as truly identical. While Hirsch declares the possibility of synonymity, he concedes that a word or text may not even be synonymous with itself, and once this concession is made, he ushers in the interpretive "chaos" he aims to oppose—the same "anarchic" state of affairs that his theory intends to protect us against. Here as elsewhere, one suspects that Hirsch's repeated statements in favor of authority, order, and an "object of knowledge" partly arise from the resemblance between his positions and those he attacks.

The ground for Hirsch's theory is his distinction between "meaning" and "significance." It is this "firm principle" that he uses both to refute Derrida's relativist claims and to avert the interpretive anarchy that some of his own insights might appear to generate. He can subscribe to what I have termed "radical" literary positions (despite his uneasiness about them) because he believes that his argument is located in an authoritative center—in a principle of order that will prevent interpretive "radicalism" from undermining unity and objectivity in English studies. Yet the origins of Hirsch's crucial tenet are again surprising. In *Validity* he emphasizes that "there is nothing in the nature of the text itself which requires the reader to set up the author's meaning as his normative ideal" (p. 24). In other words, there is no a priori necessity for treating "meaning" as the author's meaning. But for Hirsch, only "authorial meaning" can exist as a compelling standard for interpretation: "On purely practical grounds, therefore, it is preferable to agree that the meaning of a text is the author's meaning" (p. 25). This definition of "meaning" is not in any sense forced upon us by the text, but is to be preferred for its practical advantages: it will act as a defensible norm to regulate the activities of scholars and teachers. Because we require a standard to govern interpretive practice, we select—as preferable to disorder—a normative definition of authorial meaning.

While Hirsch's category of "meaning" may supply the profession with a standard, his application of it is not reassuring. In *Validity* he presents a "hypothetical instance":

> We have posited that Shakespeare did not mean that Hamlet wished to sleep with his mother. We confront an interpretation which states that Hamlet did wish to sleep with his mother. If we assert, as I have done, that only a re-cognitive interpretation is a valid interpretation, then we must, on the basis of our assumed premise about the play, say that the Freudian interpretation is invalid. It does not correspond to the author's meaning; it is an implication that cannot be subsumed under the type of meaning that Shakespeare (under our arbitrary supposition) willed. It is irrelevant that the play permits such an interpretation. The variability of possible interpretations is the very fact that requires a theory of interpretation and validity. (Pp. 122-23)

If the critic or teacher hopes for a defense against relativism and a return to authority, he or she receives it here (as Henry James would say) "full in the face." The attempt to erect and justify arbitrary authority—one which is "posited" and "assumed"—could not be more nakedly presented.

Hirsch differentiates "meaning" and "significance" to ward off the state of affairs that his terms "chaos" and "anarchy" signal. But it is important to recognize that this constitutes a desire rather than a proof. If there is only indeterminate meaning, then there is no norm for deciding among interpretations; but since we must have a norm if we ever hope to achieve objective knowledge, then we must assert that "meaning" is the determinate meaning that the author intends. Hirsch offers a variety of arguments for authorial meaning, yet too often he forgets that his choice of a "firm principle" is merely posited, not naturally grounded. His arguments for authority are the result of a need he perceives in the profession, and his proposal of the distinction between "meaning" and "significance" is chosen because it is, he feels, defensible, not because it is a truth that no one could deny. Hirsch assumes that there will be "chaos" without a standard that all of us agree to honor; he does not consider the alternative that there might exist other kinds of standards, however uncodified, which already operate to forestall anarchy in interpretation. It is not as though we now write and teach without any constraints; our academic and other forms of behavior are quite "orderly," even though they are not impelled by a fully-articulated charter of rules. As Stephen Toulmin has argued,

We can properly write from any of a number of points of view, and we can truthfully say rather different things, depending on the exact nature of both the occasion and the audience; yet that fact does not open up a complete "free-for-all." Alongside these *possible* points of view and statements, there are also countless others which would be irresponsible, libelous, or otherwise impermissible.[2]

Hirsch believes that we cannot speak of a structured and orderly discipline unless we observe an authoritative standard. But the elusiveness of a single standard should not be taken to imply that in scholarship and teaching "anything goes." We are more conscious of all sorts of standards, rules, and proprieties, and less prone to anarchy, than Hirsch's arguments suggest. Simply because there is no single standard, privileged above all others, does not mean that there are no standards at all. This is an important point, and I will return to it when I discuss Derrida at the end of this chapter.

II

The authority that Hirsch claims for his category of "authorial meaning" is far less stable than he believes. When considering the problem of "implications," for instance, he explains: "If, for example, I announce, 'I have a headache,' there is no difficulty in construing what I 'say,' but there may be great difficulty in construing implications like 'I desire sympathy,' or 'I have a right not to engage in distasteful work'" (*Validity*, p. 220). But to claim that the verbal meaning of "I have a headache" is explicit assumes that it always comes attached to an identifiable (and irrefutable) context, and that this context will immediately be the same for both speaker and hearer. The meaning intended by the author of this statement, however, depends upon whether he suffers from migraines or has had engine trouble with a new automobile or has suffered some other misfortune; the hearer or reader cannot always know in advance the appropriate context for understanding this authorial meaning. The author's intention is problematical for interpreters precisely because there *is* "difficulty" in construing what Hirsch "says" in these types of examples.

Other problems with Hirsch's distinction between "meaning" and "significance" become clear in *Aims*, where he qualifies somewhat the definitions presented in *Validity*. "Meaning" is now "simply meaning-for-an-interpreter," and "significance" is "meaning-as-related-to-something-else" (pp. 79-80). This new emphasis on the interpreter greatly enlarges the category of "meaning" and undermines the authority that Hirsch claims for it.[3] "Meaning," he argues, "now comprises constructions where authorial will is partly or totally disregarded" (p. 79). By reducing the normative power of authorial intention in this manner, Hirsch seriously weakens the forcefulness of the term "meaning" in his system. He still hopes to conceive of "meaning" as centered in the text—the interpreter finds meaning in a text because he or she is confident that it is truly "there" (p. 80). But it is "there" only because, as Hirsch often reminds us, the interpreter has constructed it. This description no longer provides for the "firm principle" of authorial will and intention: "No normative limitations are imported into the definition" (p. 79). There is thus no single, reproducible, and determinate authorial intention "represented" by the text to confine the interpreter, and the boundaries to responses to the text therefore are taken away. While Hirsch still speaks of "meaning" as a "principle" of authority, one that guides and stabilizes our interpretations, he has eliminated its impact through his own revisions.

III

The most admirable feature of Hirsch's work, one that largely accounts for his tough-minded theoretical stance, is his concern for the profession. No other theorist today speaks as passionately for "responsibility" in both scholarship and teaching, and certainly no other member of the profession so emphatically calls upon academics to address themselves to the dismaying trends in recent criticism, to the decline in writing skills among students, and to the pressures on teachers of the humanities to "justify" their performance. What disturbs Hirsch about the Derridean relativists is their impracticality and even hypocrisy. "Nobody could live" according to such theories in "his ordinary intercourse with the world" (p. 3), and no one would choose to do so even if it were possible. Derrida's thought is "faddish" and "decadent" to Hirsch not only because of its theoretical blindness to the need for authority and to the demands of the academy, but also because its proponents are not (and could not be) committed to living out the tenets of their doctrine. For Hirsch, "empirical truth is the ultimate arbiter of theories in the practical disciplines" (*Aims*, p. 80), and he emphasizes throughout his work the importance of attending to the "usefulness" of our theories (pp. 31-32), to "common sense" (pp. 39, 118), "practical questions" (p. 81), "concrete goals" (p. 127), and the "practical side of our present situation" (p. 135). There is a bottom line: "Poetry and fiction are worth studying, and if we don't keep them alive in humanistic education, nobody else will. That is the only justification we need" (p. 140).

The New Criticism committed a "philosophical error" in asserting the "centrality" and "autonomy" of literary studies; but, Hirsch adds, it owed its success to its ability to define the roles and methods of those engaged in teaching "poetry and fiction." Now that the errors and excesses of New Critical practice have been exposed, we require a new theory. We need once again to define our identities as scholars and teachers and to form our professional duties around a "center." But to find self-definitions in the writings of Derrida would, Hirsch argues, deny our communal responsibility as teachers, preclude a common object of knowledge, and trigger "anarchy" in interpretation.

Hirsch maintains that literary theories and emphases in interpretation reflect "ethical choices" (*Aims*, p. 77). We must decide what should be the "goals of interpretation" and the priorities of the humanistic disciplines, and in making these decisions "we have to enter the realm of ethics" (p. 85). The source of Hirsch's strength both in *Validity* and in *Aims* is this ethical commitment and his awareness that interpretation is never innocent of motives and goals. Whatever our theoretical allegiances, we must at the very least be conscious of their ethical grounds and measure them carefully against the ethics of those who speak from other points of view. For Hirsch the issue is clear: those who choose to ignore authorial intention are guilty of a vicious type of intellectual domination:

> To treat an author's words merely as grist for one's mill is ethically analogous to using another man merely for one's own purposes. I do not say such ruthlessness of interpretation is never justifiable in principle, but I cannot imagine an occasion where it would be justifiable in the professional practice of interpretation. The peculiarly modern anarchy of every man for himself in matters of interpretation may sound like the ultimate victory of the Protestant spirit. Actually, such anarchy is the direct consequence of transgressing the fundamental ethical norms of speech and its interpretation. (*Aims*, p. 91)

When we engage a text "solipsistically," Hirsch declares, we in effect manipulate and abuse the intentions of another person. But while Hirsch's ethical point is forthright and persuasive, it is difficult to apply it to his own theory: his category of "meaning," as described in *Aims*, is no longer restricted to "an author's words," and his position therefore is no longer strictly located in an authority that would certify his ethical judgment.

Though Hirsch's reminders about the relationship between ethics and interpretation are valuable, he does not recognize the problems of authority and ideology that these imply. In a key section of *Validity*, he recommends that interpretive debates proceed under an "advocacy system." Each critic "advocates" his or her interpretation of a certain text, and then participates in "adjudication" that will determine which is most probably correct. But it cannot be guaranteed that each advocate will voluntarily surrender a claim to knowledge; each person may remain convinced, despite the attempt at adjudication, that his or her own interpretation is the most accurate one. Hirsch's answer to this problem is to nominate a judge: "Unless advocates sometimes serve as judges, none of this activity will actually contribute to knowledge" (p. 197). Hirsch makes no provision, however, for the selection of judges, and so fails to deal with the question of authority at its most crucial point. There must be an authority to prevent the "chaotic democracy of readings" that could arise even under an advocacy system. Yet Hirsch nowhere mentions how this judge will be selected or how an intellectual tyranny will be avoided in which certain interpretations are summarily over-ruled. Hirsch's theory is in many respects bluntly dogmatic, and many beleaguered scholars and teachers will welcome it for its promise of a return to authority and legalistic supervision. But this interpretive choice may be as alarming in its implications as that which it professes to guard against.

In several chapters of *Aims*, Hirsch deals provocatively with the issues of authority and evaluation, but again his answers are unsatisfactory. He observes that "preferential criteria" in evaluative criticism are problematical for us, since we lack "institutionalized authority" or a "genuinely widespread cultural consensus" (p. 122). Since, he writes, "there is no papacy in intellectual affairs" in the modern world, we must judge literary value according to "principle, not authority" (p. 112). But when Hirsch advocates "principle," he is not offering a substitute for "authority" but instead proposing a new one. And when his "principles" lead in *Aims* to a return to the Arnoldian definition of "literature," their potential for peremptory judgments becomes striking: "Under that older conception, literature comprises everything worthy to be read, preferably the best thoughts expressed in the best manner, but above all the best thoughts" (p. 140).

The criteria for "worthy to be read" and "best thoughts" have never been obvious: does the approved canon spring up naturally (as Hirsch appears to imply), or is it decided upon by those with the authority to establish it? Later, when alluding to the Victorian critic Edward Dowden, Hirsch presents a particular evaluation of "worth": "In the spirit of Dowden it is tempting to add that in English literature of the nineteenth century, Charles Darwin is a greater and more interesting name than Walter Pater" (p. 142). Darwin's name associates nicely with the advocacy system set out in *Validity*, which Hirsch describes as "the survival of the fittest," but its ideological force is disturbing. The dangers exposed by the naming of Darwin, and by his placement (again, as though it were self-evident) in the roster of "greater" and "more interesting," must be firmly resisted. The "principles" that inform these judgments are not simply alternatives to authority, but in fact promote an authority that is ruthless: it is the survival of those who are declared to be the fittest.

In *Validity* and *Aims,* Hirsch confronts major theoretical and professional issues. His effort to preserve authority in scholarship and teaching is admirable, and his positions are often compelling and succinctly argued. But it is their persuasiveness, their skillful appeal to the need for authority, which demands that they receive careful scrutiny. Before we accept Hirsch's proposals, we should consider the practice of what he preaches.

IV

It would be unfair to Hirsch to criticize his theoretical statements without also taking a brief account of Derrida, the most influential member of the "cognitive atheists" whom Hirsch condemns. Derrida's texts are varied, allusive (as well as elusive), obscure, and difficult to summarize, and I will be forced to be selective in my references to his writings. I also want to make clear that my commentary pertains to Derrida's early work, work that strikes me as more stimulating and productive than the self-indulgent splendor that has characterized too much of the recent Derrida. *Of Grammatology* (1967; trans. 1976), *Writing and Difference* (1967; trans. 1978), and the essays published during the 1960s and early 1970s remain for me the essential texts. Those written more recently, such as *Spurs: Nietzsche's Styles* (1978; trans. 1979) and "Living On" in *Deconstruction and Criticism* (1979), are impressive and exhilarating in places, but they appeal primarily to devotees who take Derrida's writing as their special subject-matter. My interest here lies in several points: Derrida's "deconstructive" theory of literary criticism and its attack on concepts of "origin" and "center"; his particular insights about the nature of authority, and why these have proven so disturbing to Hirsch; and finally, his recognition of the constraints on his "deconstructive" method and his insistence that authority is crucial to his approach.

In the interview titled "Positions," Derrida describes "deconstruction" as the inversion of textual hierarchies and systems.[4] It "brings down the superior position while reconstructing its sublimating or idealizing genealogy, and the irruptive emergence of a new 'concept,' a concept which no longer allows itself, never allowed itself to be understood in the previous regime" (p. 36). Derrida strives to reverse the scale of authority in textual interpretation; he probes a particular text, hunting out the strand or element that serves as the "center," "knot," or "navel" for a certain reading, and then exposes it as yet another product of linguistic or philosophical conventions—as, in other words, a feature of the text whose authority should not be privileged over others that are themselves constituted by language and the assumptions of Western metaphysics. The repressed reading, the group of "other" textual elements that the former authority has subjugated, is then revealed, its structural contours brought to light.

"Deconstruction" denies the existence of a text governed by a "center" or an "original" core that organizes and authorizes a single system of meaning. When we deconstruct a text, we show that there is no "naturally" privileged center for its meanings. Rather, there is only a multiple and interwoven "play" of meanings that is not bound to observe the strictures that a claimant to centralized authority imposes. In Derrida's terms, there is no single "referent" or "transcendental signified which would regulate all of the text's movements" ("Positions," p. 37). We cannot, according to him, identify a fixed goal or endpoint for our interpretations, and hence cannot justifiably speak of a privileged authority that verifies some interpretations and rules others out of court. Interpretation never ends because it has no final destination: "The turbulence of a certain lack breaks down the limit of the text, exempts it from exhaustive and enclosing formalization or at least prohibits a saturating taxonomy of its themes, of its signifieds, of its intended meaning" (p. 37). Once we acknowledge the absence of a "center" around which the text is constructed, we shatter the notion of a text whose meanings our interpretations will eventually contain. The de-centered text excludes the possibility of a final stage to interpretive work: there can never be a complete listing of patterns and themes or a single statement of authorial intention.

The conflict between Hirsch and Derrida should be clear from this summary and set of quotations. Derrida questions the availability of the central articles in Hirsch's theory: the notion of a fixed and determinate center; the belief in a final, authoritative meaning (in Derrida's words, an "exhaustive" or "enclosing" interpretation); and the possibility that an interpretive goal can be established by combining and sifting among the "meanings" that different interpreters advocate. No doubt Hirsch is also disturbed by the disruptive thrust of Derrida's vocabulary—the overthrow of entrenched authority, the reversal of hierarchies, and the illumination of the subjugated "concepts" in the text. Hirsch fears the rebellious eruption of subjectivity and the consequent emergence of each person as an authority in interpretation. He can foresee only disorder and "chaos" in a world without a centralized authority towards which all interpreters and interpretations defer and owe their loyalty. Interestingly, Hirsch does in fact ratify Derrida's arguments when, in *Validity* and *Aims*, he acknowledges that his appeal for a "center" is not in any sense required or privileged by the nature of the text itself. But Hirsch maintains that the standard of "authorial meaning," even though it is our own creation, is preferable to the existence of a chaotic world that has no obvious standards, norms, and authorities—a world he describes as unstructured, undisciplined, and fragmented by the irreconcilable demands of each interpreter upholding a private cause.

"Constraints," however, do not disappear simply because they are left uncodified. Nor does authority fail to exert its influence after its "center" is called into question. The analysis that Derrida devotes to systems and hierarchies, and to displacing their usual priorities, is confined by the reign of language, as he himself recognizes. For Derrida, analysis never terminates, interpretation never ends, because "the hierarchy of the dual opposition always reconstitutes itself" ("Positions," p. 36). What deconstruction works to tear asunder strains to join back together again, and the reversal of authority, which the activity of the deconstructive critic brings about, is itself reversed. This "hierarchy" is never precisely correspondent with what it was before (it has been modified, adjusted, disrupted), but its previous authority is "always" restored and vulnerable to still another deconstruction. Deconstructive procedures, undertaken through language, are therefore inescapably "trapped in a sort of circle":

> This circle is unique. It describes the form of the relationship between the history of metaphysics and the destruction of the history of metaphysics. There is no sense in doing without the concepts of metaphysics in order to attack metaphysics. We have no language—no syntax and no lexicon— which is alien to this history; we cannot utter a single destructive proposition which has not already slipped into the form, the logic, and the implicit postulations of precisely what it seeks to contest.[5]

Far from being able successfully to subvert authority, Derrida realizes that he can never break free from its hold; his very intention to "destroy" and "deconstruct" is challenged by the terms in which it is expressed. He is bound to observe the authority of a centered system even when his deconstruction reveals its linguistic base and, at that moment, tries to topple it. Derrida does not believe, contrary to Hirsch's view, that authority can be made somehow to disappear completely. Its origins can be examined and its priorities reversed, but its structure "always" seeks to reconstitute itself. And it is this fact—authority tends to re-order itself under interpretive pressure—that the deconstructive critic tries, precariously, to accept and reject, accede to and resist. Although Derrida analyzes the foundations for authority, he perceives that his method must be limited to the same resources that support authority: "It is a question of putting expressly and systematically the

problem of the status of a discourse which borrows from a heritage the
resources necessary for the deconstruction of that heritage itself"
("Structure, Sign, and Play in the Discourse of the Human Sciences,"
p. 252).

The deconstructive critic's situation—testifying to authority in the
act of opposing it—demands discipline. This does not fade away under
Derrida's method, but instead becomes all the more exacting, since we
no longer have automatic recourse to a single authority that orders
interpretations for us. Again, this should not be taken to mean that we
are not conscious of, and obliged to observe, the presence of authorities;
we are never free to ignore them and do so only at great risk. When
we interpret a text and enter our interpretation into public and professional contexts, we are intensely aware of norms and standards. And
this holds true no matter how successfully we have illuminated their
claims to privilege. There are always authorities at work that govern
our behavior, whatever our illusions or pretensions about living inde-
pendently of them. As Jonathan Culler observes, even

> the attempt to "free" the process of reading from constraints imposed by
> a particular theory of culture requires one to reintroduce some rather
> powerful rules to apply to the combinations or contrasts produced by ran-
> dom extraction and and association.... Even if "emptied" by a radical the-
> ory, the center will inevitably fill itself in as the analyst makes choices
> and offers conclusions.[6]

Derrida specifically calls for "rigor" and "responsibility" in interpretation ("Structure, Sign, and Play in the Discourse of the Human Sciences," p. 252); he does not (and could not) advocate a state of affairs
where these would not be required. His arguments affirm that efforts
to dislodge concepts of authority will always end in re-instituting them
somewhere else.

Derrida's most striking insight is that we cannot "get along" without
"the center," no matter how persuasively we demonstrate its suspect
claims for privilege. "The center," Derrida states, is "absolutely indis-
pensable" ("Structure, Sign, and Play in the Discourse of the Human
Sciences," p. 271). We cannot rid ourselves of the notion of an authoritative center or reject other kinds of authorities that hold sway
over us in different contexts. And we should not delude ourselves that
we can enjoy complete freedom from responsibility—both to ourselves
and to others—in interpretation. Yet while authority cannot be overthrown in any absolute sense, it is nevertheless always subject to attempts to criticize it and unsettle the systems and hierarchies that it
promotes: "It is a question of knowing where it comes from and how
it functions" (p. 271). For Hirsch, on the other hand, once authority
is, as in his *Hamlet* example, "posited" and "assumed," then it must

remain unquestioned. The danger inherent in his position is that, in his effort to provide a "center" for the profession, he will establish an authority that does not merely limit interpretations but tyrannizes over them.

V

The most curious aspect of the theories presented in *Validity* and *Aims* is that the more Hirsch clarifies his arguments, the more radical he makes them. Hirsch argues for disciplinary order, and he articulates a position that will enable critics to defend literary study. But as he advances his arguments and labors to sharpen them, he inclines towards positions that are subversive of his own goals: he calls for authority in ways that make it more difficult than ever for him to attain. Hirsch is, in a sense, always arguing against his own skeptical perceptions, seeking to stave off the insights that keep filtering into his literary doctrine.

Early in *Validity*, for example, Hirsch states that "no necessity requires the object of interpretation to be determinate or indeterminate, changing or unchanging. On the contrary, the object of interpretation is no automatic given, but a task that the interpreter sets himself. *He* decides what he wants to actualize and what purposes his actualization should achieve" (p. 25). This shows, in a dramatic fashion, just how close Hirsch is to the "relativists" and "subjectivists" he derides. And this passage also indicates the kind of power that he attributes to the interpreter, power that Hirsch then works to hard to curtail. The key word in his books appears to be "authority," but actually he is concerned less with authority than with power and how it is (and ought to be) exercised. In the final sentences of *Aims*, Hirsch tells us "that which humanists recover, understand, and preserve needs to be preserved intact. To be useful, humanistic study, like any other study, needs to be believed" (p. 158). It is Hirsch's mission, in his theoretical inquiries, to empower members of the academy to enforce this belief and constrain those who might profess a different faith.

I now turn to the writings of J. Hillis Miller, one of Hirsch's major rivals in debates about interpretation. Like Derrida, Miller is a "deconstructive" critic, and he speaks about textual play and undecidability in a fashion that seems to link him to the "relativists" against whom Hirsch contends. But while Miller's words make him sound at times like Derrida, he is a different kind of critic. Miller is intent upon conserving what his theory appears to challenge, and he is less self-aware than Derrida about the ambivalences in his position. There is more in his work for Hirsch to welcome than to fear.

As my pairing of Miller with Hirsch will illustrate, theorists who seem to differ often share a great deal of common ground. Though Miller's rhetoric is radical, his positions on literature, criticism, and interpretation reproduce and tally with those that Hirsch espouses. Indeed, one might even suggest that Hirsch's insights about the instability of terms such as literature, literary language, meaning, and significance are as "radical" (if not more so) as Miller's. Hirsch realizes that his insights threaten the discipline, and thus he strives to control and contain them. Miller also sees that perceptions of this kind are threatening, and he too seeks forms of control; he differs only insofar as he appears initially to welcome the threat and invite us to contemplate a new world in which undecidability reigns. Neither theorist appeals for fundamental changes in literary study. Both are committed to what literary study has always taken as its province—the principled, ethically grounded interpretation of canonical authors—and both therefore participate in a heated debate where the opposition is more apparent than real.

2.

Deconstruction in

America: The Literary

Criticism of

J. Hillis Miller

Why must there be literary criticism at all, or at any rate more literary criticism? Don't we have enough already?

J. Hillis Miller, "Stevens' Rock and Criticism as Cure, II"

In a number of essays and reviews, J. Hillis Miller has argued for a new, "deconstructive," criticism. "Deconstruction" stands opposed to the belief in a "center" or "origin" that is immune from the play of language: there is no privileged position "outside" the languages of literature and criticism from which to initiate our critical discourse and upon which to base our interpretation of texts. Deconstructive critics know that their performance (their work with texts) is itself linguistically defined. They are part of the linguistic system, and thus cannot pretend to be free from its uncertainty and instability. Nor can they claim to take hold of this system, manipulating it like a tool and exercising their authority and command over it. "Deconstruction," Miller explains, "attempts to reverse the implicit hierarchy" that affirms center and origin. Its assumptions are not "monological" (logocentric), but rather "dialogical," which implies that "logocentric metaphysics" already contains its own "subversion." "Deconstruction" simultaneously adheres to an original source or center "outside" language and undermines it, testifying to its complete penetration by language.[1]

Miller's "deconstructive" theory has wide-ranging consequences. It calls into question and explodes our faith in the author (someone who is in command of language and creates the text); in the text itself (a stable entity that yields stable meanings); in interpretation (an activity that aims to extract univocal meanings from texts); and in literary, cultural, and other kinds of history (a story or narrative that "progresses" from one period to the next). It is, in fact, the burden of Miller's deconstructive labors to challenge the terms upon which his own earlier writings—*Charles Dickens: The World of His Novels* (1958), *The Disappearance of God* (1963), and *Poets of Reality* (1965)—were profitably grounded.[2] Few of the terms included in the introduction and the conclusion to the book on Dickens, for example, would now pass the deconstructive test: "the original unity of a creative mind" (p. ix); "the presiding unity hidden at the center" (p. x); "real world" as opposed to "imaginary world" (p. 328); and "a real self" (p. 329). One of the most intriguing features of Miller's recent work is that he advocates "deconstruction" at the expense of his own critical career. "Deconstruction" undercuts the possibilities for privileged authority, authenticity, and selfhood that informed his previous books.

But the threat that "deconstruction" seems to pose to other forms of criticism, including that which Miller formerly practiced, is less substantial than it seems. Miller's shift of allegiances to "deconstruction," far from implying a radical assault on our understanding of influence, literary history, authority, and interpretation, retains many of the ideas and values that it appears most vigorously to challenge. And deconstruction, at least as Miller articulates it, also falls prey to many of the same confusions that have often plagued other, more traditional, methodologies. These concern the roles of the author, the critic, the reader, and the text; the definition of the reading process; and the place of evaluation and ethical judgment in interpretation. Miller over-rates the degree of innovation that his theory introduces into literary studies, and he fails to perceive the conservative impulses that keep its subversive force in check. He believes that he is drawing on Jacques Derrida and translating this French theorist's "deconstructive" program for an American audience, and this is certainly true up to a point. But Miller safeguards and hedges in the "radical" theory that he presents, so much so that to connect him with Derrida comes to feel inaccurate and misleading.

I

As is well known, the formative influence on Miller's early career is Georges Poulet, and his recent call for deconstructive criticism can be viewed as an overthrow of this critical father. Poulet's phenomenological criticism, as Miller has described it on several occasions, privileges the authorial consciousness and regards the critic's goal to be the "coincidence" of his or her own consciousness with the author's.[3] For

Poulet, there is a "true beginning"—the Cogito of the author—that is "the ground or foundation of everything else" ("Georges Poulet's Criticism," pp. 198-99). This criticism presupposes the unity and integrity of the author's "thought" and maintains that the critic can "identify" with it. Miller has now displaced Poulet, however, along with his belief in origin, center, presence, and identity, and aligned himself with Derrida, who argues for the absence of origins and the dispersal of meaning away from the concept of a "center" that is its source of authority and principle of verification.

In the final version of his critique of Poulet's writings, Miller tries to bridge the gap between these two influences and to reconcile the different theories of criticism each has advocated. While he concedes that Derrida endangers the Pouletian enterprise, he emphasizes that the issue is more complex and interwoven than "an irreconcilable either/or" (p. 216). A "deep" and "careful" reading of Poulet's work, says Miller, reveals that "it challenges its own fundamental assumptions" in surprisingly Derridean ways. Poulet's several essays on Proust, for instance, question "the value of presence and the definition of consciousness which seem to be postulates of his work" (p. 219). But this attempt to demonstrate the affinities between Poulet and Derrida is not persuasive, because even as Miller describes their similarities, he must at the same time acknowledge their clear differences in "tone," "attitude," and intention. ("Unlike Derrida, Poulet has no desire to 'deconstruct' metaphysics" [p. 217].) This bridging of the theoretical gap is also suspect in its attribution to Poulet of insights that Miller derives from his "reading" of Poulet's critical texts. Miller assumes the self-deconstructing power of these texts, and he seems to believe (though he is unclear on this point) that Poulet himself recognizes this subversion of his own "quest." Yet he admits that Poulet "may not be entirely conscious" of these "guiding assumptions" behind his work (p. 208). Miller's essay thus does not truly indicate that Poulet shares a Derridean form of self-awareness with his critical son, but rather shows that his texts are vulnerable to deconstructive operations. Miller deconstructs Poulet's criticism, reveals that it interrogates its professed confidence in origins and presence, and then imputes to Poulet the perceptions of "absence" and "de-centeredness" this deconstruction produces.

To set Miller's essay on the "Geneva School" in *Modern French Criticism* next to passages from his recent deconstructive essays, which often herald the arrival of the "Yale School" of critics (Geoffrey Hartman, Harold Bloom, and Paul De Man), suggests the nature of the difference between his two careers. He says that "for the Geneva critics literature is a form of consciousness" (p. 279). As Poulet explains, the critic must succeed "in re-feeling, in re-thinking, in re-imagining the author's thought from the inside" (quoted, pp. 279-80); the critic must, in other words, enter from "the outside" into an intimate relationship with the mind of the author. A few pages later, speaking of Marcel Raymond, Miller observes that this critic's "genius" lies in the "extreme inner plasticity" that enables him "to duplicate within himself the affective quality of the mind of each of his authors" (p. 282).

But Miller's more recent essays renounce a movement from outside to inside, and they dispute the possibility for exact "coincidence," for repetition without a difference ("duplication"). He now contends that "any terminology of analysis or explanation is already inextricably folded into the text the critic is attempting to see from without";[4] the critic therefore cannot proceed under a naive belief in distinctions between the "outside" and the "inside" of the language of texts. This naivete also receives harsh treatment in an essay on Walter Pater, where Miller asserts that "there are no fathers, each apparent father being himself, often unwittingly, the heir of forces that have come together and then separated many times in the past. Whatever the critic reaches as an apparent beginning, as solid ground on which to base an interpretation, dissolves on inspection into a repetition."[5] For Poulet, repetition—that is, the critic's moment of "coincidence" with the author's consciousness—is a goal that the critic chooses as the "true beginning" and "ground." But for Miller, now writing under Derridean assumptions, "repetitions" are inescapable yet always differentiated, and, as a result, pure "coincidence" is impossible to achieve. Hence, the interpreter's priorities are reversed, and Miller's critical paternity is denied: "There are no fathers."

In his essay on the "Geneva School" Miller also describes, with reference to Albert Béguin, the availability of a "true self." For Béguin, as for Miller in his study of Dickens, there is an authoritative self to be uncovered and known. But Miller's new loyalty to deconstruction forbids this belief in an essential self. His overthrow of origins and points of departure and his account of the labyrinth of language rule out the "true self"—the self independent of linguistic determinations. The deconstructive critic, working with "dialogical" premises, calls into question "the notions of the mind and of the self and sees them as linguistic fictions, as functions in a system of words without base in the logos of any substantial mind" ("Ariachne's Broken Woof," p. 51).[6] Miller refuses to assent to a "self" that stands "outside" language and uses language to create forms for its "self-expression"; language is not simply expressing the self, but is fictively creating it. The self is caught in the prison-house of language and defined along with everything else as a component of the linguistic field.

Miller's two careers imply two different understandings of the self, and his formulations appear to leave only a chasm between them. But while he is quick to undermine the status of the authoritatively grounded self, he does not seem to realize that his analysis hardly precludes the desire to attain such a "self." It is possible to retain the active desire for a centered self even after its linguistic constitution is detected, still possible to strive for order and coherence in the shaping of one's self. Although the self that one creates may be fictive (defined only through language), it may, nonetheless, focus the desire for orderly, coherent behavior by still acting as an authoritative center. Miller's deconstructive rhetoric—and, as we shall discover, the rhetoric that his opponents use—often implies that there is only a dichotomy of centered self or no self at all, and this chain of strict oppositions could be extended to include the existence or non-existence of literary history, authoritative interpretation, and coherence in academic work. Neither Miller nor his critical antagonists see that the deconstruction of certain terms (self, origin, history, and so on) does not mean that the terms no longer help to organize behavior. The deconstructive undertaking does not prophesy the short-circuiting of authority and order, as Miller suggests and as E. D. Hirsch, M. H. Abrams, and others fear. For built into Miller's deconstructive platform are powerful constraints which guarantee that authority, standards, and the rule of t adition in literary studies will be preserved. These are obviously points to which I will have to return, but first I need to explore in more detail what "deconstruction" means for Miller and to examine the ambiguities in his treatment of several important issues.

II

First, the place of the author. Miller's book on Dickens assumes the presence of an authorial consciousness at the center of an imagined world, and it assigns to Dickens the power to "transform" materials into a consistent "vision of things" (p. 328). In this phase of his career, Miller allows the author the capacity to fashion experience into art. A decade later, discussing "first-person narration" in *David Copperfield* and *Huckleberry Finn*,[7] he still insists that works of literature are the "verbal expression of a consciousness," and he adds, echoing Poulet, that the critic must attempt to coincide "in an act of pure identification, with the mental structures of the novel" (p. 21). The author's presence informs the novel, and the text manifests "feelings and thoughts."

Miller's recent essays, however, detach the text from its author as a point of origin; effects are located in texts, not in the mind or intention of the author who wrote them. Commenting on *Oliver Twist* in 1970, Miller at times acknowledges an authorial presence, yet he also maintains that the text itself propagates the real dynamics and interest of the novel.[8] Dickens, he says, affirms a "repetition" based on authentic models and the similiarity of the repeated elements (the model and its copy) and rejects another form of "repetition" that testifies to the in-authenticity of models and the inescapable "difference" between the model and its copy. But, Miller contends, "the hidden energy behind the novel is the tension between the two" (p. 29). The critic discovers energies in the text that are "hidden" from the author and not "explicitly" stated; thus, the critic differentiates from, rather than moves to coincide with, the author, and, in addition, dissolves the status of an "author" who is independent of the text and comprehends it. Elsewhere in the same essay, Miller notes that the *Sketches by Boz* "turn at crucial moments on their own conventions and expose them as fictions too" (p. 35). This "turn" is similarly embedded in the workings of the text, and not in an authorial consciousness.

It is difficult to make these statements accord with the claim that "the characters have no existence outside the language Dickens has invented to describe them" (p. 32), a claim that re-attributes to the writer a personal reign over language and the power to authorize new creations. The problem for Miller is that he cannot speak simultaneously of effects codified in the nature of literary texts and of authors who "invent" special arrangements of language and induce readers to respond to their texts by their handling of linguistic devices. When Miller concludes that "for both Dickens's *Sketches* and Cruikshank's illustrations the validity of the fictive reading cannot be reached unless we are tempted into accepting and exploring the representational reading" (p. 69), his passive construction ("are tempted") conceals his movement back and forth between the author and the text.

The problem is repeated, with greater clarity, in Miller's deconstruction of *Middlemarch*.[9] He selects this text as an "example" of the "self-defeating turning back of the novel to undermine its own grounds" (p. 462); the text performs its own act of criticism and is independent of both its author and its critics. Yet the authority of the author reappears, though at one remove, when Miller names Will Ladislaw as "the spokesman" for George Eliot's "demolition" of one particular "association between history and narrative" (p. 466). Now the author is, if not present, at least represented in the text through a "spokesman." In this essay Miller wavers between recognizing the author's presence ("George Eliot presents a view of artistic form as inorganic, acentered, and discontinuous" [p. 468]), repudiating it in favor of the text's own energies ("*Middlemarch* itself, finally, is an example of form as difference in its effects on its readers" [p. 470]), and locating the issue somewhere in an obscure no-woman's land ("The metaphysical notions of history, of storytelling, and of individual human lives are replaced by different notions" [p. 467]).[10] Miller's deconstructive stance prohibits origins, but his practical criticism exposes his difficulty in enforcing this principle. Repeatedly he identifies effects *within* the language of the texts themselves, yet he continually returns to the concept of an author responsible for making the text and orchestrating its purposes and strategies.

III

Miller's confusion about the author and the text points to a related problem: his inconsistent and inadequate theory of reading and interpretation. In *The Form of Victorian Fiction*, he defines reading as the "consciousness of the consciousness of another": "Through the act of reading the reader tries to identify himself with another mind and to reexperience from the inside the feelings and thoughts of that mind. Reading a novel is form of intersubjectivity" (p. 2). Reading is the effort to achieve the "coincidence" of subject with subject, and, as Miller points out in his essay on *David Copperfield* and *Huckleberry Finn*, this coincidence requires that the reader create, as he or she proceeds from "passage" to "passage," "temporary centers" around which the rest of the novel momentarily coheres (p. 24). But the deconstruction of the self in Miller's recent work disposes of an "intersubjective" definition of reading. His analyses in this new mode do not offer a comprehensive theory of reading, and this omission leads him into imprecision when he refers to the relations, and the degrees of priority and responsibility, among the author, reader, and text.

In an essay on *Lord Jim*,[11] Miller describes this novel as containing, "like most works of literature," "elements" that are "self-interpretive" (p. 211); readers are "inveigled" into sharing "in the self-sustaining motion of an unending process of interpretation" (p. 227). This suggests that the text itself produces interpretive "elements" that readers can only "share"; when interpreting the text, readers become implicated in a process that has begun without them. Conrad's novel, Miller asserts, does not supply the reader with a structuring principle to tie together its "secrets" (p. 215). Rather, the reader's interpretation is woven into the cloth or fabric of the text's own interpretations (Miller's metaphor, borrowed from Conrad). Yet Miller can also ask: "Can this description of the form of *Lord Jim* be sustained by close examination of the text?" (p. 215). This account depicts a different role for the reader, who now structures an interpretive paradigm and then, as a practical critic, tests its accuracy by scrutinizing the text. According to this view, the reader possesses the "form" of the work in advance of textual explication. Instead of stressing a "weaving" in and out of interpretations, Miller implies here that the reader arrives at an interpretive hypothesis and then juxtaposes it with New Critical exegesis. Reading and criticism are not an interlaced design of interpretations, but (it seems) procedures that are based on comparison and analysis.

Miller presents two descriptions of the reader's and critic's activity, but he appears unaware of their contradiction. The first suggests that "new" interpretation is *already* part of the many threads of the text, while the second works by sketching the novel's "form" and then checking its correspondence with particular passages. It is also unclear whether the roles of the reader and the critic are, for Miller, the same or different. Does the critic return to the text to perform upon it operations that the reader avoids or is unaware of? Are "reading" and "critical" interpretation (acts of analysis) two different things, or does interpretation simply plot what the reader does? Sometimes Miller speaks of *Lord Jim* as though it were doing all of the interpretive work itself: "The novel creates its meaning out of the juxtaposition of its various episodes in their interplay of sameness and difference, of 'objective' facts and 'subjective' interpretation" (p. 224). In this account the novel itself, rather than the reader or critic, "creates" meaning through its own acts of "juxtaposition" and "interplay."

Miller deals at length with these issues in his well-known review of M. H. Abrams's *Natural Supernaturalism*, published in the Winter, 1972, issue of *Diacritics*. Drawing on Nietzsche and Derrida for support, he argues that "the reading of a work involves an active intervention on the part of the reader. Each reader takes possession of the work for one reason or another and imposes on it a certain pattern of meaning" (p. 12). "Intervention" connotes that readers break in upon, or interfere with, a process that is already underway; they obtrude themselves upon the text's "interplay" of meanings and "impose" themes and patterns where there were none before. But when Miller attributes to readers this Nietzschean will-to-power over the text and confers upon them the ability to create patterns of meaning, he contradicts the notion of the text that is "self-interpretive." On the one hand, there is a text that proposes its own interpretation, and, on the other, there is a reader who imports meaning into the text or, as Nietzsche declares in *The Will to Power* (which Miller cites), "projects" a sense into "facts" ("there are no 'facts-in-themselves'") and thereby brings the category of "facts" into being. Miller's priorities are jumbled: Is the reader or the text responsible for generating meaning? To state this question so crudely should not be taken to mean that there is an equally crude and unambiguous answer, but it does help to highlight a confusion in Miller's theory. In his review he refers to Abrams's "more or less unspoken methodology" (p. 8), "implicit assumptions" (p. 8), and error in taking "his writers a little too much at face value" (p. 11). But he nowhere clarifies the deconstructive theory of reading and interpretation that lies behind these phrases. What is the status of an assumption "implicit" in the text and how is it uncovered, as opposed to a "value" that rests on the "face" of the text? Though Miller rebukes Abrams for failing to take account of the "terms" of his analysis (p. 8), he falls victim in his review to the same charge.[12]

IV

Miller is also hazy about the ethics of reading and criticism. Is there a specific morality involved in the reading and interpretation of texts? What dictates the morality of an interpretation that is designed to persuade an audience and win its complicity and acceptance? What is the responsibility of the critic towards a text, and what kinds of judgments does he or she render on those who are also engaged in the interpretation of texts? In 1966, Miller observed that "it is possible to distort novels and poems in the direction of a dualism which they do not in fact express."[13] This presupposes an area of unwarranted "distortion," a twisting or perverting of the text that the critic must guard against and chastise in others. But elsewhere Miller suggests that "distortion" is an inevitable consequence of all interpretation, and not merely an error or lapse that we perceive only in some interpretations. In the preface to his book on Thomas Hardy, he says that "there is no innocent reading, no reading which leaves the work exactly as it is" (p. viii). No criticism is wholly faithful to the integrity of the text, for it invariably stands convicted of some element of "distortion." Yet he also insists, in his next sentence, that "this does not mean that all readings are equally valid or of equal value. Some readings are certainly wrong" (p. ix).

Miller's ethical point remains, but it has altered in direction and emphasis. Now the critic labels interpretations—all of which necessarily "distort"—as either right or wrong. While all criticism wrenches the text out of shape, some varieties reach "more deeply into the text than others" (p. ix). But of course the standards for judging the relative "depth" of a critical analysis are themselves shaped by critical presuppositions. The category of "deep" criticism depends upon what the individual critic judges to be either "shallow" or "deep" kinds of insights into texts, and what general kinds of criticism he or she thinks should be lamented or encouraged. Not everyone, for example, finds that deconstruction "deepens" knowledge about texts. Miller's account is confusing because he adheres to ethical signatures and standards

(right and wrong), even though his deconstructive theory cuts against
them.

In his review of the Abrams book, Miller criticizes the notion of
"rightness" in interpretation. He stamps Abrams's treatment of Nietzsche
as "plausible" and buttressed by "abundant citations," but nevertheless
replies that it is "wrong." Yet he then turns on his own judgment
(though the reader has already felt its force) and explains that "rightness" in interpretation is "one of the ideas Nietzsche most wanted to
challenge" (p. 8). Abrams does not interpret the Nietzschean texts
"wrongly," Miller contends, but instead displays his will-to-power over
them. He is not guilty of "wrong" critical conduct, since there is no
"right" conduct in interpretation, and since all readers exercise will-to-
power over texts.

This again raises the issue of the standards for Miller's evaluative
distinctions. He clearly differentiates Abrams from the interpretive line
that Derrida represents (p. 8), and the criteria for his adverse judgment
of *Natural Supernaturalism* are cogent and concise—Abrams's mistaken
attitude towards tradition, literary history, "the humanization of the-
ological patterns," and so on (p. 8). Once one agrees, however, that
"rightness" in interpretation is an "idea" to be jettisoned, Miller's critique becomes surprisingly elusive. Miller reprimands Abrams for a
number of faults and failings, and invests himself with the authority
to make these judgments. But it is not evident that, after acknowledging
as a "fact" that all interpretation is a will-to-power over the text, he
has reflected on his basis for discriminating among readings. On some
occasions, Miller flattens out the issue by noting, for instance, "that all
reading is misreading is as true of the traditions of criticism as of
literature itself" ("Walter Pater," p. 98). Yet he elsewhere urges finer
discriminations: "Critics have erred in expecting *Middlemarch* to be in
one homogeneous 'realistic' style throughout. They have misunderstood and misjudged it as a consequence, for example in what they
have sometimes said about Will Ladislaw" ("Narrative and History,"
p. 470). Miller's alignment with Nietzsche on interpretation does not
prevent him from applying ethical and evaluative distinctions. Despite
his master assertion that "all reading is misreading," he continues to
censure specific instances of misinterpretation and critical error.

One can locate a more consistent evaluative slant in Miller's work,
but its implications are troubling. Increasingly his essays, however acute
and challenging, tend towards a rigid didacticism. Texts are praised,
and high value is conferred upon them, for testifying to deconstructive
insights about language, the self, and the absence of origins and privileged authorities. After citing a passage by Michel Foucault that denies
authoritative beginnings, Miller writes that "thematically and structur-
ally *Lord Jim* is an example of this absence of origin, center, or end"

("The Interpretation of *Lord Jim*," p. 213). For the reader to "impose" on the novel "a notion of aesthetic form modeled on a cosmos with an externally existing divine center" is to "falsify" it. The truth or falsehood of criticism of *Lord Jim* is therefore dependent, in an uncomfortably strict sense, on its conformity to Foucault's statement. Foucault is taken to authorize what Miller finds in *Lord Jim*, and what he "finds" confirms and repeats Foucault's cultural diagnosis. The text is then congratulated for living up to the strictures that Miller's cited authority announces.

Elsewhere Miller suggests that our hierarchy of poets arises from their success or failure in conforming to the dictates of deconstruction. In an essay on Wordsworth, he outlines two concepts of "form." The first distinguishes between "shape and substance, origin and result, cause and effect, model and copy, mold and molded," and also assumes that what is "formed" is validated by an "original" standing outside it. Whereas the second (part of "the deconstruction of metaphysics") rejects the belief in an "origin" upon which copies are formed or modeled. "The conflict between these two concepts of form" is "central in Wordworth's poetry. His greatness may in part be defined by his role in articulating the modern changes in concepts of form. Often what appears to be a more radical later statement will turn out to have been anticipated either explicitly or in practice by Wordsworth."[14] Miller awards high grades to Wordsworth's writing because it reveals correspondences with privileged modern authorities. He enlists Derrida and Foucault as evaluative norms, and measures a writer's "greatness" ("in part") according to the foresight shown in "anticipating" them. Miller does not seem to realize that he privileges these deconstructionist "modern" writers and texts when he deploys them as guidelines for evaluation. Nor does he inquire whether deconstruction, rather than being a standard that Wordsworth "anticipates" and is judged by, might instead provide us with a new way of reading him, one that makes his texts yield what interpretive procedures (to recall Nietzsche's term) "project" into them. In this case we would not be uncovering "anticipations" in Wordsworth's texts of "modern" attitudes towards origins, language, and the self. We would instead be filling out a different Wordsworth whose dimensions are shaped by deconstructive methods of reading, and by expectations about what texts should be and what insights they should deliver. Perhaps then we would not be forced implicitly to devalue Wordsworth by suggesting that his "greatness" can be acknowledged only in the face of Derrida's and Foucault's still greater achievement in "modern" times. We might credit Wordsworth not with taking his value from Derrida and Foucault, but instead with providing the norms for modern reading and interpretation to which these later writers belatedly testify.

V

When one turns to Miller's specific defense of "deconstruction"—
what it does and what it accomplishes—one finds that he often addresses the issues of critic, reader, text, and evaluation explicitly, but
finally no more coherently than in his other published work. In an
exchange with Wayne Booth and M. H. Abrams, Miller speaks of deconstruction as a "strategy." Referring to his deconstruction of a phrase
of Booth's (cited by Abrams), he writes: "My little example of a deconstructive strategy at work is meant, moreover, to indicate, no doubt
inadequately, the hyperbolic exuberance, the letting language go as far
as it will take one, or the going with a given text as far as it will go,
to its limits, which is an essential part of the procedure."[15] In this
account the critic is responsible for the interpretive situation, adopting
a certain "strategy" or "procedure" that will "let" language and texts
"go" to their limits. But as other essays make clear, Miller's attitude
towards the control of his interpretations is ambivalent. In his essay
on Williams, he argues that "the interpreter of a given text can only in
one way or another enter inside its play of language" (p. 430). This
implies that the critic chooses to "enter" into the textual network at
some point or juncture. Yet in his essay "Ariadne's Thread," Miller
suggests that because "any novel already interprets itself," the critic is
never "safely and rationally outside the contradictory language of the
text" but "already entangled in its web" (p. 74). Is critical choice vol-
untary or enforced? Is the critic able to decide to do something with
or upon the text, making an entrance or slicing into it, or does the text
enclose the critic within the folds of its language?

Miller usually argues that the text performs its own interpretation.
But his insistence on the critic's deliberate "procedure" and "strategy"
towards the text undercuts this claim, and it also merges with his
confusions about reading, evaluation, and critical ethics to create additional problems. As Joseph Riddel has noticed, Miller's deconstructive
criticism valorizes a "literary language" that is never "mystified" about
the availability of origins and the myth of presence.[16] Indeed, Miller
always identifies the self-interpreting text, the text that enacts its own
deconstruction, as the *literary* text. Here we encounter the conservative
impulse that leads Miller to canonize "literature" along the lines that
Nietzsche, Derrida, and, as Riddel points out, Paul De Man have traced.
In his essay on *Middlemarch*, Miller states that his "chief point" is to
call attention to the capacity of novels to "undermine their own ground"
("Narrative and History," p. 462); only the literary text (the novel)
deconstructs itself. Yet a few pages later, when alluding to the deconstructive power of a text written by Walter Benjamin, Miller claims that

"both metaphysics and its deconstruction" are "inescapably inscribed in the words that we must use to speak at all" (p. 471). This insight is far more radical, dispersing deconstruction into all texts, even those that comprise our ordinary speech. Miller's Nietzschean and Derridean sources encourage this extension of the self-deconstructing text into all forms of language. But while he hints that deconstruction is intrinsic to *all* language, he persistently guards against its abolition of literary categories and administers it only to literary works. When discussing *Tess of the d'Urbervilles*, Miller explains that his method suggests "a way to read this novel or, in fact, a way to read literary works in general," and he thereby situates deconstructive "reading" within the field of literary texts.[17] However "radical" deconstruction may appear—no origins, center, or presence—its insights are only disseminated to (and therefore contained by) literature.

Miller sometimes gestures towards the full force of deconstruction, as when he speaks of the radical possibilities "inherent in the English language" ("Ariachne's Broken Woof," p. 59). But he always pulls back to trap deconstruction within the literary domain. Even when he refers to the power of "strong interpretation" to break down the usual distinction between "literary" texts (and methods considered appropriate for their analysis) and "philosophical" or "psychological" texts, his point is less important for what it dissolves than for what it retains: literary, philosophical, and psychological texts are still distinct from other, presumably more pedestrian, kinds.[18] Although Miller is aware that "self-subversion" characterizes language in general, he consistently limits his deconstructive hegemony to literature and other respectable categories: "This structure of self-interpretation is characteristic in one way or another of all literature and of all art" ("Williams' *Spring and All*," p. 416). Somewhere there is another use of language that Miller excludes because it is not "literary" or "philosophical" or "psychological"; yet this unknown X must also be, according to his own definitions, "self-interpretive."

Miller's deconstructive stance not only privileges "literature" but also reifies the literary canon as it now stands. Deconstruction does not give us a radically new literary history, and it is in fact difficult to perceive that it has engendered any substantial changes in influence and reputation. Though deconstruction provides "new" terms with which to praise Wordsworth's "greatness," it does not call into question this "greatness" or attempt to alter the current literary rankings—despite the fact that Miller refers to the aim of deconstruction as the "reversal" of hierarchies. The deconstructive critic might do well to ask why this method, for all of its "radical" mustering of terms and insights, leaves Wordsworth's authority and prestige so little changed. As I observed earlier, Miller's evaluations are problematical in their effort to show an author's conformity with Foucault, Derrida, and other "moderns." What is equally problematical is that this conformity appears almost always to be practiced by writers traditionally regarded as "great." The terms of Miller's evaluations are questionable, but it is clear that their impetus is to retain the privilege granted to certain writers by literary history as it is usually written. When Miller states that "Pater's writings, like those of other major authors in the Occidental tradition, are at once open to interpretation and ultimately undecipherable, unreadable" ("Walter Pater," p. 112), he is not laying out a "new" hierarchy of "major authors"; he is instead preserving the traditional canon, with only minor shifts in emphasis, set out in deconstructive terms.[19]

VI

Miller elaborates his deconstructive stance in greatest detail in his important review of Riddel's *The Inverted Bell* in *Diacritics* (Summer, 1975), and in the second part of his essay on Wallace Stevens. It is possible to identify and list several familiar fissures in the review of Riddel's book.

1. Literary and other kinds of texts. Miller rebukes Riddel for failing to recognize "the necessary heterogeneity of any text" (p. 30). But he does not mean to welcome all texts into the deconstructive fold, as he indicates a few sentences later: Riddel ignores the "irreducible heterogeneity of the languages of poetry, of philosophy, and of criticism." For Miller, the phrase "any text" translates into the literary and related texts that are in a special class, separated and protected from the outcast kinds.

2. The role of the reader. Miller defines deconstruction as "a version of the basic act of reading" (p. 30). But this "act" of reading, rather than being "basic," is a privileged transaction with a textual aristocracy. Miller states in his next sentence that this version of the "basic" reading experience "may be performed on any literary, philosophical, or critical text." He does not explain what "act of reading" we perform on that other (non-literary) assortment of texts that never figure in his deconstructive census.

3. The deconstructive critic and the text. Here again we discover Miller's divided sympathies. He contends that "the text performs on itself the act of deconstruction without any help from the critic. The text expresses its own aporia" (p. 31). This displaces the critic in favor of the text that interprets itself. Yet when Miller goes on to suggest that the critic is more than merely subservient to the text, his phrasing is instructive: "The heterogeneity of a text (and so its vulnerability to deconstruction) lies rather in the fact that it says two entirely incom-

patible things at the same time" (p. 30). The text possesses its own voice and speaks for itself ("it says"); yet it is also weak, "vulnerable" to the critic's deconstructive entry. "Or rather," Miller adds, "it says something which is capable of being interpreted in two irreconcilable ways." This textual voice, then, may be less than self-sufficient, for it may require interpretation ("capable of being interpreted") to bring out its "irreconcilable" character. Though Miller often stresses the self-interpretive text, with the critic slotted in a subordinate role, he rein-vests the critic with the authority to reveal the text's special "hetero-geneous" nature. "Both 'Asphodel' and *Paterson Five* are Modernist and Post-Modernist at once, and can be shown to be so," he explains (p. 31). The critic is needed to deconstruct the text precisely because it cannot "show" its own "interpretation," its deconstruction of itself.

4. Literary history. Miller argues that no text can fit into a "univocal period definition," since all "periods" are "equivocal," made up of "heterogeneous" texts. A new literary history, like those that Harold Bloom and Geoffrey Hartman have begun (p. 31), "will no doubt differ radically" from usual accounts of "periods" that "progress" from one to the next. Yet these claims for "radicalism"—putting to one side the question of Bloom's and Hartman's work—are misleading. The terms in which Miller expresses his deconstructive "literary history" may jar with those that other "histories" employ, but the canon of exemplary authors—Miller cites Chaucer, Spenser, Shakespeare, Milton, Words-worth, George Eliot, Stevens, and Williams—belies, in its adherence to traditional alignments, its "radical" posture.

When Miller returns to these issues in his second Stevens essay, he runs into similiar problems. He attacks "the notion of the self-enclosed literary work" (p. 333), but he removes one type of enclosure (the text restricted by a "fixed, identifiable meaning") only to erect a new one—literary works enclosed within, and distinguished by, their own "het-erogeneity."[20] While he speaks of the "dismantling" of the boundaries between "literary texts and other kinds of texts" (p. 334), he stakes out another boundary that limits these "other kinds" to acceptable academic ones. Miller always controls and holds in check the interpretive pos-sibilities of his theory, and he carefully preserves what a truly "radical" critique would threaten to undermine. At one point he comments on the dynamic cast of Harold Bloom's studies, remarking that "after Bloom's work we shall never be able to read Shelley or Browning, Tennyson or Stevens, in the same way again" (p. 340). This may well be the case, but if so, it argues for a redefinition of Miller's account of the self-interpretive text. When he says that because of Bloom's analyses, our understanding of these writers' texts has changed, he implies that the critic can remake and reform these texts. The critic offers new strategies for reading texts that alter their composition, making it impossible for

us to reread the texts we once thought we knew. By crediting Bloom
with changing these texts, Miller subverts the priority of the self-interpretive text and restores the preeminent place of the critic who re-
fashions the text and presents us with "new" ways of composing and
structuring it.

VII

In his second essay on Stevens, Miller alludes to the likely "institutionalization" in America of deconstruction and other types of Continental criticism. Sometime in the very near future, he observes, "deconstruction" will be taught in college courses, discussed in detail in
seminars and in the professional journals, and no doubt will suffer at
the hands of less skilled and less responsible practitioners. But the truth
is that this "institutionalization" has already occurred. Is it merely
accidental that what advertises itself as "radical" criticism proceeds
apace at the finest "institutions" of higher learning? Critical theory is
expanding at an impressive rate these days, in the form of new journals,
courses, special "schools," books, collections of essays, debates, and
translations. It is remarkable how easily this "radical" material has been
absorbed into the academic mainstream and assimilated into the intellectual channels that define responses to, and ways of dealing with,
almost everything else. Deconstruction is no more exempt from immediate "institutionalization" than other critical methods, and, as the
economic index for literary theory rises, it will surely continue to serve
as one of the idols of the marketplace.

But if Miller's theory of "deconstruction" is so mild-mannered and
similar to other types of criticism, then why have influential members
of the profession, such as Hirsch, Abrams, and Booth, risen to combat
it? These enemies of deconstruction are dismayed by the "chaos" that
it seems to promote, and they refuse to believe that texts (the "ground"
for research and teaching) lack "fixed, identifiable meaning." There is
a "core of meaning," says Abrams, and a "determinate object of knowledge," insists Hirsch, that we can agree upon and employ as a "standard" to order our scholarship and justify our role as teachers of something authoritative and concrete. Miller's deconstructive theory, it is
argued, repudiates authority, invites subjectivity and an influx of "irreconcilable" interpretations, and cripples the values of humanistic inquiry. It cannot be allowed a place among the plural voices of criticism,
because it refuses to believe in what the others are committed to: an
origin and goal in interpretation.

To polarize the issues in this way—Miller vs. Abrams, Booth, Hirsch;
no authoritative meaning vs. a fixed meaning—guarantees a lively de-

bate. But the affinities between Miller and his adversaries count more than the differences. Miller retains almost everything that his opponents fear will be removed if the reign of deconstruction arrives: the "great" Western authors and texts remain; literary language keeps its privileged position; literary history only changes its terms, not its traditional objects of study; the "object of knowledge" and principle of authority do not disappear, but turn into the "heterogeneous" nature of literary texts that the critic and teacher can "identify" (Miller's word, used in his review of Riddel's book); and the "institution," rather than being subverted by deconstruction, becomes its long-lost center, where its tenets are formulated and discussed. Miller's deconstructive theory, despite the persuasive lure of its "radical" surface, in fact bears witness to the literary and professional allegiances he shares with his enemies. He includes "enclosures" and "boundaries" that hold back the spread of subjectivity and that forestall the dissolution of authority in scholarship and teaching.

Miller and his opponents share a profound area of agreement, and their positions are, in their polemical form, unfaithful to the multiple crossings between them. Abrams, for instance, fears the disappearance of interpretive constraints and worries about the disorder that their loss would introduce into literary studies. He takes a determined stand behind a "core of meaning" to ward off what he sees as Miller's radical assault on standards and discipline within the ranks. But Miller himself reveals little sympathy for eliminating constraints; he incorporates a number of them into his deconstructive method and thereby ensures that a system of checks and balances will over-ride its potentially disruptive force. Miller's call for deconstructive criticism, far from being "radical," is bound and limited by its decision to privilege certain authorities (Nietzsche, Derrida, Foucault) and valorize "literary" categories ("literary" language and canonical texts that are self-interpretive); by its susceptibility to common confusions that have always been with us (the place to be accorded to author, critic, reader, and text); and by its appearance in professional and highly "institutionalized" contexts.

VIII

Miller is a prolific writer and is hard to keep up with. Since my critique was published, in an earlier version, in the December, 1979, issue of *College English*, Miller has written a book and a number of articles. But he has not changed his basic position, and he still does not seem aware of the ambivalences in his deconstructive arguments. He continues to make the same errors and get caught in the same confusions about authors, readers, and texts.[21]

The most interesting aspect of Miller's recent work, however, is its emphasis on the differences that deconstruction has wrought. In "Theory and Practice," he states that deconstruction has begun to bring about important changes in the institution of literature, "changes in the style and content of teaching, changes in the organization of courses, curricula, and departments" (p. 613). But the issue is not really whether deconstruction has caused "changes" in scholarship and teaching, but is instead whether these "changes" are significant. Miller is correct to say that changes have occurred, and his commentary on "character" in fiction, literary "realism," and "periodization" outline some of the adjustments that deconstruction has effected. But, as always, Miller is careful to circumscribe the "changes" and "differences" that deconstruction produces. In fact, he is becoming even more open, in his recent writings, about declaring just how "conservative" his allegiances are. He welcomes deconstruction as a positive development, and he persists in being one of its most avid spokesmen. But it is clearer than ever that Miller is willing to allow deconstructive practice to go only so far.

"My instincts," Miller observes in "The Function of Rhetorical Study at the Present Time," are "strongly preservative or conservative. I believe in the established canon of English and American literature and in the validity of the concept of privileged texts. I think it is more important to read Spenser, Shakespeare, or Milton than to read Borges in translation, or even, to say the truth, to read Virginia Woolf" (p. 12). Miller imposes deconstruction upon a base or ground that he is unwilling or unable to contest. He cannot imagine the possibility of altering or overturning the "established canon"; he can only imagine ways of interpreting that canon differently. For Miller, the measure of a theory lies in its capacity to give us "readings" of classic texts, and in this respect, he concludes, deconstruction has proven to be a great boon to the study of literature.

"The primary evidence of the value of deconstruction," Miller suggests, "is not its coherence as theory but the fact that it has made possible new insights into what is going on in particular works, even where that has been insight into the necessary blindness of the work to its own incoherence or heterogeneity and insight into the consequent inability of the critic to 'read' the work in any determinate or monological way" ("Theory and Practice," p. 610). "I still believe," Miller notes in an interview,

> in verification and validity in criticism. When I say a work is undecidable or open-ended, that does not mean that there is not a better or worse reading of the work. The best reading is the one that identifies most exactly the possible alternative meanings between which it is impossible to decide identities than through citation and discussion. The exact form of

"indeterminacy" can be determined by those means. . . . The critic does not deconstruct the text. The text deconstructs itself.... The attraction for me of "deconstructive" criticism is that it seems to account for more features that are objectively there in the literary text than other forms of criticism indicate. ("Interview," pp. 110-12)

Miller's brand of deconstruction privileges the canon, stresses close reading as the ultimate goal of criticism, preserves the notion of "validity" (some readings are more accurate and thus "better" than others), fixes meaning in the text, and preserves an object of knowledge and value that critics and teachers can defend. There is much for Miller's foes, particularly Hirsch and Abrams, to greet warmly and admire here.

"The ethics of reading," says Miller, "is not some act of the human will to interpretation which extracts moral themes from a work, or uses it to reaffirm what the reader already knows, or imposes a meaning freely in some process of reader response or perspectivist criticism, seeing the text in a certain way. The ethics of reading is the power of the words of the text over the mind and words of the reader." This, he adds, "is an irresistible coercion which shapes what the reader or teacher says about the text, even when what he says is most reductive or evasive.... The ethics of reading is the moral necessity to submit in one way or another, whatever one says, to the truth of this linguistic imperative" ("The Ethics of Reading," p. 41). It is indeed because the "preservative or conservative" and "moral" themes have grown so central in Miller's work that he belongs—and is now seen as belonging—to the main line of academic criticism. In my view, Miller has always been part of this traditional line; it is just that many readers, stricken by the assertions about "self-dismantling texts" and the like in Miller's first group of deconstructionist essays, mistakenly saw him as dangerous, as a threat to the survival of the discipline. Miller's antagonists now recognize him as one of their own, however dubious or excessive his procedures may appear to be. Robert Langbaum, for instance, has praised Miller's book on the novel, *Fiction and Repetition*, and characterized his method as "mainly New Critical close reading."[22] And this is a description that Miller himself has seen fit to acknowledge: "I'm still true to my primary interest in the New Criticism in that ultimately my real interest is in accounting for literary texts" ("Interview," p. 111).

In my next chapter, I consider Stanley Fish, who, like Miller, proposes a "radical" or "revolutionary" theory of literature. Fish concentrates on "the reader" and aims to free us from the notion of an "objective" text, a text that itself contains meaning, and that readers simply consume and critics report on. But Fish, again like Miller, builds constraints into his system even as he proclaims its liberating power, and in the process he too becomes trapped by errors and contradictions.

With the publication of "Interpreting the *Variorum*" in 1976, Fish begins to detach his theory from the constraints that formerly enclosed it. But his account then suffers from a disabling limitation: Fish describes a theory that has suggestive implications for social and ideological analysis, yet he oddly refuses to develop them. He remains mired in demystification, doomed, it seems, to keep reproducing the same insights and unable to proceed to reconstructive projects. Miller presents us with a new theory in order to repeat, in a different form, the work that has been done many times before, whereas Fish gives us a new theory without realizing the kinds of truly innovative work it can accomplish. In this respect Fish is a powerful but disappointing figure, a theorist who does not capitalize on the potential of his theory. His work allows for the kind of political, social, and historical commentary that neither Hirsch nor Miller envisions. Yet Fish is oddly uninterested at the present time in pursuing these lines of inquiry: he seems in fact rigidily opposed to moving his theory into new areas. Fish is a shrewd critic and skillful polemicist, but he leads us, as we shall see, to a dead end.

3.

Constraints and Politics in the Literary Theory of Stanley Fish

In short, the theory, both as an account of meaning and as a way of teaching, is full of holes; and there is one great big hole right in the middle of it which is filled, if it is filled at all, by what happens inside the user-student.

Stanley Fish, "Literature in the Reader"

Despite René Wellek's and Austin Warren's warning that studies of "the reader" would lead to "complete skepticism and anarchy" and eventually to "the definite end of all teaching of literature,"[1] critical theorists since the 1960s have devoted much attention to "readers" and the "reading process." Georges Poulet, Norman Holland, Wolfgang Iser, David Bleich, and Jonathan Culler have, in their different ways, displaced the text in favor of the reader and encouraged the study of topics such as "indeterminacy" in reading, personal identity and psychological defense in the reader, and the "conventions" that make reading possible. But the most influential—if also the most controversial—of the reader-theorists is Stanley Fish. He has been presenting, clarifying, and redefining his theory for more than a decade, and, as he predicted in *Surprised by Sin* (1967; reprint edition, 1971), his work has helped to make "the reader in" a familiar phrase in the titles of scholarly books and articles.

Fish's emphasis on the reader has been both warmly received—one enthusiastic admirer has compared him to Kant—and severely criticized.[2] But neither Fish's supporters nor his detractors have taken full account of the differences between the two major phases of his work.[3] In his early theoretical writings, Fish seeks to refute the charge that because his method views the "reader" as the maker of meaning, he invites impressionism and subjectivity. He builds constraints into his system (a controlling author, a "meaning-full" text, uniformity among readers) that are designed to guarantee rigor, discipline, and orderly procedure and thereby rule out the danger of merely "subjective" responses. In "Interpreting the *Variorum*," a key transitional essay, Fish resolves the problem of subjectivity not by means of these constraints, but by arguing that the problem itself is a false one. Readers, he states, do not respond in private or subjective ways, but instead act as members of "interpretive communities." Yet while the *Variorum* essay marks an advance, it also reveals a failure to confront the theory's political power and reinvokes the authority of institutions even as it seems to call them into question. Fish devises a fine analytical instrument, yet he cannot conceive of truly challenging and recreative uses for it.

I

In "What Is Stylistics and Why Are They Saying Such Terrible Things about It?" Fish criticizes the work of Louis Milic, Richard Ohmann, J. P. Thorne, Michael Halliday, and other stylisticians.[4] Their enterprise, he says, is invalid, because it lacks "any constraint on the way in which one moves from description to interpretation, with the result that any interpretation one puts forward is arbitrary" (p. 113). But Fish's case against the stylisticians is not just that their project is "impossible" (p. 114) and succeeds only because its arbitrariness ensures that it will never fail (p. 117). "My larger objection," he declares, "is that it is unworthy, for it would deny to man the most remarkable of his abilities, the ability to give the world meaning rather than to extract the meaning that is already there" (p. 134). The reader is the maker of meaning, and "human beings" should occupy the privileged place in theories of interpretation.

Fish's call for a new humanism is a limited one, however. He encourages us to recognize that "meaning is human" (p. 152), yet he does not entirely break away from a model that locates meaning in the text. Fish speaks of the reader as the creator of meaning, as an "interpreting entity" engaged in "determining what counts as the facts to be observed" (p. 148). But this argument on behalf of the reader is given alongside a different one that stresses the "cues" in the text, the reader's "interaction" with the words on the page, and the ways in which the reader is "directed" by what he or she reads (see pp. 151, 146). Fish credits the reader with the ability to determine "what counts as" meaning, but he also implies that there are meanings already "in" the text. This slide from the reader to the text also occurs when he revises the stylisticians' theories. He, too, is interested in "formal characterizations of language," but he gathers this "information" for another purpose:

"Rather than regarding it as directly translatable into what a word or a pattern means, it will be used more exactly to specify what a reader, as he comes upon that word or pattern, is doing, what assumptions he is making, what conclusions he is reaching, what expectations he is forming, what attitudes he is entertaining, in short, what acts he is being moved to perform" (p. 144). Despite Fish's concern for what a reader "does," he preserves a theory of textual meaning. Patterns exist in the text, and they prompt or lead the reader to take certain actions ("what acts he is being moved to perform"). Fish pays tribute to the scope and quality of the free reader's work, but he also makes sure that this activity is connected to what the text itself instigates and proposes.

Another problem with Fish's esteem for "human beings" arises when he describes the "informed reader." He defines this reader during his analysis of "Why is Iago evil?" a sentence taken from Joan Didion's *Play It As It Lays.* "There are at least four potential readers of this sentence," and these range from "the reader for whom the name Iago means nothing" to the reader "who is aware that the question has its own history, that everyone has had a whack at answering it, and that it has become a paradigm question for the philosophical-moral problem of motivation" (p. 146). Fish is not simply suggesting that these readers differ, for he adds that after we identify the different readers, we then rank them. The "informed reader" is the fourth one, and "his experience of the sentence will be not only different from, but better than, his less-informed fellows" (p. 146). Fish fails to explain the relation between his regard for "human beings"—all of whom have "the ability to give the world meaning"—and his insistence that their responses are to be accorded different degrees of value. When he says in an earlier essay, "Literature in the Reader: Affective Stylistics," that his concern is with "description," not "evaluation," he is only partially correct.[5] He does not assign value to texts, but he does evaluate the performance of different classes of readers: some are "better than" others and enjoy greater distinction.

Still more questionable is Fish's reference in his early work to the "constraints" that allow him to talk about the "informed reader." These are: "(1) the conscious attempt to become the informed reader by making my mind the repository of the (potential) responses a given text might call out and (2) the attendant suppressing, in so far as that is possible, of what is personal and idiosyncratic and 1970ish in my response" ("Literature in the Reader," p. 145). This argument reflects badly on Fish's call for a theory that affirms the place of "human beings." He celebrates "man" as the maker of meanings, yet advocates a method that suppresses the special features of a person's meanings. The "informed reader" is a "construct" (p. 143) that helps to keep the individual reader in line. It is also a "constraint" (p. 145) that forestalls "subjectivity" and maintains orderly procedures. The reader is free to make meaning, but only insofar as he or she shears off from response anything that is personal, idiosyncratic, or time-bound—anything, in a word, that departs from the norm that the "informed reader" establishes. As "Literature in the Reader" makes clear, the "informed reader" is only one of several constraints, and I will now turn to the others.

II

In "Literature in the Reader," Fish describes his method in detail. He wants, first of all, to guard against the charge that his theory invites an "impressionism" whereby each reader reports on personal responses. Borrowing from "modern linguistics," Fish outlines a "competence model" that assumes that "if the speakers of a language share a system of rules that each of them has somehow internalized, understanding will, in some sense, be uniform; that is it will proceed in terms of the system of rules all speakers share" (p. 141). Because these rules act as "constraints," they set the "boundaries" within which responses are registered and even make certain that response is, "to some extent, predictable and normative." Far from lapsing into impressionism, Fish argues, his accounts of the reader are based on the fact that, within a certain range, readers' responses are the same.

This argument for uniformity bypasses critical history. Not only do readers respond in ways that appear far from uniform, but their responses differ so dramatically that one might ask, as Fish does himself in his later "Variorum" essay, whether they are even reading the same text. Fish is aware of this objection and tries to answer it: "If there is a measure of uniformity to the reading experience, why have so many readers, and some equally informed, argued so well and passionately for differing interpretations? This, it seems to me, is a pseudo-problem. Most literary quarrels are not disagreements about response, but about a response to a response. What happens to one informed reader of a work will happen, within a range of non-essential variation, to another" (p. 147).

This extraordinary claim overrides the differences among readers and asserts that these fall "within a range of non-essential variation." Fish's statement is less an answer to the problem of disagreement than a means of deflecting his critics, who contend that because their responses are manifestly different, they can readily undercut Fish's claim for *the* reader's response. Faced with such readers, but bolstered by his belief in "non-essential variation," Fish replies that these other responses only "seem to be" different from his own and are really confused or misunderstood reports of a basic, shared response.[6] This is, to say the least, a problematical position, since it obliges Fish to tell readers who claim to differ with him that they are wrong and do not understand their own responses. While Fish is in an awkward place in his argument here, his statements make a certain kind of confused sense when one grasps that they are motivated by Fish's effort to constrain the interpreter's self and ward off the peril of subjectivity.

Another constraint is implicit in Fish's description of the author. We should consider, he explains, the "mistakes" that a reader makes when working through a text. A critic such as Richard Ohmann is wrong to dismiss such readerly acts as "inappropriate"; these are "a response to the strategy of an author; and the resulting mistakes are part of the experience provided by the author's language and therefore part of its meaning" (p. 144). If the reader errs or revises an earlier decision, he or she does so because the author is guiding or manipulating response. Fish realizes that this might seem to "claim too much for the conscious control" of "producer-authors" (p. 147). "I tend to answer this question," he states, "by begging it, by deliberately choosing texts in which the evidence of control is overwhelming" (p. 147). Fish's critics sometimes charge that "affective stylistics" ushers in subjectivity and does away with authority in interpretation: once we see the reader as the maker of meaning, we turn criticism into an arena where "anything goes." But as Fish's remarks on the "author" suggest, he and his critics may be closer to one another than either side is aware. While Fish does focus on the "reader," he wants to shape and limit the reader's work, and when he describes the place of the author in his theory, he worries that one of his principles of authority (the controls that the author's language provides) may be too unyielding for the readers of his essay to accept it.

Like the "What Is Stylistics?" essay, "Literature in the Reader" highlights the reader but preserves a theory of textual meaning. Fish's central question—"What does this sentence do?" (p. 125)—alerts us to the reader's response but locates its source in the text. The text is *doing something*, pushing, prodding, and manuvering the reader. Fish inclines so strongly toward textual meaning that he credits the text with an independent existence. "What I am suggesting," he says, is "that there is no direct relationship between the meaning of a sentence (paragraph, novel, poem) and what its words mean. Or, to put the matter less provocatively, the information an utterance gives, its message, is a constituent of, but certainly not to be identified with, its meaning" (p. 131). There is "information" given in the text that the reader does not make or produce, but which he or she "actualizes" and "responds" to. And this relation between the reader and the text becomes even more apparent—and still more subversive of the reader's activity—when Fish states that "meaning is a (partial) product of the utterance-object, but not to be identified with it. In this theory, the message the utterance carries—usually one pole of a binary relationship in which the other pole is style—is in its operation (which someone like Richards would deny) one more effect, one more drawer of response, one more constituent in the meaning experience. It is simply not the meaning. Nothing is" (p. 160).

Far from doing away with the text, Fish tends to make it reappear. The text guides the reader and prompts certain actions, and it thereby functions, along with the author and the "uniformity" among readers, to constrain interpretation. Contrary to the arguments made by Morton W. Bloomfield and others, Fish is not leading us towards "a morass of subjectivity,"[7] but is guarding against any tendencies in his reader-centered method that might dispose each reader to interpret as he or she pleases. In his first batch of theoretical writings, Fish may look dangerous, but on more careful inspection, he emerges as a spokesman for strict interpretive controls. He champions the need for "constraints" as much as, if not more than, he proclaims the reader's freedom.

III

In part one of "Interpreting the *Variorum*," an essay published six years after "Literature in the Reader," Fish still worries about constraints.[8] His "reader-oriented analysis" is, he claims, superior to formalism because instead of bringing more evidence forward, it asks what the evidence signifies. When reading a poem, we may form expectations that a particular line fails to satisfy; if a word in this line seems ambiguous, we should not seek to decide on its exact meaning (by gathering, like the formalists, various kinds of evidence), but should try to describe its significance "in the context" of our expectations. "That context" is

> experiential, and it is within its contours and constraints that significances are established (both in the act of reading and the analysis of that act). In formalist analyses the only constraints are the notoriously open-ended possibilities and combinations of possibilities that emerge when one begins to consult dictionaries and grammars and histories; to consult dictionaries, grammars, and histories is to assume that meanings can be specified independently of the activity of reading. (P. 468)

Fish's last sentence overstates his case: a reader's use of other texts does not in itself imply an open-ended pursuit of interpretations. Fish might reply, of course, that such a reader errs in assuming that one text provides the key to another one. But actually Fish should welcome this type of diligent reader, who consults "dictionaries, grammars, and histories" in order to become better "informed." After research, and after having purged "personal" responses, he or she can return to the text and participate more faithfully in its meaning.

Although Fish's argument in this passage may be turned against him, his motive is clear. His method has checks and limits and does not engage the critic in "the endlessly inconclusive adducing of evidence which characterizes formalist analysis" (p. 468). But if this constraint distinguishes Fish's approach from that of other formalists, a second one brings their approaches together. Fish again stresses "the reader" in this essay, yet he also speaks of the text as "doing" something. "Everything" in a line of poetry, for instance, may "create" a certain expectation about what will follow (p. 468). Like the earlier essays, part one of "Interpreting the *Variorum*" glorifies the reader at the same time that it revitalizes the text: "the reader" is the object of critical attention but the text is the true source of meaning. Fish thus continues to argue at cross-purposes. He endorses a new, liberating method based on the reader, but he also presents constraints to seal off his system from the reader's "subjective" reports. Even as Fish privileges the reader, he says that the text directs us; the author provides the language of the text and is the controlling figure behind it; readers' responses, even when they seem to differ, are basically the same, falling within a range of "non-essential variation"; and the reader-response critic, because he or she is "informed" and free from "personal" interests, does not engage in futile, "endlessly inconclusive" hunts for evidence.

In the second part of "Interpreting the *Variorum*," Fish reexamines each of the terms (text, author, uniformity of response) that act as constraints in his previous work, and he relaxes his claims for the priority of his method. He still refers to the text as steering or manipulating the reader, but he now identifies this as "the bias of our critical language" that makes us "talk as if poems, not readers or interpreters, did things" (p. 477). The truth is quite the reverse: "Interpretive strategies are not put into execution after reading (the pure act of perception in which I do not believe); they are the shape of reading, and because they are the shape of reading, they give texts their shape, *making them* rather than, as it is usually assumed, arising from them" (p. 481, my emphasis). Because a reader possesses a certain set of strategies, he or she not only reads a text, but writes it (p. 482). The text exists in the reading (which is really the writing) of it: we make our own texts.

Where does this leave the author, who was earlier seen as the guiding force behind the text? The author retains a place in Fish's revised theory but is now judged, like the text, to be a product of the reader's strategies. We are always debating and making decisions about an author's intentions in a passage, but these acts do not result from something "in" the text. Instead, we construct an author's intention, attribute it to the text, and then proceed as if this intention were embodied or realized in the text all along. "Intention," Fish maintains, "is no more embodied 'in' the text than are formal units; rather an intention, like a formal unit, is made when perceptual or interpretive closure is hazarded; it is verified by an interpretive act, and I would add, it is not verifiable in any other way" (p. 478). If Fish's early work reneged on its promise to exalt "man" as the maker of meaning, his recent work more than compensates for it. "Rather than restoring or recovering texts," Fish affirms in a reply to critics of "Interpreting the *Variorum*," "I am in the business of making texts and teaching others to make them by adding to their repertoire of strategies."[9]

This powerful claim fails to consider an obvious question: if one grants that the reader "writes" the text, where does one locate the author's writing? Do the reader's and author's writings enjoy the same status? If pressed, Fish would likely answer that while Milton, for example, is obviously an "author," our sense of him as an author (as someone who has written a text) is an interpretation. Readers *construct* the author "Milton," and it is wrong to assume that each of us does so in the same way. A living author can tell us about his or her work, and may even specify the intention of a particular text. But, Fish implies, we accept an author's word as authoritative only if we believe that what an author "says" is not itself a "reading" of the text. The highest compliment that Fish could pay to an author would be to address this person as a reader, whose interpretation of a text we may (or may not) find convincing.

Once we concede, however, that the reader "writes" the text, are we not inviting the subjectivity that "Literature in the Reader" tries to defend against? "Interpreting the *Variorum*" makes no demand for uniformity among readers, and Fish now argues that when we seem to be talking about "different" poems, we are right, "for each of us would be reading the poem he had made" (p. 482). We do read differently after all, but, Fish insists, this does not mean that the alternative to uniformity is total subjectivity among readers. Readers are grouped in "interpretive communities" that

> are made up of those who share interpretive strategies not for reading (in the conventional sense) but for writing texts, for constituting their properties and assigning their intentions.... This, then, is the explanation both for the stability of interpretation among different readers (they belong to the same community) and for the regularity with which a single reader will employ different interpretive strategies and thus make different texts (he belongs to different communities). (Pp. 483-84)

Fish now recognizes "difference" among readers and incorporates it into his system, rather than denying it and making a claim for uniformity. Since there is no single kind of response or experience, some readers agree, while others disagree.

In "Interpreting the *Variorum*," Fish no longer needs uniformity, authorial control, or textual meaning to guard against subjectivity, because he now sees subjectivity (and the threat of chaos among interpreters) as a false problem. We will never have a final agreement among readers of a text, but we are not then committed to anarchy:

> Interpretive communities grow larger and decline, and individuals move from one to another; thus while the alignments are not permanent, they are always there, providing just enough stability for the interpretive battles to go on, and just enough shift and slippage to assure that they will never be settled.... The fear is of interpretive anarchy, but it would only be realized if interpretation (text making) were completely random. It is the fragile but real consolidation of interpretive communities that allows us to talk to one another, but with no hope or fear of ever being able to stop. (P. 484)

The curious strength of Fish's revised theory is that it allows him to explain "subjectivity" and "anarchy" not as an attack on shared conventions, but as examples of them: we must have shared, conventional ways of identifying these threats for us to know when they endanger us. For anarchy to arise, interpreters would first have to know what is to count as "anarchy."

IV

"Interpreting the *Variorum*" finally makes good on Fish's promise to situate man at the center of interpretation. But despite his emphasis on the reader as a maker of texts, Fish does not repeat the humanism of his early essays. Such an appeal is no longer relevant, for Fish has removed his claims for the special place of his method; the notion of "interpretive communities" embraces not only Fish's theory, but even one that is dedicated to text-centered meaning. Fish also realizes that his earlier model is complicated, if not undercut entirely, by his new arguments about the author, arguments that can easily be extended to apply to the reader. Like the author, the reader or interpreter is both the bearer of strategies and the product of them. He or she is "textual," a construction of the readings that one's self and others project. Men and women are not freely creative interpreters, as Fish's humanistic theory had stated. Instead, they are bound, restricted, and confined by their textual character, which makes them subject to the activity of other interpreters. Not only, then, is the author an interpretation, but so is the reader, since he or she is known only through "readings."

As the textuality of the "author" and "reader" suggests, Fish's account of interpretive communities involves questions of power, authority, and the ethics of social control; a man or woman imposes readings on others, and is understood as he or she is read. But here we confront the blind spot in Fish's theory: Fish sometimes raises these questions, but he does not answer them. It is one thing to speak of an interpretive community as a state or condition based on a description: "you and I read this text in the same way"; but it is another to speak of this community as an act of choice and, necessarily, exclusion: "you and I agree to read the text differently from others." In his reply to his critics, Fish admits that his procedure, like others, is arbitrary, but explains that in his theory the arbitrariness "enters at the beginning, when a set of assumptions is adopted which subsequently directs and generates the analyses" ("Interpreting the *Variorum*," p. 195). This implies that interpretation is an act of choice, a decision about the strategies that will be invoked ("adopted") for the reading of texts. But Fish fails to explain the origin of this choice and its effect on the ability of others to make such a choice. How are we able to initiate this change in the system, making a new "beginning" and declaring our own "set of assumptions"? Is "change" of "interpretive communities" truly possible, or "is the inevitable conclusion to the formation of an interpretive community," as Edward W. Said inquires, "that its constituency, its specialized language, and its concerns tend to get tighter, more airtight, more self-enclosed, as its own self-confirming authority acquires more power, the solid status of orthodoxy, and a stable constituency?"[10]

Fish's emphasis on interpretive communities should lead him to consider the place of authority and privilege in interpretation. He fails, however, to develop these implications of his method, and when he does gesture towards them, he appears eager to dispel their force. In his important essay on Speech Act theory,[11] Fish makes an interesting, but limited, point about the role of "declarative utterances" in maintaining institutions:

> It is not that words are in force only so long as the institutions are, but that institutions are in force only so long as the words are, so long as when they are uttered hearers perform in the stipulated way (the batter returns to the dugout, the armed forces mobilize, the defendant is released from custody). If, on the other hand, hearers simply disregard a declarative utterance, it is not only that they have ceased to pay attention to the words (which still bear the perfectly ordinary and understood meanings of commands that are not being obeyed), but they have ceased to recognize—and assist in the constitution of—the institution. The moral of this is chastening, even disturbing: institutions are no more than the (temporary) effects of speech act agreements, and they are therefore as fragile as the decision, always capable of being revoked, to abide by them. (P. 997)

Fish emphasizes that a verbal agreement underlies the state, and also that this agreement can be disregarded or overturned. The next step would be to apply this insight to the "interpretive communities," to examine why in our institutions some "communities" are sanctioned whereas others are not even recognized. Fish says that the "moral" of his argument is "chastening, even disturbing"; yet what is most disturbing is his failure to apply this "moral" to his account of the "interpretive communities." To do so would suggest that they do not move and exchange places in the generous way Fish describes in "Interpreting the *Variorum*"—with "just enough shift and slippage" for us to continue the usual critical debates. Missing from Fish's work is an explicit treatment of the politics at stake and active in the ordering of interpretive communities. A community does not simply emerge with a little shift and slippage, but struggles against (and perhaps even overthrows or legislates out of existence) an earlier one; an interpretive community must clear space for itself, and define itself in opposition to others.

Fish's work is similar to Michel Foucault's in its concern for communities of discourse and conventions. But Fish touches on these issues without addressing their real impact, and without grappling with the crucial matters of authority, power, and conflict in different communities. He lacks political self-awareness, and so cannot comprehend that "interpretation" is a system of difficult exchanges, with forced entrances of new communities and exclusions of old ones. "If interpretation," Foucault observes in an essay on Nietzsche, "is the violent or surreptitious appropriation of a system of rules, which in itself has no essential meaning, in order to impose a direction, to bend it to a new will, to force its participation in a different game, and to subject it to secondary rules, then the development of humanity is a series of interpretations."[12] Like Foucault, Fish views historical development as a "series of interpretations"—there is no "essential meaning" that precedes the activity of the interpreter; but unlike Foucault, he does not consider the powerful interplays and differences among these interpretations. In a word, he seems unwilling or unable to embark upon what Foucault defines as "a critical investigation of the thematics of power."[13] Fish is a combative, aggressive theorist who writes in a commanding style and whose theory often absorbs its competitors (such as the "affective fallacy"). But despite his domineering ways, his account of "interpretive communities" is notably pluralistic and restrained; he judges interpretive debates to be a harmonious shift and slippage.

Fish's failure to consider the politics of his theory is graphically evident in a later section of his Speech Act essay, where he treats the status of "facts" and "fictions." There are, he insists, no sets of "facts" independent of conventions of discourse; a fact is not essentially different from a fiction, but is a fiction that enjoys special status. The factual or "standard" story is not the truth, tied to indisputable evidence in the world, but is the story that people agree to count as the truth. "What is remarkable" is "how little this changes: facts, consequences, responsibilities, they do not fall away, they proliferate and make the world—every world—alive with the significance our stories (standard and otherwise) create" (p. 1022).[14]

Fish rightly suggests that a change in the status of an authority does not (as if automatically) cause this authority to disappear, relieving us of the obligation to obey it. But the important point is that it *can*; once an authority is perceived to be conventional, authorized only by verbal agreement, it is dramatically changed. The thrust of Fish's theory is liberating, for he subverts the myth that an authority is a "natural" fact, and that we are forever bound to the existing shape of institutions and their practices. Yet even as Fish points towards the force of his theory, he weakens it, turning his theory's demystifying power into a restatement of authority's necessary dominion over us: he does not say whether demystification helps to create any positive or constructive differences.[15] As Fish's concern for "constraints" in his early work testifies, he is committed to order and discipline. And it is this belief in the need to preserve order, to conserve meaning within its proper bounds, that leads him to undercut his argument at its most radical point.

V

It is striking to see how closely Hirsch, Miller, and Fish resemble one another, whatever the differences among their positions. Each of these theorists is concerned about the controls and constraints that need to be placed upon interpretation. Hirsch wants to impose them; Miller incorporates them into his deconstructive program right from the start; and Fish moves from a position that trumpets its constraints to one that says we do not have to call for constraints because they already exist in the generally stable "interpretive communities." These theorists thus employ a vocabulary that often edges into politics, particularly the politics of institutions; but all of them shy away from acknowledging their interpretive politics, refuse to engage in a critique of ideology, and fail to inquire into the sociology of knowledge implicit in their "literary" theories.

Each of these theorists also stresses the boundaries that limit interpretation, and each is extremely concerned about "subjectivity." Hirsch might not think so, but Miller and Fish are as obsessed by the question— more properly, the menace—of subjectivity in English studies as he is.

For Hirsch, Miller, and Fish, subjectivity spells incoherence, the unraveling of critical and pedagogical discipline. We need to *have* discipline, they say, if we intend to lay claim to *being* a discipline, and we need to build our work upon an "objective" ground rather than locate it in the purely subjective responses of readers and critics.

The theories that Hirsch, Miller, and Fish advance are, in a very important sense, "about" the discipline of English studies. In focusing on these three figures, I am not of course arguing that they are *the* most important and influential contemporary theorists—though they doubtless would belong in any such grouping. Rather, I have chosen to concentrate here on Hirsch, Miller, and Fish—as opposed, say, to Harold Bloom, Paul De Man, and others—because they exemplify so well the relations between theoretical and disciplinary/institutional concerns. Hirsch promotes his theory in order to solidify the discipline and protect it from the invasion of relativist dogma; Miller seeks to enliven the discipline by way of new, Continental methodologies yet makes certain, at the same time, that his proposals do not endanger the traditions he values; and Fish, having seen the failings of his early reader-response enterprise, reaches a stage in his revised theory—one that entails the study of politics, culture, and history—that he seems unwilling to develop or examine further. What these theorists show us is that a theorist's ingrained sense of what English studies is and ought to be shapes the form of his arguments. They also show us—Miller and Fish in particular—why theories that appear to be radical, groundbreaking, and truly innovative are often disappointing, for they proceed from a very limited vision of what the discipline might accomplish. When one really bears down on these theories, they, like many others being promoted and discussed today, offer little that is dramatically new, however much rhetorical gestures seem to indicate otherwise.

To understand English studies and to grasp why promising theories usually have only a minimal impact, we need to know how the dominant tendencies in the discipline came into being. And this obliges us to situate contemporary theory within a more general professional, academic, and institutional context. "English" is a relatively new discipline, its emergence and consolidation having taken place in the late nineteenth and early twentieth centuries. When we analyze the various types of criticism and theory articulated since that time, we should realize their connection to this history—what it is, what it takes as its corporate identity, what it embraces and excludes as outside its borders. In the next part of this book, I will consider some of the ways in which English has been defined and defended as a discipline. I will be especially concerned with the verbal object of knowledge—the text itself—in English studies and the astonishing impact of the New Criticism on the ideas, attitudes, and discourse of the profession.

In the following chapter I explore the issue of "subjectivity," the issue to which my account of Hirsch, Miller, and Fish inescapably leads. My interests in this chapter are not so much philosophical and epistemological as they are literary/critical and institutional. What I suggest in this chapter is that we are right to feel that the discipline is in "crisis" but wrong—or at least incomplete—in our descriptions of why this has arisen. English studies is indeed in trouble—the economic and institutional facts are impossible to ignore. But once one disengages oneself from the immediate pressures of the moment, one can recognize just how protracted this "crisis" has been. As the record shows, critics and theorists have always judged the discipline to be in "crisis," complained about its incoherence and disarray, protested against its drift towards subjectivity, and sought to devise methods and systems to bring order to the ranks at last. But the reforms have never succeeded. I. A. Richards, Northrop Frye, and others invariably end up seeming to invite and foster the subjectivism that their theories aim to oppose and overcome. And the cycle repeats itself: still another theorist arrives on the scene to lament the disorder and urge a more systematic approach. "Subjectivity" has always been perceived as the major threat to the legitimacy of English studies, and the fear of subjectivity lies behind many of the most fervent calls for order and authority in the discipline. Yet it also strangely seems to constitute the value-term that members of the discipline esteem above all others, and to which they return when they seek to defend the work of English studies. It is the interpreter's self, the individual subject, that both *endangers* and *embodies* literary study.

PART
TWO

4.

Self as Subject in

English Studies

You see, what is a man who's done English as an academic, literary subject, what's he to do the rest of his life, except to write books-about-books-about-books and reviews of them? I'm agin' it on the whole.

I. A. Richards, *Complementarities: Uncollected Essays*

Edward W. Said has stated that critics "had better claim that criticism is a discipline if it is not to be an intellectual equivalent of wine-tasting."[1] But it is one thing to *claim* that criticism is a "discipline," and another to define the ways in which it *is* a "discipline," a field of study with a specific object and methodology. Critics and teachers of literature clearly want to insist that literary study is, indeed, a true discipline, not only for the sake of their self-esteem but also because their field seems today to be in such jeopardy, in dire need of defense against foes both inside and outside the profession. In political, social, and economic terms, we feel undervalued and unappreciated. Public support for the humanities has always been shaky, but is especially tentative during periods of economic decline. With parents and tax-payers facing financial pressures, and with colleges and universities encountering severe constraints on their budgets, literary study comes to look like a luxury, stimulating enough in its own right but finally expendable.

Despite their concern about jobs, careers, and economic survival, students do continue to enroll in literature courses. Some institutions have reported a decline in enrollments, but nationally the figures testify that more "undergraduate student credit hours" are taken in "English and American Literature" than in any other field. The American Council on Education reports that 16.1 percent of the total number of credit hours in the Fall, 1980, semester are in literature, as opposed, for example, to 14.1 percent in the mathematical sciences and 16 percent in the basic social sciences; the remainder are fairly evenly distributed among chemistry, psychology, history, and other fields.[2]

67

While these figures are surprisingly high, they do not really indicate, when examined closely, that the literary discipline is thriving. Nearly half (48 percent) of the total credit hours in literature are taken in two-year colleges, and only 10 percent of the total hours fall in the category of advanced or "upper-division" courses. Students are enrolling in our courses, but at the introductory level and in writing programs, in order to satisfy "distribution requirements" in literature and composition. From this point of view, literary study has a certain "disciplinary" function, helping to process students through surveys of a few masterpieces and enabling poor writers to improve and standardize their skills. But this is hardly the "discipline" to which most critics and teachers aspire and lay claim. Is the purpose of English studies to staff basic courses in poetry, fiction, and drama? Are composition courses, with an occasional seminar in "literature" included to keep our morale from collapsing, the fate that lies ahead for the "discipline"?

But to outline the problems of English studies in this form is misleading, or at least incomplete, because it ignores the extent to which the crisis in the study of literature has been generated within the discipline itself. I am not discounting the effects of our current political and economic plight: these effects are real and pervasive. But it is too easy to become smug and self-pitying as we reflect on the ways in which society victimizes us and fails to bestow upon us the honor and attention we deserve. It is tempting simply to defend the discipline by saying that we shelter human values held in contempt elsewhere, and that we thus preserve and protect the best that has been thought and said. But we cannot allow such a self-serving valuation to remain "exempt" from scrutiny, safe from the critical judgments that we are quick to impose upon the world outside English studies.

It is important to take account of exceptions, acknowledging that since the 1920s there have been a number of bold attempts to reorient the course of English studies and chart its future. Yet it is also evident that these attempts have been failures, one call for reform leading inevitably to others. These have always taken as their point of departure the confusion and disorder (tending towards "anarchy") in the study of literature, its absence of "discipline" and rigor, its lack of both an object and an objective, and especially its slippage into subjectivity. I. A. Richards, for example, in his *Principles of Literary Criticism* (1925), states that "critics have as yet hardly begun to ask themselves what they are doing or under what conditions they work."[3] And four years later, in *Practical Criticism*, he adds that "the technique of the approach to poetry has not yet received half so much serious systematic study as the technique of pole-jumping."[4] Embarking on a theoretical project that embraces psychology and neurology, Richards strives in these books to give methodological coherence—as well as a therapeutic mission—to English studies.

Although Richards's work was extremely influential, particularly in its analytical focus on texts, it did not succeed in ordering and justifying the discipline. We have Richards's own word for this, in his essay "Responsibilities in the Teaching of English," which appeared in 1949: "A connected, over-all view of the tasks, the methods, the norms, and the ends of English teaching—from the nursery school to the university, and from Bloomsbury to Yunnan—does not yet exist. Few ranges of human activity more deserve an encompassing, planetary regard; few receive less speculative attention."[5] Many people "do" English, but no one appears able to define its procedures and objectives. "Yet no study," Richards contends,

> more needs a radical questioning which would develop an explicit state-
> ment of what should be the directing implicit assumptions. The teacher of
> English, at whatever level, is oddly reluctant to discuss his principles. He
> takes them for granted. Whether they could be granted, were they avail-
> able for inspection, must be doubted until they are set forth. This shyness
> may indicate the presence of beliefs too deep to be confessed. It may re-
> sult, on the other hand, from a felt absence of any notion as to why, in
> any philosophic sense, he should be doing as he does—or be teaching
> English at all. ("Responsibilities in the Teaching of English," p. 91)

Twenty years later, in the interview from which I take the epigraph for this chapter, Richards is still charging that critics and teachers of literature engage in an ill-conceived enterprise. "English" as an academic subject seems so futile to Richards that he is led to remark, "I'm agin' it on the whole."[6]

Whenever Richards scans the work being undertaken in English studies, he sees mostly failure and disarray, groups of "uncritical" critics plodding forward without any sense of "principles" and "assumptions" that they can articulate. He is not, of course, alone, for the other major theorists of this century have similarly noted the absent center of "English" and sought a meaningful object with which to fill it. Northrop Frye, in his *Anatomy of Criticism* (1957), comments that

> if criticism could ever be conceived as a coherent and systematic study,
> the elementary principles of which could be explained to any intelligent
> nineteen-year-old, then, from the point of view of such a conception, no
> critic now knows the first thing about criticism. What critics now have is
> a mystery-religion without a gospel, and they are initiates who can com-
> municate, or quarrel, only with one another.[7]

Like Richards, Frye sees production, but no progress, no sense of a disciplined intellectual pursuit. Critics have given us scholarship and interpretations galore, but "in the growing complication of secondary sources," says Frye,

> one misses that sense of consolidating progress which belongs to a sci-
> ence. Research begins in what is known as "background," and one would

expect it, as it goes on, to start organizing the foreground as well. Telling us what we should know about literature ought to fulfill itself in telling us something about what it is. As soon as it comes to this point, scholarship seems to be dammed by some kind of barrier, and washes back into further research projects.[8]

Frye's indictment is even more stringent than Richards's, in that Frye stresses not only the lack of method and principle, but also our inability to specify just what our object is. We do not even know what we mean by "literature," nor do we have any notion of a common goal. We appear equipped only to declare preferences, each man or woman stating what appeals to private taste and fancy, seemingly unable to relate personal insight to an objective standard.

Other critics, ranging from William Empson and F. R. Leavis to Robert Penn Warren and Cleanth Brooks, have confirmed Richards's and Frye's diagnosis of the lamentable state of the discipline, and all have proposed new methods in order finally to situate English studies on firm ground. The movement we know as the "New Criticism" is in significant ways, as I argue in a later chapter, the basis or foundation of criticism as we know it today, and all of the figures I have cited, with the exception of Frye, helped to define and promote it. But the New Critics themselves quickly became disenchanted about the reforms in teaching and criticism that they instituted; even as their work was greatly influencing critical practice, they were signaling their reservations, worrying in particular that too many people were churning out "explications" without considering or caring about why they were doing so.

It is precisely this flood of "explications" that disturbs Jonathan Culler and prompts his attempt, fifty years after Richards's *Principles*, to reform the discipline. Exactly like Richards, Frye, and others before him, Culler begins by observing that teachers and critics have no true understanding of their work. "What is literary criticism for?" he inquires in the first paragraph of his preface to *Structuralist Poetics*. "What is its task and what is its value?"[9] "If there is a crisis in literary criticism," Culler explains, "it is no doubt because few of the many who write about literature have the desire or arguments to defend their activity.... What then are we to say of criticism? What more can it do?" Culler's answer to these questions is "to look to the work of French structuralists" and to develop from suggestions in their writings a means of "freeing" literary studies from "an exclusively interpretive mode." But this answer is, for my purposes here, less important than Culler's insistence on starting his interpretive project from "the ground up." Critics have been doing this for decades: surveying the state of the discipline, remarking on its rampant subjectivity and disorder, and aiming to turn criticism, in Culler's words, into a "coherent discipline" at last.

This is not simply a rhetorical move that these various theorists practice, not simply a way of launching their arguments. Our discipline is unusual, perhaps unique, in that its major theorists always feel obliged to cancel what has been done before and invoke new principles, methods, and systems that will usher in the long-awaited "coherence." In literary study, Wallace Martin points out,

> each new theory presents itself as the only sensible alternative to those that preceded it. But its predecessors remain stubbornly alive, and the new theory stimulates the production of still others intended to rectify the errors *it* has introduced. Where one is dismembered, two or more grow in its place, and the herculean task of reducing criticism to order becomes more difficult every time it is undertaken. . . . No academic discipline currently produces as many theories as the study of literature.[10]

We seem not to have made any progress since Richards's investigations in the 1920s, remaining mired, just as he believed teachers and critics were in his time, in the "chaos of competing theories." Of course our predicament is worse, as Martin's account indicates. We have not only Richards's theory and the New Critical analyses that it informed and shaped, but also the many theories that were devised to displace the work of Richards, Empson, Leavis, Ransom, Brooks, and others. There are endless numbers of theories, and many attempts to patch two or more of them together. No one who examines the critical scene can detect coherence or order amid all this labor; it remains the case, but to an even more extreme degree, that teachers and critics today are uncertain about the discipline—its basic procedures, modes of inquiry, values, and whether it is really a "discipline" at all.

In the face of this "chaos," one response might be to accept it as a given, a fact of history to which the quotations from Richards and the others attest. English studies is constituted differently from other disciplines, we might say. It does not progress in a direct course, but rather keeps circling back to questions about its own status and justification. It has never been—and can never be—made coherent in some final sense, but instead is always in the process of forming itself, undermining its foundations, and renewing itself by seeking to set a proper course. Indeed, when we consider the question of "coherence" less anxiously, an observation like John Passmore's, in his *Philosophy of Teaching*—"Of all school courses, English has tended to be the most chaotic, the most fragmented in its objectives"—seems more to describe the discipline than to evaluate it.[11]

Such a response, however, is inadequate, for it rationalizes disorder and disarray by making them appear to be ingrained and inescapable. It hardly reassures those within the discipline to tell them, when they bemoan the purposelessness of their enterprise, that teachers and critics have always felt this way. Many, maybe even most, of those serving in the field of English studies feel alienated from their students, their board of overseers in the institution, their public audience, and, in the rush of theories, from one another as well. What we feel intensely is that our discipline has never been more vexed or shabbily treated, both by its practitioners and their clientele.[12] We need now to understand how the problematical facts of the discipline—its doubts about its very validity, its unbroken record of disorder and dissatisfaction—came to lodge themselves in place so securely. And we need to grasp the ways in which the past of English studies has led us to the fear, anxiety, and self-contempt of the present.

There does seem to be evidence to suggest that the disturbances in our discipline are especially serious at the present time. To speak first in general terms, a sharp split exists within the discipline between "theorists" and "practical critics." Never before in English studies have we witnessed more kinds of theoretical inquiry, and never before has the antagonism between those who favor "theory" and those who stress the necessity—the moral obligation—of returning to scrupulous "close reading" of texts been more pronounced. Theoretical work has grown so refined and elaborate that it appears to many to be a separate discipline; it seems unconnected to the direct engagement with texts that forms the substance of critical essays ("readings" of literary masterworks) and pedagogical routine. The boom in literary theory, in fact, has reached such extravagant proportions that some of its leaders are now maintaining that "theorists" on the whole have misunderstood the central issues; and they are urging that the "theoretical enterprise should come to an end."[13] The most advanced theoretical position is to stand opposed to "theory," and thus certain vanguard theorists become allies of the close readers and practical critics whom they once attacked, and whose assumptions they sought to undermine.

This union represents one of the common patterns in the history of the discipline: advanced thinkers and spokesmen for positions strive to outdistance their rivals and eventually reach a stage in their work when the only (and, it seems, best) option is to go back to origins—in this instance, to an original ground of opposition to theory. But we need to be more precise about the effects of the emphasis on theory, and we need to probe more deeply into the reasons for the widespread discontent it has engendered in the discipline. "Theory" is nothing new. English studies has always been concerned about theoretical questions, as the writings of Richards, Empson, Frye, Crane, and others demonstrate. New Critics such as Tate and Brooks staked out powerful theoretical claims, and their colleague Ransom even spoke specifically about the requirements of "theory," noting that

the good critic cannot stop with studying poetry, he must also study poetics. If he thinks he must puritanically abstain from all indulgence in the
theory, the good critic may have to be a good little critic. Actually, it
seems reasonable to suppose that no such critic exists. Theory, which is
expectation, always determines criticism, and never more than when it is
unconscious. The reputed condition of no-theory in the critic's mind is
illusory, and a dangerous thing in this occupation, which demands the
utmost general intelligence, including perfect self-consciousness.[14]

To refuse or scorn theory altogether is to be unwilling to examine
the nature of one's work; it is, in effect, to seek permission to continue
in a kind of labor that may have no intellectual warrant. When critics
say that they are opposed to theory, they are not opposed to theory
as much as they are insistent on the right to practice the theory that
they now espouse: their theory has become so naturalized that it no
longer feels like a "theory" at all.

Yet the critics are correct to sense that the recent wave of "theory"
is particularly threatening to, even destructive of, the work that has
been undertaken in English studies for decades. It is one thing to
contend, as did W. K. Wimsatt and Monroe Beardsley in the 1940s,
that the author's intention is not available for inspection and hence is
not relevant to the interpretation of texts; this raises important questions
about authorship and authority, as Wimsatt's and Beardsley's foes realized.[15] But it is another, more unsettling thing entirely to judge, with
Roland Barthes and other contemporary theorists, that the "author" is
a fiction, that there is no endpoint or closure in interpretation, and that
interpreters can never hope to gain full access to or exercise command
over texts. "Once the author is removed," Barthes asserts, "the claim
to decipher a text becomes quite futile. To give a text an Author is to
impose a limit on that text, to furnish it with a final signified, to close
the writing."[16] Unlike Barthes, Culler appears ready to accept the possibility of a ground for and limit to interpretation, basing his theory on
the conventions that make reading possible. But he too disputes the
authority of the author, and his account in addition fails to give solace
to critics who seek to retain belief in the essential selfhood or "human-
ness" of the reader. For Culler, the reader is no more a free agent than
the author and is equally at the mercy of social practice. "The subject
who reads," he states, "is constituted by a series of conventions, the
grids of regularity and intersubjectivity. The empirical 'I' is dispersed
among these conventions which take over from him in the act of reading."[17]

Recent theory, then, has mounted an attack on the "author" and
the "reader." Culler, Barthes, and others have not merely questioned
who or what ought to be accorded priority in interpretation, but have
also—Barthes more so than Culler—challenged the concept of "privilege" in interpretation, seeing the claim to "read" the text (as we have

come to understand this act) as a delusion at best, a sign of our im-
prisonment within the folds of ideology. The arguments of Barthes and
Culler imply, and the more radical critiques of Stanley Fish and others
affirm, that nothing in interpretive work is finally stable or verifiable.
The "text," Fish announces, has no independent status, not even in
its formal features (periods, commas, and the like). Readers do not
"read" texts, but "write" texts in the process of reading them. We
sometimes complain to one another, in the midst of an interpretive
disagreement, that we seem to be reading "different" poems, and, Fish
argues, this is exactly the case, "for each of us" is "reading the poem
he has made."[18] Once this step is taken, it appears inevitable that the
judgment of "wrong" and "right" in interpretation must be dispensed
with. New Critics and literary historians once debated which approach
was "right or wrong," which most suitably equipped to illuminate the
text, but Fish rejects the terms of this debate altogether. "My fiction"
is "liberating. It relieves me of the obligation to be right (a standard
that simply drops out) and demands only that I be interesting (a standard that can be met without any reference at all to an illusory objectivity)."[19] Liberation, for Fish, lies in bypassing "wrong" and "right"
and concentrating instead on keeping the attention of one's public; the
critic is obligated only to be "interesting," as though he were an en-
tertainer soliciting the favor of his audience.

Author, reader, text, right and wrong in interpretation—recent critical theory has dramatically redefined all of these terms. It is no longer
a question of the priority of these terms—should the author, for example, be perceived as central to criticism and teaching of texts?—but
rather a question of whether they have any status as significant categories, any meaning apart from certain illusions about artistic creativity
and "determinate" interpretation we might cherish. During the past
decade, M. H. Abrams reflects, we have witnessed the "systematic
dehumanizing of all aspects of the traditional view about how a work
of literature comes into being, what it is, how it is read, and what it
means."[20] "Only yesterday," Norman Rabkin remarks,

> it was widely assumed that the critic's job was to expound the meaning
> of literary works. Today, under an extraordinarily swift and many-fronted
> attack, that consensus is in ruins. . . . For [Fish, Derrida, and others] it is
> hopeless to talk about plays or poems as if they "mean" anything, a mis-
> take to believe as not only the New Critics but the establishment they
> replaced did that one could speak for a community that looked out on the
> same world.[21]

Rabkin's reference to "community" sounds a familiar chord. The
common understanding that binds the members of the discipline together is dissolving, Rabkin and others contend, under the steady pressure of "theory." Again, what was once a matter of the right procedure

to arrive at "meaning" has been transformed into a denial that "meaning" exists, a denial that makes interpretation into a playground for subjectivity.

Rabkin does not fully grasp the complexity of the positions that he wages war against. But his and Abrams's comments do indicate the anger felt by many in the profession as they see basic terms exposed as "fictions," theory replacing criticism and scholarship, and communal agreements and conventions undercut. "Theory," especially in its post-structuralist forms, upsets many critics because its proponents seem determined to destroy the discipline even as they profit from its rewards. "Some of my colleagues," E. D. Hirsch declares,

> are indignant at the present decadence in literary scholarship, with its anti-rationalism, faddism, and extreme relativism. I share their feelings. Scholars are right to feel indignant towards those learned writers who deliberately exploit the institutions of scholarship—even down to its punctilious conventions like footnotes and quotations—to deny the whole point of the institutions of scholarship, to deny, that is, the possibility of knowledge. It is ethically inconsistent to batten on institutions whose very foundations one attacks. It is logically inconsistent to write scholarly books which argue that there is no point in writing scholarly books.[22]

Hirsch sees himself as a defender of the discipline, one who protects the "foundations" of literary study from subversion. He senses that major voices in the profession speak against scholarship and knowledge, and he feels morally compelled to oppose them. The discipline, Hirsch believes, is unraveling, as vanguard theorists strive to bring deeply-rooted traditions and values into question. Subjectivity now reigns supreme, endorsed by many of the most prestigious and respected members of the profession.

Hirsch is correct to feel contempt for faddish, nihilistic "theory," but he, like Rabkin and Abrams, errs in his diagnosis of where the real problems lie. It is not the case that high-powered theorists have deprived literary study of its "center," but rather that they have given us a new one that confirms and deepens a problem that has always plagued the profession and that we have never resolved. This new center is self-referential, consisting of theories that are endlessly reproduced and turned in upon themselves. Barthes, for instance, writes in *S/Z* that

> Flaubert . . . working with an irony impregnated with uncertainty, achieves a salutary discomfort of writing: he does not stop the play of codes (or stops it only partially) so that (and this is indisputably the proof of writing) one never knows if he is responsible for what he writes (if there is a subject behind his language); for the very being of writing (the meaning of the labor that constitutes it) is to keep the question, Who is speaking?, from ever being answered.[23]

Barthes is a very clever writer and enjoys being mischievous—it is risky to take him too seriously. But this is a grotesque argument, and it would be wrong to fail to name it as such. Why would one seek to evade responsibility for what one writes? Except for a momentary and shallow thrill, why would one aim to dodge the question, "Who is speaking?" What would be the point and purpose of undermining the "subject" and erasing its authority? Here, as elsewhere in his work, Barthes articulates an expansive notion of "text" and "author." But this critique of the "subject"—the agent who writes—is unworthy of our acceptance. Barthes keenly questions naive assumptions about "writing" as the embodiment of a subject and checks any impulse we might harbor to assign complete command over a text to the author who composes it. Yet he ought to have focused his attention on the ways in which a more flexible view of author, subject, and text can still allow for writerly "making," for shaping acts of language. Rather than follow the path of seeing "writing" as marking the dissolution of the subject, Barthes should have employed his imaginative energies to give the subject space in which to appear and become "critically" situated.

It is crucial to defend the notion of "responsibility" in speech and writing in order to preserve the possibility of specific social and political statements that each of us can make and be committed to. But my desire to affirm personal responsibility not only illustrates an essential element of critical work as I have defined it. It also gestures towards what may be the central obstacle to claiming final order and coherence for English studies and returns me to the accounts of disciplinary disarray with which I began this chapter. When the authority of our labor is challenged, when we feel that the center that organizes criticism and teaching is threatened, when we judge that our object of inquiry is under attack, and when we sense that discipline is declining into impressionism, we usually have recourse to ourselves, to our own intense affirmations of individual power, presence, and value. What seems, in one sense, to be a stirring and necessary defense of English studies is also a concession (if not an invitation) to subjectivity, to an appeal for "the discipline" that places it in the hearts and minds of its practitioners.

It is striking how often critics invoke the self as the authoritative ground for their disciplinary mission. And it is even more striking to notice that the impact of these claims fails to register upon the critics who propose them. Richard Levin, for example, acknowledges that we must try to learn from other critics, but he concludes that "criticism will never be a collective enterprise; it must always come down, in the final analysis, to the individual critic confronting the literary work in solitude."[24] This is a startling admission, one whose force Levin seems not to have felt. In his book-length review of recent trends in the criticism of Renaissance drama, Levin intends to restore good sense to scholarship, to make the discipline more "responsible" in its interpretive practice, and, above all, to halt the outpouring of "readings" in academic journals and books. Implicit in his argument is the fear of subjectivity; he stands opposed to the ingenuity—that is, the unconstrained freedom—that allows each critic to produce interpretations. But as Levin's assertion about "the individual critic" suggests, he concedes that "criticism" finally amounts to the solitary labor of "confronting" the text. Levin launches his critique on behalf of the discipline, but his statement that criticism can never be a "collective enterprise" undermines the possibility for disciplined communal inquiry: we are left with a collection of individuals.

Like Levin, many critics judge criticism to be "subjective," a matter of personal taste, decorum, and style. Certainly one of the grand paradoxes of the contemporary scene is that critics fear the outbreak of subjectivity, yet, as their arguments attest, they regularly base their claims for criticism upon the merits of the gifted individual, the distinctive personality "confronting" literary texts. "The only worthwhile literary criticism," John Bayley insists,

> is written by personalities which, when exposed to works of art, react in interesting ways: interesting, that is, in the sense that the transaction throws light not only on a work and its author but on critic and reader as well. The human situation in general appears both complicated and extended by the operation of such a personality, whose manifestation on the page is in a style. . . . What a good critic has are not principles and an area but prejudices and gut reactions.[25]

Critics of "theory" spurn methods and systems, but it is hard to regard them as defenders of the discipline, for they defend criticism and attack theory by affirming the stimulating personality of the critic. Bayley's understanding of criticism is as open-ended as Stanley Fish's, for he, like Fish, upholds what is "interesting"—the critic reacts in "interesting ways"—as the criterion for criticism. Bayley stands up for fundamental values in interpretive work and believes they have compelling authority; but these are very much the values of an "individualist" practice that privileges the solitary reader and text and that sees their encounter as the brute fact upon which English studies is grounded.

Whatever the differences between them, Fish and Bayley favor "interesting" personalities, powerful writing and reading displays, and argumentative virtuosity, and thus they bear witness to the subjective element that seeps into statements for and against the traditions of the discipline. In the writings of theorists and anti-theorists, both those I have quoted and others, there is often this return to the individual subject as the center of criticism, the basis for critical and pedagogical authority, the source of what is good and true in the interpretive world, and the underpinning for method and system. ("The method is only as good as the critic who uses it.") What might, from a different angle, amount to an admission of disorder, even "anarchy," becomes the essential truth of English studies and the tenet that nearly all members of the profession acknowledge.

The evidence for this valorization of the self is extraordinarily ample and can be drawn from the writings of theorists and anti-theorists, critics and scholars, main-line academics and eccentrics. Reading lists and interpretive styles will always be in flux, explains Leslie Fiedler, but "what does not change is a commitment, an attitude, a way of living with living literature, amateur rather than professional."[26] The basis of English studies—what makes it rich and meaningful—is neither a fixed canon nor a particular method but is, instead, the critic/ teacher. "After more than four decades," Fiedler observes,

> one of the few things I believe I really have learned is that the teacher, that professional amateur, teaches not so much his subject matter as himself. If he is a teacher of literature, he provides for those less experienced in song and story, including the reluctant, the skeptical, the uncooperative, the incompetent, a model of one in whom what seemed dead, mere print on the page, becomes living, a way of life—palpable fulfillment, a transport into the world of wonder. ("Against Literature as an Institution," p. 7)

Fiedler expresses clearly, and with the appropriate shading of sentimentality, a crucial assumption at the heart of the discipline as many define it: methods and great books to the side, we believe that we teach "ourselves" in the classroom and give voice to our individual integrity and strength of character. The critic/teacher is like a beacon, sending out a magical glow that somehow enlightens others, and his or her subjectivity thus comes to be not a liability for English studies, but is rather its informing principle and justification.

Why do these subjective terms appear so frequently in accounts of English studies and in descriptions of criticism? It may seem natural enough to place ourselves at the center of our own work, but there are deeper reasons for the persistent nomination of the self or subject as the embodiment of English studies. In part we incline towards invoking ourselves because we are uncertain about just what constitutes our subject-matter, especially during a period when key terms are being questioned and recast, and when "literature" (the "great tradition" of classic texts) is perceived to be ideologically suspect. "We know what literature is only vaguely," concedes E. D. Hirsch, "so that any attempt to remove that vagueness in a definition actually falsifies our knowledge of the word, rather than clarifies it. To define is to mark off boundaries distinguishing what is literature from what is not, but our knowledge of literature has no such defining boundaries; there are many cases about which we are not sure—important cases, not just peripheral ones."[27] We teach and criticize literature, but we are not able to say precisely what "literature" is and where its boundaries lie. Nor do we feel confident, admits Alastair Fowler, that we can specify our interpretive mission or ever hope to accomplish it, whatever it may be. We cannot assume that we can "construct an author's work without deficiency or superfluity"; in fact, Fowler notes,

> our best attempts are blurred with probabilities and approximations. We cannot even look forward, in the general case, to some distant time when all uncertainties will have been resolved—as one might resolve a particular problem, such as the quality of a rhyme. Criticism's fundamental predicament is that it inescapably concerns itself with an intended work that it must inevitably fail to discover.[28]

Fowler suggests that critics pursue the ungraspable and unknowable, and he touches on—only to dismiss—the implications of this view for the discipline: "This dilemma of our contingency should not make us despair or turn to antinomian relativism. There is plenty to be done." Fowler is anxious to leave theory behind and return our attention to interpretive and editorial projects, and with good reason, since his theoretical inquiry has led him to detect "antinomian relativism" as the unnerving truth that lies behind references to the "disciplined" community of critics and teachers.

Hirsch and Fowler paint a disturbing picture. Hirsch observes that we cannot be certain about our subject-matter; we cannot define it, he implies, and the attempts to do so issue in confusion and obscurity. Fowler implies, even more damagingly, that we can never know the object we seek to interpret, and he glimpses the possibility that English studies is a swirling sea of relativism. When theorists like Hirsch and Fowler say such things (they locate themselves in the conservative ranks in most interpretive debates), it is no wonder that many members of the discipline choose to follow Fowler's advice—getting down to work, simply "doing" criticism, for "there is plenty to be done." But just what is to be "done" in English studies has always been open to dispute. "Literary criticism" seems not to possess obvious and ongoing work to perform and appears to lack problems of its own. If there is an essential or intrinsic "problem," it is, I think, the subjectivity that emerges as both the discipline's menace and its justification. Richards, Frye, Culler, and the others who have sought to renovate literary/critical work have never properly engaged this problem, though they are, to different degrees, aware of it. In many ways this is the central problem of English studies, the one that underlies the persistent disorder in the discipline that they and many others have long complained about, the one that eventually causes the dissolution of the many methods that reformers have proposed.

Criticism, it seems, has no clear object beyond the selfhood of its practitioners. Critics and teachers are always wishing that it were otherwise and are searching for and erecting "objective" methods, models, and systems. But every theory and critical method comes to the same end; devised to forestall disorder, atomism, and relativism, it ends up seeming arbitrary and subjective, and so is, in its turn, rejected in favor of something else—something that at last will make English studies truly a discipline. And then the cycle repeats itself yet again. In a curious and unsettling irony, what keeps criticism and teaching from being a discipline is their repeated slide towards subjectivity; yet—as the passages from Bayley, Fiedler, and others attest—it is the individual self or subject to which critics then respectfully gesture when they identify the true center of the discipline.

The interpreter's self is thus first judged to be the enemy of the discipline, the threat that teachers and students must labor to oppose. Yet when critics construct "defenses" of the discipline and testify to what English teaches, values, and regards as its authority, they recur to the self: the enemy of the discipline then becomes its ally, center, standard, and distinction. The following passages are just a few of the many that could be cited in order to show how deep and pervasive this "subjective element" is:

> Criticism does remain in the end one of the liberal, not one of the mechanical, arts. The critic may *apply* certain methods. But he does not, in the end, rely on his methods. He relies on himself.

> Nowadays the teaching of literature inclines to a considerable technicality, but when the teacher has said all that can be said about formal matters, about verse-patterns, metrics, prose conventions, irony, tension, etc., he must confront the necessity of bearing personal testimony. He must use whatever authority he may possess to say whether or not a work is true; and if not, why not; and if so, why so.

> A civilized and humanized man is the only ostensive definition of the humanities— the evidence of the text we study, a living example of the meaning and value of what he teaches. What he *is* persuades or compels the student's assent to the human necessity of the text, its humanizing power. It is this man's experience that the student admires, respects, envies, tries to grasp by grasping what he believes to be its ultimate source—the work, the text, the poem, the play. He may be wrong but the impulse is natural and right.

As for methodology, over the years the humanities have accumulated an almost embarrassing number of methods, but no single method has turned up that will answer all or even most of the questions that humanists like to ask. Faced with the options of philology, historical criticism, comparative criticism, *Quellengeschichte*, stylistics, genre theory, structuralism, contextualism, myth criticism, Freudian analysis, the sociology of literature, and phenomenology, to name only a few possibilities, most humanists are inclined to sympathize with the advice given by Henry James to a young man who asked him how one writes good novels: "Be very intelligent." To James's intelligence I would add a second criterion—sensitivity—if the two are not really different sides of the same coin.

Finally . . . you are left only with yourself and with the impossible enterprise of understanding understanding; impossible because it is endless, endless because to have reached an end is to have performed an operation that once again extends it beyond your reach.

The truth is that deconstructionist theory can only be as useful as the mind that puts it to work.[29]

The unresolved problem of English studies is the problem of subjectivity. On the one hand, the study of literature is felt by many to depend on (and to glory in) the individual work and distinctive merit of each interpreter. But it is precisely this individualistic strain, so others argue, that English must erase if it wishes to nominate itself as a true "discipline," as something other than the field where subjectivity romps. English studies does not have an "object" as much as it rests upon and wrestles with a dilemma, one that, as we have seen in previous chapters, theorists as different as Hirsch, Miller, and Fish engage. How can the discipline ever hope to be objective, orderly, and founded on concrete knowledge if it is immersed in subjectivity?[30] How can we affirm the power of English to express individual merit and distinction if rigorous system and method—the bases for an academic discipline—entrench themselves? It is the self who teaches and criticizes, articulating responses to texts, who embodies and gives meaning to the discipline. What threatens to cause the dissolution of English studies also serves to preserve and promote it.[31]

When one understands the dilemma that subjectivity poses, one knows better how to situate and interpret Richards's, Frye's, and Culler's complaints, and one can make sense of certain facts and curiosities on the current critical scene. Take the reader-response movement, for example. During the late 1960s and early 1970s, Stanley Fish, Norman Holland, David Bleich, and others contended that it was time to turn our attention away from the text and towards the reader. Readers, Fish states, are the true makers of meaning, and it is dismissive of "human" activity to slight "the reader" and focus on the "text itself," as the New Critics had advised. In opposition to Wimsatt and Beardsley, Fish embraces the "affective fallacy," affirms the productive power of the reader, and downplays (though he still allows a place for) the meanings that the "words on the page" generate.

At first this movement was welcomed. Critics and teachers judged that Fish and his reader-response colleagues were acknowledging what the New Critics ignored or sought to repress—the creative work that readers perform upon texts—and were revitalizing the discipline. But no sooner did the reader-response movement start to win support than it began to fall into decline. The discipline indeed celebrates the "selves" of readers and interpreters, and it aims to refine and monitor their critical instruments. But at the same time, the discipline—in order to remain a discipline—cannot finally tolerate any method that emphasizes selves and thereby seems to invite subjectivity and the slide into chaos.

Fish did his best to demonstrate that his method was orderly and did not amount to the anarchy of "anything goes." But he could not shake the charge that reader-response criticism led to subjectivity, impressionism, and the collapse of authority; as soon as he highlighted the reader and undercut the text, he appeared to many in the profession to be subverting objective goals and standards. Fish realized, I suspect, the futility of his arguments in favor of "the reader," and he has now concentrated his theoretical labors on other matters. What made the reader-response movement seem valuable and invigorating—its concern for the individual reader—also caused its demise.

The dilemma of subjectivity also accounts, more generally, for both the dominant position of the New Criticism and the discontent that it caused and continues to engender. When Richards's *Practical Criticism* appeared in the 1920s, it disturbed many people precisely because it showed how subjective and unconstrained were the interpretations that students produced. These students, it was clear, required "training" in order to become equipped with methods that would forestall random associations and subjective wanderings. But while *Practical Criticism*, *Understanding Poetry*, and other New Critical texts were enormously successful and re-oriented the discipline, they failed to counter the threat of subjectivity. New Critical procedures did seem initially to stop the self-fixation of readers; as Ransom and others noted, the explication of texts was meant to be an exacting discipline, one that eliminated subjective responses and gave criticism an "objective" basis and the "professional" austerity of the sciences. Yet the New Criticism was unable to escape the very accusation that it had so earnestly tried to protect itself against. For all its aura of scientific rigor and objective precision, the New Criticism appeared to let loose readers upon texts, enabling each reader to interpret the text as he or she pleased. Teachers were thus striving to improve the responsiveness of readers even as they were also worrying that these same readers might become *too* responsive, *too* insistent upon personal or private meanings.

One can see the bind to which this leads. Teachers train students to become adept interpreters; these students then grow confident about the keenness of their own insights and adhere to them steadfastly. This leaves teachers in the position of seeking ways to preserve a standard, an authority, and an object of knowledge. And teachers seem unable in this position to do much more than invoke their authority as "teachers," exalting their higher perceptions, pointing to their greater training, and citing their own subjectivity to deflect that which the students display. The New Criticism therefore both opposes and constantly has recourse to subjectivity: it simultaneously guards against and encourages the place of the "self as subject" in English studies.

In my next chapter I examine the New Criticism in detail and try to account in historical terms for its extraordinary success. But before I take up that part of my story, I need to speak more directly to the nature of the "subjectivity" that the New Criticism teeters upon, and that critics and theorists today debate feverishly. I cannot answer the problem of "subjectivity," though I have sought to diagnose and identify it and have stressed its crucial position in arguments for and against the practices of the discipline. In part I do not have a wholly satisfying answer because I believe that there is indeed something distinctive in the work each critic performs—"distinctive" at least in the sense that each person, in writing and, I would claim, in teaching, engages in action that he or she "intends" and should be prepared to take responsibility for. In the best critical work, we are acutely conscious of what Richard Poirier, in his discussion of artistic performance, has finely described as "the whole conduct of the shaping presence."[32] And this phrase feels to me to be an apt description for the kind of creative virtuosity that critics as different as Leavis and Blackmur, Foucault and Derrida, display at their best, and that the rest of us perform in a minor key. To say this may at first seem a lapse into sentimental mystification of the "author," but not if we acknowledge the social, political, and institutional contexts within which the author as "subject" is situated.

As I contend in my treatment of E. D. Hirsch in chapter one, conventions, rules, institutional guidelines and procedures constrain—as well as enable and provide opportunities for—writing. The writing—and here again I would add, the teaching, which is another kind of "performance"—that the critic produces is both his own and not his own. He informs and shapes it, but it is also "shaped" by the discursive field that is the writer's limitation as well as his resource, and by the historical situation within which he is located and which he addresses. At a certain point this explanation starts to feel forced, as though one were trying to have it both ways, dodging problems rather than solving them. But what I am laboring to express here and in greater detail in my Conclusion is a more dialectical—and also a more historical—conception of the critic/teacher's behavior. If we continue to define our enterprise as ultimately, in Richard Levin's words, "the critic confronting the work in solitude," then we are never going to escape subjectivity; we will never cease being caught by the polarity that obliges us to locate "everything" in the reader (as Fish does) or in the text (as Hirsch does) or that exposes us to making confused jumps back-and-forth (as Miller does). Levin's model requires us either to lament the fact that each critic generates his own interpretation or to celebrate the liberating individualism that such a model appears to proclaim. In neither case can we transcend subjectivity and speak pointedly about the social, communal, and disciplinary function of English studies.

"Subjectivity," then, should not imply the labor of the solitary individual, but should instead refer to the condition of each "subject" as social actor and agent. We are perhaps less readers who "confront" texts than we are rhetoricians who speak and write and explicate texts in complex social settings, and who consequently deal at all times with questions of authority, power, and politics. Many in English studies oppose this view because they fear the conflict and disruption that it might engender, and they therefore seek to both privilege and isolate the "subject" by making the essential literary/critical transaction that which occurs between self and text. But to insist on the primacy of the encounter between self and text is to blind oneself to the vexed enterprise of English studies as a discipline, profession, and institution: it reflects a failure to recognize the truth about the work that we currently undertake. The discourse of the "self as subject" I have described in this chapter reports what we often say to ourselves and to others, but this discourse neither does analytical justice to what we now do nor clarifies, in historical terms, how we came to do it.

5.

English Studies and the

Emergence of the

New Criticism

The charge is pathetic. He [Alfred Kazin] has taken far too seriously the alarm of a few orthodox professors fearful of being disturbed at their footnotes. I can assure him personally that the new formalists have next to no influence in the universities.

Cleanth Brooks, writing in 1943

Near the beginning of his essay "The Two Environments: Reflections on the Study of English," Lionel Trilling summarizes the traditional goals of English studies in both England and America. "The study of literature," he observes,

> has been traditionally felt to have a unique effectiveness in opening the mind and illuminating it, in purging the mind of prejudices and received ideas, in making the mind free and active. The classic defense of literary study holds that, from the effect which the study of literature has upon the private sentiments of a student, there results, or can be made to result, an improvement in the intelligence, and especially the intelligence as it touches the moral life.[1]

Many still find this moral vocabulary to be fortifying, however much it may be in decline, and assent to the "defense of literary study" that Trilling describes: the reading and analysis of classic texts liberates the "intelligence" and fosters moral growth and maturity. But even as teachers and critics assent, they would acknowledge that this "defense" of the discipline sounds feeble, its Arnoldian echoes barely audible— and hard to take seriously—in our post-modernist age. English studies has regrettably now become an academic business and profession, a field of self-promoting "specialists" and irresponsible "theorists" who shame "literature." "The current scene," George Steiner remarks, is little short of ludicrous. In the academy and the media, the critic has a prepotent, monumentalized station. Critical methodologies, with spurious claims to theoretical profundity and performative rigor, are multiplied and offered to secondary and tertiary investigation (there are critics of criticism, journals of "dia"- and "meta"- criticism in which critics dispute the merits of each other's jargon; there are university qualifications in criticism).[2]

Even as critics exaggerate their own status, they undermine the author and make the text disappear. "In a mode of narcissist terrorism," Steiner adds,

> criticism now proposes to "deconstruct" and to "disseminate" the text, to make of the text the labile, ultimately contingent source of its own prepotent display. Such display is sustained by the construction of metalanguages of autistic violence and obscurity. The resultant terror and mist envelop the text object to the point of deliberate effacement. The act of criticism has "ingested" its object (Ben Jonson's term for parasitic consumption) and now stands autonomous.[3]

We are living in the era of the academic superstar whose energies are spent not in serving literature but in advancing a career. English studies is geared towards production, and what counts is not quality but quantity: the goal of criticism is to generate more criticism. If we measured our performance against an objective norm, we would see the far-fetched, irresponsible nature of our work, but, say Steiner, Richard Levin, and others, no one is going to jeopardize his or her own industry by exposing the hoax perpetrated by others. Since nearly everyone is engaged in dubious or marginal projects, all members of the discipline conspire to ignore the sorry spectacle.

Viewed from this perspective, the recent emphasis on literary theory is contemptible but makes a certain sort of vicious "commercial" sense. Reader-response criticism, deconstruction, and the other new modes and models ensure that English studies will continue to thrive, with new industries replacing those that have grown obsolete.[4] How should one respond to this display? The most common response is to call for a "moratorium" on the production of criticism. There is far too much criticism already, so the argument runs; like managers of a factory that has expanded too rapidly, we need to stop, or at least slow down, the assembly lines. Others respond more darkly, prophesying that the mountains of books and articles signify the imminent death of literature and culture. Thomas Roche, for example, after surveying the scholarship in his field, states that what disturbs him "is not simply the bulk of material but the stupefying realization of the intellectual and moral bankruptcy of the study of English letters."[5] Thomas McFarland, having completed a similar assignment, speaks even more ominously:

The bourgeoning contributions call into question the use and purpose of culture as such. Just as the increase in human population threatens all the values of individuality, so too does the flood of publication threaten the very knowledge that publication purports to serve. . . . Scholarly proliferation is an actual enemy of culture, not merely its excrescence. As the number of books increases, the area of feasible expertise for any scholar necessarily becomes smaller and smaller, and the likelihood of his being able to exercise significant judgment (which must rest on a broad and extended culture) becomes correspondingly more remote.[6]

The amount of material overwhelms even the most diligent reader and researcher. No one can presume to "know" a field, let alone presume to master "culture" as a whole. Criticism is produced by the ton; lectures, symposia, panel discussions, and critical "schools" proliferate; and in the process, English studies grows increasingly fragmented and chaotic, its emblem of excess the MLA Convention Program. We do not share common concerns and do not serve literature but merely puff and promote ourselves, many in the profession now say. We never consider—again I am reporting the consensus of opinion—whether the criticism we produce is truly relevant to students and in line with the mission of English studies. We have, to put it bluntly, betrayed the tradition that Trilling evokes, and defaulted on the values of "intelligence" and the "moral life" that we ought to hold dear.

The words spoken by Steiner, McFarland, and the others are heartfelt; it is hard to discount such impassioned language. But except for a few shifts in terms, they are saying nothing new. If there is, as Trilling tells us, a high-minded humanistic tradition that flows deeply in English studies, there is also a "tradition" that asserts that the discipline fails to serve humanism, literature, criticism, and culture. At least since the turn of the century, almost, that is, from the moment of its consolidation, English studies has seemed to many people, both inside and outside the discipline, to be misconceived, an activity with neither an object nor an objective, a discipline that neglects its essential duties and appears constitutionally unable to reform itself.

Critics have always believed that the production of "criticism" needs to be slowed down, and that its gross accumulation is suffocating literature. Writing in 1891 about the "periodical literature" of his day, Henry James declares a verdict that many others seconded about the work being done in both academic and non-specialist journals. "Literary criticism," James exclaims, "flows through the periodical press like a river that has burst its dykes."

> The bewildered spirit may ask itself, without speedy answer, What is the function in the life of man of such a periodicity of platitude and irrelevance? Such a spirit will wonder how literature resists it; whether literature indeed does resist it and is not speedily going down beneath it. The signs

of this catastrophe will not in the case we suppose be found too subtle to be pointed out—the failure of distinction, the failure of style, the failure of knowledge, the failure of thought.[7]

James's words are eloquent, but his sentiments are common: criticism is causing the downfall and disappearance of literature. Novelists, poets, and journalists were voicing this complaint throughout the 1890s and into the first three decades of the twentieth century, and all were urging that critics immediately reform their ways or, even better, cease publication altogether. But the protests were perhaps most fervent among teachers and critics in the colleges and universities. The New Humanists, particularly Irving Babbitt and Paul Elmer More, argued vociferously against bad teaching methods and critical over-production.[8] And the grievances sounded by what might be termed the rank-and-file academic were equally sharp and noteworthy. Here are the words of an anonymous "College Professor," taken from his article "The Pedagogue in Revolt" (1928):

> How heavy has been, and is, the weight of learned volumes, of commentary, exegesis, under which both pedagogue and student must stagger in order to fulfill contemporary academic demands. Month by month and week by week they multiply, tomes, articles, pages upon pages upon the reading of a word or phrase, discussion after discussion upon some minute point of fact, as to the authenticity of a perhaps unimportant fragment, or disputed date— discussions often inspired less by passion for truth than by the bitter joy of proving that some other scholar, in a rival university, is in the wrong.

"There is a lost sense of proportion in all this," the "College Professor" continues.

> A poem has, in many cases, become less important than the array of facts about it, genuine, or invented in order to prove an hypothesis. . . . Too often a highly prized poem is as a precious jewel, buried under a haystack of print. How can one ever find it again?. . . From the point of view of mass, the output is appalling. If huge tomes, giving an omnium-gatherum of all documents, important and unimportant, significant and insignificant, that can any way be associated with an author, increase and multiply, where will it all stop?[9]

The "College Professor"'s article makes nearly all of the points registered by Roche, McFarland, and others in the 1970s and 1980s. The "mass" of criticism is ghastly; critics have lost their sense of relevance and proportion; academic nit-picking and trivia abound; critical and scholarly books are alienating students and deforming pedagogy; and as production increases, "literature" and "culture" are undermined. "Where will it all stop?"

While the persistence of complaints about criticism is clear, it is important not to blur distinctions or too quickly detach the "College Professor'''s statement from its historical moment to make it wholly accord with what is said about English studies today. We know the basis for the arguments launched by Steiner, Roche, and McFarland— not only is there too much criticism, but it co-exists with (and is infiltrated by) extravagant "theory," deconstruction, dissemination, and the like. But what were the grounds for the disturbances about criticism and scholarship felt by so many in the early 1900s? What were the conditions, particularly within the new field of English studies, that seemed so destructive of literature, criticism, and teaching? And most important of all, how did the problems of the past usher in those we now face?

As the twentieth century began, there were two main currents in English studies, one more dominant than the other. The field was chiefly ruled by the search for "facts" and drew its inspiration from the lessons and models that German philology and positivist scholarship provided. There was little "criticism" as such; fact-centered research, based on a gruelling drill in classical and medieval languages, was understood to be the "object" and objective of the profession. Though "research" was laborious to undertake, it was felt to be easier to assess than critical reflection on the great authors. And in their rigor and precision, the philological, textual, and other kinds of scholarship gave English studies the prestige of a "hard" science, with a compelling discipline and a comparable sense of progress.

"Criticism" did exist, usually in the form of impressionistic commentary on Shakespeare, the Romantic poets, and the Victorian sages. But critics were rare, in part because they lacked the scholarly credentials to qualify for a place in any respectable department. They were also rare because it was generally assumed that students could *read* "literature"—as opposed to studying it scientifically—on their own. At most colleges and universities during the first thirty years of this century, there were no courses in American literature, modern literature, or criticism. From our vantage point, this seems absurd, and in its uncritical veneration of the past, it is absurd. Yet it is the consequence of a belief that the *reading* of literature—again, as opposed to the scientific *analysis* of literature—is not entirely an academic pursuit and pleasure. English studies at the turn of the century was hardly exemplary, and in many respects it was a grinding bore. But then at least it was imaginable that literature could live outside departments of English. What occurred within the best departments was a stern discipline and training, not to be equated with the "reading," however enjoyable and stimulating, of literary texts.

The two currents in English studies are evident in the volume titled

Anniversary Papers, published in 1913 to honor George Lyman Kittredge on his twenty-fifth year of teaching at Harvard University.[10] Most of the essays are scholarly with a vengeance, as a partial listing of the table of contents indicates:

"Caiphas as a Palm-Sunday Prophet"
"Merlin and Ambrosius"
"Human Sacrifice Among the Irish Celts"
"The Twelfth-Century Tourney"
"Notes on Celtic Cauldrons of Plenty and the Land-Beneath-the-Waves
"Medieval Lives of Judas Iscariot"
"The Breca Episode in *Beowulf*'
"From *Troilus* to *Euphues*"

All of these essays are written by members of English departments and testify to the extreme attention paid to medieval literature. Literary scholarship means delving into antique lore and accumulating facts that demonstrate, with scientific exactness, that a project in "research" has been successfully accomplished.

Several of the essays in the volume are of a different order but are no more satisfactory. These are vague "appreciations" that touch, piously and sentimentally, on the modernity of the great authors. Examples include "A Fantasy Concerning the Epitaph of Shakspere," "Johnson and His Friendships," and "The Modernness of Dante." At first sight these essays seem out of place in a volume that is weighted towards "scholarship": one might assume that the scholars would not have accepted such writing, in all its mellow imprecision, for a book dedicated to the master-scholar and source-hunter Kittredge. But the scholarship and appreciation go together, both partaking of a warmly emotional, nostalgic attitude towards the past.[11] In a less impressive form, the essays in *Anniversary Papers* bear witness to qualities of mind we see, for instance, in Henry Adams, who is, on the one hand, a scrupulous historian of fact and detail, yet who is also capable of a myth-making reverence towards the Middle Ages.

In its own strange way, *Anniversary Papers* is a notable monument in the history of English studies. But it is impossible to deny the rarified scholarship and vapid appreciation of the classics that characterize the volume. Almost from the moment of its publication, *Anniversary Papers* came to symbolize everything that was wrong and destructive in teaching, criticism, and scholarship. Nothing that we might say about the volume can outdo the bitter protest that Stuart Sherman recorded in his review, which appeared in the *Nation* in 1913. Sherman concedes that Kittredge is a diligent researcher and friend of scholars but charges that this "professor" is unable—even unwilling, it seems—to instill the "love of literature." Kittredge "has been a potent force," Sherman alleges,

> in bringing about the present sterilizing divorce of philology from general ideas. If his school has not been very prolific in important books, it should be remembered that one of his maxims is, "Anyone can write a book; the difficult thing is to write an article." This appears to be a veiled way of saying that the digestion of facts, however weighty, sinks into insignificance in comparison with the discovery of facts, however trifling.

Surveying the volume and generalizing about the state of English studies, Sherman declares that "you feel in this 'fellowship of scholars' an almost tragical lack of common interests and ideas. You feel as one wandering in an intellectual Sahara in a silence unbroken save by an investigating sparrow chirping from time to time over a kernel of musty wheat in the shroud of Ptolemy."[12]

Sherman's critique of the Kittredge volume reaffirms and extends arguments he had advanced five years earlier, in an essay titled "Graduate Schools and Literature." In words that quickly achieved classic status among foes of the academic study of literature, Sherman states that "the very best men do not enter upon graduate study at all; the next best drop out after a year's experiment; the mediocre men at the end of two years; the most unfit survive and become doctors of philosophy, who go forth and reproduce their kind. The worst thing that can be said against the graduate school is that it turns the best men away."[13] Every so often bright young men and women do enter graduate school, ready and willing to devote themselves to literature and letters. But they become disenchanted soon enough; "they are bidden to provide themselves," says Sherman,

> with an adding machine to count the occurence of "fish" and "flesh" in the poetry of the Fourteenth and Fifteenth Centuries; they are asked to hearken to the vowels and consonants singing together throughout the Dark Ages; they are invited to embrace the inspiring relics of the Gothic gospels; they are inducted into the physiology of the vocal organs; they are set astride an enchanted broomstick and sent chasing Cuchulin through the Celtic moonshine. ("Graduate Schools and Literature," pp. 37-38)

English departments seem intent on turning away "the student of real literary taste and power." "There is no branch of higher education," Sherman concludes, "that has set to work more deliberately to cut off its own nose than English. There is no department of the graduate school that has greater opportunities, or makes less use of them" (p. 39).

Many others shared Sherman's judgment about the bad tendencies of graduate study—the concentration on medieval literature, the lust for trivia, the overproduction of articles, the indifference shown towards young men and women truly committed to a life of "letters." But it was not only the state of graduate study that angered many critics of the profession. Undergraduate teaching appeared equally poor, consisting of a potpourri of "facts" spiced with impressionistic asides. There is abundant evidence of the discontent felt by students, as they embarked on the study of literature only to be beaten down and disappointed.

The fate of Miro, the protagonist in Randolph Bourne's "History of a Literary Radical," is representative. When Miro began his first course in English literature, he was given

> a huge anthology, a sort of press-clipping bureau of belles-lettres, from Chaucer to Arthur Symons. Under the direction of a professor who was laying out a career for himself as poet—or "modern singer," as he expressed it—the class went briskly through the centuries, sampling their genius and tasting the various literary flavors. The enterprise reminded Miro of those books of woolen samples which one looks through when one is to have a suit of clothes made. But in this case, the student did not even have the pleasure of seeing the suit of clothes. All that was expected of him, apparently, was that he should become familiar, from these microscopic pieces, with the different textures and patterns.[14]

With a keen wit that wonderfully catches Miro's sad confusions, Bourne describes how such training denies critical judgment.

> The great writers passed before his mind like figures in a crowded street. There was no time for preferences. Indeed, the professor strove diligently to give each writer his just due. How was one to appreciate the great thoughts and the great styles if one began to choose violently between them, or attempt any discrimination on grounds of their peculiar congeniality for one's own soul? Criticism had to spurn such subjectivity, scholarship could not be willful. The neatly arranged book of "readings," with its medicinal doses of inspiration, became the symbol of Miro's education. (P. 233)

Many other critics could be cited to reinforce Sherman's and Bourne's indictments of English studies on both the graduate level and the undergraduate level. The scholars had their defenders, notably Edwin Greenlaw in *The Province of Literary History*.[15] And it is true that despite the barrage of protest, English studies generally remained, until the late 1930s and 1940s, a combination of fact-based research and impressionism. Yet when one examines the books and journals published during the first decades of the century, one is struck by the number of satiric pieces, angry anatomies of the profession, and calls for action. Scholarly research churns along, and inept, lazy teaching persists, but even the scholars feel that the discipline needs to be reoriented, and reformers start to emerge from their ranks. Here, for instance, is Albert Feuillerat's diagnosis of the state of literary study:

> There is no end of dissecting the literary works, submitting them to the lens of our microscopes, making statistics, cataloguing, indexing, tabulating, drawing diagrams, curves, angles (all the figures used in geometry), adding facts, still more facts, weighing data, accumulating an enormous mass of *materialien*. And so exciting has been this sort of labor that we have practically forgotten that the reason why literary works are written is that they may be enjoyed by all those who read them, critics included. In fact, we no longer suppose that they can be enjoyed or, at least, we refrain from enjoying them.

"We write cards, we sort them, we argue, we demonstrate about, above, and around books," Feuillerat states. "But the books have ceased for us to have interest in themselves. By degrees we have broken away from the literary attitude of mind; we are on the point of losing all contact with literary matter. The beauty, the artistic value of the works, no longer appeal to us; in fact, those things have disappeared from our purview."[16] Feuillerat contends that scholars have buried the "books themselves" under piles of information. No one is able to see the literary works of art because so much data surround and obscure them. If we wish to revitalize the discipline and enable it to fulfill its humanistic function, we need to restore the primacy of the books in their own right—the real "literary matter."

Feuillerat is a scholar writing in the mid-1920s, and this makes his emphasis on the "literary works themselves" all the more striking. He is not alone; others, critics and scholars alike, lamented the emphasis on "facts" and positivist research and urged that the literary text be placed at the center of the discipline.[17] Scholarship still reigned in the journals, and teaching remained a mixture of impressionism and Germanic "research." But Feuillerat's and the others' words signal that a new discourse was emerging, one that displaced the historical "facts" and elected the "texts themselves" as the object of critical attention in English studies. Even as impressionism and scholarship persisted in the academy, their authority was beginning to fade. Since the early part of the century, critics and scholars had been voicing their dismay at the condition of the discipline. And as the century progressed, the key critical documents of modernism served as both stimulus and reinforcement. By 1935, the following texts had appeared, all of which shaped the emerging text-centered discourse:

T. S. Eliot, *The Sacred Wood: Essays on Poetry and Criticism* (1920); *Homage to John Dryden: Three Essays on Poetry of the Seventeenth Century* (1924); *For Lancelot Andrewes: Essays on Style and Order* (1929); *Selected Essays, 1917-1932* (1932)

Ezra Pound, *The Spirit of Romance* (1910); *How to Read* (1931); *Make It New: Essays* (1934)

John Middleton Murry, *The Problem of Style* (1920)

T. E. Hulme, *Speculations* (1924)

I. A. Richards, *The Meaning of Meaning*, with C. K. Ogden (1923); *Principles of Literary Criticism* (1924); *Foundations of Aesthetics*, with C. K. Ogden (1925); *Science and Poetry* (1926); *Practical Criticism: A Study of Literary Judgment* (1929); *Coleridge on Imagination* (1934)

F. R. Leavis, *Mass Civilization and Minority Culture* (1930); *New Bearings in English Poetry: A Study of the Contemporary Situation* (1932); *How to Teach Reading: A Primer for Ezra Pound* (1932); *For Continuity* (1933); *Culture and Environment: The Training of Critical Awareness* (1933)

Laura Riding and Robert Graves, *A Study of Modernist Poetry* (1929)

G. Wilson Knight, *The Wheel of Fire: Essays on the Interpretation of Shakespeare's Tragedies* (1930); *The Imperial Theme: Further Interpretations of Shakespeare's Tragedies* (1931)

William Empson, *Seven Types of Ambiguity: A Study of Its Effects on English Verse* (1930)

R. P. Blackmur, *The Double Agent: Essays in Craft and Elucidation* (1935)

R. P. Blackmur, editor, *Henry James: The Art of the Novel, Critical Prefaces* (1934)

Kenneth Burke, *Counter-statement* (1931)

Edmund Wilson, *Axel's Castle: A Study in the Imaginative Literature of 1870-1930* (1931)

This new discourse hardly became dominant overnight; we have the testimony of René Wellek, Douglas Bush, and others concerning the depressing condition of literary studies in the 1920s and 1930s.[18] The opposition between new critics and old-line scholars was fierce, and the advocates of new critical procedures were often reviled. Yet it did not take many years for the scholars to decline, replaced in prestige and power by those who were able to restore the "books themselves" to view, bringing back into the line of vision the texts that had "disappeared." By the 1920s, it was possible to see what one had been missing and to know how to speak about it, however hard it might be to locate a wholly sympathetic audience in the academy. Cleanth Brooks and Robert Penn Warren, for instance, were reading, drawing upon, and defining themselves against Richards's *Principles of Literary Criticism* and *Practical Criticism*; Richards supplied them with a lucid account of bad reading practices among students, and he was thus able to give distinctive utterance to the complaints that Sherman, Bourne, Feuillerat, and many others expressed. When Brooks began graduate work at Tulane, he was able to diagnose the faults of "conventional graduate study" and realize, through the new vision and discourse he was learning to possess, that critics needed to concentrate on "the interior life of the poem."[19]

The New Critical reformation of English Studies, led by Brooks,

Warren, John Crowe Ransom, Allen Tate, and others, was brilliant and courageous. Yet it was also inevitable; the new discourse, as I have termed it, was emerging on many sides, and it was only a matter of time before the "books themselves" took firm hold in the discipline. The New Critics were not really saying much that was revolutionary; they were just saying it in more concrete and determined fashion. Their achievement was to seize upon the terms already present in the newly emergent discourse and to underscore "the text itself" as the central term, and hence the central fact, of literary work. They argued that the text was the keystone of criticism, and they also recognized—I am inclined to say, could not help *but* recognize—the connection between critical and academic interests. To secure the New Criticism, to give it prominence, to make it endure, they saw that they needed to orient it towards pedagogy. As Bourne's words bear witness, students had long hungered for "the texts themselves"; when Brooks and the others attended the university, they had sought the same thing. This was exactly what people had been calling for as the essential object of English studies, and it is a sign of both the New Critics' zeal and their strategic sense that they based their reforms of the discipline on the priority of the literary text.

When the New Critics, then, began to revamp English studies in the late 1930s and through the 1940s, they were capitalizing on terms, attitudes, and goals already in circulation. By highlighting the text and refining techniques for its analysis, they succeeded in defeating both the scholars and the "appreciators" of the masterpieces. The New Critics offered what the research scholars ignored and they gave students immediate training in the fundamental skills of "close reading" and discrimination. At the same time, the New Critics made clear that their methods were "scientific" (Ransom's word): orderly, disciplined, meticulous.[20] They thus displayed (and benefited from) a love-hate relationship with science, opposing the positivist research undertaken by the scholars yet preserving the aura of "science" in order to claim "professional" rigor and superiority to mere impressionism.

There are, of course, other dimensions to the story of the new discourse that emerged in English studies. Within the academy, the crucial opposition and the most intense disputes occurred between New Critics and both scholars and appreciators. But a word should be said about the two other contenders for authority, New Humanism and Marxism, both of which enjoyed considerable attention and kindled debate during the 1920s and 1930s.

New Humanism was doomed to fail, despite the energetic labors of Babbitt, More, Norman Foerster, and others. The movement included men who were prominent in major universities—Babbitt taught at Harvard, More at Princeton, and Foerster at North Carolina and later Iowa—

and in this respect it did manage to establish an academic base of support. But this support was never deep or widespread, and in retrospect, the New Humanists appear as earnest but lonely voices speaking in an outdated language. The New Humanists privileged a very narrow canon, were hostile to modernism, and declared their lack of sympathy for nearly all contemporary literature. The movement reached a climax in 1930 with the publication of *Humanism and America*, but it almost instantly expired, its key text demolished by the rival volume, *The Critique of Humanism*, which was published in the same year.[21]

Marxism, particularly during the years of the Great Depression, had a wider appeal than Humanism. Marxism seemed, first of all, to offer an alternative to the skepticism and despair preached in the great modernist texts. And it also appeared to testify to the *power* of literature as a means of explanation and instrument for reform. Marxism affirmed the connections between literature and society, writing and revolution, and thus beckoned to intellectuals as a kind of vitalizing "true religion."

As soon as one uses the term "intellectuals," however, one begins to grasp the reasons for the failure of Marxism to enter significantly into English studies. Marxism did have its members in the academy, but their activities were veiled in secrecy and were often laughably irrelevant to the day-to-day business of teaching and research.[22] Marxism never managed to secure itself in college and university life; administrators and politicians resisted it and made abundantly clear that the academic Marxist would find his or her job in jeopardy. Intellectuals and activists—Granville Hicks, Michael Gold, Joseph Freeman, and others—fought hard for Marxism at conferences and congresses and in books and journals, as Daniel Aaron and others have noted in their studies of the period.[23] But through the National Industrial Recovery Act (1933), the Wagner Labor Bill (1935), the Social Security Act (1935), and other legislation, the Roosevelt administration was able to turn many liberal and left-leaning men and women away from Marxism and towards the New Deal. Marxism further lost supporters as a result of its endless polemics and factional rivalries between Communists, Socialists, and those who drew upon Marxist terminology but resisted membership in either party. The horrors of Soviet policy eventually rent asunder the last vestiges of a united front. Once the truth of the purge trials of 1936-1938 came to light, and once Stalin signed his pact with Hitler in 1939, it was impossible to remain a Marxist with a clean conscience. Though it sparked heated exchanges, Marxism never threatened to control or even influence the academic study of literature. As Alfred Kazin concludes, Marxism in the 1930s was "a phenomenon, rather than a body of critical thought."[24]

Several essays by Allen Tate indicate the state that criticism had reached by 1940 and trace the lines of New Critical opposition to scientific research, New Humanism, and Marxism. Tate first states his objections to "historical scholarship," arguing that

> in our time the historical approach to criticism, in so far as it has attempted to be a scientific method, has undermined the significance of the material which it proposes to investigate. . . . The historical scholars, once the carriers of the humane tradition, have now merely the genteel tradition; the independence of judgment, the belief in intelligence, the confidence in literature, that informed the humane tradition, have disappeared; under the genteel tradition the scholars exhibit timidity of judgment, disbelief in intelligence, and suspicion of the value of literature.[25]

To revive English studies and criticism, we need, Tate says, to cease scholarly accumulation and instead focus on the text, the true literary "object." "The question in the end comes down to this":

> What as literary critics are we to judge? As literary critics we must first of all decide in what respect the literary work has a specific objectivity. If we deny its specific objectivity, then not only is criticism impossible but literature also. . . . From my point of view, the formal qualities of a poem are the focus of the specifically critical judgment because they partake of an objectivity that the subject matter, abstracted from the form, wholly lacks.[26]

For criticism to exist as a discipline, it requires "objectivity," something that provides a center for interpretive dialogue and a standard for judgment. Scholarship gives much information that is useful, but also much that is useless, and it fails to cohere around a particular object. By concentrating on the text itself and engaging in formal analysis, we can "objectify" criticism, making it, at long last, an intensive discipline. As this passage testifies, Tate is eager to highlight "the form" and distance "the subject matter" from the critic's operations. This partially reflects his effort to prevent critics from abandoning the text-object in favor of excursions into biographical and historical data. But it also reflects his wariness about allowing criticism and teaching to drift into politics. Tate seeks to prevent political zealots from appropriating the poem and making it a weapon in the ideological wars of the 1930s, and so emphasizes that poetry "does not explain our experience. If we begin by thinking that it ought to 'explain' the human predicament, we shall quickly see that it does not, and we shall end up thinking that therefore it has no meaning at all."[27]

Tate's argument has had disastrous consequences. For by defending the poem against claims that it "explains" experience, he unwittingly sanctioned the belief that poetry and other forms of experience are disconnected and that "worldly" concerns sully and disfigure literature. But seen in the context of the critical campaigns of the 1930s, Tate's point makes tactical sense. Tate is fighting on several fronts: he is opposing the scholars who control literature in the academy; he is protecting literature from the New Humanists and moralists who would seek to make texts assist in ethical crusades; and he is battling against Marxist intellectuals who seem intent upon enrolling literature in the service of the class struggle. This anti-political defense of poetry dovetailed with the academic needs of English studies. In a general sense, Tate sought to save poetry from politics; but in a more particular way, he helped to focus the pedagogical aims of the literary/critical profession, intensifying the new academic concentration on "the text itself" and differentiating its concerns from ethics, politics, and other matters.[28]

The pedagogical orientation of the New Criticism, and also the errors that it unknowingly encouraged, are evident in Leo Spitzer's important essay "History of Ideas versus Reading of Poetry." Spitzer is not a "New Critic," but his essay accentuates features of the new critical discourse I have been describing, supplements key points made in Tate's essays, and demonstrates the extent to which "close reading," "formal analysis," and "the texts themselves" had become fixed as the terms for literary study. Brooks and Warren accepted "History of Ideas versus Reading of Poetry" for publication in the *Southern Review* and regarded it as valuable testimony on behalf of a new kind of critical undertaking.[29] Like others before him, Spitzer contests the reign of source-hunting, biographical research, and "background" information. We must acknowledge the needs and desires of our students, he says, and return to the "particular work of art." "Most of our textbooks"

> cram the student with the sources of a work while failing to describe
> the work itself—as if to imply that to "teach" the work of art itself
> would be an encroachment upon the personal reaction of the reader.
> Thus, on the pretext that any description of a poem must be emotional,
> personal, subjective (a pretense that perpetuates the escapist attitude)
> they fail to train their pupils to *avoid* subjectivity and emotionalism by
> learning to form and to express objective observations, to fix in their
> minds the exact contents, the relationships between the part and the
> whole, the structure and the formal qualities of a poem—all of which
> may be formulated with clarity and objectivity.[30]

Spitzer's call for "objectivity" is important, and is central, as it is also in Tate's essays, to the New Critical opposition to historical scholars, Humanists, and Marxists. In ways that we should by now recognize as common, Spitzer dramatizes the rigor and precision of his new critical method. It is, he suggests, as disciplined as any procedure devised by the scholars, and thus does not mark a surrender to impressionism. Spitzer asserts that teachers and critics should concentrate on the "form" of the work, aiming in this manner to help students describe the "exact contents" of what they see. In contrast to the New Humanists, he believes that students should not use moral or didactic principles to appraise the text. Rather, students should learn, in the most exact sense, to report on the particular work they examine and to explain its status as "art."

This same close attention to the text also serves to separate literary study from politics. Unlike the Marxist, who judges texts through the lens of party doctrine, Spitzer's teacher/critic analyzes what is concretely "there" in what he or she reads. Such a teacher/critic is armed with "objective observations" that are the product of training and experience, is equipped with a technique to convey in the classroom, is given a standard or norm by which to discriminate between good and bad readings ("bad readings" being those readings that reflect the student's "subjectivity"), and is provided with a means of determining when politics are intruding upon art and interfering with "objective" study. "It should be impressed on the minds of students of literature," Spitzer summarizes,

> that art and *outward reality* should, at least while the work of art is being studied, be kept separate—however much the artist may have derived from reality. I say purposely "while the work of art is being studied," for, obviously, our enjoyment of any work of art comes from the deeply-grounded feeling we have that art is not life, but a new architecture, built of fancy and the poetic will, apart from life and beyond life.[31]

Spitzer's words attest to what was quickly becoming "policy" for literary study, a policy that pointedly defines the object that critics and teachers take as their province: "the work of art" must be distinguished from "life" and accorded a pure examination. Many others said similar things during the late 1930s and on through the 1940s and 1950s, and they crafted a legacy that continues to hold our allegiance today. They established, and we generally remain under the sway of, a bold but narrow conception of English studies. These men articulated, in Ransom's phrase, "a strategy for English studies," and we persist in speaking their language, so naturalized has it now become. Ransom's voice is urgent and enterprising:

> It is really atrocious policy for a department to abdicate its own self-respecting identity. The department of English is charged with the understanding and the communication of literature, an art, yet it has usually forgotten to inquire into the peculiar constitution and structure of its product. English might almost as well announce that it does not regard itself as entirely autonomous, but as a branch of the department of history, with the option of declaring itself occasionally a branch of the department of ethics. It is true that the historical and the ethical studies will cluster round objects which for some reason are called artistic objects. But the thing itself the professors do not have to contemplate.[32]

Here, in Spitzer's essay, in Tate's writings, and in other books and articles published during the period, we can observe the discipline reconsolidating itself, declaring its new business, refining its product, and securing its boundaries. The study of literature occurs within "departments" of the colleges and universities; literary study means focusing on the "artistic objects" themselves; and critics and teachers must be mindful of the specifically *literary* terms of their work, terms that make clear the difference between *this* work and that which takes place in other departments. By the early 1950s, these were the tenets of English studies.

These were tenets that the New Critics constantly hammered home. W. K. Wimsatt, for instance, stressed that "the verbal object and its analysis constitute the domain of literary criticism," and René Wellek and Austin Warren insisted that "the object of literary study" is "the concrete work of art."[33] It may be true, as defenders of the New Critics sometimes argue, that Ransom, Wimsatt, Tate, Brooks, and the others were not anti-historical, and did in fact urge that other disciplines enrich the study of literature. But it is undeniable that the New Critics, in their statements of policy, underline the priority of the text itself and strive to make English studies equivalent to the analysis and explication of specific works of art.[34] When William Van O'Connor describes the New Criticism in 1949, he is clear about its principles:

> Most of them would probably agree that the critic should (1) center his attention on the literary work itself, (2) study the various problems arising from examining relationships between a subject matter and the final form of a work, and (3) consider ways in which the moral and philosophical elements get into or are related to the literary work. . . . Almost all the contemporary critics would probably agree with Robert Penn Warren's statement, in his essay on *The Ancient Mariner*, that the primary problem in examining the meanings of a work of literature is to get at its "internal consistency."[35]

This is the New Criticism, and this, more importantly, is the view of criticism in general that we still abide by. What is crucial to see is that not only did the New Criticism triumph, but so did the belief, shared by both supporters and foes of the New Criticism, that English studies means "reading" particular texts. The New Criticism was so successful in dislodging the impressionists and the old-line scholars, and its doctrines became so secure in such a short span of time, that in one important sense the New Criticism no longer could even be contested. True, the Chicago critics, led by R. S. Crane, and the myth critics, stimulated by Northrop Frye, challenged the New Critics' hegemony. But what was being challenged were ways of reading texts, not the assumption that "reading texts" and English studies were identical.

There is no doubt about the victory that the New Criticism achieved. By the late 1940s, the New Criticism was an established practice, and by the early 1950s, it was "the Establishment" itself.[36] But what made this victory possible? Why was the New Criticism so extraordinarily successful in defining the object of criticism, setting the terms and methods for teaching, and making available a "product" (Ransom's word) for the profession to sell? In part the New Criticism's rise to power resulted from the rhetorical skill and strategic genius of Ransom, Tate, Brooks, and the others; they waged an effective campaign against the scholars, New Humanists, and Marxists, and their writings inspired a generation of teachers and critics to focus directly—without the distraction of scholarly data, outmoded ethical systems, or ideology—on literary texts. But it is also important to understand that, in another sense, the New Critics simply made highly visible the terms, attitudes, and values that already existed in the writings of Sherman, Bourne, Feuillerat, and many others. The New Critical revolution was inevitable—people inside and outside the academy had been arguing for a return to the "books themselves" for decades. The New Critics, with courage and determination, speeded the process along.

In one of their most intelligent strokes, the New Critics devoted themselves not only to the reform of criticism, but also to the reform of pedagogy. Their methods were—and they remain—"teachable," more so than any other method yet devised. Neither the teacher nor his or her students require special background or preparation to begin their literary work in the classroom. From the first day, teacher and students can read and respond to poems, exchange views about tone, paradox, and imagery, and make discriminations about relative degrees of complex thought and feeling in texts. There is something admirably democratic about this procedure; teacher and students gather round a common object, and all strive to give the most detailed and sensitive reading possible. Such a method quickly enables the student to feel accomplished as a "reader"; he or she is empowered to see ambiguities and puzzles in texts never glimpsed before, and thus experiences the pleasure of a new kind of expertise. This pleasure is especially compelling when it occurs in response to the modernist writings of Yeats, Eliot, and others, difficult writings that the New Criticism was designed to explicate and open up for students.

It makes obvious professional sense to affirm, as the New Critics instruct us, that the object of criticism is the text, and that our job is to interpret it. The text is something tangible and available for study, and the readings that can be extracted from it provide us with both a goal in teaching and a commodity that suits the needs of professors who must publish books, articles, and notes in order to gain tenure and promotion. Texts, it is clear, can be explicated endlessly.

But the endless explications suggest the major weakness of the New Criticism: it generates "close readings" without apparent limit, saturating the text with so much interpretation that "the text itself"—which the New Critics sought to rescue—tends to disappear. Before the New Criticism emerged, many people argued that "the books themselves" were being lost amid piles of scholarly information, or else were being tarnished by unconstrained impressionism, insipid moralizing, and political sloganeering. Displaying a new kind of "scientific" rigor, the New Critics recovered the text, examined its formal patterns and structures, and inaugurated an English studies based on it. Yet no sooner were the texts restored to view than a chorus of complaints were heard that, once again, they were being obscured, forced into the dim background by the press of explications. And no sooner did the New Critics claim disciplinary precision for their labors than other critics and scholars declared that New Critical procedures were not disciplined at all, but rather amounted to a wholesale invitation to subjectivity. The New Criticism hence aimed to preserve literary texts but almost immediately seemed to many to be losing sight of them; and it also intended to stop the personal commentary on the masterpieces, yet it struck many as seeming merely to authorize impressionism, with each person trained to be a sensitive reader whose response counted as significant. The most curious aspect of the New Criticism is that it preserves the grounds for complaints about criticism even as it appears to answer them.

We have reached the point today where, in the words of George Steiner, Thomas McFarland, and others I quoted earlier, English studies appears to be totally corrupt. The literary texts are being slighted or ignored; theorists are spinning out their dizzying flights of fancy while refusing to descend to textual practice; and all of us—so we say in embittered moments—are grinding out books and articles while paying no attention to the needs of students, the humanistic mission of our work, and the great traditions of culture. Seen from this vantage point, the New Criticism seems admirably cogent. The discipline is racked by abuses, and many feel it is time now to remedy them by returning to the basic encounter between reader and text. Literature—"the books themselves"—must be restored to the critic/teacher's line of vision, and trained, analytical attention to the words on the page needs to replace the self-indulgent misuse of the artist's words for the purposes of theoretical showmanship. But such an appeal and attempt at reform solve nothing, for returning to the object and objective of the New Criticism also means returning to everything that critics hope to forestall—endless readings of texts, the disappearance of literature, and the play of impressionism and subjectivity. "Going back" to the New Criticism simply guarantees that the discipline will remain unstable even as it seems relocated on solid ground. More importantly still—and here is the strangest twist of all—"going back" is impossible, for we cannot return to what we have never abandoned. As I explain in my next chapter, we believe that New Critical methods have been lost and desire to restore them only because we cannot perceive how deeply embedded in our practice they already are. The New Criticism has been transformed into "criticism" in general.

6.

The Institutionalization

of the New Criticism

What is taken for granted must be attended just the same, like breathing.
    R. P. Blackmur

We are apt to be peculiarly under the influence of ideas and attitudes of which we are not fully conscious; they prevail until rejected.
    F. R. Leavis

In this chapter I shall argue that the New Criticism is alive and well. To say this may seem perverse, since there is such general agreement that the New Criticism has lost its prestige and authority. All of us are keenly aware of its failings: it ignores the reader's role, denies the importance of authorial intention, cuts off literature from history, and favors some groups of texts (metaphysical poetry, for example) at the expense of others (Romantic and Victorian poetry in particular). Attacks on the New Criticism have in fact been so sustained and, apparently, so successful that it is common today to discover references to the "decline" or "death" of the movement—as though the New Criticism were already in the grave or rapidly on its way there. Sometimes the references are slightly more charitable, as when Morris Dickstein remarks that individual New Critics exist but as a species of "toothless lion." Which implies that they possess a certain nobility, if not the power to do us harm.[1]

But we have been hearing reports of the death, decline, or harmlessness of the New Criticism for decades, and they have always been greatly exaggerated. Twenty years ago, Murray Krieger noted that "we are told on all sides that the New Criticism is dead, that a reaction has set in against it."[2] Many others said the same or similar things, and the dirge still sounds in the 1980s. Everyone agrees that the New Criticism is dead or declining and is obviously no longer an influential force. But at the same time, everyone feels obliged to keep dismissing the New Criticism yet once more. Its power is said to be negligible or non-existent, yet it still compels interest and renewed attention, and arguments for its overthrow or displacement continue to be made. Critiques of the New Criticism, even in its so-called decline or death, crop up frequently in books and journals. And it is standard practice for literary theorists to begin their discussions of "new" approaches by first assailing the New Criticism, as though its errors still needed to be exposed.

For several decades, then, critics and theorists have been saying that the New Criticism is neither vital nor influential. Even the New Critics themselves—and at a relatively early stage—expressed doubts about the movement. John Crowe Ransom observed in 1948 that New Critical "stock" was low, having taken a "dip in the market," and he suggested that a revaluation was in order.[3] A year later, Cleanth Brooks also called for a "general stock-taking," adding that the New Critical era "has come to fruition, or has arrived at a turning point, or, as some writers hint, has now exhausted its energies."[4] So widespread was this sense of closure that by 1951 Austin Warren could state as a "commonplace" that the New Critical movement "had come to an end."[5]

What we have is a curious phenomenon. The New Criticism appears powerless, lacking in supporters, declining, dead or on the verge of being so. No one speaks on behalf of the New Criticism as such today, and it mostly figures in critical discourse as the embodiment of foolish ideas and misconceived techniques. But the truth is that the New Criticism survives and is prospering, and it seems to be powerless only because its power is so pervasive that we are ordinarily not even aware of it. So deeply ingrained in English studies are New Critical attitudes, values, and emphases that we do not even perceive them as the legacy of a particular movement. On the contrary: we feel them to be the natural and definitive conditions for criticism in general. It is not simply that the New Criticism has become institutionalized, but that it has gained acceptance as the institution itself. It has been transformed into "criticism," the essence of what we do as teachers and critics, the ground or given upon which everything else is based.

The New Criticism leads two lives. Or rather, it is dead in one sense and very much alive in another. It is dead as a movement, as the many critiques and attacks demonstrate. But its lessons about literary study lead a vigorous life, setting the norms for effective teaching and marking the boundaries within which nearly all criticism seeks to validate itself. It is the New Criticism that defines and gives support to the central job of work that we perform: "practical criticism," the "close reading" of literary texts.[6] "Close reading" forms the substance of most critical essays and books, and it is reinforced in our classrooms, where we teach verbal analysis to students. It is also an evaluative principle, the norm by which we assess new theories of literature. If a new theory cannot generate close readings, if it fails the test of practical criticism, if it seems unable to make us understand the classic texts in new ways and appears unlikely to function well in the classroom, then it is usually judged to be irrelevant. A new theory, it is believed, must have consequences for the analysis and explication of texts; it can only make modest claims for itself and should serve, above all, to direct us back to the text and thus enrich "close readings." It is the single text that stands, in Malcolm Bradbury's words, as the "irreducible literary minimum," and our essential duty is to read it with as much sensitivity to tone and nuance as we can manage and to teach others to do the same.[7]

In his essay "Beyond Interpretation," published in 1976, Jonathan Culler argued against this over-riding emphasis on the "close reading" of texts. The chief and most "insidious" legacy of the New Criticism, he stated, is the "unquestioning acceptance of the notion that the critic's job is to interpret literary works."[8] Culler's argument upset many people, who, on the one hand, claimed not to be New Critics at all, yet who nevertheless insisted that the critic's function is obviously to explicate literary texts. To insist on the "obviousness" of interpretation, however, is not to refute Culler's argument but to confirm it. We are so accustomed to seeing ourselves as "close readers," and we are so committed to producing more interpretations of texts, that when we practice close reading we believe that we are engaged in the inevitable work of criticism. No one, of course, is opposed to the detailed, attentive reading of texts, and I am not making a case for its elimination. But I think it is important to recognize that what was once the aim of a particular critical movement now defines the general aims of criticism. Close reading of literary texts is the ground that nearly all theories and methods build upon or seek to occupy. And this holds true even for those that are explicitly set up in opposition to the New Criticism. To put this point another way: the New Criticism is not so much in decline or dead as it has won eternal life as the core or essence of criticism.

In a recent review article, Louis D. Rubin, Jr., affirms this identity between the New Criticism and "criticism" in general, and thereby brings into the open what most critics take for granted and leave unsaid. "If the New Criticism as a movement is concluded," he explains,

> it is because its job has been done: it has made us read poems closely and in their own right, so that we could gain access to the poetry written in English during the first half of the twentieth century. But I remain unconvinced that it is kaput, because I don't see its job as having been done. Certainly its faddishness is over; it is no longer a novelty. But in ceasing to be New it has not thereby become Old Criticism. Instead it has become simply criticism.[9]

New Critical techniques, Rubin points out, are especially suited to the analysis of difficult modern texts, the poetry, for instance, of Yeats and Eliot. But instead of highlighting the historical conjunction of modern poetry and criticism, and instead of commenting on the kinds of poetry the New Criticism cannot help us to read well, Rubin endows the New Criticism with a permanent validity. "The best criticism of literature," he concludes,

> as long as it is criticism *of* literature, will have to be that which starts with the text and, no matter how far it may stray, or whatever it brings to the text, will find its validity in the text . . . Somebody is always going to say, eventually, after the New Historical Scientist or the structuralist or the Marxist or the reader-psychologist or whatever has erected his glittering paradigm or simulacrum or manifesto or document or who knows what: "Yes, but how do you *know* it's so?" And the only convincing response will have to be "Let's look at the text."[10]

The text is our point of departure and the instrument by which we measure the accuracy of an interpretation. The meanings situated in the text will prove or disprove what we say about it, Rubin assumes, however caught up we may be in our newfangled theories. When all the preliminaries and distractions are out of the way, we will be obliged to return to the text, reading it scrupulously and hence seeing (and abiding by) its meaningful signals.

Such a "New Critical" understanding of the text is debatable at best, and it has been challenged by Gerald Graff, Richard Strier, and others.[11] But Rubin's definition of the text concerns me less than his belief, uttered in that weary voice we reserve for basic truths in danger of being forgotten, that the basic fact of "criticism" is the close reading of texts. When we undertake the task of interpretation, keeping our sight focused on the words on the page, we are not merely fulfilling the job that the New Critics prescribed. Rather, according to Rubin, we are living up to the responsibility that every right-minded critic must acknowledge. We are not practicing the New Criticism, but "simply criticism."

Rubin's argument is not unique, and it is indeed surprising to realize, in this era of proliferating methods, theories, and approaches, how widely it is shared. Even for those who scorn the New Criticism and declare that something else should replace it, the close reading of texts remains the normative procedure, the way of showing that the proposed replacement for the New Criticism is useful and worthwhile. Whenever a critic wishes to state the essential truth of criticism, or intends to demonstrate what a new theory has to offer, he or she returns to the literary text for an exercise in practical criticism. At this point the theoretical debates and conflicts are set aside, factional strife ceases, and teachers and critics urge one another to accept the facts of interpretive life—that we remain faithful to the discipline of "close reading" and to the class of specifically *literary* texts for which this skill was devised.

In his recent call for the "oral interpretation" of literature, Roger Shattuck does not present himself as a New Critic, but his argument is informed by the terms that the New Criticism canonized. He advises us to

> keep our heads, eschew intellectual fashions, avoid cleaving to one method as suitable to all circumstances, and attempt to approach a work of literature without rigid preconceptions, without a grid of theory. No, there is no "innocent reading" any more than there is an "innocent eye." But it is possible to temper experience and mastery with a kind of induced innocence—negative capability or *lacher prise*—which discourages the kind of usurpation I have been deploring. And in the domain of teaching . . . I would also favor certain kinds of exercises—busy-work even—that have fallen totally out of favor: word for word copying, dictation, reading aloud, summarizing (precis writing), memorizing, and translation. All of these activities enforce close attention to what a piece of writing is actually doing without requiring an elaborate theory of literature to begin with.[12]

This argument presents itelf as straightforward and commonsensical even as it bypasses the contestability of its assumptions. It is a paradoxical kind of argument, since Shattuck wants something and concedes that it cannot be attained, but then tries to have it anyway. He admits that there cannot be an "innocent" reading, yet he then asserts, without any explanation, that we can "induce" this innocence or something like it in ourselves and thereby guard against the perils of "experience" and the arrogant desire to "master" the text. Shattuck's words sound persuasive to many people, but his argument is not very rigorous. It is in fact loose and rather sloppy, but Shattuck succeeds in reaching his audience because his argument is based on what many teachers and critics believe as a matter of course—that we should always attend to the text and remember that *any* "theory of literature" will necessarily be "elaborate," interfering with the text rather than helping us to understand it in more complex ways.[13] Like Louis Rubin, Shattuck judges that he is reiterating commonplaces which, in our waywardness, we occasionally lose sight of but basically agree with. He knows that many of his proposals appear dated and old-fashioned, yet he also senses how appealing these will be for readers—and they constitute the majority of the profession—who are tired of all the talk about theory and are anxious to get back to the practical criticism of literature. To be a teacher and critic is to "enforce"—the word is somewhat disconcerting—the "close attention to what a piece of writing is actually doing." And this means that we should not mar the discipline with theory, non-literary topics and approaches, or even preconceptions. Just read the text closely and the disciplined nature of "Criticism, Inc." (Ransom's term) will be ensured.

"Literature," Shattuck admits, "is not autonomous and unrelated to our daily lives; on the contrary, we all to some degree live by and through it. But it does not belong to any domain outside the domain of art, and we are shirking our responsibilities if we look the other way while self-styled 'literary' critics deliver literature into the hands of one or another of the social sciences" ("How to Rescue Literature," p. 30). Shattuck states that literature is not "autonomous" and therefore *is* connected, in some way that he does not specify, to our daily lives. Yet no sooner does he make this point then he appears to take it back or at least diminish its force. Literature belongs to "the domain of art," and we are obligated to prevent traitors within the "literary" ranks from handing over "literature" to the social sciences. Once again Shattuck's words strike a high-minded tone, but this should not disguise the fact that he is concerned about the territorial privileges of English and other departments of literature. Like Ransom and the other New Critics, he seeks to keep the discipline "autonomous." A responsible critic, Shattuck insists, must affirm the autonomy of the discipline and must examine *literature as literature*, not as some other thing—and certainly not something as abstract and fussy as one of the social sciences, which traffic in the world outside the "domain of art."[14]

What is especially revealing about Shattuck's argument is his lack of confidence in the "literature" he claims to be supporting. Shattuck believes that other disciplines are making "raids" on literature, and his assumption is that these raids are dangerous, that they threaten a literature unable to defend itself. Any exchange between literature and other disciplines must occur at literature's expense, Shattuck implies. He could have maintained that literature naturally tends towards being enriched and supplemented by other disciplines; from this point of view, he could have argued that precisely because "the domain of art" is itself powerful, it enables and encourages us to move beyond its secure boundaries. But rather than emphasizing the range and resilience of literature, Shattuck worries about its weakness. Literature, to quote the title of his essay, needs to be "rescued." And this rescue mission is undertaken, as one might have predicted, by a return to the text, to "close attention" to the words on the page. This will enable us to safeguard literature or "at least delay the abduction of the text by method, theory or system" (p. 33). As this last phrase suggests, Shattuck's modest claims for the role of the critic barely conceal what is certainly a major claim: literature is best served not by method or theory but by the virtues of its protectors. Those who truly serve and strive to "rescue" literature do not require critical terms, theoretical models, or interpretive machines, but just themselves.

A similar, though more eloquent, proposal is at the heart of Helen Vendler's 1980 presidential address to the Modern Language Association. In her capacity as our spokesperson, Vendler articulates the mission that we perform as critics and teachers of literature. And she does so by repeatedly drawing upon New Critical language about the close reading of texts. "We are all, by now, scholars," she observes.

> But I would wish for us all a steady memory of the time when we were not yet scholars—before we knew what research libraries or variorum editions were, before we heard any critical terms, before we had seen a text with footnotes. It was in those innocent days that our attachment to literature arose—from reading a novel or seeing a play. In every true reading of literature in adult life we revert to that early attitude of entire receptivity and plasticity and innocence before the text.[15]

Like Shattuck, Vendler feels that there is something impure about scholarly pursuits, and she recommends that we try to recover our lost "innocence," that time before we knew "critical" terms. This is, at first sight, a peculiar argument, primarily because it seems to be directed *against* the various practices in which the literary institution deals and which, one assumes, Vendler ought to be defending: it is as if the products of research and scholarship were, for her, consequences devoutly to be wished away. But while this appears to be an anti-institutional argument, it is actually one of the oldest, most institutionalized arguments of all. The New Critics first made this point in the 1930s when they stated that literary history, source study, and the like were overwhelming the literary texts. For the New Critics, the essential truth about literary experience is that it puts the reader into intimate contact with a particular text. And this is a belief that Vendler, Shattuck, and Rubin share: we cherish the literary text, seek always to return to it for close reading and practical criticism, and view this task as the ground upon which discipline is constructed. This belief enables us to reaffirm our sense of mission and justify our work to the world.

"No matter how elementary or specialized the written inquiry," Vendler adds, "it originated in problems raised by human submission to, and interrogation of, a text" (p. 344). Nothing, perhaps, seems more understandable, in the face of institutional chores and routines, than the desire to escape our consciousness of them and "revert" to purity and innocence—Vendler even characterizes the reading of texts as, at its best, a "state of intense engagement and self-forgetfulness." But this desire signifies a form of nostalgia that was itself institutionalized a long time ago, so much that it has become the basis for our conception of ourselves as teachers and critics. We read texts, poems in particular, because we feel that they are far better, richer, more deeply textured and organically unified than any world that we know from daily experience. Returning to the text means, in this sense, turning away from the world and dwelling within the verbal structures that literature provides.

I do not want in this essay to seem unfair or ungrateful to Ransom and his colleagues. The New Criticism made a necessary case against the bad effects of a certain kind of excessively "historical" approach, and in this sense it was truly liberating. But the spirit of reversion, withdrawal, and isolation remains deeply rooted in literary studies, and the New Critics are in large measure responsible for it. Once the Agrarian movement failed, Ransom and the others focused their attention on the reform of criticism and teaching. These reforms required, first, that "English Studies" be separated from other disciplines, and second, that literature not be made impure by contact with the world—the world that the New Critics, in their Agrarian phase, had sought to reform but now thought beyond repair. When Ransom was asked to organize and edit a new journal at Kenyon College, he insisted that such a journal deal exclusively with literature and the other arts, and he did so despite the fact that the president of Kenyon College had originally proposed and hoped for a journal that would examine philosophy and public affairs as well as the arts.[16] "It seems to me," Ransom stated in a letter to Allen Tate (December 10, 1937), "that our cue would be to stick to literature entirely. There's no consistent, decent group writing politics . . . and in the severe field of letters there is vocation enough for us: in criticism, in poetry, in fiction."[17] Ransom's determination to stress literature and criticism in the new review hearkens back to his earlier desire, again expressed in letters to Tate (September, 1936), to establish an "American Academy of Letters," which would bear the title "Institute of Literary Autonomy and Tradition," and which would focus on questions of style, form, and technique.[18] As Ransom's symbolically charged decision implies, the injunction to return to the text and the privileging of literary experience are not, contrary to Vendler and others, *anti*-institutional. These do not allow us to escape from the hindrances of the literary institution but rather establish what the literary institution *is*, what it assumes as its central job of work, and what it regards as its justification.

"We love in *King Lear*," Vendler affirms,

> precisely what distinguishes it from *Hamlet* or *Doctor Faustus*, the quality that makes it not simply a Renaissance tragedy, not simply a Shakespearean play, but the single and unrepeatable combination of elements we call *King Lear*. It is from the experience of one or two such works that we are all led to the place where we are now, and it is from that original vision—of the simple, unduplicatable, compelling literary object—that we

must always take our final strength in university life and public life alike, whatever combinatorial tactics prudence may occasionally recommend. ("Presidential Address," p. 348)

Vendler inherits her conception of our submissiveness before the literary text from the New Critics, and the zeal that is evident throughout her essay suggests her feeling for the text's importance. It is not the case, however, that she is addressing an audience that needs to be won over to her view. Most teachers and critics already share it, for their attitudes, too, have been formed by the New Criticism. An extremely gifted reader herself, Vendler is thus speaking to an audience that was converted long ago. New Critical beliefs and practices, though no longer in fashion, are also no longer in dispute, because they have been widely accepted as the foundation for criticism. Vendler does not name herself as a New Critic, but that is part of my point about her, and about Rubin and Shattuck as well. The New Criticism is so woven into the fabric of critical discourse that its assumptions are not recognized as assumptions at all.

This emerges with unusual clarity in John M. Ellis's essay "The Logic of the Question 'What is Criticism?'" Ellis contends that most of the criticism being written today is wrongheaded and contemptible. As he surveys the critical landscape, he sees battles and disagreements that are fought without real point or purpose. The main problem is that many critics now view their enterprise as a "creative" one, in competition with the literature that criticism ought in fact to be serving:

> Modern critics seem less and less inclined to let the text speak for itself, through close attention to *its* emphases; they seem far more concerned to impress than to allow the text to do so, readily substituting their own ideologies and conceptual systems for those of the literary work. They seem often to be trying to rival the uniqueness of literary language by their own dazzling conceptual pyrotechnics, and to display their own erudition and intellectual feats instead of the literary text's subtle individuality. Never have we been so faced with criticism which so obviously strains for originality at all costs. Critical essays by well-known and well-regarded critics seem often to ramble from one ill-defined but grandiose concept to another, attempting to enrich a vacuous argument with fashionable jargon and names, as well as bons mots and aphorisms of questionable relevance. The result is a veritable caricature of discussion, a reduction of criticism to an entertainment for scholars, a narrowly clubby kind of discourse.[19]

The issues are clear, Ellis believes. Critics should not impose their systems (or their personalities) on the literary text, but should "let the text speak for itself." If criticism is to lay claim to being a discipline, then its practitioners need to recall that it is the literary text, not the critic, which is our foremost concern. The goal of "actual criticism" is to "discern the unique emphasis of a given text." Some people, Ellis concedes, will judge such an emphasis to be "old-fashioned," a throwback to the "New Criticism." Yet "nothing will be as enduring as the plain confrontation of reader and text, the fundamental literary experience which will still be going on long after our current critical fads are forgotten" ("Logic of the Question," p. 27). Like Rubin, Ellis advocates a return to the text itself; like Shattuck, he hopes to rescue the literary work from the theorists and self-serving critical performers; and like Vendler, he regards the "plain," direct encounter between the reader and the literary text as the essential truth to which the critic must remain loyal. These four critics doubtless disagree about many things, but all of them are in agreement about the necessity of "close criticism" and its central place in the study of literature.

Rubin, Shattuck, Vendler, and Ellis are to be commended for their efforts to reorient and justify the "discipline" of criticism. But their arguments on behalf of criticism suggest why criticism is in trouble and accorded little respect. Literature departments suffer from the pressures of the faltering economy: the stock of "Criticism, Inc." appears even lower today than when Ransom and Brooks worried about it in the late 1940s.[20] Obviously we need to renew the discipline and vitalize the work that we perform, making clear the value of our labor and the importance of its survival. Yet even as literary study seems to be collapsing and in dire need of basic repairs, many of the most prestigious critics devise sophisticated theories, draw upon philosophy and the social sciences to buttress their interpretations of literary texts, and pay scant attention to the texts themselves. Must criticism, Rubin and the others ask, be so rarified and detached from literature? Isn't it time to get back to the fundamentals and reacquaint ourselves with specific texts? Criticism, it is argued, should return to the text, concern itself with close reading, and resist the temptations of theory, ideology, politics, social and cultural commentary. It is the encounter with the literary text—and not anything else—that establishes the discipline of criticism and gives direction to our common pursuit.

But to see the dispute as one that sets practical critics against vanguard theorists, close readers against deconstructionists, advocates of a return to the text against proponents of French and other Continental methods, is misleading. Whatever their differences of opinion on other matters, both sides share a commitment to "close reading" and the production of more analyses of texts. Most of the major theorists, including Paul De Man, Geoffrey Hartman, and J. Hillis Miller, seek to demonstrate the usefulness of their speculations in the "reading" of texts. As the spate of books and articles testify, these theorists and their disciples have created an industry in new kinds of textual explication. The results are not "New Critical" in any obvious sense: the form of the analysis differs; the terms vary; and the philosophical rationale is not the same. But the aim is identical—to generate more close readings, and to describe this activity as the inevitable job of the critic. Miller's defense of deconstruction makes this abundantly clear: "The ultimate justification for this mode of criticism, as of any conceivable mode, is that it works. It reveals hitherto unidentified meanings and ways of having meaning in major literary texts."[21] Deconstruction feeds the growth-rate of literary studies, assuring us that still more readings can be gotten out of the classic texts that critical exegesis might seem to have exhausted.

Thus it is no accident that deconstruction, of all the new theories, has gained the largest group of supporters and become a cultural phenomenon. Deconstruction can be readily acquired by anyone versed in the techniques of the New Criticism, and it holds out the promise of something radical and innovative even as it fits comfortably into the standard ways of doing business. It is also no accident that of all of the theories being advanced today, deconstruction is the one against which the so-called practical critics fight most strenuously. They recognize a certain—perhaps one should say a sneaking—kinship between the usual forms of "close reading" and deconstruction; but they cannot understand why the explication of texts needs to be theorized about—why invoke the terms of a theory to justify the basic procedure of criticism? And this in turn helps to explain why De Man, Miller, and the others are praised for the rigor and intensity of their analyses *and* chastized for their pretensions and overblown rhetoric; their readings are often stimulating, but their theories, it is charged, are foolish and extravagant. The deconstructive critics are pretentious in many ways, but not for their philosophical grandeur as much as for their insistence that they are breaking free from the New Criticism and moving beyond formalism. As Edward W. Said has remarked, these "new New Critics," like their predecessors, "confine literature to language and the problems raised by language."[22] Deconstruction has not made a decisive change in our understanding of the discipline, but has merely enabled critics to refine familiar techniques, generate more close readings, and indulge in controversy without consequences.

My argument tends towards an obvious and double-edged conclusion. First, that the New Critics' placement of close reading at the center of English studies was mistaken, however necessary it might have seemed at the time; and second, that we are wrong to assume that this New Critical practice defines the essential task of criticism. But "close reading" is clearly here to stay, and I cannot pretend that I wish it could be dislodged. This chapter is not, as I have already indicated, a plea for the end of careful, detailed study of specific texts. But I do believe that we need to acknowledge the costs of our too often single-minded emphasis on textual interpretation of the masterpieces: the rejection of other methods and other kinds of texts; the misguided attempt to define (and thus defend) the *teaching* of literature as, above all, "close reading"; the skepticism shown towards literary theory; and the refusal to see other disciplines as having relevance for "literary criticism." It is not that "close reading" is itself misconceived but rather that the case for it has always been made at the expense of other important things. In making arguments for the discipline, we invariably exclude too much. We seek to defend criticism, but in fact restrict and delimit it. Literary studies are at once exalted (they alone can teach us to read closely and perceive the powers of language) and diminished (they become tainted when they are involved with theory, other analytical techniques, other disciplines, and the burdens of worldliness).

During the 1930s and 40s, when Ransom and the New Critics were clashing with literary historians in America, F. R. Leavis was conducting a similar campaign in England. He, too, felt that useless data about sources, backgrounds, and influences were overwhelming "literary texts themselves"; and he also argued that it was time to focus on the "words on the page" and acquire practical skills in analysis and judgment. In terms that remind us of Ransom and his fellow New Critics, Leavis contends that we must examine "poetry as poetry," and he envisions a program for criticism that wrests control from the enemies of literature—both the pedants inside the institution and the journalists outside it. Criticism, both Leavis and the American New Critics stress, must be firmly grounded in the close reading of literary texts.

But Leavis differs significantly from the New Critics. Though he values "close reading," he distinguishes between "elucidation," which he associates with Brooks and the New Critics, and "criticism," which he seeks himself to practice. "Criticism" foregrounds judgment and discrimination, whereas "elucidation" too often amounts simply to the tracing of images, patterns, and ambiguities for the sake of the exercise, one where nothing seems to be at stake.[23] Even more importantly, Leavis sees the "close criticism" of literature as leading to serious work in other disciplines, to the study of literature written in other languages, and to the criticism of culture, society, and contemporary civilization. Leavis states these proposals in a number of books and articles, of which *Education and the University: A Sketch for an "English School,"* published in 1943, is the most concrete and compelling example. And this book is all the more illuminating when it is read in conjunction with Ransom's and the New Critics' writings during this period. Leavis's proposals indicate a significant road not taken in the charting of the American "New Critical" institution.[24]

Like the New Critics, Leavis emphasizes the necessity of defining

"English" and distinguishing it from other disciplines. But he then stresses that the study of English demands that we engage in historical research, cultural analysis, and social commentary. We take our bearings, he contends, in literary criticism, in the interpretation of particular texts, and then we proceed, inevitably, to other, more general studies. We are critics of both literature and more than literature, and viewing ourselves as concerned with the first job should not prevent us from doing the second one as well. To affirm that literature must be studied in its historical richness, its relevance to the present, and its relation to modern society is not to weaken or disfigure the integrity of criticism. It is, rather, a sign of our confidence in the power of literature and criticism that we feel able to teach and write "critically" in other ways and through other disciplines. This confidence will seem misplaced only to someone who is so defensive about the discipline—to say nothing of being defensive about literature itself—that he or she judges the best argument for criticism to be the one that describes it in the most exclusive terms.

There were, of course, a number of important American critics in the 1940s and 50s who, like Leavis in England, sought to progress beyond the close reading of texts. Here are three representative statements:

> Like every other agent in this life, the critic has to be understood from what he does, what changes he effects or seeks to effect in the world . . . The critic cultivating too zealously his critical autonomy may be consuming a great deal of energy defending himself against a threatening situation of which he does not want to be too conscious. We know that in life a man is sometimes most victimized by his fellows when he seeks to remove himself from them.

> The New Critic's attention to the text is valuable in so far as he does not resemble the ostrich, with his head in the sand while round his oblivious baser parts sweep the contentious gales of personality and culture. . . . A viable critical movement needs its own idea of the artist as a type of moral man living in or out of a type of culture; and the New Criticism should have developed such an idea.

> In becoming a general critic, the literary critic does not betray his vocation but fulfills it. The "pure" literary critic, who pretends, in the cant phrase, to stay "inside" a work all of whose metaphors and meanings are pressing outward, is only half-aware. And half-aware, he deceives; for he cannot help smuggling unexamined moral and metaphysical judgments into his "close analyses," any more than the "pure" literary historian can help bootlegging unconfessed aesthetic estimates into his chronicles. Literary criticism is always becoming "something else," for the simple reason that literature is always "something else."[25]

While these and similar statements by Philip Rahv, Alfred Kazin, and others should not be discounted, they finally represent no more than a fervent minority report. It was the New Criticism, and not a social or cultural or historical criticism, that became, in Richard Foster's words, "the dominant Anglo-American" literary movement of the twentieth century. It not only survived but "absorbed" its adversaries, Foster explains, making it "now almost impossible to identify the individual species *New Critic* as something distinct from the general run of competent literary academics." This was written in 1962, just when Krieger and others were observing the the New Criticism had died.[26]

"One of the virtues of literary studies," Leavis argues, "is that they lead constantly outside themselves," and we should remember this whenever we are inclined to defend the "autonomy" of the discipline. "While it is necessary" that literary studies "should be controlled by a concern for the essential discipline, such a concern, if it is adequate, counts on associated work in other fields" (*Education and the University*, p. 35). "Close reading," Leavis emphasizes, is obviously important, "but a serious concern for education in reading cannot stop at reading": "Practical criticism of literature must be associated with training in awareness of the environment—advertising, the cinema, the press, architecture, and so on, for, clearly, to the pervasive influence of this environment the literary training of sensibility in school is an inadequate reply" (p. 138). This marks a commitment that the American New Critics and their successors generally do not share. For Ransom and those who have followed him, the critic's task is to post the boundaries of the discipline and to work within them, whereas for Leavis, "literary" criticism is simply what we begin with. Indeed, it is precisely because we know the strengths of the literature that we study, and also have faith in our own discipline, that other disciplines and procedures do not threaten us. We can and should relate literary/critical skills to other studies and allow them to inform interpretive work. The "literary training of sensibility," in and of itself, is not adequate to the goals of criticism.

Leavis's words appear to make very good sense. Criticism ought to mean more than simply *literary* criticism, for surely the explication of classic texts needs to be supplemented by other modes and methods of analysis. Yet the situation today, as Rubin's, Shattuck's, Vendler's, and Ellis's essays attest, still reflects an extreme anxiety about any kind of criticism that seems non-literary, interdisciplinary, abstract, theoretical, or not primarily devoted to "close reading" particular texts. Most people do acknowledge that the New Critical movement erred in limiting itself to the words on the page, and, in some cases, they may even concede that we should not "return" to New Critical procedures that have lost their theoretical validity. But at the same time, New

Critical practice retains its potent influence because it is firmly in place as the natural form for "criticism" to take. It is true that many departments of literature include in their course offerings the study of topics and issues similar to those to which Leavis refers. But many do *not*, and most of us condescend towards such courses: they are not "literary" and are therefore unserious and to be tolerated only for the sake of departmental enrollments. The "close criticism" of literature is our means of explaining and justifying the discipline to ourselves—this New Critical habit dies hard. It disturbs us to feel that the survival of "literature" departments depends on courses in media, popular culture, contemporary critical theory, interdisciplinary studies, and the like. And this has the effect of making public calls for a return to the close reading of literature all the more vigorous—as if by promoting "practical criticism" passionately enough, we could recast criticism and make it once again a discipline nearly autonomous.

Invoking this New Critical tenet is the wrong way to defend English studies. For it is the New Critical determination to identify the discipline as one that features "close reading," to the exclusion of all else, that has led to the crisis which many feel so acutely. To put the matter as directly as possible: "close reading" is the problem, not the solution. It is unquestionably basic to the discipline, but is not the discipline itself and does not specify the only or the essential task that the teacher/critic undertakes. "Literature" forms one group or body of texts that we study; there are other kinds of texts, and we turn to them because we realize, as Leavis points out, that the practical criticism of literature is not enough to fulfill the demands of a responsible, truly critical mind. Criticism cannot be purely "literary." Other studies should enrich interpretive work, and we involve ourselves in them in order to extend critical practice, turning it, finally, into more than just the close reading of classic texts. Instead of perceiving interdisciplinary, theoretical, and cultural studies as interfering with the real business of criticism, we should see them as further evidence of how capacious and wide-ranging criticism can be. However much we cherish literature, it is not what Ransom suggests that it is—"the best of all possible worlds."[27]

In his account of a revised plan for the English Tripos, Leavis notes some of the areas and issues that criticism should embrace. His list concentrates on the seventeenth century and is too lengthy to quote in its entirety, but it consists of more than twenty topics—for example, "the rise of capitalism," "economic individualism," "the changing relations between sophisticated and popular culture," "the rise of the Press," "general comparison with French development" (*Education and the University*, pp. 52-53). Undertaking this work as a natural outgrowth of training in literary criticism prepares and shapes the mind as a "coordinating consciousness" (p. 55). Such a critical enterprise attempts to integrate various kinds of analysis and research, and it strives to demonstrate the relationships among the materials that are now divided up according to the discipline that claims the sole right to study them.

Identifying criticism with the close reading of classic texts has not served us well, and we ought to be aware of the cost that such an identification exacts when we seek to ground English studies upon it. Many students—to say nothing of their teachers—are skilled at textual interpretation but are at a total loss when asked to speak in a critically informed manner about their politics, attitudes towards history, and "awareness of the environment" in which they live. They are at a loss, at least in part, because we confine criticism to literature, devaluing other techniques and other kinds of texts and materials. No wonder it sometimes seems to students that their critical thinking ends when there are no more literature courses to be taken in school: it is as though the close reading of the classics is the only way in which criticism may be exercised, as though the only "criticism" is the New Criticism.

The essays by Rubin, Shattuck, Vendler, and Ellis might appear to indicate otherwise, but there have been signs in recent years that the New Critical reign is at last coming to a close. Much contemporary theory can be dismissed as a set of passing fads and fancies, but the revival of "history" as an instrument for criticism is a truly important development. This has come about through the labors of a number of theorists and critics, including Michel Foucault, Edward W. Said, and others. What they have shown is that "history" does not have to imply—as it did for the scholars the New Critics attacked in the 1930s—a narrow and naive review of sources, backgrounds, and influences. For Foucault and those influenced by him, "history" means the formation of an archive, the building up of a rich and complex discursive field. The ground for criticism is not the classic literary text, but intertextual configurations and arrangements. "Criticism" thus entails the study of power, political uses of language, and orders of discourse. As I explain in more detail in my Conclusion, this seems to me immensely productive, and the research that has begun to emerge is extremely promising. There is reason to hope that the kinds of suggestions made by Leavis in the 1940s can finally be realized, and in ways far more sophisticated than anything he could imagine or doubtless would wish to sponsor.

But it is precisely because certain signs are hopeful that I see all the more reason to be wary and suspicious and all the more need to recognize that the lines of resistance to significant change are still strong. In the years ahead, as the profession confronts the hard realities that accompany living in a diminished world, we will be urged by people, both inside and outside the institution, to get back to basics—a core curriculum, expository writing, and "close reading" of the masterpieces.

This will tighten the hold of the New Criticism upon us, and it will become increasingly difficult to give more than momentary attention to other programs and proposals. As in the past, other forms of criticism may appear for a time to displace the New Critical hegemony. But the New Criticism always seems able to outlast its competitors and to draw upon their methods to reinforce the techniques of "practical criticism." It furnishes the rhetoric through which many voice their opposition to "newer" modes, and which many capitalize upon when the discipline seems to require a unifying gesture, something that will "return" us to common sense and bedrock reality. The New Criticism has been extraordinarily resilient and has survived many challenges. Even as it is declared dead or on the decline, it remains powerfully present— alive and well, "simply criticism."[28]

The success of the New Criticism in "institutionalizing" its methods and values is the major story of modern criticism. But I do not want to seem to be too tightly forcing everything that has occurred in theory and criticism during the past decade into this single mold. Many teachers and critics do indeed remain sympathetic to the New Criticism— now defined as simply "criticism"—and many vanguard theorists reaffirm New Critical practices even as they appear to be challenging them. But finer distinctions are required for my book to have the range and validity I seek, and so I turn now to a three-chapter account of key books in criticism and theory that were published or reprinted in the 1970s and early 1980s.

In what follows I examine important trends and issues, including the politics of interpretation, the influence of Derrida and Foucault, the effect (or lack of effect) of structuralism and post-structuralism on "traditional" scholarship (in this case, the scholarly work on Milton), and the decline of evaluation. I deal with these matters by focusing on specific theoretical and critical books. This enables me to reconsider or else draw attention to books that I judge to be noteworthy and significant, as well as allows me to criticize books that are flawed and misleading, however influential and celebrated they might be. Though "theory" is a thriving business, one with many workers, it still has not reached many members of the profession, and it is necessary, for these readers, to discuss what has been happening in "theory" and reflect upon its major figures, books, issues—to provide, in a word, a "reader's guide" to a confusing (and often confused) field.

Those who are well versed in theory can also profit from reflection upon the work that has been done. One of the paradoxes of theory and criticism today is that it exhibits both extreme self-consciousness and a total absence of self-consciousness. Theorists busily produce more and increasingly sophisticated texts yet all too often fail to ask whether they are truly serving social needs and interests, or are simply laboring to make theory a glamorous enterprise, one for ambitious professionals who want to transform themselves into their special domain and subject. A great amount of material gets published in contemporary theory and criticism, but few theorists seem able or willing to make discriminations. No one wants to interfere with the blossoming of reputations, or to raise the possibility that theory as it is presently being "done" may well have out-lived its usefulness. My aim, then, in the following chapters is not to gather "book reviews" but is instead to "re-view"— to re-examine and revaluate—a wide range of important and influential texts, and to show how they illustrate both the promise and disappointment of literary theory in the 1970s and 1980s.

I begin by discussing four modern critics—Lionel Trilling, F. R. Leavis, Kenneth Burke, and R. P. Blackmur—whose relations to the rise of structuralism and post-structuralism are, as I shall explain, intriguing and very much in need of commentary. I admire and have learned from other critics, including Wilson, Richards, Winters, and Frye, but though I allude to and cite these critics, they do not bear in prominent ways on my concerns in this book. Wilson, as I remark in my Introduction, is an exemplary man-of-letters, but he worked outside the academic and professional contexts that orient and shape my treatment of English studies. Richards is one of the pioneers of criticism and theory, and he urged crucial reforms in the techniques of the discipline. But by the 1940s and perhaps even earlier, Richards was less a critic and theorist than a seer and prophet. His career is a fascinating one, and he demonstrates boundless reach and vision in his many books and essays. But his later writings did not receive much attention from those working in English studies, and in this respect he, like Wilson, lies outside the major developments that I have been tracing.

Winters, in his crusty individualism, and Frye, in his astonishing grasp of the whole of literature, are both significant critics. But Winters is too eccentric to warrant sustained attention here, and Frye is too ensnared in his conceptual system. Both are powerful and impressive writers, and each displays strengths that illuminate the other's shortcomings. Winters labors mightily to winnow and exclude, whereas Frye seeks to remain as capacious as possible in his response to the totality of literature. Winters, one feels, often makes his style wounding and mean-spirited as a pointed strategy for undercutting settled reputations, while Frye wants to preserve sympathy, generosity, and catholicity and so refuses to judge and discriminate. Though I respect these critics and feel that they deserve to be studied in their own right, I do not think that they tell us much about the main currents of English studies at the present time. To see the critics to whom those in English studies have turned in the 1970s and 1980s, we have to look elsewhere, to Trilling, Leavis, Burke, and Blackmur.

PART
THREE

7.

Reviewing the State
of Criticism, I

*Every man who enumerates the catalogue of his acquaintance is privately conscious,
however reluctant to confess the inferiority, of a certain number of minds which do
outrun and command his own, in whose company, despite the laws of good
breeding and the fences of affectation, his own spirit bows like the brothers' sheaves
to Joseph's sheaf.*

Ralph Waldo Emerson, *Journal* entry, 1822

Trilling in Our Time

Robert Boyers. *Lionel Trilling: Negative Capability and the Wisdom of
Avoidance.* Columbia: University of Missouri Press, 1977.

When Roger Sale reviewed *Sincerity and Authenticity* in
1973, he observed that reading Lionel Trilling "in bulk" bears "certain
affinities with eating a meal consisting entirely of Thousand Island
Dressing," and he commented on this critic's irrelevance for readers of
the present day.[1] In Sale's opinion, whatever Trilling's talents at reciting
the tale of "High Culture," his essays of the 1950s and 60s now appear
flaccid and repetitive; his social and political concerns are no longer
able to command respect; and his critical voice—once thought to be so
masterful—is woefully out of touch with our literary and cultural interests.

Sale's intemperate manner has not been widely admired, and even
readers who complain about Trilling's attachment to the Big View may
wince at his conclusion: "If Trilling's moment of highest fame and
respect has passed, it is not likely to return, because he just does not
write well enough, care enough for words, to outlive the world he
received and in which he flourished" (p. 247). But despite Sale's polemical aims, his critique should be welcomed, if only for its refusal to
lapse into Trilling's stately cadences. Few would quarrel with the moral
and stylistic norms that Trilling commends—moderation, balance, and

125

the "tone of the center"[2]—but such an Arnoldian ambience is not the
best one for an appraisal of his work. Unfortunately, Robert Boyers, in
his *Lionel Trilling: Negative Capability and the Wisdom of Avoidance*, suc-
cumbs to this temptation to imitate his subject's style, and this fault
gravely weakens his attempt to renew Trilling's value for modern criticism and culture.

Boyers argues that Trilling is preoccupied with "ideas" and "the
process of thought." "The object of this study," he says, "is to work
through the most important of those ideas in a way that will be generally
helpful" (p. 3). He frames the central "ideas" as "questions" that govern
his analysis:

> What is the point at which the idea of negative capability needs to be
> joined to the idea of will in order for either of them to yield what Trilling
> thinks it should? How much did Trilling's explicit reliance on the idea of
> tragedy mask an unwillingness to acknowledge fully the presence in his
> thought of other ideas that more truly address his concerns? Why should
> an idea of political reality in Trilling be so helpful in getting at certain
> aspects of cultural life and so inadequate to deal with others? (P. 4)

These "questions" reflect a curiously oblique engagement with Trilling's writings, and they bypass the themes—the place of the liberal
imagination and the teaching of modern literature, for example—to
which Trilling is most directly and frequently committed. Even more
curious is Boyers's decision to limit his treatment of these "questions"
to three texts: two short stories, "Of This Time, Of That Place" and
"The Other Margaret," and the essay on *The Princess Casamassima* included in *The Liberal Imagination*. He devotes too much space to these
stories and over-values their claims on our attention. The choice of the
Casamassima essay, on the other hand, is a good one, and Boyers traces
some interesting relations between Trilling and James. But he does not
move beyond the confines of this single essay to discuss the companion-
piece on *The Bostonians* in *The Opposing Self* or the essay on James and
Hawthorne in *Beyond Culture*. Nor does he address cogently and con-
cisely the strengths and weaknesses of the critical mind at work here.
Boyers admires the "tone of the center," and he feels great affection
for its status in Trilling's texts, praising Trilling on his first page for
having "done more" than any critic of the past fifty years "to make of
his calling an honorable and distinctive mode of literary expression,"
and stating on his final page that Trilling's work provides "one of the
consistent pleasures of literary experience." But this admiration has led
Boyers to ask poor questions and make dubious decisions about which
texts to emphasize. The "aggressive engagement" (p. 74) he hopes to
bring to his review of Trilling is rarely demonstrated.

The shortcomings of Boyers's study are best measured by the fine perceptions he sometimes registers, but which, because they lie outside his chosen tone and texts, he does not pursue. He points out that Trilling's "success" depended in large part on knowing "what he was meant to handle" (p. 5). Another, possibly more damaging, way of putting this might be to say that Trilling's themes are few and remain constant from his books on Matthew Arnold (1939) and E. M. Forster (1943) to *Mind in the Modern World* (1972): the modern writer's alienation from other artists and the contemporary culture; the modern self's antagonistic stance towards society; the contempt shown by writers and their readers for the values of the family and social group; and finally, the complexity and pain of living the "moral life." Much to the irritation of Sale and others, these themes reappear in essay after essay with minimal advance in sophistication and insight. If Boyers intends to press his case for Trilling's staying power, then he will have to consider whether the books and essays possess a range of themes and variations to challenge us consistently.

Boyers also praises Trilling's determination "to establish a view of things that would serve his purpose as a writer and artist in the en- trenchment of attitudes he took to be good for all of us" (p. 7). But how comforting is it to know that Trilling's paternal care is always being exercised for our "good"? How much condescension towards his audience resides in that "tone of the center"? Boyers should have inquired more carefully into Trilling's attitude towards his readers. And he might also have profitably examined the many occasions when Trill- ing's "view of things" leads him to impose his authority on texts, remaking them in his own image. In *The Opposing Self*, for example, he asserts that Milton welcomed Adam's and Eve's fall and expulsion from Eden, since this opens up "the human drama" of a "strenuous world of freedom."[3] But this assertion fails (or refuses) to acknowledge the "strenuous" moral discipline that Adam and Eve freely exhibit at every moment they obey God's command not to eat the forbidden fruit. It is not so much that Trilling "misreads" Milton, but rather that he advo- cates an outdated critical line on the poet (formulated by E. M. W. Tillyard and others) because it records an appealing distinction about moral values in the modern world.

Elsewhere Boyers states that Freud is "surely Trilling's intellectual hero" (p. 14). Yet he does not engage the influence of Freud on Trilling's work or examine this critic's several essays on psychoanalysis. Though Trilling stresses Freud's achievement, his own interest in psychoanal- ysis is ambivalent, and he scrupulously avoids deploying its methods with full rigor even where the material might seem to warrant it. De- spite, for instance, twice alluding to Freud in the famous essay on Keats's letters, he does not ask whether Freudian ways of thinking help to account for Keats's "pervasive" and "extreme" "ingestive imagery" and relation to his mother.[4] As for the individual essays on Freud, they prosecuted an important case for the relevance of psychoanalysis to literary studies, but they are period pieces that offer little insight and sophistication today.

Twice in his study (pp. 26, 50), Boyers cites Leo Bersani's provocative book on character and desire in literature, *A Future for Astyanax*.[5] Yet he does not notice the major challenge that Bersani's work offers to one of Trilling's concerns—the authority of the morally "centered" self. Bersani would agree with the statement in *Beyond Culture* that "in its essence literature is concerned with the self."[6] But whereas Trilling's criticism privileges the centered or integrated self, *A Future for Astyanax* emphasizes the "deconstruction" of the center and the substitution of radically "dispersed" selves. In the past decade, post-structuralist theories of literature have become increasingly important in the writings of American critics, and it is this new style, articulated in different ways by Barthes, Derrida, and others, that Bersani's book exemplifies. When one considers this trend, Boyers's insistence on Trilling's "negative capability," "feeling," "sensibility," "taste," and "disinterested contemplation" (all of these terms occur on pp. 44-45) seems set in a distant past. The new theories might not hearten Boyers, but if he intends to demonstrate Trilling's significance, he will have to take account of them and prove his critic's superiority. Boyers realizes the contrast between Trilling and Bersani, but he does not probe its implications; he does not show that Trilling's criticism survives such an encounter with post-structuralism, nor does he persuade us that the terms he draws from Trilling—"sensibility," "taste," and the others—should command our assent. Like other critics, Boyers opposes post-structuralist theory but does not engage it fully enough to make his arguments convincing. He has immediate recourse to a set of privileged terms that evoke literary value and the moral life. Invoking them "feels" to be a natural way to counter current trends; the terms are so powerful, and he is so habituated to them, that he cannot imagine anything being able to measure up to their authority.

Boyers is well attuned to the ambiguities of Trilling's political views, noting "the large margin of sheer sentiment" he often "allowed himself" (p. 55). But again Boyers neglects to follow through on his initial perceptions, and instead presents an awkward defense of Trilling's political stance. On one page he maintains that Trilling does not speak for an "ideological conservatism" (p. 63), only to remark on the next one that such a position makes clear "that there are problems in the world, that it is useful to be aware of them, and that very few are susceptible of social or political solutions." Maybe this is, as Boyers claims, "politically liberal and meliorative" rather than "conservative"—such terms always leave room for slippage. But the point of view recommended here—whatever terms are chosen for it—comes close to detachment and inaction in political life, and it should not be so warmly endorsed. Like Boyers, I do not accept the "politics" implicit in much contemporary theory and criticism; it is intense but unserious and self-promoting. But the failures of today's interpretive politics do not oblige us to incline towards and welcome what Trilling offers. We should commit ourselves to finding better language than we now possess to speak about the political, literary, and cultural network. Trilling is useful up to a point, but his worried withdrawal from the world he sees too often turns his critical detachment into mere distance and disengagement.

Trilling admired George Orwell for "his virtue of not being a genius, of fronting the world with nothing more than one's simple, direct, undeceived intelligence, and a respect for the powers one does have, and the work one undertakes to do."[7] When Trilling writes badly, it is often because he is trying too hard to reveal his own affinities with writers like Orwell. Similarly, Boyers's poorest writing occurs when he adheres too closely to his subject's moral line and middle tones. Like most of Trilling's work, Boyers's study is admirable in its lucidity and poise, but too frequently it fails to arrive at precise terms and evaluations. Though he alludes at one point to Sale as that "mean and envious fellow" (p. 2) and hopes to rebut disrespect for Trilling's "sensibility," Boyers neither discriminates the good from the bad in Trilling's work nor deals with the contemporary context in which this "sensibility" could rediscover its place.

The Rest of Wholeness: F. R. Leavis

F. R. Leavis. *Thought, Words and Creativity: Art and Thought in Lawrence.*
New York: Oxford University Press, 1976.

When F. R. Leavis wrote *D. H. Lawrence: Novelist* (1955), he grounded his argument in two distinct but interdependent points. The first was the necessity of exposing "the grosser and absurder falsities"—that Lawrence was wildly obsessed with sex and the proponent of a male will-to-power whose closest affinities were with Nazism—that had attached themselves to this novelist's name. Other charges had also become common currency in discussions of Lawrence—his crudity, irresponsibility, lack of intelligence, and inadequate education and background—and these too had to be cleared away. But Leavis's second and more important point was "to win clear recognition for the nature of Lawrence's greatness" by demonstrating through critical argument that his work stands among the major achievements of literature and has a positive value for "life" that misrepresentation and falsehood have for too long obscured.[8]

Leavis's book gets much of its energy from intermittent attacks on T. S. Eliot, Bloomsbury, the literary and cultural "elite," and ill-informed journeymen of letters, all of whom "retarded" the appreciation of Lawrence's genius. Eliot in particular is roundly condemned. For Leavis, he is "the essential opposition in person" (p. 303), who in *After Strange Gods* and elsewhere "did all that his immense prestige and authority could do to make the current stupidities about Lawrence look respectable" (p. 22). Yet, Leavis argues, the truth is that while Lawrence affirms life, health, and creativity, Eliot—ranked so much higher by the literary circles of his day—offers only "human and spiritual nullity" (p. 26), contempt for life, and disgust with the individual. Our age in literature "may fairly be called the age of D. H. Lawrence and T. S. Eliot," but Lawrence is "immensely the greater genius" (p. 303), with the more acute insight into modern civilization and the far more powerful faith in human love and community.

Leavis also devotes his attention to Lawrence's "diagnostic" treatment of the spread of industrialism and its corruption of "standards," and this of course sharpens his polemical edge. But despite the polemics, Leavis's focus, as his title implies, is on Lawrence as novelist and artist. His individual chapters deal with characters and themes, and with the novels' "range" and "flexibility" of formal organization, and he continually highlights Lawrence's technical originality, skill as a comic writer, and assured "dramatic" handling of scenes. These formal analyses support and reinforce Leavis's evaluation that "Lawrence is incomparably the greatest creative writer in English of our time" (p. 18). His major novels, *The Rainbow* and *Women in Love*, are assigned the preeminent position among works of English fiction, and his short stories and tales are ranked alongside Hawthorne's and James's.

These claims will be familiar to students of Lawrence's work and the modern novel, and few—even those who disagree with Leavis's manner and method—will deny that *D. H. Lawrence: Novelist* is one of the most important books on this writer. But it is necessary to reacquaint ourselves with Leavis's aims and formal preoccupations in this first study, so that we can be clear about the different intention and approach in *Thought, Words and Creativity: Art and Thought in Lawrence*. Leavis is surely one of the dominant critical figures of this century, and his dedication to literature demands that response to his criticism be exacting and precise, as a measure of respect for a committed critical career that spans fifty years.

Thought, Words and Creativity surveys territory that is covered in more detail in *D. H. Lawrence: Novelist*. The first chapter deals with Lawrence's "discursive" thought in *Psychoanalysis and the Unconscious*, and additional chapters treat *The Plumed Serpent*, *Women in Love*, *The Captain's Doll*, and *The Rainbow*. Here Leavis's "analyses"—though later we will have to qualify this term—take their cue from Lawrence's dictum that "art-speech is the only speech." We cannot separate Lawrence's "thought" from his "art," Leavis contends; they are organically related, each giving "life" to the other. As a great "creative" writer, Lawrence uses language as it has been developed and formed by "continuous collaborative creativity" (p. 31). It is therefore impossible to distinguish between Lawrence's success as an artist and his insights as a "discursive" thinker: his "genius is that of a supremely great novelist—which is to say that his art is thought and his thought art" (p. 64). Later, Leavis explains that in fact Lawrence's "use of the English language as a creative writer" is significantly opposed to the "discursive" norms of "logic" and "clarity": "It does what language can't do when put to expounding discursively with strictly and narrowly explicit logic" (p. 82).

For Leavis to be faithful to his belief in the organic relationship of Lawrence's "thought" and "art," he must forego what we usually call "analysis"—an examination of the formal features of the text that reveals ("discursively") how the "art" functions. Many readers will no doubt complain about the amount of paraphrase and quotation in *Thought, Words and Creativity*, and both are excessive. But Leavis's insistence on the "organic" quality of Lawrence's writing requires that the critic reaffirm and repeat the unfolding of his writer's text. In Leavis's terms, the critic of major "creative" works cannot pretend that his analysis could ever do justice to the richness of their "art-speech." When discussing *Women in Love*, Leavis alludes to the impossibility of defining the word *life* in an expository way: "The live, the living nature itself of Lawrence's thought soon brought out its unamenableness to orderly exposition of that kind. One might say that the complex totality of *Women in Love* is needed to convey the superlative force and nuance, the supreme value, the word 'life' has for his comprehensive creative thought" (p. 94). The nature of the text, Leavis maintains, undercuts our attempts to present a critical account of its themes and structures. The true (and only) recourse for the critic is not to analyze *Women in Love*, but to read it once again and recommend its organic texture to others.

Leavis repeatedly says that the "wholeness," "living integrity," and "organic unity" of Lawrence's work prevent us from achieving an "expository ordering" of its formal operations (pp. 113, 121, 123, 131). So what then does he intend to accomplish by returning to Lawrence's texts? At several points he refers to our failure to apprehend Lawrence's "art" and "thought," and he trusts that this new book will help to bring about better "perception" and "recognition." Here, and also in those places where he speaks of the "real readers" who truly "understand" Lawrence (pp. 10, 27, 140), Leavis is asserting the presence of an interpretive community dedicated to "Laurentian" values of "life," "health," and "wholeness," and opposed to the neo-Benthamite forces of the "anti-human and anti-life" (p. 11). He represents Lawrence's texts in the hope that others will join this community of "real readers" and stand against the decadence and materialism of the "Americanized" majority-culture. His book invites readers to respond as Leavis himself does to Lawrence's texts, testifying once again that "he has readers who understand him" (p. 145).

Thought, Words and Creativity is structured on principles of repetition—quotation, review and retelling of the plot, continual fading of Leavis's voice into Lawrence's (the critic repeating his author), and references to "Laurentian" values in Lawrence's own texts. When Leavis diagnoses Gerald's problem in *Women in Love*, he sounds like Lawrence: "He lacks the creativity that comes from the source—from the inlet through which the unknown, without access to which there is no creation, enters" (p. 89). And his commentary on texts often reads as tautology: *Women in Love* "has positive Laurentian value" (p. 62); its opening chapter is "superbly Laurentian" (p. 63); and its vocabulary includes "Laurentian terms" and words used in "a special Laurentian sense" (p. 67). Because Leavis believes in the organic bond between "art" and "thought," he cannot detach himself from the novel, locating terms outside of (and foreign to) its texture and imposing them on its "living integrity."

The formal concerns of *D. H. Lawrence: Novelist*—theme, character, imagery—are almost entirely absent from *Thought, Words and Creativity*, and Leavis's remarks on the conclusion to *The Rainbow* register this difference. In the earlier book he writes: "There is something oddly desperate about that closing page and a half; the convalescent Ursula's horrified vision, from her windows, of the industrial world outside, and then that confident note of prophetic hope in the final paragraph— a note wholly unprepared and unsupported, defying the preceding pages" (p. 142). This lack of an "inevitable close" ruptures the movement of the novel; it suffers from—though it is not disabled by—this formal inconsistency. But when Leavis returns to this scene in *Thought, Words and Creativity*, he omits his structural criticism and instead emphasizes the significance of the "unprepared" and "unsupported" hope. The "rainbow" bears witness to Lawrence's faith that life will endure against all odds: "The paradox was the life in him which perceived, and fought against, the irreversible drive, the lethal upshot of which seemed certain, and at the same time cherished the certitude that life would refuse ever to suffer final defeat. The Laurentian rainbow of the title was the assurance" (p. 139). Even though Lawrence perceives the "irreversible" menace that industrialized civilization poses to "life," he affirms that "life" will always be "cherished" and retain its value.

There is, Leavis concedes in *Thought, Words and Creativity*, "no rainbow" in *Women in Love* (p. 139). In this novel, Lawrence (through his spokesman, Birkin) articulates his awareness of the "inevitable disaster towards which our civilization is taking us" (p. 140). But Leavis still wants to maintain the possibility for "life": "No rainbow, then. Yet Ursula was with him, and there is every sign that the problem of marriage was, for them, solved—solved permanently" (p. 140). Here Leavis takes possession of the novel and projects upon it a life-affirming message that the text cannot sustain. The novel's concluding pages, which record Birkin's regret at Gerald's death and his disagreement with Ursula about his need for a male friend, do not convince us that "for them" all of the problems of "marriage" are "solved permanently." Nor is it possible to absolve Birkin of his withdrawal from further efforts to contribute to the community. He feels no commitment to his profession as a school inspector or any urge to undertake a career as social reformer—a refusal that strikes against Leavis's own deep involvement in teaching, education, culture, and society. In a powerful, contentious, and self-deceived way, Leavis misreads the ending of *Women in Love*, finding more life-affirming intensity than the text warrants.[9]

Thought, Words and Creativity is a highly personal book, and often it reads as a testimony to Leavis's own literary and cultural concerns. By "personal" I don't mean simply his anecdotes about *The Calendar of Modern Letters* (the literary review published from 1925 to 1927), his correspondence with a scientist about Lawrence's critique of the "scientific correctness of asserting that 'water is H2O'" (pp. 46ff.), and the like. Far more "personal" are those moments when Leavis's commentary on Lawrence voices his own beliefs. When he refers to Lawrence's "troubled concern for the survival of civilized humanity" (p. 63) and his "unshaken invincible faith" in "creativity" (p. 137), he is also describing—and reassuring—himself. In *D. H. Lawrence: Novelist*, Leavis concludes that "in some moods," Lawrence's account of industrialism in *Women in Love* "may very well strike us as something like the essential human history of the decades" since this novel was published (p. 164).

In *Thought, Words and Creativity*, the general forecast is much darker and the qualification ("in some moods") is taken away. Materialism and Philistinism have now acquired their own momentum, and have instilled in us "an economic dependence" that "we shouldn't dare to destroy if we could" (p. 13). The consequences of a breakdown in the social and economic machine are, Leavis warns, even more frightening than its continued operation. We are therefore faced in our time with "the supreme anti-human triumph of the technologico-Benthamite spirit"

(p. 142). And even more disturbing is the bitter fact that there are no grounds for "faith" that things will ever change for the better: "That faith was possible for Lawrence in his time, but we, in the present age, can hardly share it, nor would it comfort us if we could" (p. 156). But despite the evidence to the contrary, Leavis believes that we must have "faith"—there remains no choice for us but to defend "life." "Who can be sure?" he observes in his final sentences. "Logic and automatism, impossible as it now seems, may yet be robbed of their final victory; the decisively new and unforeseen may yet reward us" (p. 156). Against what he judges to be overwhelming opposition, Leavis persists in upholding the supreme authority of literary "creativity."

My acknowledgment of Leavis's distinction, here and in chapter 6, should not be taken as a full endorsement of his position. His value judgments (however "responsibly" he feels they are presented) and his polemics tend to dismiss other judgments and approaches, shutting down disagreement and ruling out the "collaborative" activity he advocates. Though he claims that the ideal response to one of his evaluations is "Yes, but," his presentation too often confers merit only on those who agree immediately, and it denies intelligence or insight to those who hold other opinions. Leavis posits a critical aristocracy, with centralized powers of judgment and evaluation, to which the public-at-large looks for its "standards." He does not recommend—nor can he even imagine—a democratic criticism that finds a place for all contributions, but rather enforces a point of view that allows no room for rebuttal and correction. As *Thought, Words and Creativity* makes abundantly clear, Leavis holds "democracy" in both literature and society in contempt. Men should not be judged as "equals" (pp. 26, 45, 142), since this obliges the individual to "conform" to others. But this advocacy of individual fulfillment applies only to the privileged few who establish the "standards" to which others must be loyal. Not all will agree that Leavis and his followers should be empowered to define the final criteria for "valid thought" (p. 41) and "the most important kind of thought" (p. 92). Again the danger is that Leavis, in entrusting to himself the authority to determine "validity" and "importance," will cut off all possibility for the "creative" exchange he seeks to preserve. While he calls for an open and cooperative community, he also intends to control its norms and limit its membership.

We owe Leavis our gratitude for his dedication to value and principle, and in studying his books we should appreciate his continued testimony to Lawrence's achievement and his own "faith" in the exemplary power of literary works. But admiration for Leavis should not preclude the inspection of his proposals. However much we emphasize their virtues, we should not allow them to restrict the freedom to disagree.

Leavis's Authority

Francis Mulhern. *The Moment of "Scrutiny."* London: New Left Books, 1979.
R. P. Bilan. *The Literary Criticism of F. R. Leavis.* Cambridge: Cambridge University Press, 1979.

F. R. Leavis encourages us to respond as much to his personality as to his critical work, and he regularly returns to the personal injustices that he claims (with no lack of evidence) to have suffered. But once we are captivated by the personality, we lose contact with Leavis as a literary critic, and our judgments become concerned not with the quality of his writing but with our estimate of the man. No one disputes Leavis's influence, but few seem able to explain it or to account for the hold that he exercises on readers in the United States and England. At times, especially for English readers, Leavis's influence seems to burden intellectual change and growth; his evaluations impose limits on what can be taken to merit study, and opposing voices must first contend with his prestige. Francis Mulhern and R. P. Bilan examine Leavis's authority and influence, and both generally do well in the difficult task of reviewing his career respectfully yet critically. But one finishes their books feeling that still sharper judgments are in order.[10]

Mulhern has the wider angle of vision. He is interested in Leavis's "power of disturbance" and "pervasive influence among English literary intellectuals, teachers, and journalists" (p. viii). But he also believes that to understand the impact of "Leavism" we must examine the journal *Scrutiny*, which Leavis edited for most of its two decades of existence (May, 1932, to October, 1953). Mulhern begins by describing the political and economic state of post-war Britain, the rise of journalism and advertising, and, most important of all, the reform of English studies at Cambridge, which he sees as both a "revolution in the discipline" and a "revolution of literary criticism against the palsied cultural regime of post-war England" (p. 28). Mulhern's opening chapters are informative and detailed, exploring F. R. and Q. D. Leavis's early writings and the major themes of the *Scrutiny* group—the damaging effects of industrialism, the decline of standards in literature and life, and the corruption of the language in modern times. He notes, for example, that the "typical gesture of Leavisian criticism" is "recognition." Leavis and his collaborators, Mulhern argues, were unable or unwilling to identify precisely the kind of "community" they valued. "The perimeter of the [*Scrutiny*] circle," he stresses, "marked the limits

of persuasion: what *Scrutiny's* audience did not 'know already,' it could
not be told" (p. 175). Here one recalls Leavis's famous refusal, in his
debate with René Wellek (*Scrutiny*, 1937), to articulate the central tenets
of his theory or even to define his key terms. His community of the
like-minded could herald "values" and recognize their presence in others,
but the community could not persuade others to join its ranks since it
denied that its values could be defined, its deep meanings made available to discursive argument.[11]

Mulhern is also helpful in showing the importance of the novel for
Leavis. Lawrence's novels in particular provide Leavis with a "pre-text"
for "a generalizing discourse on human existence in the modern world"
(p. 293). Marriage, politics, tradition, English history, the conditions of
human existence (the question of "what for")—these are Lawrence's
major concerns, and the truly "responsible" critic must address them
in Lawrence's spirit, celebrating "life" and "health" and refusing to
surrender to the second-rate and merely fashionable. In writing about
Lawrence and the other novelists of the "great tradition," Leavis assumes the role of critic-as-cultural-spokesman. His criticism thus evolves
into a discourse that leads constantly towards "other studies," "becoming psychology, sociology, ethics and, at the limit, ontology" (p. 293).

The Moment of "Scrutiny" has its shortcomings. Mulhern lapses too
often into tedious summaries of the writings of Leavis and other *Scrutiny*
contributors, and he suffers on occasion from a form of critical blindness. He offers us several pages that summarize Marius Bewley's work
on American literature, observing that Leavis's different approach suggests a "dispute" between "national" styles of criticism. But Mulhern
does not develop this, and oddly states that "it is not feasible here to
explore fully the issues raised in the dispute between Bewley and Leavis"
(p. 265). Elsewhere he quotes the crankiest and most outlandish Leavisite judgments, such as Q. D. Leavis's attack on Virginia Woolf's "bou-
doir scholarship" and conception of "the art of living" as that of a
"social parasite," yet he does not pause for any comment. Or else he
lists what Leavis and the others were writing (e.g., p. 138) but gives
no analysis of what they were actually saying or any indication of what
he thinks about it. Along with the dull summaries and failures of
judgment, there is also the problem of Mulhern's New Left jargon. He
has fine things to say but the reader must labor to disentangle them
from the clotted prose.

Mulhern does not examine *Scrutiny's* contribution to literary criticism.
This is the issue that interests most readers, but he touches on it
infrequently and even declares it out of bounds: "A full account and
assessment of *Scrutiny's* literary-critical production is not feasible in this
study" (p. 134). For R. P. Bilan, however, the criticism is what counts;
Leavis is "primarily a literary, rather than a social, critic" (p. 4). Patiently
probing the entire range of Leavis's writings, Bilan deals very well with

his critic's views on language, literature, and continuity and basic attitudes towards "the idea of criticism," the need for "standards," and the "educated public." But the chief value of Bilan's book is his skillful analysis of Leavis's work on the novel and his eighty-page survey of "Leavis on Lawrence." In these parts of his study, Bilan provides us with some of the best writing that we are likely to get on Leavis.

But here we also encounter a queer gap in Bilan's procedure. He shows Leavis's serious weaknesses as a critic of the novel, yet he never grapples with the question of how they qualify or subvert Leavis's authority. Bilan maintains that the concept of "the great tradition" is "unsatisfactory and perplexing in many ways" (p. 145), notably in its placements of James and Conrad. Leavis is also guilty of over-simplifying (and perhaps over-rating) *Hard Times* by focusing almost exclusively on its "values" and identifying the characters with them. Still more disabling, Bilan adds, is Leavis's contemptuous dismissals of Gaskell, Trollope, Meredith, and especially Hardy from the "tradition"—dismissals that make no attempt to explain and justify themselves. When Bilan deals with the books and articles on Lawrence, he demonstrates that Leavis misrepresents the novelist in order to enthrone him as an "affirmative" writer; and he also uncovers Leavis's confusions in trying to portray the novels and stories as essentially "normative."

Bilan fails to see that his criticisms unsettle his claims (e.g., pp. 3, 61) for Leavis's "greatness": he does not recognize the damaging effects of his own analyses. "At times," he says at one point, "Leavis offers us a slanted or distorted view of Lawrence; he reads his own values and attitudes into Lawrence's work and then offers us these as a source of health. In particular, Leavis reads into Lawrence's work his own insistence on the importance of education, culture, and the critical intelligence" (pp. 231-32). But if Leavis's failings loom so large, why has he had such an impact on Lawrence studies? How does one account for the phenomenon of a critic who so dramatically transcends the limitations of his writing?

Bilan's reference to "reading in" raises other questions. There is much melodramatic talk these days about "the necessity of misreading," and usually it occurs with little awareness of what such a claim implies. But it is true that we both represent and recreate the texts we criticize, and it is also true, as Northrop Frye once remarked, that critical writing is a form of intellectual autobiography. This, of course, suggests a cluster of theoretical dilemmas. We strive to be faithful to the text even as we stand committed to our own interpretive interests and values; and we also find ourselves enlisting literary texts—as Leavis does so often—in common cause against social and cultural disturbances. Bilan's account of Leavis's strategy of "reading in," then, is apt but needs to be situated in a more detailed theoretical context. Other critics may be guilty of the same charge—which turns "reading in" from a judgment on Leavis to a more general description of what interpretation entails.

Though it seems strange to say so, Leavis is an elusive figure and is difficult to write about in an appropriate tone. In discussing him, it is always hard to avoid sounding like either a disciple or a carping member of the establishment he assails. Leavis's work in the 1960s and 70s poses an especially rankling problem. Except for some sections of *Thought, Words and Creativity* and *The Living Principle*, these books written at the end of Leavis's career make for depressing reading. The barbed voice has become shrill; the key terms are used without inspiration; and the once trenchant prose sits inertly on the page. Too eager to preach Holy Writ, Leavis's worst faults run unchecked, such as his habit of deploying his select group of writers to beat down the claims of others. By singling out Lawrence, Blake, Dickens, and Shakespeare, and by exalting their "art-speech" so fervently, Leavis narrows his range of critical responsiveness and never gives Woolf, W. H. Auden, and others a fair hearing.

Leavis also casts off old allegiances and is bullying and brutal towards T. S. Eliot. As *Revaluation* and *New Bearings in English Poetry* show, Leavis learned a great deal from Eliot's criticism. But in the late essay "T. S. Eliot as Critic," Leavis hammers away at the inadequacies of "Tradition and the Individual Talent," stating that it is "notable for its ambiguities, its logical inconsequences, its pseudo-precisions, its fallaciousness, and the aplomb of its equivocations and its specious cogency."[12] For admirers of Leavis, nothing could be more painful than the spectacle of this powerful mind so drastically limiting itself and severing its intellectual ties. It is even more tragically disappointing than that. "In setting the highest form of art immediately in front of himself," Robert Garis reflects, "Leavis has been blinded by the sun": "The intense directness of Tolstoy's, Shakespeare's, Lawrence's enactment of the quest for significance has blinded him to the point where the kind of 'feeling towards' significance represented in *The Europeans* (and so finely honored in Leavis's essay on that wonderful work) has come to seem hardly 'questing' at all. Rarely has the best . . . been a more implacable enemy of the good."[13] By the end of his career, Leavis admires texts only if they resonate with "Laurentian" significances, and he thus defaults on the Arnoldian project of "seeing the object as it really is" that he once carried out superbly.

Yet interest in Leavis is as pronounced as ever. Since 1976 there have been eight books on his criticism, and more are on the way. In part this is a reaction against post-structuralist critiques of authorial presence, the speaking voice, value judgments, literature as a form of knowledge—the very things to which Leavis staunchly testifies. But Leavis's major value rests, I think, in his commitment to teaching and criticism as essential activities, and in his belief that literature bears directly on "life" and "community." Threatened by uncertain prospects for the future, our work and dedication to literature have never seemed more in jeopardy—or more irrelevant. In Leavis's criticism we hear the importance of literary studies persistently affirmed. Hard times or not, the literary critic and teacher, Leavis insists, never needs to offer any apology for the centrality of English studies. Though Leavis's own criticism is flawed, his passionate concern for the place of literature and criticism in society retains its forcefulness: his authoritative presence still gives meaning to our common pursuit.

The Kenneth Burke Problem

Kenneth Burke. *The Philosophy of Literary Form.* 1941. California Library
   Reprint Series, no. 45. Berkeley and Los Angeles: University of
   California Press, 1974.

Many would agree with Wayne Booth's statement that Kenneth Burke is "without question the most important living critic."[14] But there are dissenters, notably Grant Webster, who declares in his massive study of "postwar literary opinion" that Burke, "largely ignored or rejected," is best regarded "as an old-time American crank inventor who might have been Edison except that his work lacks any relation to reality outside his own mind."[15] Burke's critics have often differed in their judgments, but here the disagreement is especially sharp. Booth sees Burke as a verbal wizard, the designer of a great verbal system, while Webster describes him as a solipsist, adding that "Burke's system is explicable only in its own terms, but no reason is given for adopting them, over, say 'Jabberwocky'" (*The Republic of Letters*, p. 325).

There is a Burke "problem" that accounts for these opposite evaluations. Burke's career is one of the curiosities of modern literature, and though he has been written about often, he, like F. R. Leavis, has not been written about well, in the right tone and with the proper critical leverage. He is either accepted wholeheartedly—by, for example, Stanley Edgar Hyman and Howard Nemerov—or else he is dismissed out-of-hand, as when Marius Bewley accuses him of being trapped in a rarefied vocabulary and engaged in producing books that we read "with something of the fascination with which one studies the combination of aimlessness and purpose that characterizes life in an ant hill."[16] While there are reasons for the "problem" that Burke sets for his critics, there are not easy or satisfactory ways of resolving it. Burke's writings both stimulate and frustrate us; he is and will remain a problematical figure, difficult to approach and evaluate.

Burke is hard to pin down as a critic because he works in many fields, including literature, sociology, economics, psychology, and political science. His range is intimidating, and he strikes us at times as a "veritable one man department," moving forward with his labors unmindful of what friends and foes say about him.[17] Having created his own subject matter—"Burkology" is the best name for it—Burke appears not to need the contributing presence of other critics. His system, laid out in his *Grammar and Rhetoric of Motives*, is so intricate that he alone knows how to use it, and only he can speculate about new areas into which it might be launched.

The more Burke writes, the more imposing and isolated he becomes: his "dramatistic" system almost seems to be controlling him, rather than the other way around. His texts possess their own momentum, and his many prefaces, forewords, introductions, expansive footnotes, and interviews signify his effort to subdue his swirling system.[18] Perhaps, however, it is misleading to depict Burke as a prisoner caught, like the hero of one of Chaplin's films, in the gears of his own machinery. He may now seem a lonely if heroic figure, victimized by his terms and no longer in touch with his readers. But then Burke's critical identity and relation to his audience have been troubled and uncertain since the beginning of his career. One question in particular, as Merle E. Brown observes, presses on us as we read Burke: "To whom could he possibly be writing?" "His audience is never included actively in his writing; it is never specified with precision."[19] Brown's question is tough to answer because Burke is equal parts virtuoso and poseur. More successfully than most critics, he manages to keep his reader off balance and unable to anticipate the course of his critical explorations. To borrow Richard Poirier's well-known phrase about Mailer, Frost, and other of the most interesting American writers, Burke is very much a "performing self," "dramatically" present in his texts, acting out roles, buoyantly trying on and testing attitudes. So interested in "dramatism" himself, Burke is intensely dramatic in style, as he strives to entertain, cajole, and baffle his reader's attempts to keep pace with him.

Burke's thought is always in motion, if not always in progress or slanting in a direction that we can chart. It spirals with suggestions, alternately amazing and disappointing us. There is considerable unevenness in Burke's work, and his reader must be patient. Sometimes our investment of time and energy is unprofitable: we can read Burke for many pages and not feel we have gotten anywhere. Then we will catch him in an inspired moment, and he will delight us with the pointed aside or startling conjunction of terms (his "perspectives by incongruity"). When Burke is read for the systematic argument he is straining to present, he can be tedious, even interminable. But when he is read and valued for his marvelous intuitions about form and structure, and appreciated for his "dance" (one of his favorite words) of mixed solemnity and whimsy, seriousness and jocularity, he can provide us with an experience that is unique in criticism.[20]

The Burke "problem" is even more vexed than my description has so far suggested. Despite his productive career and despite having generated much commentary, Burke has not had much influence. He is one of a kind, and this underscores his limitation as well as his distinction. Though harsh in its directness, Fredric Jameson's assessment is difficult to quarrel with: "This immense critical corpus, to which lip service is customarily extended in passing, has—read by virtually everybody—been utterly without influence in its fundamental lessons, has had no following, save perhaps among the social scientists, and is customarily saluted as a monument of personal inventiveness and ingenuity . . . rather than as an interpretative model to be studied and a method to be emulated."[21] As Jameson suggests, there is plenty of nodding in Burke's direction. Particularly during the 1970s and 80s, we have heard a good deal of vague talk about Burke having "anticipated" French structuralism and post-structuralism. Some readers want to give credit where it is felt to be due. Others, however, seem to believe that structuralism and its offshoots will be made less menacing, less disruptive of our critical habits, if their insights about "language" and "system" are located in Burke, the critic who has "been there already." If this leads to a rereading of Burke, it is worth encouraging, but not if it is simply another effort to dismiss or domesticate new modes of criticism. Such a ploy is unfair to Burke and will likely issue only in more calls for his rediscovery and gestures towards him as the great (and still misunderstood) forerunner of avant-garde criticism. Many insist that we need to rediscover Burke and see the relevance of his work, but no one has yet tackled the assignment and shown how and why Burke bears on criticism today.

Burke's *Philosophy of Literary Form* is the best place to begin such a revaluation. Originally published in 1941, it contains what the inveterate punster Burke describes as "thirty-minded" pieces. Most are essays and reviews, but there are also two forewords, an "Instead of a Foreword," letters to the editor, a "Dialectician's Hymn," and the long (137 pages) title essay, first printed in its entirety in this book. The *Philosophy* is typically Burkean in that it both absorbs and irritates the reader. It is often bracing in its suggestiveness, as when Burke tosses off comments about sacrifice, scapegoating, and ritual. But the *Philosophy* has many dull stretches where Burke deals at length with books that have been forgotten or seem negligible—for example, Neurath's *Modern Man in the Making*, Ludovici's *Secret of Laughter*, Chevalier's *Ironic Temper: Anatole France and His Times*. When Burke rehearses and analyzes the argument of these books, we feel little obligation to follow him. The

Philosophy also falters when Burke focuses on texts or documents—such as the exchange between Malcolm Cowley and Archibald Macleish on "art" and "propaganda"—that are mildly interesting but too limited for us by their historical situation. Sometimes the dated quality of this book is slightly disturbing, if also rather quaint, as when Burke refers to "the soundings that the Japs are said to be taking of our Western coast line" (p. 151).

The dated parts of the *Philosophy* are a problem today, but they do not explain Burke's failure to influence his contemporaries in the 1940s. The start of Burke's career coincided with the rise of the New Criticism, yet he was never a member of this or any other movement. Many of his principles in fact go against the grain of the New Criticism and help to clarify the reasons for his marginality. In a foreword, Burke explains that he prefers not to deal with "the internalities of a work's structure." This is too much like what a "reporter" does, and he is instead concerned with the "general problems" of structure and the "function" of characters and scenes. Unlike Cleanth Brooks, for instance, Burke focuses primarily on general, theoretical issues; he does not limit himself to the single text, and indeed he warns us that if we are looking for "the specific criticism of books" we might be disappointed. But by aiming to provide a "theory of criticism of books," Burke locates himself outside the boundaries of the New Criticism. And this both separated him from the critical orthodoxy of his time and ensured that his work would not affect pedagogy. Brooks, Robert Penn Warren, Robert Heilman, and the other New Critics make analytical tools available to their fellow critics and teachers. Their methods can be taught readily and learned easily, whereas Burke's schemes are difficult to master and harder still to apply. Burke builds a system, embracing science whenever it seems rewarding to do so. The New Critics, on the other hand, rely upon the trained sensibility and power of individual judgment, standing opposed to science, system, and interpretive machines that violate the organic unity of the text. "Virtually everybody," including the New Critics, reads Burke. But his writings have been conspicuously without influence on practical criticism and classroom teaching, where critical methods win legitimacy, privilege, and continuity.

Burke does not entirely forego the "reading" of texts. In the *Philosophy*, he offers analyses of *Julius Caesar* and *Twelfth Night*. But both essays are less valuable for what they say about the plays than for what they indicate about Shakespeare's keen awareness of the audience's expectations and his means of "persuasion." Neither of these essays is intended as a complete reading; both are instead meant to "illustrate" (Burke's word) theoretical concerns and problems in method. Both of the essays are also quirkily conducted, as Burke—performer extraordinaire—assumes the roles of Antony in *Julius Caesar* and the Duke in

Twelfth Night, transforming these characters into "critical commentators" on Shakespeare's rhetoric and "process of appeal." Burke's procedure is not only theoretical but also exuberant and eccentric. He flaunts our sense of critical decorum and refuses to adopt the New Critic's methods of explication. While such freedom, playfulness, and brisk approaches to the text may be attractive to us, they made his New Critical readers uneasy and unsure about what he was up to, and hence made Burke all the more a critic to be admired but not imitated. His tones and attitudes, however stimulating, come across as not serious enough—not serious, that is, in the New Critical manner. He does not appear deeply enough engaged in disciplined textual analysis, and he is not willing to subordinate his verbal flights to the authority of "the words on the page."

Many of the readings in the *Philosophy,* especially in the title essay, are devoted to Coleridge's writings. But to say this is somewhat misleading, since Burke's comments on specific Coleridge texts are scattered and undeveloped. Again moving outside the field selected by the New Criticism, Burke explores "Coleridge himself" rather than his texts. Though he stresses that he bows to no reader in admiring the "structure" of these texts, he wants to "commune" with the writer, to get "inside his mind" and discover what the poems "do" for the poet. Referring at one point to "The Ancient Mariner," Burke observes that

> to grasp the full nature of the symbolic enactment going on in the poem, we must study the inter-relationships disclosable by a study of Coleridge's mind itself. If a critic prefers to so restrict the rules of critical analysis that these private elements are excluded, that is his right. I see no formal or categorical objection to criticism so conceived. But if his interest happens to be in the structure of the poetic act, he will use everything that is available— and would even consider it a kind of vandalism to exclude certain material that Coleridge has left, basing such exclusion upon some conventions as to the ideal of criticism. The main ideal of criticism, as I conceive it, is to use all that there is to use. (P. 23)

Eminently sensible as an ideal, Burke's statement here cuts against New Critics' emphasis on the text itself. Again he stamps himself as an outsider, opening up the text to biography and everything else "there is to use," even as Brooks and the other New Critics are insisting on steady concentration on the verbal object.

For Burke, understanding the "psychology of the poetic act" calls for knowing about and drawing upon biography, social background, historical context. And many of his remarks about Coleridge "use" the poet's drug and marital problems to gloss the poetry. But Burke does not often succeed in enriching the poems through this line of analysis, and he frequently simplifies texts and badly reduces the complexity of the poet's mind. In dealing with "The Ancient Mariner," for example, Burke crudely aligns details from Coleridge's life with scenes in the poem. "Do we not," he inquires,

> find good cause to line up as one strand in the symbolic action of the poem a sequence from marriage problem, through the murder of the Albatross as a synecdochic representative of Sarah, to the "blessing of the snakes" that synecdochically represented the drug and the impulsive premarital aesthetic (belonging in a contrary cluster), to an explicit statement of preference for church, prayer, and companionship over marriage (with the mariner returning to shore under the aegis of the praying Hermit, and the poem itself ending on the prayerful, moralizing note that has annoyed many readers as a change in quality)? (P. 72)

This is little more than a verbal logjam. Burke is sketching one-to-one correspondences between "The Ancient Mariner" and Coleridge's life, and he disfigures both poet and poem. Severely limiting his range of vision, Burke divides the text into "levels," which he then places in slick relation to one another. His performance is impressive after a fashion, but for what it reveals about his own ingenuity and addiction to terms, not for anything that it enables us to perceive in the poem or discover about Coleridge. As so often happens when Burke interprets a text, he is crippled by what Benjamin DeMott has aptly called his "iron inattention to tone."[22]

Burke's interpretive practice is disappointing, and this brings us close to the center of the Burke "problem." His ideals are compelling in their exploratory breadth and open-mindedness, and when set down in order, they read like a primer in how to move beyond the New Criticism:

1. In all our inquiries, we ask "leading questions" and "structure" the field that we investigate. "Every question," Burke asserts, "selects a field of battle, and in this selection it forms the nature of the answers" (p. 67). We do not make objective reports about the text, but rather introduce interpretive contexts that shape and structure it.

2. Literary texts share in the same kinds of concerns that "motivate" other texts. We adopt labels—literature, history, economics, and so on—for purposes of classification, but finally there are just "texts," all of which can be treated as "strategies."

3. Criticism is practiced on all texts, not merely on the special group we call "literature." "The analysis of aesthetic phenomena," Burke claims, "can be extended or projected into the analysis of social and political phenomena in general" (p. 309).

4. We make "symbolic acts" in our lives as well as in texts. Literature is by no means divorced from life, but is involved in, bound to, and fundamentally "like" life. "The question of the relationship between art and society," Burke stoutly adds, "is momentous" (p. 235).

5. A true critical method gives "definite insight into the organization

of literary works," but it also "automatically breaks down the barriers erected about literature as a specialized pursuit" (p. 302). To essentialize and privilege literature is ultimately to trivialize it, to divorce it from everything with which it shares forms and values. Valorizing "the literary" is the surest way to transform a rich area for study into just another "academic" pursuit.

Burke does not proceed from these fine principles to authoritative commentary. He has an acute sense of linguistic strategies, but no feeling for verbal detail. He can assemble complex machines, but, given to applying hammer-blows to the texts that he interprets, he is unable to respond to subtlety and delicacy in language. Burke's interests are broad, and his aims make many readers sympathetic to his general critical project. Yet then one confronts his mediocre analyses of "structure" and sees poems buried by layers of terms and categories. Burke's goals are invigorating, but his practice as a critic is too often bruisingly heavy-handed and subverts the potential richness of those goals. The *Philosophy* fails to give us really illuminating, powerful interpretations. And it is this failing that sets Burke a notch below Leavis and Empson, the other great independent-minded critics of this century. Their work is uneven, sometimes coarse and objectionable, but their engagements with texts are dynamic and incisive. We accept their limitations as critics and go on reading them because they confirm their authority, time after time, in their interpretive work.

Much of Burke's best critical writing in the *Philosophy* and his other books, especially *Language as Symbolic Action*, deals with Shakespeare. But it is one measure of his shortcomings that none of these essays commands the attention we devote to Leavis's writing on *Othello* and *Measure for Measure* or to Empson's studies of *King Lear, Othello, Hamlet, Measure for Measure*, and other plays. To be fair to Burke, he does insist that he desires a "theory" about the criticism of books, as opposed to the detailed reading of specific texts. And as I argued in chapter six, I am aware that it is the New Criticism's hold upon us that impels me to look for deft "readings." But Burke himself claims that his method provides "definite insight" into literary works—this is a key point for him. And to focus more on his theory than on his practice simply exposes the limitations of the theory—its crudity, mazes of terms, and odd rhetorical figures. Burke has been constructing his theoretical engine for half a century; but the more he complicates and tinkers with it, the more he removes it from our understanding and sympathy. The final volume in Burke's trilogy, the *Symbolic of Motives*, has been promised for almost three decades. One cannot help but wonder whether Burke's theory has led him to a dead-end, where elaborations and adjustments might be made, but not any progress, and not any hookup with literature and criticism outside the system.

So the Burke "problem" persists. He is truly one of a kind—ingen-

ious and inventive, a performer with a flair for the dramatic and surprising. But he probably will not influence contemporary criticism in a
profound way. He will continue to be read by "virtually everybody,"
yet will always remain on the verge of being rediscovered. His pro-
ductiveness, his resistance to the New Critical orthodoxy, his arguments
for relating literature and other disciplines, and for tying literature to
life—all this makes him an important and admirable figure. But Burke's
system is too grandiose and unwieldy, and his interpretive practice
swerves too often into reductiveness. Reading Burke can be a marvelous
experience, but he is likely to stay a marginal critic.

A Critic's Burden: R. P. Blackmur's Reading of Henry Adams

R. P. Blackmur. *Henry Adams*. Edited and with an introduction by
  Veronica A. Makowsky. Foreword by Denis Donoghue. New York:
  Harcourt Brace Jovanovich, 1980.

One of the curiosities of modern criticism is that a number of its
major works were never written or were not completed. One thinks of
T. S. Eliot's study of seventeenth-century poetry, F. R. Leavis's systematic account of "the elements of practical criticism," Kenneth Burke's
monograph on Coleridge, and John Crowe Ransom's book on aesthetic
theory, "The Third Moment." Each was announced, and its publication
declared to be imminent. But though parts and chapters did appear in
journals, these were works that their writers were unable to finish or
see through to publication. Other books took precedence as the critic's
career moved forward, or else the studies undertaken by other critics—
this seems especially true in Eliot's case—made the planned job un-
necessary.

R. P. Blackmur's book on Henry Adams is the most famous—and
also the most infamous—example of this peculiar genre. Blackmur's
first piece on Adams appeared in 1931, and other essays and reviews
soon followed, all of which seemed to forecast that the publication of
the book-length study was just a year or two away. But as each in-
stallment appeared, it became ever more obvious that Blackmur had
neither stopped working on Adams nor gotten any closer to wrapping
up the book. So doubtful did the book's publication come to seem that
Blackmur's colleagues and acquaintances began to treat the project as
a kind of farce, joking about the advances that he had received from
his publisher and the deadlines he kept failing to meet.[23]

There is admittedly something amusing as well as depressing about
Blackmur's long struggle to complete the task he started in the 1930s.

He often insisted that only a little more time and money would enable him to conclude his work at last. But it is apparent that this was no ordinary scholarly book, and that Blackmur was involved in much more than a critical analysis. In examining and meditating upon Adams, Blackmur saw reflections of himself, and he used his subject as an opportunity to locate terms for his own life and brood upon their meanings. He felt a kinship with Adams's sense of failure, loss, and inability to secure a satisfying life and career within society's institutions. And he was also drawn to Adams's vivid and sometimes grotesque forms of irony and sense of distance between the truly intelligent observer and the events that occur around him. Blackmur's favorite name for himself was "the outsider," the man without a place or vocation.[24]

Blackmur's identification with Adams is sometimes overbearing and arrogant. Though Blackmur is an extremely self-conscious writer, he does not often direct the bemused remark or ironic aside against himself or search into the nature of his obsession with Adams's ideas. He does not appear to recognize the degree to which he has accepted Adams's myth of "failure," despair about human achievement, and pessimism about the course of history: it is as though these are doctrines to which one is obliged to pay homage. But Blackmur's kinship with Adams also has its sadly self-punishing side. In 1941 this headnote preceded one of Blackmur's essays: "Scheduled for publication in 1941 are two critical studies, *The Spoils of Henry James* and *Henry Adams: A Critical Portrait*."[25] It is eerie, comical, and disturbing all at once to witness Blackmur putting such pressure on himself; as if the Adams project were not onerous and oppressive enough, he burdens himself with a second book, equally challenging and complex. This is the act of an ambitious critic, gifted beyond measure, who sets high goals for himself and voices them publicly even as he knows that he will not be able to attain them. It is, one might say, the act of a man who needs to feel the pain and inescapability of failure. "Failure" perhaps was more meaningful for Blackmur than success, and he seems to have construed it as a sign of authenticity. "Failure" carries the mystique that Adams assigned to it: it is the genuinely perceptive man who realizes that the "expense of greatness" is to fail, and who understands that his most significant aspirations are those he cannot fulfill.

We owe the publication of *Henry Adams* to Veronica A. Makowsky. It is not the book that Blackmur intended to write, and in its omission of important material, it might even be judged as unfaithful to his design. As Makowsky points out in her introduction, the revised outline for his study that Blackmur wrote in the late 1940s divides it into two sections. The first would begin with Adams's education at Harvard and would survey his life and career until the turn of the century, just before the major books, *Mont-Saint-Michel and Chartres* and *The Education of Henry Adams*, were composed. The second section would consist of a detailed analysis of both texts, with additional commentary on Adams's other, later, writings and theory of history, and it would conclude with a biographical review of Adams's final years.

Henry Adams, as Makowsky has organized it, is almost entirely focused on the second section of Blackmur's projected work. It opens with "The Expense of Greatness: Three Emphases on Henry Adams," a brief general account that first appeared in the *Virginia Quarterly Review* in 1936 and that Blackmur included in *The Expense of Greatness* (1940) and *The Lion and the Honeycomb* (1955). The next part of the book is titled "The Virgin and the Dynamo" and is more than 250 pages in length. Most of this material appears here for the first time and provides us with Blackmur's interpretation of *Mont-Saint-Michel and Chartres* and the *Education*. Blackmur's manuscript for this section breaks off in midsentence, and at several points in the text, he refers back to chapters that either he did not complete or Makowsky has not included. At times "The Virgin and the Dynamo" reads like work-in-progress, in need of the revision and reshaping that Blackmur could not bring himself to perform. Part three, "King Richard's Prison Song"—the title is taken from a medieval lyric that Adams loved—is also mostly new, though a section of it appeared in the *Kenyon Review* in 1940 and was reprinted in *A Primer of Ignorance* (1967). The book's fourth and final part, never published before, is titled "At Rock Creek: Adams: Images: Eidolon." It is six pages in length and represents Blackmur's attempt to imagine Adams's meditations at his wife's graveside, next to the monument sculpted by Augustus St. Gaudens.

Much has been omitted. Blackmur left among his unpublished papers essays that deal with Adams's *History of the United States of America during the Administrations of Jefferson and Madison*, the journalistic writings, and the biographies of Albert Gallatin and John Randolph. Makowsky decided not to include any of these four essays. In her introduction she contends that this kind of historical criticism does not display Blackmur at his best, and adds that much of the analysis is based on sources which more recent scholarship has superseded. Also omitted are three essays on "Foreign Affairs, 1895-1908," one of which appeared in the *Hudson Review* in 1952. Nor will the reader find reprinted in this volume Blackmur's essay on Adams's novels, *Democracy* and *Esther*; his review of Marian Adams's letters; his comparative study of Henry and Brooks Adams; and his treatment of Adams's letters to his niece, Louisa Hooper. For this material we will still have to consult Blackmur's other collections of essays (not all of which are in print) and the scholarly journals.

Even with these omissions, *Henry Adams* is a 350-page book. And no doubt economic factors influenced Makowsky's and the publisher's decision not to give us, in a single volume, everything that Blackmur wrote about Adams. Still, one's gratitude for the book is tempered by what has been left out. It may well be true, as Makowsky argues, that Blackmur rarely labored as a historian, and that formalist criticism is where his real strength lies. Yet this might suggest an excellent reason for including samples of historically grounded work in the book. *Henry Adams* obviously appeals to readers who are interested as much in Blackmur as in Adams; we are anxious to discover more about this critic's style and approach as well as acquire new insights about his subject. To fail to include any of the material on foreign policy and politics is to narrow Blackmur's range, to portray him as more of a pure formalist than is actually the case. In addition, Makowsky too quickly assumes that Adams's writings of the 1900s constitute his best and most enduring work. There is, of course, a good deal of support for this judgment; B. L. Reid, in fact, has recently stated that the *Education* is "the single book of highest distinction ever produced by an American."[26] But other critics have maintained that both *Mont-Saint-Michel and Chartres* and the *Education* are seriously flawed masterpieces, too often playful without purpose, marred by eccentricity, and excessively burdened by Adams's unremitting sense of irony. William Dusinberre, for example, in his stimulating *Henry Adams: The Myth of Failure*, has described the *History*, rather than the later books, as Adams's major achievement, one that rivals the work of Gibbon and Macaulay.[27] We can only regret that Blackmur's analysis of Adams's superbly crafted nine-volume *History* remains unpublished, still consigned to the Princeton University Library archives.

But until a second editor gathers the other writings on Adams, the book that Makowsky has constructed is the closest approximation we have to the book that Blackmur never finished. Much of Blackmur's commentary is, without question, very thoughtful and penetrating. Blackmur is wonderfully skilled at treating the patterns, imagery, and formal systems of a text, and no critic has shown more distinctly the complex symbolic structures that Adams created in *Mont-Saint-Michel and Chartres* and the *Education*. Blackmur's argument cannot be summarized, in part because of the density of his writing, but even more because he is not, in this book, actually arguing his case and developing specific points. Denis Donoghue, in his foreword to the present volume, refers to Blackmur's criticism as a "supplication of texts" (p. viii), and this seems especially true of the writing on Adams. Blackmur is carefully and patiently attending to Adams and serving the manifold organization of the texts. Blackmur might even be seen as engaged in his own act of re-creation, as he strives to reshape and illuminate the great symbols of the Virgin and the Dynamo in his own prose.

When Blackmur succeeds, the results are impressive. His analysis is shrewd, yet phrased in a manner that reveals a deep sympathy for, and sensitivity to, his subject. Sometimes Blackmur is merely repeating commonplaces, but even these are stated with just the right feeling for tone and nuance, as when he observes that Adams "had not the faith; only the apprehension of its need which made him struggle toward it all his life" (p. 17). Blackmur is also acute in noting Adams's "doubts" about his audience but ultimate faith in his symbols: "The waywardness of form and lightness of tone reflected doubt of his audience—doubt of the possibility of any bridge between the audience and himself— but of the validity of the symbols toward which he worked he had no doubt at all" (p. 28). Blackmur never managed to deal at length with Adams's response to his wife's suicide in 1885. But he does comment in detail on the "gap" in the *Education* between the twentieth and twenty-first chapter, a gap that excludes from Adams's life story the years of his marriage, his wife's death, and his efforts to recover from the shock of the blow. "In leaving out twenty years," Adams

> is not only making an enormous understatement; he is bringing to bear on all his later chapters the force of the unaccountable—the sum of all that had happened which is not recounted—by means of deliberately inexplicit or only partly explicit symbols. The feeling is thus thicker than the prose: the meaning continues after the words have stopped because it was active before the words began. We have thus a recapitulation, here and there in these chapters, of material that was never given in the book and yet refers both the readers and Adams to it with all the more strength because of its deliberate disguise as the shared unaccountable. (P. 96)

Blackmur has often been praised for his ability to demonstrate how words are used in literary texts. As this passage suggests, he is also alert to the power generated in texts by what a writer leaves unspoken. In an early chapter of the *Education*, Adams characterizes the writing he did as a young man at Harvard by saying, "At best it showed only a feeling for form; an instinct of exclusion."[28] For Adams, to "feel" the formal patterning of a work is to be aware of what must be excluded from it: the text receives its greatest intensities from the facts and feelings that the writer does not express in words. Adams's critics, including Blackmur, have often examined the content of the *Education*— its ideas, themes, and historical generalizations. But Blackmur is exceptional in seeing that Adams's exclusions inform what is explicitly "said." The form of the book is permeated by Adams's sense of the formless, chaotic, and inexplicable. His deepest feelings are expressed not in words but through significant gaps, exclusions, and silences that exist precisely at what might have been, in a different book, its most verbally active and fluent part.

When Blackmur addresses the later chapters of the *Education* and considers Adams's theory of history, his discussion is often incisive. Yet while Blackmur's kinship with Adams often leads him to say intelligent things, it also encourages him to identify so closely with Adams that his writing loses its critical poise. As often happens when Leavis deals with Lawrence or Trilling with Arnold, Blackmur is not able to detach himself from his valorized subject and preserve a critical distance from the texts that he is analyzing. Because *Henry Adams* is often stimulating, I hesitate to stress its shortcomings, but these do exist and are serious.

In some stretches, *Henry Adams* is long-winded and wearying. There is a great deal of paraphrase and summary, not enough quotation and analysis, and too many occasions when Blackmur's attempts to write prose-poems transform his usually careful style into a series of bad lyrics. Blackmur is also guilty of an excessive solemnity in this study; sometimes one feels that the critic's piety, exaltation of Adams's symbols, and respectful attention to the theories about man and the cosmos are more appropriate to a funeral oration than to a critical work. Blackmur is constantly raising questions that he does not answer, leading up to crucial arguments that he then dodges, and referring to passages that he either touches on briefly or does not examine at all.

Henry Adams suffers from a lack of proportion and judgment, a lack that is all the more striking when one recalls the early essays that Blackmur wrote on modern poetry. In these essays, he is very aware of the need to build an argument, to distinguish the good from the bad, to focus on and evaluate basic techniques, ideas, and structures. In *Henry Adams*, however, Blackmur appears so absorbed in his subject that he can propose critical judgments only if he is certain that he can then diminish or explain away their impact. At one point Blackmur concedes that "there is a little plain nonsense" in Adams's symbols, "a little *hoc est corpus* turned hocus pocus" (p. 71). But instead of taking hold of this issue, Blackmur in effect sidesteps it by saying, in his next sentence, "Yet nonsense has a right in one's symbols; for there is nonsense at the center of the major as well as the minor contradictions in man's mind." How much "nonsense" is contained in *Mont-Saint-Michel and Chartres* and the *Education*? How much does it damage the books? Does its presence reveal something about the tragic self-imprisonment of Adams's mind in his later years? These are the questions that Blackmur's remark about "nonsense" implies, but he passes over them, settling for wordplay (sense and "non-sense") and generalizing the problem in such a way that he is not required to confront it. The nonsense that we may feel at times in the *Education*, he maintains, is not peculiar to Adams but defines the mind of man.

Even more disturbing is Blackmur's willingness to adopt Adams's

terms as a means of interpreting the modern world. When he does
this, his attitudes become shabby and his language toneless. "To preserve the absolute values in the new relation" was Adams's "true
problem,"

> and he was right to insist on it even if his view of the new relations was
> prejudiced and erroneous. It would have altered only his exaggerations and
> nothing of his judgments, had he seen how the population problem of India
> and Southeast Asia under the impetus of a mild injection of artificial energy
> in the absence of Western resources suggests the *need* of a mechanization
> of sex there. Even war, in itself, no longer cuts population much in areas
> dominated by new forces, and its effect on race in Russia is doubtful. Further,
> inertia of race among the decimated Jews seems to have intensified. Thus
> Adams was righter than he might have thought. (P. 251)

If George Orwell had known of this passage when he was writing
"Politics and the English Language," he might have included it as an
example of the relationship between deformed language and skewed
thinking. Blackmur begins by noting the errors in Adams's diagnosis
of social problems, but then concludes by affirming that whatever the
errors, Adams was "righter" than he could have realized. Here and
elsewhere in his book, Blackmur criticizes or corrects Adams only to
progress to new reasons for admiration. And this produces a callousness
in his voice that apparently he cannot hear. As Makowsky observes in
her introduction, much of Blackmur's work on Adams was done in the
1940s and 50s. It was performed, that is, during the period when the
war raged in Europe and the terrible truth of the Holocaust became
public knowledge. These facts of history make Blackmur's generalizations, layered in Adams-like language, all the more insensitive. To refer
to the "decimated Jews" in such a shallow way, and to leave unexamined the question of Adams's notorious anti-Semitism, are glaring
failures of critical responsibility.

Blackmur's uncritical relation to his subject manifests itself in other
ways. While he comments well on the formal design of Adams's texts,
he is sometimes inattentive to the resonances of particular passages.
Blackmur's absorption in his material here exacts its cost, for it prevents
him from being skeptical and suspicious about Adams's language. A
whole set of questions that this critic raises in his treatment of the
modern poets is not introduced in this book. Blackmur does not tell us
in detail what Adams's language sounds like, how it moves from phrase
to phrase, how sentences and paragraphs are put together and function.
He appears to believe that Adams presents us with sacred texts that
the critic cannot handle without violating their sanctity. And so the
business of the critic never gets done.

Far too frequently in *Henry Adams*, the reader is disappointed, let down by Blackmur's failure to provide the necessary analysis and make the essential discriminations. A notable case in point occurs when Blackmur quotes Adams's account of his feelings after hearing the news of his sister's death. "Impressions like these," Adams writes,

> are not reasoned or catalogued in the mind; they are felt as part of violent emotion; and the mind that feels them is a different one from that which reasons; it is thought of a different power and a different person. The first serious consciousness of Nature's gesture—her attitude towards life—took form then as a phantasm, a nightmare, an insanity of force. For the first-time, the stage scenery of the senses collapsed; the human mind felt itself stripped naked, vibrating in a void of shapeless energies, with resistless mass, colliding, crushing, wasting, and destroying what these same energies had created and labored from eternity to perfect. Society became fantastic, a vision of pantomine with a mechanical motion; and its so-called thought merged in the mere sense of life, and pleasure in the sense. The usual anodynes of social medicine became evident artifice.[29]

Blackmur offers a few sentences about this passage, but they are more in the nature of ardent paraphrase than actual analysis. Adams's writing is impressive and grand here, and it is hard not to be awed by the effect. But it is the very sublimity of the passage that one cannot help wondering about. The rush of the participles ("colliding, crushing, wasting, and destroying"), the alliteration, and the other stylistic devices are very much on the surface. This is not, clearly, an instance of an art that seeks to conceal itself: the style, in all its brilliance, is as much or more at the center of our attention as the feeling that Adams is evoking. As one reflects upon the craftsmanship, the motives and aims of the passage become puzzling. It is not clear whether Adams's effort is primarily to stress the horror of his sister's death or instead to dramatize how intensely he responded to it—as though he alone could feel what the death meant, in its reverberating madness and cosmic significance. Adams's description is also informed by his specialized vocabulary of energy and force, which may be faithful to his sense of his response, but which may, in addition, point up his attempt to incorporate this death, like the other incidents of his life story, into his theoretical patterns and schemes. The sister's death confirms the deathly tendencies of Nature, Adams believes, and his loss both horrifies and captivates him.

As one reads this passage and others in the *Education*, the foregrounding of Adams's own "evident artifice" is sometimes difficult to fathom. Passages strike us as imposing and brilliant, yet when they are looked at carefully, they appear evasive in intention and elusive in meaning. In part this is a shortcoming in Adams's book; as Tony Tanner has argued, in the *Education* "the feeling of verdict preceding evidence, of experience being subtly deformed by dogma, is sometimes very strong."[30] Yet it is also true that Adams revels in the complexities of his artifice and takes great pleasure in the depth of his ironic performances. Adams sees his act of writing as an act of incessant irony, role-playing, masking, and imposture; and it often happens that at just the moment when Adams appears to be finally revealing himself he is, once again, hiding his intentions and practicing still other forms of evasion.

In his *Education*, Adams is always provoking his reader to ask questions, note disparities, and contemplate what is irrational and inexplicable. And he also wishes to make us pursue lines of force and sequences in his own narrative, to make us, in other words, see the relationships that group one incident or person with others. Adams's description of his sister's death, in all its stylistic power and extravagant feeling, is intensified by the fact of Marian Adams's suicide. The sister's death occurred in 1870, the wife's in 1885; one is rendered, the other not at all. It is the second, as Adams constructs his narrative, that the first might be seen to prefigure. And it is the memory of the second death that informs the first one and heightens it. The language used to evoke the sister's death is extreme, highly dramatized and elevated. And this makes the absence of language at the gap in the narrative, which leaves the wife's death in silence, all the more painful: here, imagination and language fail.

What we have in *Henry Adams* is a book that is both insightful and seriously flawed. Blackmur studies the formal structure of Adams's masterpieces more cogently than any other critic has done. Yet at the same time, it must be said that he does not sufficiently consider Adams's ironic stances and profound play with language, and is too enmeshed in Adams's theories and ideas. It is because *Henry Adams* presents such extremes of distinction and failure that final assessments about it prove difficult to make. Depending upon one's point of view and approach, the book will seem an achievement of the highest order or a disturbing example of the ways in which excessive sympathy interferes with the tasks of critical judgment. Possibly Blackmur might have eliminated the failings in his book if he had been able to revise and restructure it. But I think that the problems in *Henry Adams* tell us something important about Blackmur's criticism taken as a whole. His critical writing combines an extraordinary awareness of formal structures with an inability to perceive what they contain. As many sections of *Henry Adams* demonstrate and as his later work generally testifies, Blackmur is interested in ideology, politics, international affairs, and related topics; he is, in this respect, much more than a critical formalist. But his efforts to get beyond formalism are not often successful, both because they are filtered through Adams's terms and because they are themselves "formalist" in their orientation. Though Blackmur does treat issues and ideas, and not just technique and style, his analyses invariably take a "formal" direction. He nearly always is concerned to explain how values, beliefs, and attitudes function in texts—how, that is, they serve to undermine textual structures or make them more coherent. It is, for the most part, formal questions and considerations to which he gives his sharpest scrutiny.

No sooner does one say this than one feels obliged to qualify it. In several essays in *The Lion and the Honeycomb* and *A Primer of Ignorance*, Blackmur deals with "the economy of the American writer," the "American literary expatriate," and other social and cultural matters. And he discusses them in a way that his formalist predilections do not distort. When you write about Blackmur, you always have to be prepared to take back what you say. He is difficult to characterize, for, like Adams, he appears anxious to avoid settling into a single role or position. It is not merely the case, however, that Blackmur wants to keep us off-balance and parry attempts to place him as one kind of critic or other. There is also a good deal of uncertainty and contradiction in Blackmur's work. He recognizes that formalist studies of a writer's craftmanship suit his talents. Yet he also feels constrained by a criticism that binds him to the words on the page, and so he seeks to devise a more elaborate style and devotes himself to the religion of art.[31] When Blackmur acts as a high priest of criticism, his essays are obscure, silly, and seem a throwback to the aestheticism of Pater and Wilde. But—as if matters were not confusing enough—this is only part of the story, for Blackmur's sacramental essays sit in his collections alongside provocative work on politics, economics, and the state of culture. In *this* work, Blackmur is a valuable commentator on society, not at all a decadent escapist from it.

Like many contemporary critics, Blackmur wants to make major claims for the critic's activity but is ambivalent about how extra-literary these should be. Sometimes he seems to propose a direct engagement with social problems, while on other occasions he implies that the best response is absorption in the mysteries of art. In his 1961 essay "The Chain of Our Own Needles: Criticism and Our Culture," Blackmur stresses that we need to "relate" the connections between literature and society, art and the modern world.[32] But except for some remarks about poetics, rhetoric, and the like, he is not able to explain the means by which we might articulate these connections. It is one thing to insist that literature and society ought to be brought into conjunction in critical discourse, and another to define the various ways through which this should be accomplished. And still another to commit oneself to acting on the basis of these definitions and the aims that they embody.

By laying out the difficulties in coming to terms with Blackmur's work and describing our problems in making judgments about it, I am going against the consensus of opinion. There is a standard account of Blackmur's career, one that few have questioned. He began, it is said, as a New Critic in the 1930s and produced his best essays, including those on Stevens, Moore, Lawrence, and other poets, during these years. It is this period of Blackmur's career, when he was most purely a formalist, that the majority of his readers admire. Laurence B. Holland states that Blackmur is "the most brilliant and durable of the New Critics"; A. Walton Litz concludes that he "was in many ways the most satisfactory literary critic of his generation"; and Russell Fraser, most boldly of all, asserts that *The Double Agent* (1935) and *The Expense of Greatness* constitute "the best literary criticism produced in our time."[33] These citations could be supported by many others. Nearly everyone agrees that Blackmur is the best of the New Critics and that his formalist essays of the 1930s have achieved a classic status.

But to characterize Blackmur as *the* New Critic is inaccurate, for he transcends this category as much as he belongs in it. John Crowe Ransom, it is true, did point to Blackmur as the typical "New Critic" in his preface to *The New Criticism*, a book that appeared in 1941 and assigned a name to the movement as a whole. And like many of the New Critics, Blackmur is indeed a "close reader" of texts. But unlike the others, he rarely engages in lengthy explications; his analyses often concentrate only on parts of texts, or are strategically placed to nail down a general argument about a poet's ways of working. Cleanth Brooks's "readings" of poems by Donne, Pope, Gray, Wordsworth, Keats, and others in *The Well Wrought Urn* (1947), which proceed through the text image by image, sometimes even word by word, are more representative of the usual New Critical procedure. This is not the kind of analysis that Blackmur prefers to engage in, however well equipped he is to carry it out when it does fulfill his purposes. Blackmur's verbal analysis generally involves other, more theoretical, problems: "authority" in Hardy's poetry, the relation between literature and belief in Eliot's writing, or the nature of artistic "consciousness" and dramatic "form" in Melville's novels. Again in contrast to Brooks, Blackmur does not gear his criticism towards pedagogy, which the New Critics generally emphasize and see as the testing ground for their interpretive tools.

Blackmur once wryly noted that "whenever any of my own work is attacked I am attacked as a New Critic. Usually when people wish to make more pleasant remarks about me they say how it is that I have departed from the New Criticism."[34] As "the outsider," Blackmur felt uneasy about being a member of a movement and did not wish to be portrayed as one of the leading executives in the business that Ransom described as "Criticism, Inc." In at least two essays, "The Lion and the

Honeycomb" and "A Burden for Critics," Blackmur treats the New Criticism harshly, condemning its narrow canon, its development of methods that are "useless" when applied to Chaucer, Goethe, Racine, and Dante, and its bad effect on creative writing.[35] He is not a spokesman for New Critical doctrines in his theoretical writings; he does not confine his practice to textual explication as such; and when he does refer to the New Criticism and its advocates, he calls attention to defects and misplaced emphases.

Many contemporary critics nevertheless have a great stake in praising Blackmur as the exemplary New Critic. This may reveal little, finally, about Blackmur but much about the state of criticism today. Robert Boyers, for example, honors Blackmur for his skills as a close reader, and like Holland, Litz, and Fraser, he singles out the early essays on the modern poets as Blackmur's best work. In his concentration on poetic detail and "technical dynamics," Blackmur provides us, says Boyers, with a "model" for our own practice. "The early writings" demonstrate "right thinking" in action, the kind of sensitive response to the text that is rarely seen in "critical discourse."[36] As Boyers's frequent complaints about contemporary criticism suggest, he is opposed to the spread of literary theory and hopes to return criticism to the exchange between poet, text, and reader. For Boyers—and many others agree with him—criticism is, by definition, the type of formalist analysis that Blackmur undertakes in his early essays. Critics should not stray from the text itself, should not write "creatively" (as though they were artists themselves), and should not overwhelm the poem and the reader with theory and methodology. Boyers's assumptions— and again, many share them—show the extent to which the New Criticism has become institutionalized and won acceptance as the foundation of criticism itself. And these assumptions strongly determine the praise that Boyers bestows on the early Blackmur.

These assumptions also determine Boyers's hostile commentary on Blackmur's later work, as gathered in *The Lion and the Honeycomb, A Primer of Ignorance*, and *Eleven Essays in the European Novel* (1964). Like many before him, Boyers has nothing good to say about these essays. "Blackmur came to believe," he states,

> that he too had better things to do than to write the best essays on poets and poetry that anyone had ever written. He bought the notion that an ambitious critic was well advised to move away from texts, to discover Ideas, to talk about things instead of allowing his discourses to be penetrated by the voice and thought rhythms of poets and their verses. He pretends, in his position papers, to be as attached as ever to "technical judgment" and to be interested still in "recreating . . . a verbal sensibility capable of coping with the poetry." But he ceased effectively to write about poetry by the late

forties, and much that he wrote in the period between 1950 and his death in 1965 is simply unreadable.[37]

In Boyers's view, there is only one Blackmur, and that is the critic who produced the formalist analyses and did not wander into the thickets of literary theory. When Blackmur stopped seeing himself as a formalist and sought to enlarge his conception of the critic's job of work, he stopped being a good critic.

It is precisely the later writings that have earned Blackmur the acclaim of a different group of contemporary critics—the critics whom Boyers has in mind when he laments the state of the discipline and nominates Blackmur's early writings as an alternative. Geoffrey Hartman has described Blackmur as "perhaps the first of our witch critics," whose "involuted style betrays an extreme awareness of how the mind is textured by texts and how the critic's, if not the poet's authority is always under the shadow of imposture."[38] Even more extravagantly, Edward W. Said has proclaimed that Blackmur is "the greatest genius American criticism has produced."[39] For Hartman, Said, and others, Blackmur's greatness lies in his ability to travel beyond the boundaries set by the New Criticism and in his willingness to expand the critic's commerce with other disciplines and social concerns. From this perspective, Blackmur's later criticism, where he strives to do more than treat the "technical dynamics" of poems, is the essential Blackmur. Here, his critical approach is "creative," and it aligns him with those who argue, as does Hartman in particular, for a critical style as sophisticated, dexterous, and allusive as the primary text that it takes as a point of departure.

Blackmur is held in high esteem these days. Most readers still prefer the early essays, but now that a number of prominent critics and theorists have highlighted the later work, these essays too will win new admirers. The more one reflects upon the nature of Blackmur's reputation, the more it seems that it involves not only a debate about his career, but also one that concerns the definition and authority of the critic's role. If you propose ambitious "creative" tasks for the critic, and if you believe that criticism must move beyond the words on the page, then your emphasis will fall on the later Blackmur. If, on the other hand, you equate criticism with "close reading," then you will judge Blackmur's early work to be his best and regard his later writings as a catastrophic decline, as misconceived and unreadable. Blackmur is a brilliant, subtle interpreter of texts, and, in my view, there is no denying this aspect of his achievement. But as Adams observes in the *Education*, "one sees what one brings" (p. 387), and this applies not only to Blackmur's reading of Adams but to our readings of Blackmur as well.

Criticism and the Academy

One of Blackmur's most memorable essays is his "Notes on E. E. Cummings' Language," which appeared in 1930. What makes this essay memorable is the precision and severity of Blackmur's judgment on Cummings's poetic practice. Here the critic is not explicating a text, but is rather explicating and unfolding a judgment; he is prosecuting an argument, not giving a "reading" of a poem or group of poems.

Blackmur's critical behavior in the Cummings essay was rare in the 1930s, and it has become even rarer in recent decades as criticism has grown increasingly "professionalized" and "academic." There is so much pressure to produce readings that few people seem able or willing to make judgments upon the body of material being interpreted. Everyone feels obliged to seize upon an author or authors to serve as his or her field; and because everyone is driven to pursue the same goal, no one desires to interfere with or jam the process by considering the value of what is being intently examined. Many critics and teachers even believe there is something admirable about refusing to make judgments. This refusal even takes the form of a principle, one that encourages the production and play of all responses in the hope that, slowly but surely, the truth will emerge. Such a refusal to judge and discriminate would doubtless shock Leavis, Blackmur, and most of the other major critics of this century. It amounts to intellectual surrender and turns the discipline into a preserve where a marketplace mentality—the more readings, the better—can reign supreme. As I have tried to show in this chapter, Leavis and Blackmur make mistakes. But this fact should not rule out the act of judgment altogether, and it ought not to sway us from the example that these critics establish. The decline of evaluation is unfortunate, and to its bad effects—as well as to other disturbing tendencies in contemporary theory—I direct my attention in the next chapter.

But one or two more general reflections are in order here. The critics I examine in this chapter—Trilling and Leavis in particular—are now becoming the object of meticulous study, and it is difficult not to have ambivalent feelings about this trend. These are important, influential critics; they obviously merit rereading and reassessment. Yet one knows that there are other, less disinterested, reasons why scholars now attend to them in such detail. They furnish us with a host of texts to analyze and explicate, and thereby provide fertile territory for those unable or unwilling to hazard "readings" of so-called primary texts. The critical texts are "there"; they form a more or less coherent group. Is it not natural that they should be surveyed and studied in articles and books?

Perhaps it is both natural and inevitable that these kinds of analyses should proliferate, yet it is queerly ironic that all four of these critics should now figure in the scholarship that professional academics produce. With the possible exception of Trilling, these critics saw themselves as outsiders, marginal to the workings of the academic institution. Even Trilling, especially in his later years, cultivates the voice of the detached observer and brings to bear on "culture" the vision of moral centrality he judges the majority to have abandoned. Not only do these critics take note of their marginality, they insist upon and seek to preserve it. Leavis is the most compelling instance of this, of course; but it also applies to Blackmur and Burke (one might add the names of Yvor Winters and William Empson), who are uneasy about their membership in Anglo-American academic institutions.

It is a measure of Leavis's power and arrogance that he regards himself as the very embodiment of the true university: he represents the university in its most distinguished form. In this respect Leavis perceives himself as the outsider who is in fact the insider, the one who bears steadfast witness to the values and traditions that the apparent insiders (those in positions of authority) betray. Leavis's self-perception sometimes damages his work, most noticeably in the books he wrote towards the end of his career. He could never let go, it seems, of this image of himself as the persecuted outsider, not even when the facts of his reputation and influence were manifest. Yet one can understand why he invests so much in the story of his marginality. Like others, if in a much more vivid fashion, Leavis resists incorporation by the university, resists being absorbed by the institution he often celebrates and strives to reform. When critics praise his excellence as a reader and teacher, Leavis emphasizes that he has been badly misunderstood; when others testify to the extent of his influence, he makes clear that this "influence" is either minimal or a distortion of his real meaning.

Leavis exemplifies a dilemma that troubles many critics and theorists today. How does one work within the academic system without being taken over by it? Is it possible to capitalize on the resources of the institution without becoming its servant and falling victim to its practices—the same practices one initially challenged and sought to revise? What kind of critical and pedagogical independence can one enjoy when one is an insider, a professional, an academic critic and teacher? These questions point towards others that are even more significant. Is the role of true "intellectual" available for the academic man or woman? Are the compromises too great? Are the burdens of the institution too severe, too much of a limitation on the wide-ranging social and cultural commentary to which the intellectual aspires?

It is unclear whether the role of "intellectual"—the role that Gramsci, Benjamin, and others occupy—is one that most teachers and critics can hope to attain. I have suggested in this book that we should instead see ourselves as "intellectual workers," a term that affirms the primacy of intellect while acknowledging the fact that we are workers within an institutional setting that both *constrains* and *provides opportunities for* innovative labor. Critics and teachers have often desired to be something other than what they are, something that will enable them to get "outside" the academy and occupy a place of greater distinction and public prominence. The problem may lie, however, not with the place where they now situate themselves, but with the faulty vision of what it necessarily entails. If being a critic and teacher means being an explicator of the masterpieces, then it is no wonder that many people chafe at the role and seek to transcend it. And if explication of texts is our destiny, it is also no wonder that still others glorify this role and cling to it tenaciously, making a vocation out of an apparent necessity. If we conceive of our work differently, then we will not feel so inclined either to escape it or uncritically to embrace it. Being on the "inside" of the academic institution will feel less threatening once we define what transpires there in different terms.

In speaking of the insider/outsider Leavis as I have in this chapter and elsewhere, I do not mean to single him out as a model, as though *his* terms are those we should adopt and construct the discipline upon. He is a powerful and admirable figure, but I hope I have made clear that his work is too flawed and over-bearing to serve as a model for critical and pedagogical performance. His emphasis on criticism and judgment (as opposed to mere "elucidation") and his concern for general "critical consciousness" (as opposed to academic specialization and disciplinary enclosure) are inspiring and important. But in other respects—his very narrow canon, over-valuation of Lawrence, dismissal of dissent—Leavis is too rigid and dogmatic to stand as the exemplary figure for English studies. He is a critic from whom we can learn much, and whose theoretical statements—though he would bristle at the notion of himself as a theorist—about community, collaboration, and interdisciplinary study are suggestive. He is, however, finally too intractable for me to describe him as a model, and I want to counter that impression.

It might seem at first glance that a "model" critic might be drawn from aspects of the work of each of the writers I discuss in this chapter. Ideally, one might say, we should combine Leavis's moral passion, Trilling's social consciousness, Burke's drive for system, and Blackmur's formal virtuosity. This makes a certain kind of obvious (and generous) sense, but it feels rather lame as a conclusion and seems to falsify somewhat our manner of engagement with powerful critics. Though we may at times believe otherwise, most of us do not teach or write in this integrative manner, trying to be a combination of Leavis, Trilling, Burke, and Blackmur, or Derrida and Foucault. "Combining" traits from different critics would be likely to leave us in disarray, in a muddle that goes by the name of pluralism.

We are more likely, I think, to model ourselves first on one critic and then another, as we suddenly discover someone whose work appears to give us the central insight or method. In part this reflects a readiness to follow the fashions of the moment, but it of course also testifies to the authentic power of these writers. They speak, to borrow James's phrase, with "commanding Style," and compel us to imitate their practice; they pre-empt and dislodge the critics we followed before, and they make converts quickly. This can give our work a sharper edge, but the danger here is that we will become over-zealous and uncritical in promoting the discoveries of a master-figure. Especially at the present time, with the discipline seeming so unstable and authority difficult to locate, critics and teachers are prompt to take up a new, forceful vocabulary and serve as its spokesmen. The enthusiastic response to Derrida and deconstruction is the most obvious instance of this tendency, and it illustrates the hazards. What begins as a source of new vitality soon degenerates into its own form of orthodoxy and into an inability to criticize (or even to see) ungainly writing and self-preening thought. The "model" critic does not succeed in helping to open up inquiry in a lasting way—though he succeeds in doing so for a time—but limits it and grows increasingly controlling and prescriptive. Judgment and common sense disappear.

8.

Reviewing the State

of Criticism, II

A few conjectures, a supply of admonitions, many acute isolated observations, some brilliant guesses, much oratory and applied poetry, inexhaustible confusion, a sufficiency of dogma, no small stock of prejudice, whimsies and crochets, a profusion of mysticism, a little genuine speculation, sundry stray inspirations, pregnant hints and random aperçus; of such as these, it may be said without exaggeration, is extant critical theory composed.

I. A. Richards, *Principles of Literary Criticism*

Making Judgments: Criticism Past, Present, and Future

Richard Ohmann. *English in America: A Radical View of the Profession*. New York: Oxford University Press, 1976.
Frank Kermode. *The Genesis of Secrecy: On the Interpretation of Narrative*. Cambridge: Harvard University Press, 1979.
Harold Bloom, Paul De Man, Jacques Derrida, Geoffrey Hartman, and J. Hillis Miller. *Deconstruction and Criticism*. New York: Seabury Press, 1979.
Eugene Goodheart. *The Failure of Criticism*. Cambridge: Harvard University Press, 1978.
Lionel Trilling. *Prefaces to the Experiences of Literature*. New York: Harcourt Brace Jovanovich, 1979.
Lionel Trilling. *The Last Decade: Essays and Reviews, 1965-75*. New York: Harcourt Brace Jovanovich, 1979.
F. R. Leavis. *The Living Principle: 'English' as a Discipline of Thought*. New York: Oxford University Press, 1975.

An astounding amount of criticism gets published these days, and the recent boom in literary theory adds still more volumes to the scholarly stockpiles. A good deal of this material is second-rate or worse, but much of it is excellent—a fact often ignored by those

163

who call for a "moratorium" on the writing of criticism. (But not on the writing of novels, stories, poems, plays?) Yet the "moratorium" advocates have a point. Though impressive work is done, it doesn't seem to matter much. Or to put this another way, the production of criticism matters to those who serve on tenure and promotion committees, to reviewers of grant proposals, friends of the writer, and colleagues. But the primary emphasis remains on the production itself, not on any values that it might foster, and not on any body of knowledge that it deepens and extends. Criticism abounds, seemingly propelled by its own momentum. The more critical writing we do, the less anxious we are even to consider questions about value. Thirty years ago, in one of his essays published in *The Lion and the Honeycomb*, R. P. Blackmur warned against certain tendencies in "the modes of understanding—both of criticism and scholarship—by which we use literature," and his words sound with an unsettling forcefulness today: "What we are very largely up to in practice, and to a considerable extent in theory, is the hardening of the mind into a set of unrelated methodologies without the controlling advantage of a fixed body of knowledge, a fixed faith, or a fixed purpose."[1]

Evaluative criticism—a criticism based on the making of judgments and striving for concrete knowledge—has just about disappeared. Texts exist in order for us to write books and essays about them. We do not usually make judgments, nor do we encourage fellow critics and students to believe that some works are more important, more alive in and for our time, than others. Once it was crucial for poets and critics to know whether Donne, for example, was receiving more or less attention than he deserved. Critics explicated his texts and formed judgments about them, comparing Donne's merits with those of Milton and the Romantics. We should read Donne, F. R. Leavis maintained, "as we read the living," as we study and appraise the writings of contemporaries. But Leavis's kind of evaluative criticism is not practiced much anymore. Each of us needs an author, a piece of the literary landscape. We do not want to be told that our work is not worth the trouble, and we do not have the time, and perhaps not the rigor and commitment, to criticize the pursuits of others.

Though worth repeating and pondering, none of this is exactly news. Most of us realize that the state of criticism is part of a general crisis in the humanities and need no reminders about low morale. Our energy level seems to rise only when we are chastizing ourselves or deploring our present condition:

> Of all the areas in colleges and universities that will feel the assaults of inflation, the shrinking numbers of students, the devastated job market, and particularly the growing vocationalism of the young, the humanities will be the hardest hit.

Less than a hundred years ago, English studies hardly existed. Moreover, when they replaced classical studies, that discipline passed quickly into disuetude while hardly anyone noticed. It is not at all inconceivable, given the history of the humanities, that English studies, though at present the seemingly irreplaceable guardian of the Western cultural tradition, should decline to the current marginal status of the classics.

American teachers are engaged in guerilla war with their own society. And it is a war they are losing. At present, the best they can envision is to create some of the terms of their surrender.

Our situation is dispiriting, and we spend much time together complaining. The natural and social sciences have displaced the authority of the humanities; students are concerned about jobs and careers, not the classic texts of the Western tradition; and while we know that we are in trouble now, we expect harder times ahead. Answers and solutions are difficult to come by, and so we continue to do what we have always done, without common direction or purpose.[2]

But to speak of the loss of purpose in the academy, argues Richard Ohmann in *English in America*, is too easy and self-indulgent. "Most such talk" about the "plight of the humanities" is, he contends, "cripplingly ahistorical, and far too narrow in scope—as if the humanities were hermetically sealed, flourishing or sickening apart from the rest of the universe." If we intend to "cure" the humanities, we must study the connections between the universities and "industrial culture," realizing that literary work is in complicity with the demands and goals of advanced capitalism. "Recall," Ohmann observes, "some of the things we have traditionally attempted to teach":

> organizing information, drawing conclusions from it, making reports, using Standard English (i.e., the language of the bourgeois elites), solving problems (assignments), keeping one's audience in mind, seeking objectivity and detachment, conducting persuasive arguments, reading either quickly or closely, as circumstances demand, producing work on request and under pressure, valuing the intellect and its achievements. These are all abilities that are clearly useful to the new industrial state, and, to the extent that English departments nourish them—even if only through the agency of graduate assistants—they are giving value for society's money. (Pp. 301-2)

Ohmann states his case with admirable vigor, and his analyses of Advanced Placement Exams, freshman composition texts, the Modern Language Association, and the rise of the New Criticism are often shrewd. But to assert that the skills we teach—"conducting persuasive arguments" and the like—aid and promote the goals of capitalism is a misstatement. Such skills may indeed serve capitalist designs, but they would do the same for any form of social organization. Is the ability to fashion a "persuasive" argument something that only the modern industrial system values? If we change society as Ohmann wishes, then must we renounce respect for "the intellect and its achievements"? For Ohmann to conduct his argument in these terms is the surest way for him to deny his case a serious and sympathetic hearing. His principled commitment to Marxism is commendable, but here he says what he cannot truly believe—that valuing the intellect and its achievements binds us to the capitalist state. In this instance at least, his Marxist terms and tenets badly weaken his argument.

"We either teach politically," Ohmann concludes, "with revolution as our end or we contribute to the mystification that so often in universities diverts and deadens the critical power of literature and encysts it in our safe corner of society" (p. 335). But what does it mean to teach "with revolution as our end"? This is a powerful and courageous affirmation, but Ohmann fails to tell us what "revolutionary" teaching and scholarship look like and how they are to be undertaken. At times he comes close, but he leaves the basic question unanswered: "The literature we are to preserve includes works by Milton, Voltaire, Rousseau, Swift, Goethe, Byron, Blake, Shelley, Carlyle, Shaw, and others of that rebellious ilk. Beyond that, I think it is accurate to say that every good poem, play, or novel, properly read, is revolutionary in that it strikes through well-grooved habits of seeing and understanding" (p. 48). Is the text "good" because it is "revolutionary," or do we compile the list of "good" texts on some other basis and then discover that they are "revolutionary"? I am uncertain whether "good" precedes "revolutionary" (which implies that Ohmann retains his humanistic loyalties) or whether "good" equals "revolutionary."

Nor am I able to grasp what Ohmann means by "properly read," which he tucks between the commas. To call for "proper" reading is far from a "revolutionary" gesture, and this seems to link Ohmann with those servants of capitalism who affirm a "right" and "objective" way to read literary texts. Conspicuously absent here is any account of the manner in which one teaches and guarantees fidelity to "proper reading." Faced with recalcitrant students, would Ohmann be willing to enforce his call for the proper reading of texts? Probably not—which would then imply serious limitations on the effort to teach "with revolution as our end." Ohmann does not perceive that his daily practice as a teacher and critic complicates and cuts against his theory and desire for "revolutionary" action. Ohmann resists authority, yet as a teacher, he possesses a potent form of authority and may well lean towards invoking it—as a matter of principle—in order to encourage "proper" reading among his students.

Though Ohmann's book is flawed, he should be praised for his labors. As Patricia Meyer Spacks has noted, *English in America* has the "real value" of making us consider "tormenting issues too often blandly ignored."[3] In *The Genesis of Secrecy*, Frank Kermode also speaks of the "institution" of literary studies and comments on the "constraints" and "controls" on interpretation. He gives us a book filled with acute and sensitive exegesis, ranging widely among texts that include the Gospels, *Ulysses*, and Henry Green's *Party Going*. Yet he frequently punctuates his analyses with fashionable moanings about the "disappointments" of interpretation. Here are Kermode's final sentences:

> World and book, it may be, are hopelessly plural, endlessly disappointing; we stand alone before them, aware of their arbitrariness and impenetrability, knowing that they may be narratives only because of our impudent intervention, and susceptible of interpretation only by our hermetic tricks. Hot for secrets, our only conversation may be with guardians who learn less and see less than we can; and our sole hope and pleasure is in the perception of a momentary radiance, before the door of disappointment is finally shut on us. (P. 145)

"It may be" is the key phrase: it frees Kermode from having to take seriously his brooding about that disturbing "door of disappointment." "It may be" that this is the way of both the world and the book, but then again it may not be. I find little conviction in Kermode's voice, as he intones the latest dark truths about the human condition ("we stand alone" before world and book). This is a severe judgment, but I do not think that Kermode truly believes what he says here and elsewhere about the disappointment and impossibility of interpretation. To help prove my point, I would simply refer again to the many fine pages of textual criticism in *Genesis of Secrecy* and in the other stimulating books that Kermode has written.[4]

Critics today are addicted to exalted language and appear most contented when reflecting on the "abyss" of meaning, the grave fate of reading, and other somber matters. The so-called Yale Critics—a term made famous by J. Hillis Miller—meditate with much solemnity in their collection of essays, *Deconstruction and Criticism*. Miller, Harold Bloom, Geoffrey Hartman, and Paul De Man all contribute to the book; for readers with a lifetime to spare, there is also a 100-page essay by Jacques Derrida, dealing with a subject yet to be determined. De Man's and Hartman's essays are subtle and rewarding; Miller's, which concentrates on Shelley's "Triumph of Life," is also admirable when it stays focused on the text, for he is a skillful interpreter of the complex workings of figurative language. But Miller gets into trouble when he describes the value of deconstruction: "The ultimate justification for this mode of criticism, as of any conceivable mode, is that it works. It reveals hitherto unidentified meanings and ways of having meaning in major literary texts" (p. 252). This is the triumph of the academic mind: to be able to advocate a theory of interpretive "paralysis" and "undecidability," yet to be reassured that the business of criticism will still bustle along. Deconstruction, Miller emphasizes, "works," in that we now have a new tool for generating more essays on the "major literary texts." Reading and interpretation may be "undecidable," but no one need fear that the traditional canon will be displaced, or that the wheels of criticism will stop turning.

Bloom's "The Breaking of Form" is the most intriguing piece in *Deconstruction and Criticism*. He begins by outlining once again the basic features of his theory of poetic influence, pausing at times to reply to his critics, mostly "British academic journalists" faithful to the legacy of Matthew Arnold, "greatest of School Inspectors" (p. 7). To show his scheme of terms and ratios in action, Bloom closes by interpreting John Ashbery's long poem "Self-Portrait in a Convex Mirror." Bloom is easy to mock, and few appear able to resist the temptation to have fun at his expense.[5] But the truth is that he almost begs to be mocked. Compare two passages:

> Freedom, in a poem, must mean freedom of meaning, the freedom to have a meaning of one's own. (P. 3)

> What is weak is forgettable and will be forgotten. Only strength is memorable; only the capacity to wound gives a healing capacity the chance to endure, and so to be heard. Freedom of meaning is wrested by combat, of meaning against meaning. But this combat consists in a reading encounter, and in an interpretive moment within that encounter. Poetic warfare is conducted by a kind of strong reading that I have called misreading, and here again I enter into an area where I seem to have provoked anxieties. (P. 5)

Both passages suffer from Bloom's prescriptive tone, but the second is more irritating than the first. His point about "freedom" is suggestive and even moving, but then he quickly falls into grandiose phrasing and murky pathos: it is as though he feels that his insights reverberate only when the critic's voice sounds like the lower register of a church organ.

Yet it is also true that much of the criticism of Bloom's work is irresponsible, founded on little reading and less thought. Bloom is deeply responsive to poetry, and his writings reveal an uncomfortably intimate feeling for poetic creation and influence. His major problem is not so much his solemn phrasing and self-important preaching as it is the split in his books between his theory and his practical criticism. Even his detractors often refer to Bloom's incisive reading of texts, however disenchanted they might be with the theory's terms, charts, and ratios. But the reverse seems to me closer to the truth: Bloom's theories about poetry are far more interesting and persuasive than his actual readings of poems. And it is because the textual interpretations offered in *A Map of Misreading* (1975), *Poetry and Repression* (1976), *Figures of Capable Imagination* (1976), *Wallace Stevens: The Poems of Our Climate* (1977), and other books are badly rendered and unconvincing that Bloom is confronted with an "influence" problem of his own: everybody knows about his theories, but no one can remember (or even understand) his remarks on individual poems.

Bloom has been articulating his theoretical tenets for years, yet he appears oddly incapable of applying them to specific texts. This is not, as it might seem, a reflection on the inadequacy of the theory of poetic influence itself; when Bloom addresses problems of "form," "allusion," "misreading," "poetic freedom," and "traditions," he is very interesting. It may be simply that Bloom and his readers wrongly expect that his theory must validate itself in practical criticism, the kind of "close reading" that has become familiar to us through the work of the New Critics and their successors. Bloom may yet devise a practical criticism that testifies to the uncanny rightness of his theory. Right now, however, he is trying to provide what he and his readers expect to find— "practical" examples that authenticate the theory—and not succeeding.

Bloom's contempt for Matthew Arnold would surely dismay Eugene Goodheart, whose subject in *The Failure of Criticism* is the collapse of "humanist criticism." "Humanist criticism," he explains, "which has as its object the quality of life as well as works of art, no longer has authority" (p. 8). Carlyle, Ruskin, and Arnold represent this tradition in the nineteenth century, and its modern exemplars include F. R. Leavis, Lionel Trilling, Raymond Williams, and Ortega y Gasset. But this great tradition has lost its power, undercut by the triumph of "modernism" in literature and criticism. "Humanism," Goodheart argues, "is rooted in moral values or pieties, which radical modernism with its profound passion for uncovering the amoral process of reality is bent on destroying" (p. 15). "Modernist virtues act as corrosives, subverting all tacit, unexamined acceptances and beliefs. The impulse to bring everything into the light, to rationalize the world, may represent a will to knowledge and mastery (an ambition of modernism), but it also may undermine deep, unquestioning commitment to institutions, activities, and people, the kind of commitment that sustains life" (p. 13).

Goodheart states his verdict sharply, but his phrasing slides into vagueness. An "unquestioning" commitment? To what kinds of "institutions, activities, and people," and in what measure should each be endorsed? The description is too general to have much point. "Sustains life" is admirable, but also empty; the looseness of Goodheart's writing here is a serious shortcoming in his book as a whole. He is a sensible critic, and his project in *The Failure of Criticism*—demonstrating the effects of modernism on critical authority—is well conceived. But my respect for the conception keeps being strained by passages like this one:

> Contrast is the mode through which Arnold's irony manifests itself—and that irony presupposes a secure conviction about different and opposed realms of value. The conviction animates not only the critical essay but also the imaginative literature which criticism sustains, reflects, and understands. Implicit in Dickens's *Hard Times*, George Eliot's *Middlemarch*, Lawrence's *Women in Love* are those contrasts which appear so vividly on the surface of the essays of Arnold and Leavis. (P. 3)

It is questionable whether these novels can be grouped in this way, seen to be informed by a "secure conviction" about opposed value systems. Lawrence's novel, for example, is a far more turbulent text than Goodheart's argument allows. As Scott Sanders, Roger Sale, Leo Bersani, and others have shown, one of the most fascinating things about *Women in Love* is Lawrence's doubt about what he values and his uneasy recognition that value systems cannot be securely separated from and set against each other. *Women in Love* begins with questions, debates, and disagreements, and it ends with more of the same. Too anxious to enlist Dickens, Eliot, and Lawrence in common cause with Arnold, Goodheart blots out the significant differences among them and clouds their writings with "humanist" phrasing.

One of the dangers of humanist criticism is that it reduces complex texts in order to make them serve social and cultural aims. Important distinctions are blurred, as very different writers, such as Arnold and Lawrence, are invoked as spokesmen for the same tradition and values. Nowhere is this danger more evident than in the writings of Lionel Trilling, whose reputation seems to be on the verge of a renaissance after a period of decline. Goodheart refers to him approvingly, and books and many essays have begun to appear on his work.[6] The major monument is the twelve-volume "Uniform Edition of the Works of Lionel Trilling" that is being published by Harcourt Brace Jovanovich. *Prefaces to the Experience of Literature* and *The Last Decade* are the two most recent volumes in the series, and both have already been acclaimed. Both, however, strike me as weak and disappointing, and they reflect significant failings in Trilling's work. As I indicated in chapter seven, many teachers and critics in these post-structuralist and deconstructionist times feel drawn to admire what Trilling appears to represent so well: the humanist critic, attuned not only to the classic texts but also to the dilemmas of culture and society in the modern age. But Trilling should not be the writer we choose as our authority.

Roger Sale once remarked that Trilling is much better in the actual reading than in the memory. But for me, the idea of Trilling, which one vaguely recalls from the reading, is far more attractive than what one receives in the reading itself. In *Prefaces*, for instance, Trilling comments well about *King Lear*, noting that "one way in which the play manifests its intention of assault is by its refusal of artistic economy in favor of redundancy and excess" (p. 11). But most of the commentary on other plays and novels is extremely generalized, condescending in tone, and out of touch with the language of the texts. When Trilling does engage the text in his section on poetry, he is often strangely blind to what is going on. He observes that the "erotic content" of "To His Coy Mistress" is of "a quite explicit kind" (p. 203); yet he then wonders and worries about the phrases "roll all our strength, and all our sweetness, up into one Ball," and "the Iron Gates of Life" without displaying any awareness of their sexual impact. For Trilling, texts rarely have verbal toughness or edge. Concerned with always presenting the grand overview, he glides over the words that enable us to see it in the first place and ends up simplifying the texts.

Prefaces consists of short essays that Trilling wrote for an anthology he edited; in fairness, it should be remembered that he was writing for an undergraduate audience. But these essays merely make more obvious the flaws and tendencies in the rest of Trilling's criticism. In *The Last Decade*, he talks down to his readers as though they were undergraduates in the lecture-hall: the disquieting truths about the modern world have rarely been stated in such well-lubricated prose. His essay "Why We Read Jane Austen" (pp. 204-25) is greatly admired, yet it is an embarrassing performance that proceeds from the disingenuous assumption that the 150 students who showed up for Trilling's seminar on Austen were more interested in her novels than in taking a class from Columbia's best-known man-of-letters. Trilling is very much a performer; his style is that of a distinguished eminence whose authority and reputation place him above the fray. Most of his essays, however, have dated badly. Little force remains in the writing, and what looms largest is Trilling's desire always to make the authoritative statement, in mannered cadences, on whatever problem wins his attention. *Sincerity and Authenticity* (1972) is probably his best book, but even here he takes advantage of the texts he treats, misreading and under-reading them in order to fit them into the overall scheme. The famous final chapter of this book, which closes with an attack on Norman O. Brown and R. D. Laing, is powerful. But Trilling knows that we will welcome his words: he has chosen an easy target. This does not mean that his convictions are insincere but does suggest, to me at least, that he should not be roundly applauded for expressing them. His audience's assent is never in doubt.

In returning to Trilling in this chapter after having already judged him severely in the previous one, I will doubtless strike some readers as being guilty of overkill. But I think a two-pronged critique is required, not because it gives me pleasure to evaluate this eminent critic in harsh terms twice but because his work is tempting a good many readers into accepting a pious and sentimental conception of their enterprise. What Trilling offers is very seductive, and when he is at his best, the moral vision he articulates compels respect and allegiance. But a plodding quality often enters into Trilling's prose—this is evident in both his critical books and his novel, *The Middle of the Journey*—and it is at these moments that one feels the limits of his concerns and the conservative temper of his thought. It is not that one necessarily objects to his conservatism, but more that one senses that Trilling is presenting it in the form of a liberal openness to writers, ideas, and trends that the die-hard conservative would disdain. There is indeed something admirable about Trilling's encounters with Freud, Nietzsche, and the other modern masters, but there is something exploitative as well—a determination to enlist these authors to serve Trilling's own jaded view of the times.

F. R. Leavis has also received considerable attention recently, and I want to return to him in this chapter as well.[7] Many of the same people who admire Trilling also hold Leavis in high esteem; criticism and the moral life, culture and society, the horrors of modernism—these are their shared concerns. But Leavis's writings have more successfully stood the test of time, and he is the superior critic. The last part of Leavis's career is admittedly a problem; his final books are too often shrill, intolerant, hectoring in tone, and drastically reduced in their range of responsiveness.[8] But during his long and productive career, Leavis wrote several of the major critical books of this century, and one way of distinguishing him from Trilling is to compare *Revaluation, The Great Tradition, D. H. Lawrence: Novelist*, and *The Common Pursuit*, which are still provocative today, to any three or four of Trilling's books, which seem books of their time, not our own.

The Living Principle, while sometimes strident in its language and sour in its attitudes, is nevertheless an important book. It collects several of Leavis's best essays on "judgment and analysis," framing them with a long introduction and a detailed treatment (running to 100 pages) of *Four Quartets*. But the book's importance lies less in what it says about Shakespeare, Lawrence, and Eliot than in its status as an act of testimony on behalf of literature and English studies. "In major literary works," Leavis insists, "we have the fullest use of language" (p. 44); "literature [is] the supreme creative art of language" (p. 49). Leavis is committed to "English" as a "discipline of thought," and he declares its continuity to be essential for the "health" of society. No modern critic speaks more forcefully about the value of studying literature, and it is a sign of our depleted condition that many of us shrink from, or feel an uneasiness about, or (worst of all) mock and mimic Leavis's affirmations.

Leavis's principles, as I suggested in chapter seven, are more admirable than his practice. Early in *The Living Principle*, he refers to the "form" in which judgments should be expressed: "The form of a judgment is 'This is so, isn't it?', the question asking for confirmation that the thing is so, but prepared for an answer in the form, 'yes, but—', the 'but' standing for corrections, refinements, precisions, amplifications" (p. 35). This is a fine plea for open-mindedness and tolerance, and it shows that critical exchange is central to (really constitutive of) the Leavisite notion of "community." But when Leavis judges a text in practice—and here one recalls his infamous remarks about the writings of Hardy, Woolf, Auden, Eliot, and others—he slashes off the "but," forestalling any impulse we might have to argue with him. "Yes, but" implies a give-and-take in critical exchange and debate; positions are stated, are wrestled with, and alter their shape through dialogue. "Judgment," a process worked out in time, thus has a real and rich historical dimension. Unfortunately, Leavis's statements of his own acts of judgment are almost always firmly closed, as though not needing any revision. The later Leavis writes for those who already agree with him; his style is not a technique for persuasion, nor does it seek to extend its scope by inviting "additions" and "corrections." One of the reasons for the badness of much of the later Leavis is that he believes his audience is small in number; he has become so pessimistic about his audience that he speaks more to himself than to others. He sounds at times like an Old Testament prophet, keeping the faith not because he assumes that anyone will heed his words but because of an urgent sense of duty.

While Leavis's case reveals the hazards of making judgments, it does not mean that judgment is not a necessary part of critical practice. Evaluative criticism has obvious risks; in our roles as critics and teachers, we can easily turn into new forcers of conscience. But to deny the place of judgment, and to dismiss it (as does Northrop Frye, for example) as comprising the "history of taste," is to devalue the discipline. Though we should not take our authority lightly, we should be confident enough to express it—confident enough to say where we stand and to argue for what we believe is good, remembering the "but" at the end of Leavis's prescription. Judgment is "necessary"—as necessary as it is difficult.[9] And Leavis's example should serve as both an inspiration and a warning. His judgments are vitalized by a dedication to literature and criticism we ought to emulate, but they are also a display of power, one that repels the creative "collaboration" that his principles encourage.

Leavis's judgments must be met with questioning and resistance, even if his critical tactics do not readily allow for them. By engaging in this kind of exchange, and by defining and explaining our valuations, we can help to restore the critical function of English studies. Judgment-making and debate have their dangers: one wishes neither to tyrannize nor to lapse into veneration of "the best that has been thought and said." But making firm judgments is clearly preferable to the vagueness we find in Trilling and Goodheart, and clearly better than the melancholy posturing of Kermode and the deconstructionists. Among the critics I have reviewed, perhaps Bloom, so profoundly different from Leavis, offers the best example of passionate judgment. Bloom is engaged in canon-formation, though his fascination with terms and categories obscures this aspect of his work. He does not fully articulate his judgments and their impact on a revised canon, but these are evident in his books, as when he compares Yeats and Stevens with Eliot and Pound. Much more than merely stating preferences is needed for any evaluative act to be persuasive and make an impact: evaluation does not mean an inventory of one's likes and dislikes. But as these examples testify, Bloom is mapping a new literary history that is opposed to the poetic "great tradition" that Leavis describes. These two critics can therefore be seen in a critical dialogue and dispute that we can join. Evaluation is not final, made once and for all for us simply to follow. Because making judgments is tied to the formation of the literary canon, the life of our critical community, and the value and immediate relevance of our work as teachers, it is a necessary part of ongoing critical labor.

It is a curious fact of critical history in this century that the major "evaluative" critics, the critics whose judgments decisively altered our understanding of poetic tradition, either were non-academics—Eliot, Pound—or were academics—Leavis is the best example—whose relation to the institution was marginal. The absence of judgment-making among academics is striking, though perhaps understandable (if still unacceptable) when one realizes what it means to have a "field of specialization" and how this affects critical work. Choosing an author or period as one's field obviously represents a commitment that bears on the shape of one's career, opportunities for promotion and tenure, outlets for publications and lectures. One can select a field either because one loves the material or because one knows what the rewards will be. One hopes that neither of these reasons for choice will necessarily exclude the other; it is an inevitable part of institutional life that motives are usually "professional" as well as scholarly. But it is nevertheless important to acknowledge that specialization entails, most of the time, a loss of the ability to speak generally about literature and criticism, a loss of the capacity to interpret and judge the common practices of the discipline as a whole.

Certain fields have become so massive—they are industrial kingdoms—that judgment and discrimination play almost no part in them; in the face of such an outpouring of material, judgments are unlikely to do much good or have significant effect. Usually these fields consist of work by and about major authors: Shakespeare, Milton, Melville, James, Lawrence, Joyce. There are societies and journals devoted to these authors, and as the academic economy expands on its upper levels—even as it contracts on its lower levels—we will undoubtedly see many other authors treated in this fashion. It is hard to press this observation without seeming anti-intellectual, as though one were opposed to the intensive study of texts and the production of commentaries. But I think that the unfortunate truth is that this policy of ever-narrowing fields, already ingrained in the discipline and becoming more deeply so, tends to eliminate judgment as an essential aspect of criticism. Critics and teachers too often end up asking only the questions about authors and texts that their "field" legitimizes. They do not benefit from the enabling insights—and necessary sense of relative value and proportion—that result from extensive knowledge about other fields and the practices of other disciplines.

I now turn to the field of Milton criticism, which exhibits some of the disturbing tendencies I have noted: the lack of contact with other fields and disciplines, the decline of true rigor and judgment, the repetition of familiar debates and arguments. Several of Eliot's and Leavis's most influential essays focused on Milton, and interpretations of his poetry helped to redraw the map of literary and critical history. It is a depressing commentary on the form and direction of much academic labor that "Milton criticism," now consolidated as a field of specialization, has shown a marked falling off in vitality, power, and cultural impact.

Reflections on the Milton Industry

Milton's poetical reputation stands today as high as ever. Yet Milton needs to be defended from his defenders almost more than from the declining band of his enemies.

Christopher Hill, *Milton and the English Revolution*

Robert Crosman. *Reading Paradise Lost*. Bloomington: Indiana University Press, 1980.

James A. Freeman. *Milton and the Martial Muse*. Princeton, N.J.: Princeton University Press, 1980.

Murray Roston. *Milton and the Baroque*. Pittsburgh, Pa.: University of Pittsburgh Press, 1980.

Roland Mushat Frye. *Milton's Imagery and the Visual Arts: Iconographic Tradition in the Epic Poems*. Princeton, N.J.: Princeton University Press, 1978.

Edward W. Tayler. *Milton's Poetry: Its Development in Time*. Pittsburgh, Pa.: Duquesne University Press, 1979.

G. K. Hunter. *Paradise Lost*. London: George Allen and Unwin, 1980.

Though the numbers of new books and articles might appear to suggest otherwise, Milton criticism is in bad shape. All of the books examined here are informative, and the historical research in several of them is impressive. But I find the experience of reading and writing about these books to be a dispiriting task, because they do not, on the whole, say much that is really new and insightful about Milton's major poems.

These books are disappointing for two reasons. The first is that almost none of the writers seems aware of the work in literary theory and methodology that has been done in the past two decades. Barthes, Foucault, Derrida, Althusser, Lacan—these figures and others are absent from nearly all of the books. If one were to go by the state of Milton criticism, one would have no inkling that recent theoretical discussion has dramatically changed the way we understand poetic "influence," "tradition," "authorship and authority," the literary "canon," and related topics. Other fields—nineteenth-century English and American literature, for example—have greatly profited from this theoretical work. But Milton studies remains as conservative as ever, doggedly refusing (or else simply unable) to ask questions about methodology. And in this respect, it demonstrates that theoretical modes and models—however foregrounded they appear to be at present—have not affected all fields of study to the same degree.

It is, of course, a difficult task to shift the terms of a field as entrenched as Milton criticism, where the debates and arguments about the texts are clearly marked. But a wholesale change in terms is not required as much as a re-examination of those that are being used now. Milton criticism makes the largest assumptions about theory and method with cavalier ease. And because one writer after another follows these same assumptions and seems unwilling to question terms, the work in the field comes to strike the reader as strangely dated at the very moment of its appearance.

More than just a lack of theoretical awareness accounts for the dismaying state of Milton criticism. To an extent that is unusual in critical writing, the field is dominated by the issues raised in two books: A. J.

A. Waldock's *Paradise Lost and Its Critics* (1947) and Stanley Fish's *Surprised by Sin: The Reader in Paradise Lost* (1967). Though generalizations are difficult to make about the densely populated world of Milton criticism, it is true, I think, to say that most books on Milton's poetry defer to, supplement, or quarrel with Waldock and/or Fish. These two critics have focused the key issues and debates, and they have obliged other critics to follow their leads.

Waldock's book is the major piece of what might be called anti-Milton criticism. Ezra Pound, F. R. Leavis, and T. S. Eliot had sniped at *Paradise Lost* in essays and reviews and had clearly shifted appraisals of the poem, but it was Waldock who presented the case against Milton in a sustained manner. He argued that *Paradise Lost* is "divided" and at odds with itself. Milton adheres to a doctrine that condemns Satan, yet he responds positively to the fallen angel's courage, energy, and refusal to surrender. The narrative thus tends in one direction, while the poet's doctrinal commitment takes both him and his reader in a different one that is "counter" to the forceful narrative through which Milton relates Satan's exploits. This opposition or split, Waldock contends, can be found everywhere in the poem; another way of putting this is to recognize the gap between Milton's aims and his achievement:

> In reading *Paradise Lost*, we must not always expect to find that Milton's intention is perfectly matched by his performance—that what he meant to do in any given case has always its exact counterpart in what he did. Similarily (it is another aspect of the same principle) we must not always expect to find that what he has done is perfectly matched by his theory of what he has done; it is quite possible that the view he wishes us to take of a certain matter—the view, perhaps, that he himself, because of the prescriptions of his theme, is compelled to take—may not be in exact accord with the matter as he has actually presented it.[10]

In *Surprised by Sin*, Fish observes that Waldock is responding to something that is "there" in *Paradise Lost* but insists that Milton intends these effects. Milton seeks to "educate" his reader, to make his reader perceive that the divisions and conflicts that appear to lie in the poem are, in fact, reflections of our fallen nature. Milton demands that the reader confront the fact that human corruption and sinfulness lead us astray; we admire Satan, feel angry at God (William Empson once referred to Milton's God as "Uncle Joe Stalin"), and identify with Adam and Eve to the point of wanting to defend their sinful choice. On his first page, Fish neatly summarizes his argument and clarifies his dispute with Waldock: (1) The poem's center of reference is its reader, who is also its subject; (2) Milton's purpose is to educate the reader to an awareness of his position and responsibilities as a fallen man and to a sense of the distance that separates him from the innocence once his;

(3) Milton's method is to re-create in the mind of the reader (which is, finally, the poem's scene) the drama of the Fall, to make him fall again exactly as Adam did and with Adam's troubled clarity, that is to say, "not deceiv'd." Whereas Waldock objects to the deployment of doctrine in the poem, Fish embraces it.

> Submitting to the style of the poem is an act of self-humiliation. Like all heroic acts it is a decision to subordinate the self to a higher ideal, one by-product of which is the discovery of the true self. The imperative is "read" and by not giving up, by not closing the book, by accepting the challenge of self-criticism and self-knowledge, one learns how to read, and by extension how to live, and becomes finally the Christian hero who is, after all, the only fit reader. In the end, the education of Milton's reader, the identification of his hero, and the description of his style, that is, of its effects, are one.[11]

The relations between narrative and doctrine, poetic effect and intention, are obviously weighty and problematical aspects of *Paradise Lost*, and Waldock and Fish have done an admirable job in setting out the basic arguments. But they may have done their job too well, if the books re-viewed here are any indication. Milton's critics keep returning to Waldock's and Fish's books, quoting the same speeches—Satan's declamations in book I, for instance—and making only minor adjustments in answering the familiar questions: Is there a separation between narrative and doctrine? What is Milton's intention and what does he actually achieve? What is (or should be) the response of the reader? With the form of the debate determined by Waldock and Fish, and with Milton criticism cut off from advances in literary theory, it is no wonder that reading new books on Milton can often feel more of a burden than a pleasure. As Milton often warns us, appearances can be deceiving, and an array of books, dealing with a wide range of subjects (the baroque, visual arts and iconography, imagery), does not necessarily imply that a field of study is vital, modern in its orientation, and truly moving forward.

Robert Crosman's *Reading Paradise Lost* is indebted to Fish's examination of the reader's role. In his preface, Crosman characterizes *Surprised by Sin* as "a classic of literary criticism" (p. xi) and adds, a few pages later, that it is "the best book ever written on *Paradise Lost*" (p. 13). Crosman has also learned from Fish's theoretical articles, in particular "Literature in the Reader: Affective Stylistics,"[12] to which he acknowledges "a large intellectual debt" (p. 250). And so his book confirms one trend in Milton criticism—the special place accorded to *Surprised by Sin*—and also seems to be an exception to the rule that Miltonists are anti-theoretical and not alert to methodological issues.

Crosman offers stimulating analyses of the poem's "paradoxical techniques," narration, and interplay between Christian and epic norms. He discusses the forms of self-division that appear in the speeches of the "fallen" characters, pointing out that this "inner dialectic, the charge and counter-charge of a soul at war with itself, is the style Milton reserves for fallen beings" (p. 90). Crosman's concluding chapter on the final books of *Paradise Lost*, though dependent on Fish's study of them, is also excellent, and provides a fine overview of Milton's attitudes in the poem towards "reading" and "interpretation." But while Crosman gives us valuable analyses of specific episodes and scenes, he has larger ambitions, hoping to present a "fresh look" at Milton's epic and revise our understanding of the "reader." It is here, in the theoretical and methodological part of the book, that Crosman gets into trouble.

Crosman sees his work as liberating us from the problems that beset other analyses of the "reader." Other critics, he states, "prescribe responses," "imposing" on modern readers a definition of the seventeenth-century reader. *Surprised by Sin* is marred by Fish's determination to force his modern reader into a Christian mold: "Fish suggests that Milton's fit reader come equipped with an entire baggage of seventeenth-century Puritan habits of mind" (p. 11). Crosman is certainly right to raise the question (though it has been raised before—by Lawrence Hyman, for example) of how Milton's Christian epic ought to be read and interpreted in a secular age.[13] But he seems oddly unaware of the ways in which his argument against "prescriptive" forms of criticism can be turned on his own approach. He repeatedly chastises critics who "impose" and "prescribe" responses. Yet over and over again, Crosman engages in the grandest kinds of prescriptive criticism.

"Instead of prescribing responses," says Crosman, "we can describe them." Well and good. But the kicker arrives in the next sentence, when he declares that "this is possible because of art's universality, and because of the common humanity all readers share" (p. 15). Apparently Crosman finds nothing prescriptive here at all: he feels he is simply reporting the truth. *Reading Paradise Lost* contains sweeping, heavy-handed statements about poets, art, and readers, and at no time does Crosman imply or acknowledge that he is imposing his own views about literature on his audience. Here are just a few of many examples:

> One quality of superior art is its capacity to disorient the reader, to surprise him and undermine his preconceptions, without of course losing him completely. (Pp. 6-7)

> Rhetorically speaking, the purpose of art is to address the basic human being, to make him see and feel not simply the local issues of particular time and place, but the underlying problems that repeat themselves in changing forms throughout human history. (P. 15)

We ordinarily come to literature to dispel the ambiguities of "real life"; in *Paradise Lost* we find them exacerbated. (P. 32)

Crosman is to be praised for his attempt to bring theoretical sophistication to Milton criticism. But his book shows how far Miltonists have to go in order to achieve an awareness of what it means to be a self-conscious critic, sensitive to the implications of one's statements and methodological moves. Crosman offers no apologies for his method (p. 17) but does not realize that the claim he modestly makes is the biggest claim of all: his "method," he explains, "is not much more than common sense and common experience applied with determination" (p. 17).

Theory and methodology hold no interest for James A. Freeman in *Milton and the Martial Muse*. "There has been debate," he remarks in a footnote about halfway through the book, "about the notion of a poet's audience" (p. 113). Freeman tells us that he does not wish to get involved in "taking sides here," but will "simply assume that often-repeated ideas indicate an interested public"; he then gives references to essays by Walter Ong and Robert Crosman (whose authority as a theorist might be questioned). Freeman is making a major assumption, one that bears directly on the relation that he seeks to establish between the "European traditions of war" and the audience that Milton is attempting to reach in *Paradise Lost*. Yet he phrases this assumption in such loose terms that he drains it of all force and impact, and fobs off the responsibility on Crosman and Ong. *Milton and the Martial Muse* is a cogent review of Renaissance attitudes towards combat, soldiering, and military heroism, and is the product of diligent research. But the book suffers from an impoverished sense of its own terms and method, as the phrases quoted above suggest. It is as though it were enough merely to juxtapose the research and the relevant passages of the poem, without attending to the nature of the correspondence, what it takes for granted, and what kinds of interpretation it ought to be subjected to.

Too often in *Milton and the Martial Muse*, Freeman gathers his source materials in order to make a straightforward and unsurprising point. In his chapter on Satan, he presents an interesting account of military leadership as described in the "martial manuals" and argues that the fallen angel embodies many characteristics of such a grand leader. "Reacting to his defeat in the manner recommended," Satan "composes himself, musters his despondent legions, harangues them optimistically, consults with his staff, announces new strategy to the assembled troops, and sets off on a scouting expedition" (p. 113). This is an accurate summary of Satan's behavior, but it is also a basic one; we can accept it whatever our response is to the historical information that Freeman has provided. Freeman has not done much more than confirm the obvious. Readers of *Milton and the Martial Muse* will be grateful for this excellent survey of the terms and concepts of Renaissance warfare. Interpretations of *Paradise Lost*, however, will stay pretty much intact.

The same point applies to Murray Roston's *Milton and the Baroque* and Roland Mushat Frye's *Milton's Imagery and the Visual Arts*. Both critics clearly love Milton's poetry, have read and absorbed all the scholarship, and, particularly in Frye's case, have expended tremendous time and energy in laboring to recover the "contexts" and "back-grounds" for Milton's epics. But I both respect these books and am disappointed by them; in keeping with nearly all writing on Milton, they show little awareness of theory and methodology and make no effort to consider the form and implications of their analyses.

Frye's book is much more substantial than Roston's, and hence its shortcomings in this regard are more to be lamented. Frye's contention is that "if we are to understand and appreciate Milton's visual descrip-tions," we "must look not only to the natural world but especially to the great panorama of paintings, mosaics, and sculptures which rep-resent the same subjects and personalities which form the center of Milton's epic concern" (p. 3). Frye has many stimulating things to say. His discussion of the influence of landscape gardening on Milton's conception of Eden is excellent, and his commentary on the physical appearance of Adam and Eve is often illuminating. He notes, for ex-ample, that "a curious exception to the general likeness of Milton's Adam to the Adams of the Renaissance and later art is what Milton refers to as his '''parted forelock','' adding that "we know two men who wore their hair with a parted forelock just like that of Milton's Adam: they were Oliver Cromwell and John Milton" (p. 272). He also maintains that Milton's "repeated descriptions of Adam and Eve walk-ing hand in hand" are a "striking innovation, for which there was only the slightest pictorial precedence and reinforcement" (p. 285). These are significant details that testify to the intimacy that Milton feels for his characters, and it is in these sorts of curiosities and discoveries that the achievement of Frye's book primarily rests.

In a provocative essay, Joseph Wittreich has listed Frye's errors, oversights, omissions, and simplifications.[14] The major shortcoming in *Milton's Imagery and the Visual Arts* lies, however, not in the kinds of evidence that Frye collects, but in his minimal attention to what the evidence signifies. Frye assumes that Milton was "influenced" by the visual arts, that he "depended" on them, that they were a "stimulus" to his imagination, that he drew from many "sources and analogues," that his poetic descriptions have many "parallels" in Medieval and Renaissance art. Frye goes about his business in an informative way, but it is regrettable that he never speculates about the meaning of these terms. Nowhere does he cite and deal with the work of Harold Bloom,

Edward W. Said, Claudio Guillen, and others who have explored the meaning of influence, origins, and sources. Many critics—the most impressive being Michael Fried—have investigated the relations between verbal and visual arts, but Frye appears unaware of their writings. Though there is much to admire in *Milton's Imagery and the Visual Arts*, it is at times frustrating to read, because while a great amount of material is brought forward, it mostly remains barely interpreted, analyzed, and judged. Passages from *Paradise Lost* and *Paradise Regained* are quoted, and then compared, usually in a superficial way, with paintings, mosaics, and sculpture that Milton might have borrowed from. Frye then moves ahead to the next passage, again not pausing to comment on the verse in detail and failing to treat the complexities of his examples from the visual arts.

After reading Freeman, Roston, and Frye, I am inclined to suggest that Miltonists study Barthes's *Critique et Vérité* (1966), Foucault's *L'Ar-chéologie du Savoir* (1969) and *L'Ordre du Discours* (1971), Said's *Beginnings: Intention and Method* (1975), and Jameson's *Marxism and Form* (1971). They can then proceed to Culler's *Structuralist Poetics* (1975), Graff's *Literature against Itself* (1979), and Lentricchia's *After the New Criticism* (1980). Unfortunately, Miltonists seem to pride themselves on not falling for the "theorizing" that has affected work in other fields; even as I make my suggestion, I am aware that it is not likely to be taken seriously: the anti-theoretical habits of Milton's critics are proudly held. But this refusal to reflect upon methodology and theory damages the books that are now being written. The historical research is valuable, but it is barely investigated, scrutinized, puzzled over. Too often it sits like an "untransmuted lump" (to borrow C. S. Lewis's unkind phrase about the final books of *Paradise Lost*). The critics assume a self-evident rightness and relevance about the material they gather, and hence feel no obligation to query what it means. Thirty years ago, A. S. P. Woodhouse—a fine historian himself—complained about the absence of any real "theory" for the historical criticism he and others practiced. "Historical students of literature," he remarked, "have tended to work by a silent instinct of accumulation like the bee."[15] The theoretical debates about criticism and history have advanced and become more contentious since Woodhouse's essay appeared. But you would never know this from reading Freeman's, Roston's, and Frye's books. They are just the kind of thing that Woodhouse, back in 1951, was talking about.

Edward Tayler's *Milton's Poetry: Its Development in Time* and G. K. Hunter's *Paradise Lost* show that all is not lost in the world of Milton criticism. Both are excellent, and it is a pleasure now to turn to them. Neither critic views himself as a theorist, but both Tayler and Hunter are subtle and self-conscious writers, and as a result, they demonstrate a more analytical and rigorous attitude towards their key terms than do the other Miltonists I have discussed.

Tayler examines Milton's themes of "time and eternity" and indicates the complex ways in which the poet strives to "comprehend" them in his verse. As he acknowledges, Tayler is indebted to Barbara Lewalski, Frank Kermode, and others who have explored the poetic "representation" of time, "fictions" of the end, chronos and kairos. But Tayler's treatment of these subjects, as well as his related commentary on allegory and typology, is informed and judicious. He is a solid historian and knows how to make use of his source materials and references, as his perceptive study of the use of scriptural echoes in "Lycidas" reveals. Tayler is also a thoughtful reader of texts and is particularly good on "juxtaposition and enjambement" in *Paradise Lost*. His account of "proleptic form," irony, and "riddling images" in *Samson Agonistes*, and his analysis of Milton's concept of "heroism" in *Paradise Regained*, are also noteworthy.

Milton's Poetry: Its Development in Time is weakened by two omissions, the first in Tayler's critique of books XI and XII of *Paradise Lost* and the second in his chapter on *Samson Agonistes*. In surveying structures of time and eternity in *Paradise Lost*, Tayler quickly comes to focus on the final books, describing their representation of Milton's "visionary" attitude towards history and the promise of salvation. But Tayler surprisingly refrains from dealing with one of the most puzzling sections of these final books—the description of the Flood and the terrible end of Paradise. In His goodness, the archangel Michael tells Adam, God allows the "one just man," Noah, to escape the Flood and save himself from a "world devote to universal rack" (XI, 818, 821). "No sooner he with them," Michael explains,

> of Man and beast
> Select for life shall in the Ark be lodg'd,
> And shelter'd round, but all the Cataracts
> Of Heav'n set open on the Earth shall pour
> Rain day and night, all fountains of the Deep
> Broke up, shall heave the Ocean to usurp
> Beyond all bounds, till inundation rise
> Above the highest hills: then shall this Mount
> Of Paradise by might of Waves be mov'd
> Out of this place, push'd by the horned flood,
> With all his verdure spoil'd, and Trees adrift
> Down the great River to the op'ning Gulf,
> And there take root an Island salt and bare,
> The haunt of Seals and Orcs, and Sea-mews' clang.
> To teach thee that God attributes to place
> No sanctity, if none be thither brought
> By men who there frequent, or therein dwell.

(XI, lines 822-38)

Here Milton depicts the destruction of the Mount of Paradise, but even more painfully to the point is that this passage displays the poet imagining the violation of what he himself has created—the Eden portrayed as a place of teeming vitality and wonder in the earlier books of the poem. Coleridge once observed that when we read Milton, we feel his "presence" in "every line," and perhaps this is nowhere else brought home to us so vividly. These are grim and relentless lines, their surging energy driving towards the doctrinal lesson that "sanctity" lies in men, not in places. There is something fiercely courageous—if also self-punishing—about Milton's determination to make clear what happened to Eden: he emphasizes what doctrine tells us at the expense of the Edenic landscape he has created. "No poet compares to Milton," Harold Bloom has stated, "in his intensity of self-consciousness as an artist and in his ability to overcome all the negative consequences of such concern."[16] And this "self-consciousness" is bound up with Milton's willingness to act critically, even self-destructively, towards his own writing. He presents magnificent fictions and then undoes them as forcefully as he can.

Tayler does not adequately examine the deep ironies of the close of *Paradise Lost*; books XI and XII seem more embittered and hard-edged than his account suggests. In his discussion of *Samson Agonistes*, he shows a better awareness of the implacable ironies of the text, but here again he does not go far enough. He sees the play as always directing us towards the future, towards "the 'Divine prediction' that Samson 'Should Israel from Philistian yoke deliver'" (p. 39). "Samson has fulfilled, between the pillars at the hour precise of noon, the hope that Milton, at the age of twenty-three, had held for himself: that if man has 'the grace to use it so', 'all is' in time 'as ever' in the eye of the eternal task-master, whose 'Still and Silent Path' may be searched only in riddling fashion until the 'last Close' that coincides with the tempestivity of time" (p. 122). Tayler underestimates the uncertainty and doubt that vex Samson's (and the reader's) efforts to know when the "last Close" occurs. In an act that Woodhouse has described as "savage revenge," Samson pulls down the temple on the Philistines and himself; the problem that the play sets for its hero and its audience is the nature of this act, what motivates it, what it implies about God's justice, what it says about the possibilities for human initiative. One might in fact argue that in *Samson Agonistes*, "the last Close" is beyond the capacity of our interpretive power to know; God's ways are mysterious, and we, like Samson, can only *hope* to know them. Manoa and the Chorus do indulge in a good deal of mutual self-congratulation about their place in the Providential scheme of things. But their glowing words about the clarity of God's ways highlight, by contrast, the solitary attempt that Samson makes to know what God intends for him to do.

At the "close" of *Samson Agonistes*, Samson does seem to fulfill the promise that he will deliver his people from the Philistines. "But the Bible tells us," Northrop Frye recalls,

> that in a few years the Philistines were stronger than ever. In the Book of Judges, the account of Samson is immediately followed by another story about the Danites in which, after appearing in a most contemptible light as idolaters, thieves, and murderers, they vanish from history. In Jacob's prophecy of the twelve tribes at the end of Genesis, Dan is described as treacherous, and in the list of the twelve tribes in the Book of Revelation the name of Dan is omitted. For Milton this would practically mean being erased from the book of life.[17]

Tayler's understanding of *Samson Agonistes* is complex, and I do not want to downplay his awareness of the text's ironic structure. But he appears too intent upon validating the Chorus's final statement of "calm of mind, all passion spent" (line 1758), and this leads him not to follow through on key questions about the place of Samson's act in time.

Tayler finely treats the ways in which Milton's poetry reveals temporal moments bearing the sign or impress of "eternity." But as G. K. Hunter suggests in his study of *Paradise Lost*, Milton's art is, paradoxically, luminously clear and darkly problematical. *Paradise Lost* is "poised," "formally as well as doctrinally, between the search for causes and the perception that cause, history, progression are temporal irrelevancies, as incapable of explaining freedom as time is of explaining eternity" (p. 63). Milton believes in, and is committed to demonstrating, the truths of Christian doctrine. Yet he also recognizes, and never tries to conceal from his reader, that doctrine often fails to satisfy us as a system of explanation. God is eternally present in time, but this knowledge does not, for all-too-human readers, remove the difficulties of interpreting His ways and learning to act upon them. Rather than diminishing the burdens of action, the fact that we know that God informs time deepens and intensifies them. Hunter is very helpful on problems of doctrine, and he deals well with the pressures that they exert on the "form" of Milton's text. He also provides first-rate commentary on the epic genre, and on *Paradise Lost*'s similarities to and differences from the *Iliad*, *Odyssey*, and *Aeneid*. Since one of my purposes here is to note the absence of theoretical discussion in Milton criticism, it is humbling to concede that Hunter seems no more aware of trends in theory and methodology than the others I have treated. But Hunter is more theoretically minded than might appear at first glance. He is interested in *Paradise Lost* as "a drama of authorship" (p. 76), and he analyzes strategies and techniques in the poem: "authorial intervention and audience correction" (p. 11), "repetition and variation" (p. 12), "flashback and prophecy" (p. 36), "narrative dispersion and accumulation" (p. 46). His generalizations are always acute, as when he focuses on Satan's speeches in book I: "The inability of the will to face up to what the syntax has been showing us all along—that the individual perception is unreliable and incomplete—is as much a defeat as a triumph. The syntax allows us to see, behind the energy of the speaker who drives meaning in one direction or another, the limiting conditions within which fallen meaning can be asserted, the strictly hypothetical nature of human statement" (p. 114).

Hunter's *Paradise Lost* also merits praise for its imaginative and innovative entry into the poem. Instead of taking the predictable course of starting with book I, Hunter begins by examining Milton's concept of "heroism" in book VI, and then proceeds, in his next chapter, to compare the "fallen" Satan and Beelzebub in II with the "fallen" Adam and Eve in X. He also deals interestingly with books XI and XII, and with the poet's description of "creation" in VII and VIII, before finally concentrating on "the heart of the poem"—Adam and Eve in books IV and IX. Organizing the analysis in this fashion does lead to some confusion and repetitiveness in Hunter's argument. But Hunter's continual return to the important themes of human freedom and responsibility holds the book together. "The real protection of the Garden," he reminds us,

> does not lie in the wall or the angelic squadrons but in the perpetual vigilance of the human minds. This is the price of freedom, then as now. The prelapsarian and post-lapsarian situations are not, of course, identical. The fixing of human will in obedience to God's will was then all that was required to sustain blessedness. But God's will is not presented as simple or programmatic; it requires self-scrutiny and self-control to know how best to please the Father in Heaven and merit the advancement to a home in heaven with the angels that is the vaguely promised reward for a consistent performance in the early tests. (Pp. 181-82)

Others, including Barbara Lewalski and Boyd Berry, have stressed the continuities between life before and after the Fall.[18] But Hunter's way of stating this issue is especially apt; Adam's and Eve's "situations" are not the same, and obedience in Eden may seem easier. Yet even in their life together before the Fall, Adam and Eve are still faced with the work and discipline of knowing how best to obey, serve, and please the Father. E. M. W. Tillyard once asserted that if Milton himself had been placed in Eden, he would immediately have eaten the apple and "written a pamphlet to justify it." To say this is to assume that Adam and Eve are not doing anything productive before the Fall, whereas in Milton's terms, they are doing something intensely real, productive, and heroic at every moment that they continue to choose to obey God. It is this persistence in their faith and "perpetual vigilance" that is "the price" of Adam's and Eve's "freedom."

It may seem exceedingly odd to discuss Milton criticism at such length in a book on literary theory. But as I said at the outset, my point is less to survey Milton's critics than to take special note of their lack of contact with major theorists, debates, and trends, and to show how this limits and disfigures their work and restricts their judgment. Eventually Miltonists will grudgingly acquaint themselves with contemporary theory; there will be the usual MLA panels, special issues of journals, and the like. But it is almost certain to be the case that this activity will produce little more than the imposition of a variety of "methods" on Milton's texts, and that the results will be clumsy and unpersuasive. Theory will not be drawn upon and incorporated in truly resourceful ways, but will be invoked only to generate "readings," readings that are sure to prove so jarring and awkwardly conducted that Miltonists will then feel justified in dismissing theory as just a fad after all. Miltonists will not go to theory to challenge what they do but to reinforce and supplement what they do. Deconstruction, Speech Act theory, and other "methods" will enable Miltonists to fashion new explications, and these will be the object of some curiosity for a time. But the readings will prove too strange to secure real interest and sympathy, the theories will fade into the background, and the basic structure of the field will remain unaffected.

I may seem here to be contradicting myself, urging, on the one hand, that Miltonists study literary theory, yet observing, on the other hand, that Miltonists are unlikely to benefit from theory if and when they do discover it. But the contradiction is only an apparent one. Miltonists, like those in other fields, should read and reflect upon important trends and movements in theory; if they do not, they risk cutting themselves off from stimulating ideas and basing their inquiries on assumptions that theory has contested or modified. But neither Miltonists nor others in their fields of specialization should go to theory *uncritically*, in the hope of locating a new interpretive grid that they can then impose on texts. Theory can aid and enliven scholarly work, but it can also reduce, distort, and coarsen it, particularly when scholars see theory as a repository for global interpretive schemes and paradigms. Deployed in this mistaken way, theory invariably catches the writer in all sorts of confusions and misunderstandings; the theory is skimmed, barely grasped, and then used to process a new "reading." When this occurs, we witness a "thematizing" or "allegorizing" of the text as it is taken as an occasion for rehearsing a system or vocabulary in vogue.

Theory often proves to be most helpful when it serves to alter or deepen one's sense of method, procedure, and disciplinary practice— when it serves, that is, *not* to mold (or give terminology for) the scholar's "reading" but to extend and shift his understanding of what it means to "read" texts. What I am suggesting here is that theory can profit work in a field when it operates in local and specific instances, causing a significant adjustment in the manner by which the critic or scholar gathers evidence, assembles source materials, views the relation between canonical and non-canonical, literary and non-literary, texts. Theory will not cause a field to change overnight—this is an error that both the opponents and the enthusiasts of theory consistently commit. Nor will it prove worthwhile if it is geared only to interpreting primary texts. It enables us to revise habitual assumptions, practices, conceptions. Theory teaches us, for example, to resist distinctions between primary texts and "source" or "background" texts; these texts cannot be drawn upon simply to boost or add to the interpretation of a primary text but must themselves be interpreted, probed, analyzed. Theory also enables us to see that the history of criticism is not a record of "response" to an unchanging work (the classic text), but instead testifies to an ongoing effort to recreate, renew, and remake the work. It obliges us, furthermore, to perceive our fields more critically, as something other than neutral territory where each laborer is free to contribute objectively to the progress of scholarship.

Critics—and Miltonists are an obvious case in point—should take their fields far more seriously than they do. I would like to see studies of academic fields of interest that would examine how these were constituted; how they prospered or suffered during the periods when new methods, systems, and theories emerged; how they represent, testify to, or contrast with more general developments in criticism and culture. Milton was a political revolutionary and a heretic, and his rebellious energy captivated Blake and Shelley. Yet in this century Milton has mostly stood as the champion of conservative values, institutional rigidity, and Christian humanism. C. S. Lewis, Douglas Bush, and others succeeded in transforming this most iconoclastic and visionary writer into the defender of classical balance and restraint. How was this transformation accomplished? What kinds of commerce and connection existed between Milton criticism and the overall shape and structure of the discipline? What, in a word, made it possible for Leavis to observe as late as 1958 that "Miltonists rule the academic world"?

Directions for Criticism: Geoffrey Hartman and Stanley Fish

Geoffrey Hartman. *Criticism in the Wilderness: The Study of Literature Today.* New Haven, Conn.: Yale University Press, 1980.
Stanley Fish. *Is There a Text in This Class? The Authority of Interpretive Communities.* Cambridge: Harvard University Press, 1980.

Geoffrey Hartman and Stanley Fish are two of the most important contemporary theorists, and so it seems natural to examine their books together in order to trace shared themes and interests. But while Fish and Hartman are usually seen as members of the critical vanguard, and are often viewed as posing similiar kinds of radical threats to the institution of criticism, they are very different—in style, approach, preferred subjects, concerns—and hence reading and reviewing their books at the same time makes for an odd, if stimulating, experience.[19]

What is most noticeable to the reader, right at the start, is the sharply different prose styles of these two theorists. Fish writes with the force of a piledriver, hammering home his points and rarely letting up the pressure on his reader. Hartman eschews argument; he is oblique, indirect, both elusive and allusive. His touch is much lighter, his range is wider, and he borrows freely from and works with the ideas and vocabularies of Walter Benjamin, Jacques Derrida, and other European theorists. Fish's motto might be Whitehead's axiom that "narrowness is the price of intensity," for he maintains a steady grip on his own theory and its antagonists; unlike Hartman, he does not often probe theories that he admires and has learned from.

Rigorously organized and methodical, Fish is always striving to tighten his arguments, which, it seems, is just what Hartman is anxious to avoid. At one point in *Criticism in the Wilderness*, Hartman says outright that "in terms of systematic thought I have nothing to add" (p. 268); and later, after a rare burst of straightforward prose, he apologizes for what he has done: "I am so unused to this open kind of rhetoric that having written the above words I wish to cross them out" (p. 287). Ordinarily we grant each critic the right to prosecute his case in the way that is most fruitful for him, and then we assess what his chosen mode has led him to discover. But as one considers these books, one finds oneself wishing that each writer had greater measures of the other's virtues. With a better sense of argument, Hartman would satisfy us more; he does not deliver as much as he promises, and reading him often proves disappointing. Hartman does not perform the analytical tasks that best suit him, nor does he realize the disparities and confusions in his call for a "philosophical criticism." Fish provides us with the argumentative power that we miss in Hartman, but his writing is so goal-oriented and energetically in pursuit of its conclusions (the ideas all clicking into place) that he appears not to see some of the major implications of his arguments on behalf of "interpretive communities."

Often in *Criticism in the Wilderness*, the reader notes fine insights and connections. Hartman comments well on F. R. Leavis's relation to Carlyle and Ruskin, resistance to philosophy, and moral commitment driven by ferocity and disdain. He also touches intriguingly on the need for an "American" criticism based on Emerson, William James, and Peirce, and reflects on the major "revision" and revaluation of the Romantics that has occurred in recent decades. These and other observations are valuable, and the same can be said for Hartman's brief but incisive "readings" of poets (Yeats, Wordsworth, and Dickinson, among others), theorists (Frye, Burke, Bloom), and philosophers (Heidegger, Wittgenstein, Derrida). But it is precisely because Hartman is often suggestive that we expect more from him. Often he provides keen perceptions and references but does not fully explore and develop them. The reader is never offered the the type of focused interpretation of writers, texts, and literary movements that Hartman practices in *Wordsworth's Poetry, 1784-1814* (1964) and in many of the essays in *Beyond Formalism* (1970) and *The Fate of Reading* (1975). In reading this book, we are tantalized, momentarily rewarded, and then dismayed as Hartman makes one move after another in his allusive game.

A typical instance is Hartman's meditation on the "involuted style of Richard Blackmur," where he proposes that this critic "betrays an extreme awareness of how the mind is textured by texts and how the critic's, if not the poet's authority is always under the shadow of imposture" (p. 176). The final part of this sentence needs unpacking, and the reader expects that Hartman will clarify his insights as the passage unfolds. But Hartman's next sentences are coy and enigmatic, and his paragraph on Blackmur ends by dissolving into allusion and question-begging: "Blackmur's close reading expresses a laboring mind, for which writing is travail—'A Long Way Round to Nirvana,' to adapt the title of Santayana's essay on Freud's *Beyond the Pleasure Principle*. Lionel Trilling, it is true, sought to restore the essay to a certain decorum, and perhaps to exempt it from the disappearance of pleasure that he feared was the 'fate' of literature. Did he succeed?" (p. 176). There is a lot swirling around here, and many interesting lines of thought that could be traced and connected. Blackmur is among the best "formalist" critics, and one would like to hear what Hartman has to say about him. As Hartman is surely aware, Blackmur was greatly influenced by Santayana, was interested in but wary about Freud, and wrote a short but spirited piece, "The Politics of Human Power," on Trilling. These are commanding figures, texts, ideas; to study and relate them is hard work, much harder and more demanding, yet also more rewarding, than what Hartman produces in this passage. He generates mostly flash and flair, and one fears that the appearance of deep thinking is an illusion.

Of course Hartman would object that he is not interested in mounting full-fledged arguments. If there is a thesis in *Criticism in the Wilderness*, it is that criticism should be seen as within literature, not "outside" it, and thereby opened up to more playful forms of discourse.

Today . . . critics carp at critics while paradoxically accepting almost any style the creative writer throws their way. Defensive about their function, they normalize criticism at the price of mystifying creative genius. It is as if the literary field were being crassly divided into permissive creativity (fiction) on the one hand, and schoolmasterly criticism on the other (P. 233).

There is no reason why all criticism should be of the reporting or reviewing kind. Even if we prefer plain-style writing, should we reduce critical prose to one pattern or delude ourselves that a purely utilitarian or instrumentalist mode of communication is possible? This attitude would have expelled the more demanding critics from Plato's Republic as poets in disguise. It could even now lead to a thorough ideologizing or levelling of the critical spirit. (P. 236)

This is what Hartman believes, but it strikes me as weirdly over-stated and self-serving. It is less an argument than a caricature of one, and in this way it reflects a favorite device in the rhetoric of much contemporary theory and criticism. The opposing side is described in absurdly reductive terms: it accepts anything and everything thrown its way; it "crassly" divides the literary field; it conceives of the one right style of criticism as "reviewing" and "reporting"; and it generally labors to bring down criticism to the most mind-numbing level imaginable. To write as Hartman does here is clever and effective in some respects; he pushes us towards his position by depicting what everybody else does as a kind of disease. Fearing contagion, we quickly dissociate ourselves from the ranks of the reporters, reviewers, and plain stylists. But reliance on such tactics means that serious efforts at explanation and persuasion have long ago been left behind. Hartman's appeal is fervent yet without real content.

Hartman is to be commended for envisioning a more expansive role for criticism. Leavis, Blackmur, and other of the important critics of this century speak in different and often opposing voices, and as Hartman suggests, they teach us to recognize that criticism is not a single thing, with methods and values that we can readily agree upon and legislate for others to follow. But Hartman's advocacy of a wide-ranging, flexible "philosophical criticism" is too often purely rhetorical, inclined to browbeat the reader even as the calls for open-mindedness and freedom are being made. "No wonder," Hartman states,

some are scared witless by a mode of thinking that seems to offer no decidability, no resolution. Yet the perplexity that art arouses in careful readers and viewers is hardly licentious. It is the reality; it is only as strange as truth. It recalls the artificial nature or purely conventional status of formal arguments or proofs; the fact that human agreements remain conveniences with the force of law, metaphors with the force of institutions, opinions with the force of dogma. It recalls the prevalence of propaganda, both in open societies that depend on conversation, jawboning, advertising, bargaining, and in controlled societies that can become sinister and inquisitorial, adding to their torture chamber the subtlest brainwashing and reiterated lie. Can any hermeneutics of indeterminacy, any irony however deeply practiced and nurtured by aesthetic experience, withstand either society while they are still distinguishable? (P. 283)

In its grand self-indulgence, this passage helps to show why *Criticism in the Wilderness* frequently disappoints and frustrates the reader. Hartman's affirmation of the power of art is vehement, but the passage seems out of control. Its middle section is feverish, almost frantic, and by the end, it seems quite obscure, its affirmations phrased in jargon (a "hermeneutics of indeterminacy") that the reader cannot make contact with. Once again, Hartman tags the opposition as blind, cowardly ("scared witless"), and unserious; they cannot understand "creative" criticism, are unnerved by modes of critical thinking that refuse "decidability" and "resolution," and fail to grasp what art truly means. Both art and criticism, Hartman contends, are powerfully creative and revelatory; a critic who limits the domain of criticism will be unable to value art properly. But it is not likely that any critics among the unspecified group that Hartman is attacking would accept (or even recognize) this as an accurate description. Hartman exalts the superior understanding of his critical theory and practice by setting up a particularly woeful crew of straw men. He depicts them in simplified and simpleminded ways and then defines himself against them, amid much rhetorical energy and splendor.

This passage makes clear that Hartman is unwilling to engage in serious argument; instead, he proffers high-toned speechmaking and assertion. As it and other passages demonstrate, Hartman is not aiming to persuade his reader, but is forcing the reader to choose between the enlightened elite and the nefarious bunch that denies the power of art. Hartman everywhere seems to take for granted that major articles of his position do not require argumentative support; they do not, it appears, even need to be explained. "There is," he remarks, "no presence; there is only representation and, worse, representations" (p. 281). This may well be true, but one would have thought that such a claim merits more than a mere statement that implies no one could ever think otherwise. Hartman counts on our not quarreling with him, because he assumes that we endorse the teachings of Derrida and Paul De Man on "absence" and the illusion of "presence" in texts. At first, one might balk at Hartman's assertion, but then who would want to be exposed as hopelessly naive and unfamiliar with deconstructive principles? It's either agree that this statement cannot be contested or face being exiled to the outer darkness with the other "scared" critics.

The more one reads and studies *Criticism in the Wilderness*, the more perplexing it seems. Hartman makes an eloquent, if not always coherent, case for a philosophical criticism that strives to be "creative" and rises to the challenge of new writers, texts, and ideas. Yet while this sounds admirable as a project, it does not fully explain Hartman's discontent with criticism today and his appeal for new, more expansive kinds. In a number of places, he grumbles about "mass education" and its bad effects on teaching and scholarship. Faculty, he observes, are beleaguered and "service-ridden," but even more disturbing is that

> we are acquiring a new and corrosive sense of the mortality of books. They are in danger of being routinized or contaminated by endless readings forced out of industrious hordes of students. A photosensitive surface can become overexposed; so a work, insofar as it is language-sensitive, becomes unreadable when subjected to a stream of verbal comments. It is this blankness of the written page that is to be feared as much as the white, virginal horror afflicting Mallarmé. But perhaps the two types of blankness are related. (P. 230)

If one sees one's job as "forcing" readings from students, and if one views these students as an "industrious horde," then it is no wonder that teaching and criticism can appear to be a depressing spectacle. "Mass education" has caused problems, but are matters this desperate at Yale? Surely Hartman himself cannot feel comfortable with his imagery of "contamination" and "mortality"; teaching is difficult to do well, but it will be even harder to accomplish for someone who conceives of his work in these terms. Though presented as a diagnosis of our plight as teachers, this passage veers towards a sublime of self-pity.

In the final and best essay in the book, titled "A Short History of Practical Criticism," Hartman at last presents a sustained argument, surveying the beginnings of "practical criticism" in England under the leadership of Richards, Empson, and Leavis, and summarizing its influence on American teachers and critics. Hartman acutely points out that the "new" and "practical" critics made major claims for the specialness of literature but never explained what that "specialness" consisted of. Literature was not science, history, psychology, or some other thing. But just what it was no one seemed able or willing to say. "No theorist of the time," he explains, "was able to define" literature in exact terms or describe its subject-matter and relevance to society and institutional life. We are now paying for this failure of definition—which is also a failure to specify our role and purpose. Our conception of the "practical" is too narrow; we feel ourselves cut off from the modern "mainstream," share little with other disciplines and professions, and appear helpless as we watch graduate students joining the unemployment lines and the brightest undergraduates leaving us for other departments. Hartman is to be admired for confronting these problems, but one wishes that this final chapter in his book were instead the first one, and that the effort at inquiry and analysis he makes here characterized *Criticism in the Wilderness* as a whole.

Hartman's proposals are peculiar. He repeats his advocacy of a philosophical criticism, maintains that we must attend more to literary theory, and states that, as we achieve these goals, we will improve the state of the arts in general and enable the profession to "rejoin the humanities." There is nothing intrinsically wrong with such a program, but it will not assist much in remedying the situation that Hartman describes. To speak of the economic realities facing the humanities, and then to advise that we pay more heed to the "concept of representation" (p. 299), seems manifestly impractical. The relation between Hartman's statement of the problem and sketch of a solution is askew, oddly insightful and blind at the same time.

Denis Donoghue has referred to Hartman's proposals in more severe terms, labeling them "bizarre" for ignoring the "communicative" function of teaching and criticism—getting others to read well, learn respect for the imagination, and participate in the freedom that this reading and exploration bring. While Donoghue's point is well-taken, it misses the most disquieting feature of Hartman's argument. Where Hartman sees the potential for expanded horizons for criticism, I am inclined to fear the likelihood of greater specialization and new kinds of narrowness. *Criticism in the Wilderness* is a notable instance: it rejects argument, spurns direct engagement with its audience, lights on issues that are not explained and elaborated, and continually gestures to the knowing coterie of post-structuralists. Even as Hartman declares that we must widen the range of criticism, he restricts his notion of its audience; and even as he affirms that we must reach other disciplines and professions, he guarantees that we will have grave problems in doing so if we follow his example. "Unless we find some doors, revolving or not, that lead from the humanities into society, and unless some of our graduates go into other walks of life than teaching, or remain in touch with us even though they are in the nonacademic professions, the humanities are bound to become service departments to other divisions of the academy with more obvious and effective social outlets" (p. 288).

Hartman envisions humanities programs coupled with the study of law and business, and says that we must devise ways of securing relations with social institutions and structures. But it is surprising that Hartman can profess to see and seek bonds between the humanities and corporate America in view of his many references to the "radical" power of art (e.g., pp. 98, 115), emphasis on the ironic and trangressive powers of literature, and claims for the disruptive force of language.

Will his "philosophical criticism" provide "social outlets"? I agree with Hartman that despite the work that Frye, Burke, and others have done, "art's contribution to the political sphere remains difficult to formulate" (p. 98). But if he intends to speak of business, law, and other professions as places for humanists to locate themselves, then he is obliged to tackle hard questions about the politics of literature, teaching, and criticism. Hartman is in effect telling us to enter into forms of social organization that, according to his own definitions, "art" opposes and threatens to undermine. The pattern is all too familiar: the intellectual believes that society does not recognize and reward him, and he explains this oversight as the result of social failures and distortions such as "mass education." To alter this state of affairs, the intellectual proposes neither to disengage himself from society nor to pledge himself to be an activist and reformer; instead, he enlarges his commerce with the "mainstream." It has its advantages, and so he desires admission into what in many ways repels him.

Political issues are implicit throughout Stanley Fish's work, and in attempting to come to terms with it, one of the most pressing questions is why Fish does not treat the "politics" of his theory of interpretation directly. But before commenting on this omission in Fish's writing, I want to stress that *Is There a Text in This Class?* is extremely challenging and impressive. Fish is unfailingly lucid in his arguments and thus is an exception to the practice of most contemporary theorists, who appear to regard stylistic clarity as a scandal. *Is There a Text in This Class?* collects Fish's theoretical essays written during the 1970s along with a seventy-page study of "interpretive authority in the classroom and in literary criticism" that was originally delivered as the John Crowe Ransom Memorial Lectures at Kenyon College in 1979. For each of the essays, Fish provides a headnote, detailing his response to the essay today, its strengths and weaknesses as he sees them, and its prefiguration of issues that he would later refine. In its own right, each essay is tightly constructed and argued; taken together, the essays comprise a larger argument that culminates in the long concluding section. But the book is nevertheless open-ended, for Fish also points out the complex enterprise—an analysis of the "institution" of literature and criticism—that follows from his interest in the structures of authority that govern interpretive work.

Ralph Rader, Jonathan Culler, and others have criticized Fish's theoretical statements about meaning, interpretive communities, the roles of the reader and text, and I have advanced my own criticism in a previous chapter. But the most interesting feature of Fish's theory in this book concerns what he does not state or discuss in explicit ways. Though his theory—especially the account of interpretive communities—resonates with political implications, these are not addressed; either Fish is not aware of them or is deliberately suppressing them. His theory is nearly always gaining in interpretive range and in fact usually absorbs its earlier embodiments. And so it seems all the more surprising that this forceful theorist and writer fails to capitalize on potential powers in his arguments.

Fish's references to politics are infrequent and raise more questions than they answer. In his introduction, for example, Fish reviews what he discovered in the process of writing the final essays in the book:

> The business of criticism was not (as I had previously thought) to determine a correct way of reading but to determine from which of a number of possible perspectives reading will proceed. . . . The business of criticism, in other words, was not to decide between interpretations by subjecting them to the test of disinterested evidence but to establish by political and persuasive means (they are the same thing) the set of interpretive assumptions from the vantage of which the evidence (and the facts and the intentions and everything else) will hereafter be specifiable. (P. 16)

The Vietnam War and Watergate have brought home to us that "persuasion" and "politics" are certainly related; perhaps, as Fish insists, they are even identical. But Fish's claim obliges him to expand and clarify it, and this in turn would require him to ask several crucial questions. Is politics no more (and no less) than persuasion? Should we also equate persuasion with power? Is political persuasion the form of power, or does it need the exercise and display of power to achieve its ends? How does one decide upon the true ends of power and discriminate among competing rhetorics? Dealing with such questions might well be a lifetime's work, and no one would maintain that Fish or any other critic can easily answer or comprehend them. But they are implicit in the identity that Fish establishes (that is, takes for granted) between politics and persuasion; and because one hears something offhand and brazen in Fish's tone here, one feels compelled to insist that he recognize the impact of his statement.

In several places Fish seems to be making political judgments, as when he argues that Ralph Rader denies the relevance of the reader's efforts to make meaning "because his wish for a world whose only morality is univocal efficiency cannot tolerate it" (p. 145), or when he warns that "there is something of the police state" in M. H. Abrams's adherence to determinate meaning, with its "posted rules and boundaries, watchdogs to enforce them, procedures for identifying their violators as criminals" (p. 337). But Fish's political remarks are not fleshed out, and they stay on the margins of his analyses. In his critique of Speech Act theory, "How to Do Things with Austin and Searle," Fish examines Coriolanus's "banishing and counter-banishing" in Shakespeare's play and reaches this conclusion: "It is not that words are in force only so long as the institutions are, but that institutions are in force only so long as the words are. . . . The moral of this is chastening, even disturbing: institutions are no more than the (temporary) effects of speech-act agreements, and they are therefore as fragile as the decision, always capable of being revoked, to abide by them" (p. 215).

More needs to be said about this "moral." Institutions, Fish suggests, are the product of verbal agreements, and hence their continuity is not by any means a natural fact that we are unable to change; it lies within our power to alter or terminate the agreement and substitute new ones. What Fish has seen is this: not merely existing institutions, but any that we might subscribe to in order to counter them are the product of verbal agreements, are, that is, linguistically based. This is the truly chastening moral that he is drawing, and one assents to its logic even as one resists it. Fish demystifies both our present institutions and any others to which we might commit ourselves. Such a declaration is liberating and confining at the same time, for it exposes the fragility of existing social structures (they rest on verbal agreements) and also requires us to see that this applies as well to other structures we might nominate.

To call this argument a disturbing one is, if anything, to underestimate it. If one's commitments to institutions are as suspect as those that one challenges, then their seriousness and capacity to inspire loyalty are open to question. Fish does not elaborate on the type of political commitment that his theory might leave available to us. Nor does he suggest the nature of the political stance from which he measures the police-state mentality of Rader and Abrams. He can and does criticize these theorists, but one consequence of his views is that he can castigate the politics of others far more readily than he can uphold and testify to his own. Others, he protests, wrongly assume that their political commitments and institutional practices are independent of "verbal agreements" instead of being constituted by them, and this is an error that Fish is always prompt to rebuke. But this same awareness and drive to demystify also cause Fish's silence about the political allegiances to which his own theory might lead.

No doubt Fish would reply that his recent work offers us a way out of this apparent abyss, and that it is tied to his emphasis on and understanding of "belief." Being aware of the verbal conventions that ground beliefs does not mean that these beliefs are any less strong. More precisely,

> I will argue for my position with all the confidence that attends belief even though I know that under certain conditions at some time in the future I might believe something else. Another way to put this is to say that the fact

that I am subject to the same challenge I have put to my predecessors is not a weakness in my position but a restatement of it. The idea of a position that was invulnerable to challenge makes sense only if you believe in the possibility of a position innocent of assumptions; this of course is exactly what I do not believe in and therefore the fact that my assumptions are capable of being dislodged does not refute my argument but confirms it, because it is an extension of it. (Pp. 369-70)

Fish is maneuvering brilliantly here, but a close inspection of his words reveals the gaps and problems in his argument. He bears witness to his beliefs and to their power, yet it is a queer kind of belief that is already informed by the possibility of unbelief. Even as Fish announces the intensity of his commitment to his views, which he says he holds with the force of a "belief," he is already imagining a position "outside" or "other" than the one he now occupies. Fish maintains that this is the way it is: we have to conceive of "belief" in his terms, or else admit that we want our position to be "invulnerable to challenge" and "in-nocent of assumptions." But to characterize the issue in these terms is misleading. Having faith in (being truly committed to) one's beliefs does not mean that one is invulnerable to challenge, nor does it need imply that one is "innocent" of assumptions. Rather, a believer is aware that he might be challenged but knows he is right and thus can meet such a challenge; as Milton, one of Fish's favorite writers, might say, a believer knows he is "in the truth," and because he is in the truth he claims not that he is without assumptions but that his assumptions are right. He may be opposed, but he is a true believer and will remain one.

This difference in phrasing is slight but significant. In Fish's account, he asserts that he is talking about belief but seems more to be describing a process of self-persuasion and maybe self-deception: you convince yourself that you truly believe in a position even as you remind yourself that you might believe otherwise at some time in the future. Political acts undertaken in this spirit are perhaps best not thought about. But actually the prospect for political action, if one construes "belief" as Fish does, may not be likely, since the degree of one's commitment is qualified by the recognition that the future may undermine what one believes in now. Judged in these terms, Fish's theory of interpretation and belief might seem to forestall foolhardy action, but the more urgent question is whether it could *allow* for action. To put this as sharply as possible: what we now believe to be vicious, exploitative, sexist, or racist might, we know, seem otherwise in the future. Does this knowl-edge free us to act or encourage us not to?

Fish's demystifying intention is inclusive, and he makes it difficult for us to grasp the meaning of social involvement, political commitment, and institutional allegiance. He does not consider these complex and important issues explicitly; a larger dimension, primarily a political one, is missing from Fish's work. Either he does not acknowledge or does not wish to address the politics of his theory, and possibly this is the case because he knows on some level that his positions about the verbal foundation of social agreements and beliefs are more disruptive than he would like to contemplate. Interestingly, Fish insists that institutions and beliefs, even if we accept what he says, persist as powerfully as ever; they remain in force, verbally grounded or not. But then one is uncertain whether this is a fact that is worrisome or one that should be greeted with a sigh of relief, since it provides little sense of knowing or hoping to discover what is to be done. Fish's theory is potentially subversive, but one no sooner says this than one has to take it back; the theory exposes, unsettles, and demystifies, yet it also conserves. In deep and unnerving ways, Fish portrays the fragility of beliefs and institutions while at the same time remarking on their power and our lack of any real basis for rejecting them in favor of something else.

Fish's and Hartman's work takes us to the center of one of the knottiest set of questions that demand our attention. What are the politics of interpretation? What does it mean to speak of the power of literature, criticism, teaching, interpretive theories? What are the relations between political power and the practices of the academic institution? What is at present—and what should be—the nature of one's commitment to criticism and teaching? Does such a commitment entail some form of political engagement, and if so, does this deepen or endanger one's writing and teaching? These are extremely difficult questions that one might prefer to dodge, but they are compelling because of the uncertainty many feel today about the discipline. Like Hartman, many academics have an uncomfortable sense that society does not recognize the value of their work, and they feel disturbed by their marginality. Hartman represents one mode or means of dealing with these problems; he is alienated from society yet seeks more direct entry into it. He describes the importance of securing such an entry even as he phrases his account of the humanities in narrow and private terms (the terms of the privileged few) and deploys rhetorics of trespass and transgression. It is a curious but crucial fact that Hartman's references to radical forms of irony and indeterminacy, his often cryptic style, and his expressions of social and cultural discontent work against his desire to win a wider recognition for the humanities. If we want society to recognize us, then we have to give it reasons for doing so; it is unlikely that Hartman's terms and ideas can persuade those in the social "mainstream" that they need and ought to attend to us.

Fish's response is also problematical, but in a different way. His theory provides us with arguments that undercut habits of seeing certain institutions, and of accepting certain forms of action, behavior, and respect for authority, as natural, inescapable, unavoidable. What seems to us to be the most "natural" is often the most deeply conventional—it is just that we have forgotten about or blinded ourselves to its origins. This is an argument that is both profound and disconcerting: one cannot chart the course that it might take, or speculate on the positive commitments in teaching and criticism towards which it might direct us. Fish's theory is a technique for demystifying other theories, claims to authority, and entrenched positions of power. But it is also a technique that is self-dismantling, in that it declares its own insights to be as vulnerable to criticism as anything that it demystifies. Though we can be committed to the theory, it is hard to know what the theory itself is (and could ever be) committed to.

Beyond Formalism: The Politics of Criticism

Catherine Belsey. *Critical Practice*. New York: Methuen, 1980.
Tony Bennett. *Formalism and Marxism*. New York: Methuen, 1979.

Catherine Belsey's *Critical Practice* is a stimulating book, one that offers a fine assessment of recent work in literary theory and a suggestive account of new directions for criticism to take. Belsey's study has not received much attention. So many books get published that the good ones are sometimes lost in the shuffle or are overwhelmed by others that are more heavily advertised. But *Critical Practice* ought not to be allowed to disappear. Though overstated at times, it is an excellent piece of critical analysis and deals cogently with provocative questions that concern the power and politics of both literature and criticism.

Belsey argues that despite the thrust of current trends in literary theory, the majority of teachers and critics still believe in a "common-sense" approach. "Common-sense," she explains, "assumes that valuable literary texts, those which are in a special way worth reading, tell truths—about the period which produced them, about the world in general or about human nature—and that in doing so they express the particular perceptions, the individual insights, of their authors" (p. 2). Common-sense also assumes that "critical theory" is not an essential part of English studies. From a "common-sense" perspective, theory appears "as a perfectly respectable but to some degree peripheral area, almost a distinct discipline, a suitable activity for graduate students or perhaps as a special option for undergraduates, having no necessary connection with the practice of reading itself" (p. 2). This disdain for theoretical pursuits is, Belsey declares, merely an excuse for failing to consider the assumptions behind the "common-sense" view. By scorning theory and refusing to address the implications of its own beliefs, the "common-sense" attitude "evades confrontation with its own presuppositions, protects whatever procedures and methods are currently dominant, and so guarantees the very opposite of objectivity, the perpetuation of unquestioned assumptions" (p. 4).

Belsey's attack on the common-sense school and her defense of literary theory are incisive, and they are especially needed at the present time. Common-sense instructs us in one way to go about the business of interpretation but does not legislate the only way. By being so steadfastly loyal to it, we greatly restrict the scope of critical work and underestimate the power that the discipline makes available to us. Criticism is neither purely "literary" nor "autonomous." It is entangled in questions of theory, power, and politics, and it is a far more complex and "worldly" enterprise than common-sense accounts imply. "Any conceptual framework for literary criticism" has "implications which stretch beyond criticism itself to ideology and the place of ideology in the social formation as a whole. Assumptions about literature involve assumptions about language and about meaning, and these in turn involve assumptions about human society. The independent universe of literature and the autonomy of criticism are illusory" (p. 29). For Belsey, there is no doubt that literature and criticism are enmeshed in society and have powerful roles to play in the shaping of social thought. What is bracing about Belsey's argument is that she does not even pause—as most other critics would—to wonder whether or not criticism is "connected" to the world. These connections, in her view, exist in dramatic and intricate forms, and it is our job to acknowledge and analyze them. We should never pretend that they do not exist. Which means that we should not pose to ourselves (and worry about) the false problem of how we can "relate" literature to the world. Literature is already, and is inescapably, implicated in "worldliness" (Edward W. Said's term), and in historical contexts and social formations.[20]

Belsey has learned from Barthes, Lacan, Althusser, Macherey, and other Continental theorists, and their ideas and procedures inform her discussion. But one of the impressive things about Belsey is that, unlike other disciples of these theorists, she does not opt for fashionable pessimism or self-indulgent references to the "abysses" and "aporias" of interpretation. Her stance is critical, exploratory, and productive; she does not rely upon the catch-phrases of current theory to do her thinking for her. At one point she states, in line with Barthes and others, that "language speaks us" and displays an infinite range of meanings. But Belsey stresses that the resourcefulness of language does not defeat interpretation or make it impossible. Rather, it is precisely because language is endlessly meaningful that we can draw upon it. Being "caught" within the linguistic system does not connote that we are its "victims," but instead enables us to capitalize on the tools that language provides:

> We are not enslaved by the conventions which prevail in our own time. Authors do not inevitably simply reiterate the timeworn patterns of signification. Analysis reveals that at any given moment the categories and laws of the symbolic order are full of contradictions, ambiguities and inconsistencies which function as a source of possible change. The role of ideology is to suppress these contradictions in the interests of the preservation of the existing social formation, but their presence ensures that it is always possible, with whatever difficulty, to identify them, to recognize ideology for what it is, and to take an active part in transforming it by producing new meanings. (Pp. 45-46)

Like Said, Belsey seeks to make a place for the imprint of the individual and resists the argument, made by Michel Foucault in some phases of his work, that the order of discourse greatly restricts (and may even rule out) authorial initiative. She needs, however, to explain in more detail just how the individual author or agent brings about "change" within the system of conventions. She is right to stress the importance of (as well as the possiblility for) change, and I value her insistence on the kinds of "critical practice" that we can authorize and take responsibility for. But she does not confront the relationship between authorship and change as directly as one might wish, and so leaves a significant gap in her analysis.

There are other shortcomings in Belsey's book. She says very little about Derrida; she is sometimes guilty of characterizing the positions she opposes in reductive terms; and she does not fully examine the ways in which the academic institution imposes constraints on "critical practice." But Belsey herself takes note of the "incomplete" state of her inquiry and is aware that many "questions" remain (see pp. 143-46). And because she recognizes (and aims to redress) the limitations of her study, I do not want to push them too hard. *Critical Practice* is a challenging book, and, as Belsey remarks, the omissions and flaws in her arguments should not be "a reason for retreat." They simply indicate to us that much more work needs to be done.

Tony Bennett's *Formalism and Marxism* is also excellent, and is even more radical, in its political orientation and its arguments, than Belsey's *Critical Practice*. In his opening chapter, Bennett deals very well with the relations between "criticism and literature"; and in the middle chapters, he presents one of the best critiques of Russian Formalism that I have encountered. But the most provocative aspect of Bennett's book lies in his discussion of Marxist criticism, where he defines the limits of the Marxist critical tradition and outlines his revisions of it. "Marxist criticism," Bennett concludes,

> has hitherto proceeded on the assumption that every literary text has its politics inscribed within it and that the role of Marxist criticism is to enunciate this politics, to give it voice by making it explicit. This political essentialism must be broken with. The text does not have a politics which is separable from the determinations which work upon it or the position it occupies within the disposition of the field of cultural relations. The task which faces Marxist criticism is not that of reflecting or of bringing to light the politics which is already there, as a latent presence within the text which has but to be made manifest. It is that of *actively politicizing* the text, of *making its politics for it*, by producing a new position for it within the field of cultural relations and, thereby, new forms of use and effectivity within the broader social process. (Pp. 167-68)

Marxists have mistakenly assumed that texts carry their own political meanings, and that it is the job of the critic to unpack and comment on them. There is no such thing as a text that "intrinsically" possesses political meanings. The critic *makes* the text political, creating the politics *for* it.

This argument has dramatic consequences not only for the Marxist tradition but also, more generally, for an understanding of the role of the reader, the task of the critic, and the political dimension of critical work. For Bennett, criticism entails conflict and appropriation; we impose meanings on texts and engage in a struggle to gain acceptance for our "reading"—which means making it gain sway over other readings that compete with our own. "The activity of criticism" is

> itself a pre-eminently *political* exercise. For the texts on which Marxist criticism works are, in a sense, already "occupied." They are already filled with interpretations. The way in which they are appropriated is already determined by the uses to which they are put in the social process. Given this, the quest for an objective "science" of the literary text is illusory. The literary text has no single or uniquely privileged meaning, no single or uniquely privileged effect that can be abstracted from the ways in which criticism itself works upon and mediates the reception of that text. In this sense, literature is not something to be studied; it is an area to be occupied. The question is not what literature's political effects *are* but what they might be *made to be*—not in a forever and once-and-for-all sense but in a dynamic and changing way—by the operations of Marxist criticism. (P. 137)

This represents a curious blend of Marxism and the reader-response criticism that Stanley Fish has developed. Bennett nowhere mentions Fish, but his Marxist theory of interpretation has clear affinities with the theory of the reader's construction of meaning that Fish articulates in *Is There a Text in This Class?* Like Fish, Bennett argues that the reader makes meaning and, in effect, "produces" the text. The reader constructs the text, decides upon the traditions within which it will be located, determines how it will be put to use, and "projects" into it the values that it will affirm. As I have already noted, the major shortcoming in Fish's work is the absence of political analysis; his theory is laced with political issues and problems, but he never reflects upon (or even calls attention to) them. At first sight, Bennett's study seems to remedy this blind spot in Fish's theory, for Bennett sees the reader's "creative," "productive" role as implying, necessarily, a politics of interpretation. But Bennett retains a commitment to the text, despite his many references to the power of the reader, and he thus advances Fish's work in one direction only to modify and perhaps undermine it in another.

Bennett's declarations on behalf of the reader are forthright. His theory defines "reading" as a powerful act of "political intervention":

> It does not restore to the text contradictions which were "always there" but hidden from view; it *reads contradictions into the text*. It does not *reflect* a work of transformation on ideological forms that literary texts can be said always to have possessed, like some secret essence which criticism has only recently discovered; it *makes* such texts effect a work of transformation on those forms of signification which are *said to be* ideological. (Pp. 146-47)

> Ultimately, there is no such thing as "the text." There is no pure text, no fixed and final form of the text which conceals a hidden truth which has but to be penetrated for criticism to retire, its task completed. There is no once-and-for-all, final truth about the text which criticism is forever in the process of acquiring. The text always and only exists in a variety of historically concrete forms. . . . It is in this deep and radical way that each age, by producing its own texts, produces its own literature. (P. 148)

In these passages and others, Bennett assigns "productive" power to the reader who intervenes in the text and generates its politics. But in still other passages, he slips in statements that attribute meaning to the text—as though the text does contribute, after all, to the creation of a meaningful politics of interpretation. Often these statements are barely visible in Bennett's writing, for they occur in the midst of his affirmations on behalf of the reader. Bennett says, for example, that while the "literary text may, by virtue of its intrinsic properties, determine to a certain extent the way in which it is 'consumed' or read, it does not do so entirely" (pp. 134-35). Later, in his final chapter, he observes that acts of reading are conditioned, "in part by the text it is true, but also by the whole ensemble of ideological relationships which bear upon the incessant production and reproduction of texts" (pp.

174-75). Bennett's major emphasis is clear: he directs attention towards the productive acts that the reader performs. Yet the text keeps sliding back into his theory; it has "intrinsic properties" and at least partially "conditions" how we read. Bennett exalts the reader as the maker of meaning; his political radicalism depends on viewing the reader as a powerful agent that authorizes interpretations and imposes them upon the text. But at the same time that Bennett advocates a form of reader-power, he also stresses the meaningful capacity of the text and the informing presence of "ideological relationships." Both cut against his desire to place full faith in the reader's productive role.

The difficulty here is not that Bennett errs in attributing power to the text and to ideology, but rather that he fails to explain how *this* power influences or detracts from that wielded by the reader who should intervene and read political meanings into the text. These moments of contradiction in *Formalism and Marxism* occur, I believe, when Bennett perceives and then pulls back from the implications of his radical program. Giving all the power to the reader sounds, from a politically activist standpoint, militant and compelling; but it also may imply a degree of radicalism that Bennett himself does not wish to contemplate. To credit the reader with interpretive power, and to state, as Bennett often does, that there are no such things as "texts," suggests that criticism is a spectacle of conflict without a solid ground. Bennett does not, understandably, want to imply that interpreters wage battles over a void or blank space; he resists being forced into the political silences that Fish's "text-less" theory creates. And so he fills the category of the "text" even as he is laboring mightily to empty it and designate the reader as the maker of meaning.

A reader-based politics is a thrilling prospect, but an alarming one as well, as Bennett's contradictory account implies. Bennett has to highlight the text in some way; otherwise, he risks suggesting that readers do not strive to occupy "something," but rather construct and produce "something" out of nothing. This would lead to the view that there are no texts, just readers competing for pre-eminence and seeking to impose their interpretations in order to make others produce the same texts that they do. It is this view of interpretive conduct that Bennett glimpses, in the midst of his heady calls for creative, interventionist reading, and that he cannot accept.

Politics and Interpretation

Literary critics and teachers have always been edgy about politics, and usually strive to distance or detach politics from their discipline. But in recent years, the politics of interpretation, fed by a growing interest in Marxism, has begun to emerge as an important concern. Richard Ohmann, in a passage I cited earlier, has stated that we must "teach politically with revolution as our end." Fredric Jameson has argued for "the priority of the political interpretation of literary texts." And Edward W. Said, Michael Ryan, Gayatri Spivak, and others have contributed to this political debate. Belsey and Bennett, in their different but related ways, also engage the political problems that interpretation raises.[21] But while it is necessary to acknowledge the "politics of interpretation" as a field for study, we should realize—and guard against— the dangers of understanding literature and criticism in wholly political terms. Perhaps the foremost of these, as Gerald Graff has observed, is equating literary analysis with political analysis, and assuming that a "radical" *literary* theory illuminates, in some real and compelling manner, a *political* fact or dispute. Literary politics can all too easily become a substitute for an actual politics.[22]

Work on the politics of interpretation is now underway, but it is mostly in its early stages. All of us are aware that teaching and criticism have a political dimension and impact, yet we still do not possess a "language" that will enable us to describe just how politics informs and emanates from what we do. The kind of teaching that we favor, the type of criticism that we write and promote, the inclusions and exclusions evident in reading lists—all of this testifies to a political stand or commitment. But to say this merely gives us a point of departure for conducting an analysis of the politics of interpretation and the political power of the "institution" of English studies. We are still in the process of discovering the areas of our work where politics are truly present and vitally important—the areas where politics enters practice in significant ways, dictating or determining the slant of interpretations. And we are still devising and refining a discourse that will enable us to describe the politics of interpretation cogently—a discourse that is insightful and revelatory, and that remembers the differences— even as it seeks the relationships between—politics and literature.

"Every relation of force," Foucault aptly remarks,

> implies at each moment a relation of power (which is in a sense its momentary expression) and every power relation makes a reference, as its effect but also as its condition of possibility, to a political field of which it forms a part. To say that "everything is political," is to affirm this ubiquity of relations of force and their immanence in a political field; but this is to give oneself the task, which as yet has scarcely even been outlined, of disentangling this indefinite knot.[23]

The project to which Foucault refers—"disentangling" the relations of power and politics—is a crucial one for literary critics and theorists to undertake, one that has been ignored for too long. Yet it is important to realize the vastness and difficulty of such an enterprise. This is not to imply—as some might wish to believe—that it cannot in fact succeed and hence ought to be abandoned in favor of more traditional tasks. But it is to suggest that a great deal of specific, detailed research is going to have to occur before we can become truly knowledgeable about interpretive and pedagogical politics. There has been some encouraging work in this direction, notably Ohmann's *English in America*, a book that is, as I have indicated, flawed and overbearing in sections, but a book that musters much valuable detail about critical traditions, pedagogical practices, institutional habits and values. Yet it is striking that no other books have followed Ohmann's lead. No one has yet moved to refine, supplement, and elaborate his arguments or assembled further groupings of fact and testimony. Political rhetoric and position-taking abound, but regrettably we have seen very little concrete research.

Teachers and critics err, I have argued, when they seek to erect enclosures around English studies. This is not a good way to protect the discipline; it manages only to devalue it. Nor are such enclosures defensible, for they invariably make "English" into a home for privileged masterpieces that function to exclude counter-statements, minority voices, and non-canonical texts. To enclose English studies is to isolate and deform it, and ensure that complaints about its irrelevance and unworldliness will continue. But having said this, I want to urge that care be taken in how we introduce "politics" into the reformed practices of the discipline. We need much more research and far less rhetoric, more scrutiny of past and present procedures and fewer declarations of political right-mindedness.

As it now exists, the debate on the politics of interpretation is generally unproductive and, in many ways, shamefully unreal. Rather than receiving for study a number of focused analyses, we are witnessing heavy-handed linkages between theoretical and political positions; intolerant dismissals of any work that seems less than pure in its political attitudes; and the formation of various groups, programs, and itineraries that claim to be politically enlightened but that are narrow, self-serving, and self-congratulatory. Many teachers and critics are anxious for the quick fix; having suddenly discovered that there is indeed a "politics" in their work, they then conclude that true wisdom lies in affirming one's own political insight and exposing those whose political fidelity might be in doubt. They bypass all the intermediate steps—they do not "disentangle" the "knot" to which Foucault alludes—and hasten to prove that they are political activists and not merely literary critics. This guarantees that the politics will be pretentious and shallow, and that significant changes in criticism and teaching will not take place.

What happens too often at the present time—and here I return to my point of departure in this chapter—is that the critics and theorists who debate "politics" rarely display much capacity for true judgment. Many apparent expressions of judgment figure in this area, but nearly all are extremely coarse and crude and have an air of unreality to them. There is an irresistible need to discover and attack certain people for the "political" failures of their work, and for their seeming affiliation, in the tenets of their theory, with the formulators of government policy. The work may indeed reveal political shortcomings that we ought to address. Yet one senses that when Gerald Graff, M. H. Abrams, and others are roughly handled, they are in fact serving as stand-ins, as substitutes, for the politicians and corporate executives that academic criticism neither affects nor concerns in the slightest. I have my own objections to Graff and Abrams, and I think that their writing is flawed in ways we might term "political." But the case being made against them and others on the so-called theoretical "right"—this is a very naive designation—is over-wrought. It is misguided to view the "politics of interpretation" as somehow involving the tracking down of enemies or the search for equivalences between certain theorists and Ronald Reagan. Surely we can do better than that.

Learning to address the politics of interpretation is not something that occurs overnight. It is thrilling to regard oneself as the torch-bearer for theoretical radicalism, and to attack other critics and theorists for political impurity. But if we intend to deal with politics effectively and convincingly, we are obliged to engage in specific projects that show true tactical sense. Such projects will define in detail the network that binds pedagogy and politics; explore the precise political orientation of a particular theory, model, or system (it will not do simply to apply labels such as "reactionary" and "neo-conservative"); examine the political choices inherent in canon-formation; probe the relation—assuming one exists—between scholarly and political expertise; and illuminate the forms through which one might make teaching politically adept and meaningful without curtailing freedom and choice.

Taking Foucault's work as his methodological point of departure, Said has scrutinized the "politics" of literary and other kinds of discourse. In his critique of "Orientalism," he studies the discursive practices that have imposed cruel and destructive stereotypes on the people of the Middle East and that have encouraged political oppression and control. In my next chapter, I begin by discussing Said's work, noting in particular its reliance on new theories of criticism, theories that prove illuminating but that are also subversive of Said's moral commitments. I then proceed to other important theorists and critics, including Gerald Graff, Frank Lentricchia, and Ihab Hassan, who have also attempted to bring the politics of interpretation into focus and chart new courses for criticism. There is much in this large body of work to commend and learn from, but also a good deal that is confused and in need of re-examination.

9.

Reviewing the State
of Criticism, III

Maybe the most certain of all philosophical problems is the problem of the present time and what we are in this very moment.

Michel Foucault, "The Subject and Power"

Edward W. Said. *Orientalism.* New York: Pantheon, 1978.

To assess Edward W. Said's account of "Orientalism," we must first understand what he means by the term. "Orientalism," Said explains in his introduction, refers to "several things, all of them, in my opinion, interdependent" (p. 2). The first is "Orientalism" as an academic field of study. It originated in France and England in the late eighteenth and early nineteenth centuries, rapidly acquired a special vocabulary and set of doctrines, and soon hardened into a method for imposing its terms on "the Orient" that scholars claimed to be studying "objectively." But Orientalism is more than an academic discipline. It is also "a style of thought based upon an ontological and epistemological distinction made between 'the Orient' and 'the Occident'." Writers as different as Aeschylus, Dante, and Marx assume a sharp distinction between East and West, and use it as a "starting point" for literary, historical, and other kinds of texts. Said's third meaning of Orientalism relates these "academic" and "imaginative" ones. Orientalism is "the corporate institution for dealing with the Orient—dealing with it by making statements about it, authorizing views of it, describing it, teaching it, settling it, ruling over it: in short, Orientalism as a Western style for dominating, restructuring, and having authority over the Orient" (p. 3).

Borrowing from the theoretical writings of Michel Foucault, Said describes Orientalism as a linguistic and institutional "order" that enables the West to control—and even to "produce" (p. 3)—the Orient. *Orientalism* portrays Orientalist discourse as a means of exercising power, as a form of mastery and domination. In a rich and provocative way,

Said surveys the history of "Orientalism," in all its inter-related meanings, and he exposes the dangers of failing to perceive (and be responsible for) the social, political, and ethical implications of scholarly work and pedagogical tradition. *Orientalism* is the product of an agile and powerful intelligence, one familiar with the most advanced work of Continental theorists, including Foucault and Jacques Derrida. Said's skillful deployment of theoretical terms and methods gives his book a special kind of interest for literary critics and cultural historians. But *Orientalism* is also of special interest because it reveals Said's ambivalent feelings about the new methods that he uses well and esteems highly. As his book progresses, Said depends on influential theorists and yet commits himself to values that these theorists expressly disallow.

In his introduction, Said examines the remarkable "internal consistency" of Orientalism. For hundreds of years, Orientalism has interpreted and judged the Orient according to its assumptions about what the Orient must be "like," and has done so despite the lack of correspondence between the Orientalist's terms and the "real" Orient (p. 5). The most important of these assumptions is that the Orient cannot "represent" itself. It cannot, that is, speak in its own voice and articulate its desires and ideals, but needs the Orientalist to speak *for* it. Said's first chapter, "The Scope of Orientalism," touches on a range of Oriental "representations." From Arthur James Balfour and Lord Cromer to Henry Kissinger, Western diplomats and policy-makers have felt obliged to speak for the Orient. It is not the case, Said observes, that these men invoke Orientalist assumptions about a backward, depraved, uninformed Orient to justify a colonialism that already exists (for example, in the Middle East). Rather, the terms of Orientalism justify a colonial exploitation "in advance" (p. 39). Because the Orient "is" backward, the West has a duty, even a right, to control it, and to force Occidental culture upon it.

Chapter one also traces key events in the history of Orientalism: the Napoleonic invasion in 1798, the building of the Suez Canal (which was opened in 1869), and the growth of European societies and periodicals for the study of the Orient. As Said reviews the development of Orientalism, and discloses its pernicious effect on contemporary social and political thought, his tone becomes indignant: "Arabs, for example, are thought of as camel-riding, terroristic, hook-nosed, venal lechers whose undeserved wealth is an affront to real civilization. Always there lurks the assumption that although the Western consumer belongs to a numerical minority, he is entitled either to own or to expend (or both) the majority of the world's resources. Why? Because he, unlike the Oriental, is a true human being" (p. 108). The legacy of Orientalism, Said states, is "dehumanized thought."

Said's second chapter, "Orientalist Structures and Restructures," concentrates on nineteenth-century Orientalism, analyzing the work of its "inaugural heroes" Silvestre de Sacy and Ernest Renan, and showing its relation to the new interest in philology and scientific classification. Early in the rise of Orientalism, two points became clear. First, the European scholar studies the texts of the Orient and explores its languages from a "superior" position; Renan, for instance, examines the Orient in order to point out "defects, virtues, barbarisms, and shortcomings in the language, the people, the civilization" (p. 142). Second, these cultural generalizations about the people of the Orient are never seen to involve questions of power, exploitation, and control, but are instead judged as objective, truthful products of scientific research. "Cultural generalization" acquired "the armor of scientific statement and the ambience of corrective study" (p. 149). Even when Western scholars, such as Edward William Lane and Sir Richard Burton, or writers, including Chateaubriand, Lamartine, Nerval, and Flaubert, traveled to the Orient and lived among its people, they remained bound to Orientalist assumptions: whether you stayed in Europe to study the Orient's texts, or journeyed to the Orient as a pilgrim and explorer, you retained "Orientalism" as the one valid language for your experience. By the late nineteenth century, "Orientalism was fully formalized into a repeatedly produced copy of itself" (p. 197).

In his final chapter, "Orientalism Now," Said maps the history of Orientalism from the 1870s to the present. Returning to one of the themes of his first chapter, he depicts Orientalism's "new sense of worldly mission in the service of colonialism" (p. 205); as the British statesman Lord Curzon observed in 1909, Oriental studies had become "a great Imperial obligation." Combining with racial theory and belief in the white man's natural superiority, Orientalism served the purposes of colonialism. And colonialism took place despite the tenets of English and French "liberal culture," which Said ironically defines as "full of concern for its vaunted norms of catholicity, plurality, and open-mindedness" (p. 254). In a series of penetrating critiques, Said reveals Orientalist thinking at work in the writings of William Robertson Smith, T. E. Lawrence, Maurice Barrès, A. R. Gibb, Louis Massignon, and others. Both Lane's and Lawrence's narratives demonstrate "the defeat of narrative by vision" (p. 239). The Orientalist embraces "vision"—a comprehensive, static account of the Orient—and spurns or resists "narrative"—a detailed story that allows for change, disruption, and movement. If the Orientalist presented his text in the form of a true narrative, he would imply that the Orient is *not* composed of unchanging traits. More importantly, he would be forced to concede that his "scientific" vision of a whole people is a will-to-power over them—an attempt to contain the Orient by seeing it exclusively through Western eyes.

Despite new and sophisticated work in the human sciences, Orientalism is still "methodologically and ideologically backward" (p. 261). In the popular press, in colleges and universities, in master-works like *The Cambridge History of Islam*, the dogmas of Orientalism retain their power. These are, first,

> the absolute and systematic difference between the West, which is rational, developed, humane, superior, and the Orient, which is aberrant, undeveloped, inferior. Another dogma is that abstractions about the Orient, particularly those based on texts representing a "classical" Oriental civilization, are always preferable to direct evidence drawn from modern Oriental realities. A third dogma is that the Orient is eternal, uniform, and incapable of defining itself; therefore it is assumed that a highly generalized and systematic vocabulary for describing the Orient from a Western standpoint is inevitable and even scientifically "objective." A fourth dogma is that the Orient is at bottom something either to be feared (the Yellow Peril, the Mongol hordes, the brown dominions) or to be controlled (by pacification, research and development, outright occupation whenever possible). (Pp. 300-301)

Not only do these dogmas provide the terms for Western thought about the Orient, but they also influence the contours of *Eastern* thought. As young people from the Orient come to England and America to study, they absorb these dogmas themselves. Perhaps the greatest human tragedy of Orientalism is that "the modern Orient" now "participates in its own Orientalizing" (p. 325).

Said's methods are illuminating and enable him to deal impressively with a complex topic. But Said's methodological premises also lead him into difficulties. One of these is implicit in his phrase "Oriental realities," which occurs in his summary of Orientalist dogmas. As Said exposes the failings of Orientalism, he builds up a need on his reader's part to know what, then, is the "real" Orient. Said is aware that he has created this expectation, and addresses it late in his book. He argues, somewhat surprisingly, that "it is not the thesis of this book to suggest that there is such a thing as a real or true Orient (Islam, Arab, or whatever)." True to his belief in the scholar's power to "constitute" (to design and be responsible for) his or her field, Said contends that "the 'Orient' is itself a constituted entity" (p. 322). But his claim that he is not arguing for a "real" Orient jars against phrases such as "brute reality," "empirical reality," and "brute everyday reality"; these phrases are taken from several pages of Said's introduction (pp. 5-10), and there are many other examples.

Said tells us that the Orient is always "constituted"—the interpreter creates and produces it. Yet he repeatedly insists on the presence of Oriental "reality" or "realities," implying that an Orient exists that is not the work of interpreters. Throughout *Orientalism* there is an ambivalent relation between Said's commitment (he is an Arab Palestinian himself) to the manifestly "real" people of the Orient, and his assumption that all areas of experience and knowledge are "constituted." He upholds his theoretical belief—which questions the "real"—but also affirms sympathies that are real and immediate. No one would wish to dispute Said's personal stake in his work, yet his terms for it are discredited by the theories that he embraces.

In his first chapter, Said mentions the "common human failing to prefer the schematic authority of a text to the disorientations of direct encounters with the human" (p. 93). But if the scholar is always constituting, creating, shaping what he sees, then can he ever engage other men directly, in an unmediated encounter? By "constituting" his field of study, the scholar necessarily views others through preconceptions, never directly. This does not mean that all preconceptions and representations are equal, and that Orientalism thus should be excused for its vicious narrow-mindedness. But it does mean that Said cannot argue, theoretically, for the scholar's inevitable shaping of his field, and then invoke "human realities," "direct encounters," and so on. Said's theoretical and human allegiances are at cross purposes. On one page he declares that "there is no such thing as a delivered presence, but a re-presence, or a representation" (p. 21); yet on another he complains that "even in Burton's prose we are never directly given the Orient" (p. 196). If Said truly believes his first point, then he cannot make his second one.

Said's relation to Foucault's work is also ambivalent. Said has examined Foucault's "archaeologies" of social and political power on several occasions, and he greatly admires Foucault's emphasis on the importance of institutions, the constraints on discourse and knowledge, and the structural "formations" that exist among vast numbers of texts.[1] But Said differs sharply with this theorist on the question of the "author." "Unlike Michel Foucault, I do believe in the determining imprint of individual writers upon the otherwise collective body of texts constituting a discursive formation like Orientalism" (p. 23). Despite the massive presence of a particular discourse, an author does possess authority; he or she can make choices about the structure of texts and can produce a difference and displacement in the discursive system. Because Said credits an author with authoritative power, he is able to describe Sacy, Renan, and Lane as "builders of the field" of Islamic studies, "creators of a tradition, progenitors of the Orientalist brotherhood" (p. 122).

Said does not always maintain the author's authority, however, nor does he always express his difference from Foucault so clearly. At several points, he refers to the "inevitability" with which Orientalist terms and assumptions appear in an author's text (for example, pp. 69,

96). But if the text (or some part of it) must "inevitably" be structured in a certain way, and if the order of Orientalist discourse forms an author's writing, then how does an author's authority manifest itself? Said asserts that an author can make influential choices and decisions, and hence can deploy "writing" to make profound and meaningful differences. Yet Said also emphasizes that Orientalism is powerful enough to preclude, to rule out, individual choice. Orientalist texts "can create not only knowledge but also the very reality they appear to describe. In time such knowledge and reality produce a tradition, or what Michel Foucault calls a discourse, whose material presence or weight, not the originality of a given author, is really responsible for the texts produced out of it" (p. 94). Now Said assigns "responsibility" to texts, and he removes the author's authority that he elsewhere affirms.

Said is caught in a bind that has trapped many critics and intellectuals today. He has learned from and respects the work of Foucault, Derrida, and other Continental theorists, yet he resists their displacement of the individual (the "I" who writes). Said embraces their principles about language, institutions, and discourse, but balks at accepting their severe limits on the author's contributions to texts. If he agreed that the author lacks authority, then he would risk implying that his own work—whatever the intensities that impel it—is self-defeating, almost an exercise in futility, because he does not exercise control over, and is not "really responsible" for, his texts. Despite his loyalties to (and borrowings from) Foucault and others, Said promotes originality, initiative, personal authority, and responsibility.

Related to Said's confusion about the author is one that concerns his category of the "human." Many of his pages refer to "human realities" and attack Orientalism for failing to respect the "human" nature of its subject. Yet it is hard to know exactly what Said means by the term he uses so often and reverently. When Foucault and Derrida criticize the "author," they do so as part of their attempt to displace "human" categories that judge man to be the measure of all things and locate us in a position distinct from the linguistic order. As Said's indictment of "humanism" suggests, he agrees that we should not exalt the "human," for this turns, all too easily, into exalting one kind of "human" over another. In the conclusion to his final chapter, however, Said proposes that we should adopt "human freedom and knowledge" as the norm in scholarship. We should remember that "the study of man in society is based on concrete human history and experience"; we should foster "human community" and identify with "human experience" (pp. 327-28).

This is to make a ringing endorsement of a very problematical kind. It depends upon the existence of profoundly "real," "directly present," "human" concerns, precisely the concerns that Said advocates but that his theoretical premises prohibit. I share Said's desire to profess personal responsibility and human community; but I do not see that Foucault's and Derrida's work (at least the phases of that work which Said cites) generally encourages them. When we "affirm" these values, we may be obliged to do so through an act of individual testimony, because we cannot demonstrate that they follow logically from the theories that we draw upon. Foucault and Derrida provide Said with powerful tools for investigating Orientalism, but they do not offer a hierarchy of values to take its place. Said provides these values himself, and he is to be commended for that even though his provision conflicts with sentences like this one: "My project has been to describe a particular system of ideas, not by any means to displace the system with a new one" (p. 325). Here Said aligns himself with Foucault and Derrida and joins in their refusal to substitute a new set of values for the old. His words are methodologically astute, but it would be difficult to imagine a more dramatic statement of limitation and weakness. If this is where the Continental theorists lead us, we would do well to continue our affirmations of "human realities."

Gerald Graff. *Literature against Itself: Literary Ideas in Modern Society.*
  Chicago: University of Chicago Press, 1979.

In this stimulating book, Gerald Graff examines the function of "literary thinking" (p. 1) at the present time. His judgment is stated sharply:

> Almost as if a formal partition-treaty had been negotiated, the creative faction (or the creative side of the individual) has renounced its claim to be a seeker of rational understanding and identified itself with an outlook that makes rational understanding sound contemptible. There is no deterministic theory of degeneration at work in my diagnosis. Our literary thinking has gone wrong because we have, by our own free will and conscious reasoning, sold ourselves a certain conceptual bill of goods. (Pp. 28-29)

Teaching and scholarship are in disarray, and Graff charges that we bear the responsibility. We tolerate the decline of critical standards in academic journals and in the classroom; we allow beliefs and principles to change according to the tastes of the moment; and we produce scholarly work in abundant measure, and debate the most rarefied questions of literary theory, without asking ourselves what is the meaning of all this industry. Perhaps the most disturbing fact about our work as teachers and scholars is, Graff emphasizes, our willingness to divorce literature from culture and society. Even as we arm ourselves with extravagant theories, we insist that literature has nothing of value to say about the real world: the more sophisticated the terminology, the more irrelevant it seems, and its irrelevance is seen not as a limitation, but as a necessity. Eugene Goodheart has observed that "humanist criticism, which has as its object the quality of life as well as works of art, no longer has authority."[2] After reading Graff's book, and reflecting upon the declared tenets of many in the profession, one is tempted to claim that *no* criticism carries firm and clear authority. Few critics and teachers—or at least few on the vanguard of today's critical movements—believe that "literary thinking is bound, in a crucial and resourceful way, to thinking about culture and society."

Graff describes *Literature against Itself* as an "argumentative" book, and it suffers from the common failings of other books in this mold— the repetition of points made several times before, the selective quotation of the opposing side to make the argument even stronger, flagging energy in the final chapters, much more diagnosis of the problems than advice about how best to cure them. But *Literature against Itself* tackles the right issues, and unlike many books on critical theory, it is not imprisoned in its own vocabulary, and is not unmindful of the social and institutional contexts for the work we do (or fail to do). Graff's analysis is wide-ranging and detailed, covering modernism and post-modernism, New Criticism, the state of the discipline (which Graff explores by reviewing Richard Ohmann's *English in America: A Radical View of the Profession*), structuralism, and deconstruction.

Graff is particularly good at tracing the continuities between New and "Newer" Criticism. We often assume that deconstruction as practiced by Derrida, Paul De Man, and others, marks a full-fledged assault on the legacy of the New Critics. But while there are obvious differences between the two critical movements—John Crowe Ransom and his allies would surely scoff at the verbal pyrotechnics and obscurity of the deconstructive style—they both devalue, even renounce, the ties between literature and the world. The New Critics maintain that the text exists as a discrete object and stress that we should monitor its subtleties and patterns without attending to the author's intention or historical period. The brute realities of the world, the New Critics imply, should not distort the literary text. With the coming of post-structuralism, Graff notes, this position is not reversed or overthrown, but rather taken to its logical conclusion. Derrida, Roland Barthes, and others argue, like the New Critics, that the text does not refer to reality, and then proclaim a "liberating" corollary to this point: reality is not so much separate or different from literature, but "textual" itself. Textuality is disseminated everywhere; as Said once observed, there is nothing but discourse— "wall to wall." According to this view, when we describe the power of literature to "refer" to the real world, we are naively failing to perceive that statements of "the real" are always a form of "textual" interpretation. Reality is, at bottom, just another fiction; it is never something other than a text, never something towards which a literary text revealingly gestures.

Literary critics thus subvert the possibility of their own enterprise. Objective thinking is said to be impossible; textual and fictional categories can never be transcended; and "reality" and "reference" are simply other names for the illusions that interpretive desires generate. As Graff shows, many advanced theorists are oddly pleased with themselves for deciding that analysis is futile and that the real and true are whatever perceptual strategies and conventions make them. "At the very moment," he states, "when external forces have conspired to deflate the importance and truth of literature, literary theory delivers the final blow itself" (p. 26). As critics and intellectuals, we often define ourselves in opposition to the established culture. Yet we now act in league with the society we claim to be opposing. We agree that the study of literature is not a valuable use of one's time, for literary discourse lacks the explanatory power to make statements about the world in which we live.[3]

Literature against Itself is part of a major critical tradition that includes the writings of Lionel Trilling, F. R. Leavis, and Raymond Williams, who share a deep respect for the value of "literary thinking," whatever their differences in temperament and method. But while Graff prosecutes an important case, he encounters difficulties at the center of his argument for the "referential" capacity of literature. Like other foes of unsettling trends in the profession, Graff is caught between admirable goals and dubious arguments for attaining them. And like Said in particular, he reveals the difficulties that critics and theorists face when they talk about the "real."

Graff believes that we must adopt a referential theory of literature in order to relate literary study to the real world. There is a "reality" independent of interpretive categories, and literary modes of thinking can help us to understand and strive to change it. By splitting off literature from the world, and by refusing to move beyond texts and fictions, we rule out the possibility for change. We have no basis in fact for challenging very real evils: "injustice, poverty, triviality, vulgarity, and social loneliness" (p. 101). "The notion," Graff contends, "that there exists an objective reality 'out there,' independent of our perceptions of it, far from being an ideological rationalization for the existing order, is a prerequisite for changing the existing order, which has to be understood before it can be altered" (p. 27).

But later Graff shifts his arguments about literature and reality. We must have standards and principles, he insists, or else accept chaos and "radical cultural relativism." "Is there no standard of good reasons," he asks, "that can be invoked to show that democratic freedom constitutes a wiser choice than genocidal extinction?" (p. 38). It is one thing, however, to emphasize the presence of an "objective reality," and another to appeal to "good reasons" or persuasive formulations (p. 89) or "extremely convincing" readings (p. 159). Here, Graff is describing verbal constructs, techniques of persuasion, language used as an instrument of power—in a word, rhetoric. And it is precisely the burden of the history of rhetoric that its verbal means are not always tied to the "real" and may even (as Plato warned) substitute for it. When we enlist language as a means of persuasion and capitalize on its rhetorical force, we are attempting to solicit support for our way of seeing things; this is not necessarily the same as asserting an "objective reality" for statements.

Graff is, of course, aware of the "power" of language, and he knows too that our post-Kantian heritage concludes we understand reality through perceptual categories. Yet even as Graff testifies to the ways we form and construct reality, he also talks about objective, "disinterested" reports of the "facts." He says that "value-free objectivity is a necessary first stage of making of value judgments—the descriptive, disinterested determination of what it is that is to be judged" (p. 86). This is an admirable goal, but it cannot be accepted if one endorses Graff's other remarks about *interested* perception and interpretive categories. At one point Graff tries to have his argumentative cake and eat it too: "That we cannot conceive of a fact without *some* interpretive paradigm does not mean that this fact can have no independent status outside *the particular paradigm we happen to be testing at the moment*" (p. 202, Graff's emphasis). Again, this signals a praiseworthy effort to maintain a reality separate from our interpretations, but the obvious question is, where and how do the "facts" exist when distinct from interpretation? What is their status? Graff proceeds, on the next page, to call upon Ralph Rader (who is summarizing Karl Popper) to buttress his position. But he discusses his lengthy quotation from Rader by first describing it as an "argument" and then as an "assumption." The quoted passage does not seem to me to constitute an "argument," and it is less an "assumption" than a desire for a certain state of affairs, where a galaxy of independent facts spotlights the truth or falsity of interpretations.

Without a firm basis in "fact," an objective reality, then "anything goes" (pp. 39, 50). This is a common fear, shared by E. D. Hirsch, Wayne Booth, and M. H. Abrams. But we should ask ourselves if it is truly the case that "anything goes." Though Graff may not be satisfied by my answer, I would suggest here, as in my critique of Hirsch in chapter one, that there are always limits and constraints on interpretation: it is never the case that "anything goes." We practice interpretive work within an institution, and while its norms and codes may be elusive, confusing, and even objectionable, they are nevertheless pres-

ent and influential. Many things "go" (not all of them good) in interpretation, but not just anything at all. Interpretation is never totally
random or arbitrary, and as Graff's own analysis often suggests, we
should not underestimate the institutional pressures that regulate our
work. As Foucault, Stanley Fish, and Jonathan Culler have suggested,
no one can say just anything, because there are contextual boundaries
to what one might say in a particular situation. These constraints are
not easy to specify; they are not the same for all situations; and it is
possible to amend or oppose them—though we usually pay a price for
doing so. In a curiously apt phrase, George Meredith once referred to
the "unwritten but perceptible laws binding [us] in consideration one
to another." Their shape is not absolute or unchanging, but they never
disappear, and never leave us in a chaos where "anything goes."[4]
Graff's ambitions in *Literature against Itself* are laudable, but at several
key stages, his arguments are as over-stated or misguided as those he
rejects.

To bring order to literary studies, Graff proposes that we should
encourage "a historical view." We must return "the student to his
history" and show the critical perspective "from which to assess the
richness and poverty of the contemporary, to see what has been gained
from this break with the past and what has been lost—and might be
regained" (p. 124). English teachers should work in "collaboration"
with teachers in other departments and thereby indicate to students
the complex nature of what may seem at first to be purely "literary"
issues:

> The fact that scholars do not agree on the nature of history
> does not defeat such a program, for its purpose would
> not be to indoctrinate the student with a single theory
> but to bring him into the debate, to introduce him to
> the issues, and to equip him with the means to form his
> judgment of them and see his personal connection with
> them. The point is not to destroy pluralism but to
> transform it into a pluralism defined by a community of
> debate rather than a pluralism of incommensurable
> positions. (P. 125)

Like much of Graff's writing in *Literature against Itself*, this declaration
strikes a responsive chord. But even as one welcomes Graff's commitment to historical understanding and pluralistic debate, one wonders
how he will make a place for "judgment." If this recommendation is
to be taken seriously, then Graff must explain what it is directed towards—what better "reality." Without such a referent, he comes close
to the position that he rebukes in Sontag, Barthes, and the rest, crippling
the power of literature because it is denied the right to enunciate precise,

truthful judgments. How do we embrace a pluralistic program without falling into the defeatism that Graff warns us about in others? How do we avoid "the patronizing of diverse viewpoints" that characterizes "contemporary society" and that reflects "a contempt for ideas, which are seen as impotent, and not of a disposition to take them seriously" (p. 213)? Graff is often perceptive in noting when two apparently different positions share common ground, but he misses the most vexing of these correspondences. Because his proposal for "a historical view" lacks concrete definition and reference, it returns us to the weak forms of "literary thinking" he attacks.

Frank Lentricchia. *After the New Criticism*. Chicago: University of Chicago Press, 1980.

Frank Lentricchia's *After the New Criticism*—"an exposition and an evaluation of the course of critical theory in the United States for roughly the past two decades" (p. xi)—is difficult to review. It is clearly a major book, offering a pointed and very stimulating critique of recent work in literary theory. Yet it is also flawed and confusing, its failings tangled with its successes. Some of the problems concern Lentricchia's procedure and organization, while others raise significant questions about the nature of his arguments. Often judicious and illuminating, *After the New Criticism* is, on other occasions, uneven and overbearing, and puzzling in its repetition of errors that Lentricchia rebukes in others.

Lentricchia divides his book into two sections. The first, devoted to "A Critical Thematics, 1957-77," begins with Frye's *Anatomy of Criticism*, proceeds to careful treatments of Frank Kermode, Georges Poulet, Jonathan Culler, and others, and closes with a detailed account of major structuralist and post-structuralist theorists, including Barthes, Derrida, and Foucault. Much of Lentricchia's analysis in these chapters is first-rate and enlivened by his polemical intention. He shows, for example, the lingering traces of "New Critical" principles in the various theories, notably Frye's in *Anatomy of Criticism* (1957) and other books and Kermode's in his *Romantic Image* (1957) and *Sense of an Ending* (1966), designed to counter them. Common to nearly all literary theory since the New Criticism is, Lentricchia observes, the desire to "essentialize" literary discourse, distinguishing it from other types of discourse and saving it from the taint of historical, political, and social contexts. Lentricchia skillfully explores the dangers of opposing "fiction" and "reality," and he demonstrates that this dichotomy, perhaps best exemplified in the influential poetics of Wallace Stevens, privileges literature even as it removes it from relation to the world: we find our values and make our home in "fictions," not in stubborn, demanding "reality."

Lentricchia's argument is powerful, and he highlights a disturbing willingness on the part of many important theorists to undercut their discipline and subject-matter. They describe literature as divorced from reality, see it as unrelated to and uninvolved in history, and dismiss its political and social engagements, yet still insist that literature ought somehow to retain our respect and allegiance. As Lentricchia rightly points out—and here he echoes Gerald Graff—literary theorists have been subverting the grounds for teaching and criticism for decades, and in the subjectivism and nihilism touted by certain contemporary figures, we witness the logical next step in this self-crippling process.

Lentricchia does many other things well. He deals capably, if at times murkily, with the philosophers—Kant, Nietzsche, Sartre, Husserl, Heidegger—who have influenced contemporary theories of literature. He is also effective in reviewing Saussure, Barthes, Derrida, and Foucault, and he indicates how badly both their supporters and their antagonists have misunderstood them. The "Yale Derrideans," Lentricchia remarks, are a case in point. Even as they align themselves with Derrida's "deconstructive" strategies, they privilege literary discourse (which, they claim, is "self-deconstructing" and thereby not "mystified" about itself) and refuse to recognize Derrida's arguments against privileging one discourse over others. Lentricchia states that these American appropriations of Derrida, so unfaithful to his deconstructive texts, isolate the critic from society, allowing him or her to sit self-absorbedly in the halls of the academy:

> American post-structuralist literary criticism tends to be an activity of textual privatization, the critic's doomed attempt to retreat from a social landscape of fragmentation and alienation. Criticism becomes, in this perspective, something like an ultimate mode of interior decoration whose chief value lies in its power to trigger our pleasure and whose chief measure of success lies in its capacity to keep pleasure going in a potentially infinite variety of ways (P. 186).

In part two of his book, Lentricchia concentrates on the four "exemplary" theorists—Murray Krieger, E. D. Hirsch, Paul De Man, and Harold Bloom—who have, he believes, "the strongest claim to being the major theorists in American criticism since about 1957" (p. xii). Lentricchia's analysis in these chapters is again trenchant. He notes acutely, for instance, Krieger's strained effort to concede the principles of post-structuralism yet stay committed to his views about the poem's special discourse and presence—views that post-structuralists deny. Lentricchia also describes Hirsch's misunderstandings of Saussure, Gadamer, and Heidegger, criticizes De Man for his intellectual arrogance, "Olympian stance," and "crafty rhetorical maneuvers," and suggests that Bloom, whose theory could lead to a productive return of

222 THE CRISIS IN CRITICISM

poets and poems to "history," "has chosen to articulate his position in ways that guarantee hostile rejoinder" (p. 343). Despite some local shortcomings and overstatements, Lentricchia's critique of these theorists is very sharp and persuasive.

Lentricchia's important book has serious failings. First of all, Lentricchia's scholarship suffers from unfortunate gaps. Though he knows his primary texts well, he appears unaware of the many commentaries and reviews that exist about them and hence misses opportunities to supplement and strengthen his arguments. Lentricchia's section on Culler's *Structuralist Poetics* is suggestive, but it is repetitive in some places and incomplete in others for readers who know Michael Ryan's review (*Philological Quarterly*, 1976, pp. 294-96) and Paul Bové's review article (*Boundary 2*, 1976, pp. 263-84), both of which anticipate Lentricchia's arguments about Culler's attempt to "domesticate" post-structuralism. Lentricchia's polemical thrusts are keen and sometimes wickedly barbed, but on occasion he is too anxious to condemn the theorists that he opposes, and his tone then sounds hectoring. When he discusses Stanley Fish's work, almost every sentence is derisive. This would be less of a problem if the sentences did not themselves distort and misrepresent Fish's position.[5]

This raises a larger question about the proportions and emphases of Lentricchia's study. He devotes only three pages to Fish, in contrast with the forty pages he spends on Krieger. The proportions are skewed here, and I think that Lentricchia is mistaken about the relative importance and influence of these two theorists. Krieger is an excellent critical historian, and his *New Apologists for Poetry* (1956) remains a classic text on the New Criticism. He is also a sensitive interpreter of texts, as his *Tragic Vision* (1960) and *Classic Vision* (1971) demonstrate, and he provides us with good accounts of the state of criticism in his *Theory of Criticism* (1976) and *Poetic Presence and Illusion* (1979). Yet this prolific writer has not exercised much influence on literary theory; his achievements are considerable, but not in the area of a powerful, original theory. He has not altered and reshaped our understanding of major authors and traditions, and this is precisely what Fish has done in his books on Milton (1967) and Herbert (1978), and in *Self-Consuming Artifacts* (1972). Fish's work in literary theory has affected practical criticism and pedagogy, and the field of "reader-response criticism" owes much to his authority. His work has limitations and blind spots, as I have made clear in previous chapters, but it is unfair and misleading for Lentricchia to brush him aside and instead lavish such respectful attention on Krieger. To view the critical scene in this fashion is to misperceive it.

There are more basic problems with Lentricchia's arguments. In a number of places, he attacks theorists for their defeatism, pessimism, and surrender to a faddish despair about the disorder of the modern world (pp. 26, 33, 54, 57). Yet when Lentricchia outlines his own proposal for a new literary history based on his reading of Barthes, Derrida, Foucault, and others, he edges into a defeatist posture himself. He says that a variety of potent and complex institutional practices kept poets like Frost and Robinson from being heard during the late nineteenth and early twentieth centuries. With the "modernist revolution," these poets finally did receive an enthusiastic hearing. But, Lentricchia adds, if we are true to Foucault's insights and vigorous anti-humanism, we will not be cheered by this shift in poetic history: "Robinson and Frost were not liberated from incarceration by the modernist revolt; they were merely taken into new quarters of confinement, where under the authority of a different kind of repression their kinds of expression were granted the privilege of the poetic, even as other kinds were excluded and relegated to the status of the 'old-fashioned'" (p. 199).

If one form of repression replaces another, it is hard to avoid feeling the kind of pessimism about history and society that Lentricchia sternly argues against. Are there no discriminations that can be made—assuming for the moment that Foucault's terms are appropriate—between these different structures of repression? No differences among the forms of social organization that we can articulate and fight for? Lentricchia appears willing to accept Foucault's despairing vision of the repressive "order of things." Yet he also uses phrases such as "our human concerns," "an integrated human context," "obvious fact of our critical experience," and "normative principle," all of which move us in quite another direction. Lentricchia's feeling for this vocabulary and what it implies about our common labor as critics is exemplary. But I do not see how it can coexist with his sketch of an endlessly repressive history, where "human" values and "obvious" significances stand for just another form of confinement.

Lentricchia's sympathies are divided, and here he resembles both Graff and Said. Lentricchia is properly impatient with Frye, Kermode, Poulet, and others, and cleverly exposes the failings of their theories. One of the reasons for his skill as a critic and polemicist is that he has carefully read the writings of Derrida, Barthes, and Foucault, acquiring from them some powerful tactics and arguments. But while Lentricchia has learned much from the post-structuralists, he retains the "humanistic" loyalties that their work radically questions. If not altogether impossible, this humanistic revision of post-structuralism is at the least deeply problematical and conflicted. Lentricchia wants to turn the post-structuralists into advocates of a new, more sophisticated humanism, whereas their "deconstructions" and "archaeologies" rebuff humanist modes of inquiry.

Lentricchia's position reflects many of the theories he attacks, for it is founded less on logic and reasonable exposition than on a desire for a certain, preferred state of affairs. "Where," he inquires, "has de Man left things? Even should we agree that in the world of wall-to-wall discourse the aporia is inevitable—and I believe it is necessary to agree to this and to the post-structuralist problematic upon which the idea rests—we must resist being pushed there" (p. 317). Lentricchia knows that the strongest arguments veer away from the position he wishes us to occupy, yet he stresses that it is crucial that we occupy it anyway. Falling victim to the same charges that he mounts against others, Lentricchia, like De Man, asserts rather than proves the validity of his statements, and like Krieger, he maintains a position that he realizes is without argumentative backing. So interesting and provocative in many ways, *After the New Criticism* thus becomes an example of the contradictions that, says Lentricchia, plague the critical scene. He bears witness to humanistic ideals even when, according to the post-structuralist doctrines he espouses, there is no place left for them.

René Girard. *"To Double Business Bound"*: Essays on Literature, Mimesis, and Anthropology. Baltimore: Johns Hopkins University Press, 1978.
Hayden White. *Tropics of Discourse*: Essays in Cultural Criticism. Baltimore: Johns Hopkins University Press, 1978.

René Girard's *"To Double Business Bound"*: Essays on Literature, Mimesis, and Anthropology collects work that has already appeared in journals, including essays on Dante, Camus, Lévi-Strauss, Dostoevsky, and others; a long review article on Deleuze's and Guattari's *L'Anti-Oedipe*; and a thirty-page interview with Girard that was published in *Diacritics* (Spring, 1978). It mostly recapitulates the major themes of *Violence and the Sacred* (1972; trans. 1977), in which Girard examined the place of imitative desire, rivalry, and victimage in literature and society. But this new book heightens as well as repeats Girard's claims: he now insists on the centrality of his "hypothesis" for all studies of religion, myth, and culture. "Unanimous victimage," he maintains, "is the generative mechanism of all religious and cultural institutions." It is "the one mechanism truly able to supplant and supersede all the earlier solutions to the paradoxes of human culture and the human subject" (pp. 199, 218).

Briefly stated, Girard's argument is that desire is always "mimetic": one person "imitates" the desire of another person, deciding that he or she must possess a certain object because the other person has "designated" it to be desirable. As two or more persons come to desire the same object, they become rivals, copying one another's gambits and strategies in an effort to attain their goal. This struggle quickly intensifies, as the rivals grow more and more "like" one another (even as they strive to be "different" from one another), and it produces a "reciprocal violence" that threatens to destroy the community. "Once there is nothing left but the doubles in confrontation," Girard states, "the slightest accident, the tiniest sign can cause all reciprocal hatred to be fixed on one of them" (pp. 103-4). Joined in a common bond against the "scapegoat victim," men and women then violently restore unity to the society. But how does the society prevent the outbreak of another mimetic crisis? "Prohibitions" are one method; a second, Girard explains, is "ritual," which re-enacts conflict in a "safe" form, limiting the violence and controlling it.

In studying mimesis and victimage, we must remember several important points, Girard observes. First, there is no "privileged object" for desire. Contrary to Freud, for example, the male child does not naturally or instinctively desire the mother, but rather desires her because he is imitating one element of his father's desire.[6] Second, "it is truly impossible to fix the origin of and responsibility for desire, whose inexhaustible source is mimesis" (p. 91): we cannot pinpoint what triggers the desire to imitate desire, but can only witness its effects. Finally, the selection of the scapegoat, which ends the spiralling conflict, is always "arbitrary," the result of a random choice. Yet while this victim is "arbitrary," the community must, Girard emphasizes, see him or her as "real" and not randomly chosen. The community could not re-unite if it perceived the arbitrary status of the victim—for then everyone would be deserving of the victim's fate—and so the community refuses to acknowledge or "forgets" the arbitrariness. After the victim has done sacrificial work and brought peace to the community, he or she is exalted as beneficent, metamorphosed into the "sacred."

Girard argues that his "hypothesis" is preferable to all others— Freudian, Marxist, structuralist. It "organizes all the elements" in a clear, commonsensical way, and with "an economy of means" that must be judged as "prodigious" (p. 54). Yet, Girard remarks, it is not likely that his work will be taken seriously (p. 57), since it opposes the current and ill-informed intellectual order. The social sciences, he concludes, are "impotent," because they do not see the revelatory power of "the great literary masterpieces" that Shakespeare, Dostoevsky, and others have written (p. xi). Scholars in all fields also remain tied to the "myths" of Freudian analysis; even Deleuze and Guattari confirm the Oedipal complex that they attempt to overthrow. We are unwilling today to accept that the findings of "common sense" (which Girard identifies with his own work) are often the most "truly revolutionary" (p. 197).

The most disabling of our assumptions is, according to Girard, the self-referential text, which traps us in the prison-house of language and reduces all knowledge to a type of "solipsistic idealism" (pp. 174-75).

"Linguistic structuralism" does not escape from the "traditional mission" of criticism, but actually embraces it, "saying and re-saying meaning, paraphrasing and classifying significations," as critical work has always done (p. 43). When the post-structuralists argue that we cannot get behind or beyond language, they are really indulging in "cognitive nihilism" and pursuing the intellectual fashion of the moment at the expense of "decisive results" and "significant truths" (pp. 118, 194).

Girard's polemical manner and energetic attack on his critical competitors obscure the vexed nature of his discoveries. Girard believes that culture is menaced by "the complete disintegration of sacrificial protections" (p. 207): because we have lost belief in the "sacred" (p. 220), we no longer possess the cultural safeguards that ritual once provided. Violence is not limited, "safely" channeled into ritual, but breaks out in increasingly destructive forms (the price of advances in technology). The workings of the "scapegoat mechanism" now lie exposed, for we realize today that the victims are arbitrary, not necessary. Yet Girard himself is engaged in the very de-sacralization of the sacred that so disturbs him: his analysis of the entire "mechanism" speeds up its disintegration, making us all the more acutely aware of how we choose our "scapegoats."

Girard is thus in a peculiar position. He laments the loss of "sacrificial protections"; we now know the arbitrary procedures of ritual sacrifice, and, without ritual, we lack the means to check the spread of violence. But while Girard testifies to this cultural loss, he also affirms his argument's positive force—its power to demystify persecution. Jews, blacks, and other "scapegoats" are always arbitrary victims, Girard forcefully reminds us; and the texts that describe the persecutions of such "scapegoats" refer to real murders (texts do have referents)— disturbingly real ones—in the world. This takes us to the unnerving center of Girard's work, and it is a center he does not examine. Girard stresses that the victims are arbitrary, picked out for persecution by the dominant culture, yet he also argues that victimage (with its arbitrariness hidden from view) is necessary if the culture is to survive. Victimization *must* exist for the community to sustain itself and remain able to resolve its outbreaks of "violence"; the community must attach responsibility for "violence" to some other person or group and *needs* its victims. Girard has thus given us a theory that exposes the arbitrary nature of victimization yet that suggests victimization must continue in order to guarantee social order. Which leaves us with an interesting analysis and an impossible conclusion.

Like *"To Double Business Bound,"* White's *Tropics of Discourse: Essays in Cultural Criticism* includes studies of individual writers (Vico, Croce, Foucault, and others) and develops the themes of a previous book, *Metahistory: The Historical Imagination in Nineteenth-Century Europe* (1973).

White begins with "The Burden of History," a skillful review of the modern revolt against the "historical consciousness." In writers as different as Nietzsche, George Eliot, Ibsen, Camus, and Sartre, we see a powerful assault against history's rule over the individual. For the individual fully to realize the self, he or she must break free from the tyranny of past systems of thought. Because the historian recovers and restores the past, "historical" work hence is an obstacle to self-fulfillment in the present. Historians, White declares, must admit that this "rebellion against the past" (p. 41)—and also against the methods for studying the past—is justified; as a "discipline," history is methodologically backward, hostile to theory, and unwilling to "participate actively in the general intellectual and artistic life of our time" (p. 48).

Borrowing from literary theory and philosophy, White hopes to alert historians to the true nature of their enterprise. The past is not at all a "given," but is "constituted" by our choice of governing metaphors, tropes, figures of speech (pp. 3, 72). The historian does not recover "facts" from the records of the past; rather, he or she determines what is "to count as factual" through the perceptual framework applied to research. We never portray the past "objectively," nor do our histories remain free from their own "metahistories"—the "web of commitments" that the historian makes in the choice of "modes of emplotment, explanation, and ideology" (pp. 70-71). The historian *writes* history, composing, selecting, and arranging material to form an account of the past that is essentially "fictive," not "objective" or "factual."

White does not shirk from stating what his theory implies: "There is, of course, no escaping the determinative power of figurative language-use" (p. 105). And he is aware that his claim for this "determinative power" runs the risk of "relativism," where all interpretations of history are equal because all are equally figurative and fictional. He insists, however, that his argument does not lead to relativism and to the absence of real knowledge. We can always "distinguish between good and bad historiography" by falling back "on such criteria as responsibility to the rules of evidence, the relative fullness of narrative detail, logical consistency, and the like" (p. 97); and we also should expect the historian to be self-critical and self-questioning, sensitive to the "composed" nature of history. But White is raising more problems than he solves, since, as his own theory of tropes instructs us to see, categories such as "self-consciousness" and "responsibility" are also the product of verbal fictions (we cannot "escape" them), and are very much the reflection of the critic's or historian's ideology. To say that we can "fall back" upon these categories assumes they are constant for everyone; but because all categories are "constituted," as White encourages us to recognize, they will vary according to the figurative structure and ethical charge that each of us assigns to them.[7]

White tries to turn the dangers of relativism into the advantages of pluralism. Each historian offers "one way among many of disclosing certain aspects of the field." "There are many correct views, each requiring its own style of representation" (pp. 46-47). The "good professional historian" reminds readers that work is "purely provisional" (p. 82), never the final, authoritative word about the subject. He or she provides us with "a history that will educate us to discontinuity more than ever before; for discontinuity, disruption, and chaos is our lot" (p. 50). As this statement intimates, the other side of White's critique of the historian's craft is his uneasy awareness that the historian, caught in the abyss of tropes, can never say anything that is truly authoritative—can never, that is, get beyond the "purely provisional" and translate the "chaos" into more than one person's view of how it may be figuratively structured. In his essay on post-structuralism, "The Absurdist Moment in Contemporary Literary Theory," White refers to "the general want of confidence in our ability to locate reality or the centers of power in post-industrial society and to comprehend them when they are located" (p. 264). But if this comment bears on Derrida, Foucault, and Bataille, it also hits at the tenets of White's own work, with its sense of fragmentation and disorder, and its gestures towards the presence of (and need to embrace) "many views."

"Pluralism," which White supports, and which the Chicago critics (R. S. Crane, Wayne Booth, and others) have long advocated, appeals to many critics and scholars today. It claims to welcome an open, various criticism that allows us to speak our piece in our own critical "language." But its professed open-mindedness is less heartening than it appears, for its form of liberation can quickly become an enclosure: no interpretation is to be preferred, and no value (except for pluralist inquiry) unites us in a common cause. Political action—and here "pluralism" crosses with the demystifications Stanley Fish performs—seems futile, ruled out in advance, because any analysis of the reasons for change is just another "view." Perhaps this helps to explain why pluralism has become so attractive during these difficult times for the academic profession. It excuses scholars from examining the social and political implications of their work and does not require them to raise larger questions about the social life to which their labor contributes— or to which it fails to make any difference. When you see (and accept) your work as one kind among many, you are not obliged to consider its relevance or worth, can continue in the settled course of business as usual, and can persuade yourself that the political study of literature is the concern of someone else among the pluralist ranks. This is, to say the least, a disturbing prospect. Have we truly reached the point where critics and historians agree with White that "our interpretations of history and society can claim no more authority than our interpretations of literature can claim"?[8]

A pluralist presents himself or herself as tolerant and holistic, but in assembling "many views," pluralism serves to keep its material in separate compartments and functions to prevent the appearance of any method that regards social practice as something other (and more demanding) than "one more interpretation." An interpretation that claims or holds title to authority may be, as White suggests, "fictive," grounded on figure and trope. But its status as a verbal fiction does not mean that its power is diminished: authority can still be a source of power, command allegiance, and exclude forms of opposition, whatever our insistence on its linguistic character. White's argument might be turned around: if the dominant authority is not factual, not a given, then we are free to dissent from and change it.

Wayne Booth. *Critical Understanding: The Powers and Limits of Pluralism.*
Chicago: University of Chicago Press, 1979.

The critique that follows violates the first commandment of reviewing: do not criticize an author for failing to give us a book he never intended to write. But I see no getting around the fact that Wayne Booth's *Critical Understanding: The Powers and Limits of Pluralism* is misconceived. It is over-written, organized on highly questionable lines, and committed to solving problems that do not exist, at least not in the terms that Booth uses to describe them.

From one page to the next, Booth's writing is careful and lucid. But his book stretches over far too many pages, as he tediously returns to the same arguments in favor of a "limited pluralism" and, in the final chapters, studies texts by James, Goldsmith, and others in order to make simple points at great length. And the pace is not quickened by Booth's odd tics and mannerisms (typical examples occur on pp. 102-3 and 164-75) that attempt playfulness and stylistic self-consciousness, but that are forced, pretentious, and often silly. In setting out the "plurality of modes" as a critical problem, Booth discusses Auden's "Surgical Ward," laying out a number of possible ways to interpret it. More than one hundred pages into the book, Booth is still worrying this mildly interesting poem to death and talking about the various critical "languages" that could apply to it.

Booth's organizational difficulty is evident in his choice of representative "pluralists." R. S. Crane, Kenneth Burke, and M. H. Abrams are examined in separate chapters, their writings explored to show the different pluralisms available to us and the impossibility of harmonizing them "into a single intellectual world" (p. 203). Crane receives sixty pages, while Burke gets half that amount—an allotment that seems to me exactly wrong. I respect Booth's devotion to Crane as his former teacher, but in re-reading *The Languages of Criticism and the Structure of Poetry* and the two-volume *Idea of the Humanities and Other Essays*, I find Crane's work to have dated badly. He prosecuted an important case against dull historicism and New Critical reductiveness during the 1930s and 1940s, and was the guiding spirit of the Chicago neo-Aristotelians in the early 1950s. But his concern for "precision" in critical languages leads in his own work to pompous, deadening writing. Crane's analyses of other critic's arguments and literary texts are labored, moving like a glacier as they self-importantly promulgate their status as "serious thinking" (the "real" thing). Burke, on the other hand, is an inventive critic and theorist whose writings have not received the critical attention they deserve. As Booth comments in a note, the admirers of Barthes, Derrida, and others might be surprised to discover the range and orig-against dull historicism and New Critical reductiveness during the 1930s *Motives* (p. 361). But Booth's stimulating remark does not belong in a lonely note at the back of *Critical Understanding*. As I have argued in chapter seven, Burke's work is rich and in need of a re-assessment, but Booth plods along in his chapter about Burke-as-pluralist, missing opportunities and once more speculating about "Surgical Ward."

There are other stylistic and tactical problems in *Critical Understanding*. Booth's heavy-handed use of "warfare" and "killing" as metaphors for critical debate is irresponsible. And when he refers to Barthes, Fish, and others, he usually misunderstands or distorts their positions. He observes that contemporary theorists often proclaim a form of "liberation," "as when Roland Barthes explicitly seeks devices for combating the boredom he would feel if he confined himself to the meaning that Zola actually put into the novel" (p. 215). But the passage from *Le Plaisir du texte*, cited in Booth's note, reads: "Lisez lentement, lisez tout, d'un roman de Zola, le livre vous tombera des mains." Barthes is not "explicitly" opposing authorial intention here (though he does so in other places), but attesting to the creativity of the reader, who cuts into the text at different points and stitches or weaves together a "pleasurable" reading. Like other theorists on the intellectual vanguard, Barthes is mistaken or misleading on many issues. But if Booth intends to chastise Barthes and the others, he should not misrepresent them. Booth does discuss Barthes briefly in several sections of *Critical Understanding*, and he sometimes even praises this theorist, if in terms that are notably hollow. For some reason, however, Booth decided not to treat Barthes's writing in detail, even though his work, as Booth notes himself, is influential today—certainly more so than Crane's. Barthes, Derrida, Fish, J. Hillis Miller, and De Man foster the "relativism" and "skepticism" that Booth finds disturbing, yet he fails to study any of them.

He lumps together all of these critics (except for De Man) in a single paragraph, summing up their views in a sentence apiece (p. 216). This is simply unfair, and it is unlikely to persuade readers that Booth grasps the full meaning and import of what he obviously dislikes. A few pages later, he states that critics regularly fail to do justice to one another's work, and he refers to his own page 216 as an example—which leads me not to commend Booth's honesty, but to wonder why he breaks a law of which he is well aware.

Booth's previous books addressed real, significant problems, such as rhetorical techniques in fiction and definitions of irony, and his achievement in these books is a distinguished one. But *Critical Understanding* concerns itself with problems that are badly formulated at the outset, and that result in the wrong kind of analytical procedures and strategies. Booth contends that "contemporary literary criticism" is an "immensely confusing world" (p. 3), blighted by "utter confusion," "chaotic warfare," "many quarrels," and the general absence of "fruitful exchange." There appear to be no limits to the number of "critical languages" and no way for us to meet on common ground to reach an "understanding." "How," Booth asks, "can we reduce meaningless critical conflict?" The answer is that we should promote "vitality," "justice," and "understanding," and fair-minded, productive debate. For readers tempted to wander from the right path, Booth provides "A Hippocratic Oath for the Pluralist" in an appendix.

Booth's vision of things is mistaken. First, he ignores the extent to which critical "conflict," far from being "meaningless," is very meaningful, testifying both to the density of (and contested relations among) texts and to the power of critical discourse to generate new, provocative interpretations. Critics like De Man and Harold Bloom are, in Booth's terms, "monistic," and they are surely too preoccupied with their own interests and rhetorical flights. But their writings have clearly enriched our "understanding" of the Romantic tradition, irony, allegory, and particular texts. "Strong" and "exclusivist" readings do not necessarily close down or prohibit critical exchange, but rather extend and vitalize it.

There is an even more fundamental objection to Booth's argument. He nowhere examines the social and institutional force of literary studies—though he has treated this matter elsewhere—and this omission from the pages of *Critical Understanding* suggests why it is misguided, dedicated to answering questions that no one has been asking. We teach and produce criticism within an institution, and our work is "limited" and controlled. Many different modes of criticism exist, but surprising family resemblances can be discerned among them, and nearly all reflect general agreement about the rules of critical decorum. Booth and others are indignant about "deconstruction"—it's as though the enemy is no longer at the barricades, but actually inside the fort. But Booth over-estimates the disruption that a deconstructive essay causes, and he perceives it to be far more threatening than is actually the case. Deconstruction is not the last word on a critical subject, and we are not obligated to accept its arguments as either authoritative or as signaling the downfall of English studies. Booth is correct in judging deconstruction to be important, but he mistakenly allows it to loom too largely in his survey of the theoretical scene. Here as elsewhere, he loses perspective on the issues he deals with, and fails to attend to the institutional and professional networks within which deconstruction and post-structuralism have emerged.

What usually happens in criticism is this. One critic "deconstructs" a text, and then another comes along to restate or revise the deconstruction. Still other critics challenge and dispute the deconstructors' practice. Debate ensues, and critical exchange proceeds in a slightly different—but still recognizable—shape. Like others before him, Booth seriously under-rates the power of the institution (for better or worse) to dictate procedures, to determine what will or will not be allowed as a critical statement, and to absorb what professes to challenge it. In simplest terms, the vaunted radicalism of deconstruction, which Hillis Miller preaches and Booth fears, is tamed right from the start by its appearance in a respectable scholarly journal or university press book. This state of affairs is both encouraging and disheartening: institutional procedures and entrenched interests are difficult to dislodge, and the other side of the institution's stability is its resistance to change.

Criticism is produced for many reasons, not all of them ennobling. Anyone who complains about "meaningless critical conflict" and the glut of publications needs only to glance at the next MLA job-list to see what departments are now expecting of prospective junior faculty. Hiring, tenure, promotion, and grants—for senior and junior faculty alike—depend primarily upon publication. This is, of course, no great news, but as a factor in accounting for the state of literary criticism, it is conspicuously absent from *Critical Understanding*. Booth may be right to deplore the numbers of "critical languages" that are being spoken today, but they are the result of social, economic, and institutional facts. While much of the critical writing is bad, a great deal of it is valuable and part of a "fruitful exchange." Criticism remains "meaningful" in a variety of ways and for a variety of reasons. *Critical Understanding* does not help us in perceiving either the ways or the reasons.

Grant Webster. *The Republic of Letters: A History of Postwar American Literary Opinion.* Baltimore: Johns Hopkins University Press, 1979.

In *The Republic of Letters*, Grant Webster provides a detailed account of the "New Critics" and the "New York Intellectuals." He supplements these central sections of his book by analyzing the nature of critical "schools" and "careers" and by supplying an excellent bibliography and series of "life and works" sketches of major American critics. His chapters on René Wellek, Lionel Trilling, Irving Howe, and Philip Rahv are informative, and he does a good job treating the rise of the literary quarterlies, particularly the *Partisan Review* and *Sewanee Review*. But while there is a good deal to admire in *The Republic of Letters*, it is finally a very unsatisfactory book. Helpful and enlightening on occasion, it is more often shallow and badly written.

The problems begin in the preface, where Webster declares his intention to cause "a revolution in the history of criticism" (p. xi), one that he hopes to accomplish through his model of "a new historical science of criticism." By studying and adapting Thomas Kuhn's theory of "paradigms," Webster argues, we can trace the growth of "charters"—he prefers this term to "paradigms"—in "the world of literary criticism." This model is not compelling. It offers little that is new, aligning terms and categories that repeat obvious and well-worn points. "A critic breaks in," Webster intones, "by having his reviews or essays published in critical quarterlies, where after a time he makes a name for himself" (p. 29). This is true enough, but it is odd to see Webster making such pious statements of the obvious and unexceptional. Any person with his or her eyes open knows the rules and does not require this kind of instruction.

At times Webster's fascination with—or else his inability to recognize—the obvious seems almost eerie. "The purpose of studying the history of criticism," he maintains, "in the absence of total truth toward which one can progress, is to inform oneself of the possible vocabularies and values, the human responses, that critics of the past have used to interpret literature" (p. 45). Once again, this is quite true, but is so true that I cannot understand why Webster bothers to say it. He furnishes us with technical terms, intricate models, and charts, all of which proclaim that he is doing something innovative. Yet on page after page, he also makes the flattest, most banal statements, which indicate to me that his ideas are not nearly so new as the jargon and references to "revolution" make them sound. "Memoirs and reminiscences," Webster observes, "make the past live in the present. In this kind of writing the critic functions as historian of himself, and his recollections are uniquely valuable as a record of time that is gone by one who was there" (p. 37). True enough, but this is hardly a revelation.

With oppressive solemnity, Webster fills his book with such truisms, lamenting at one point the vanity of human wishes:

> In a sense, recognition of obsolescence is a pessimistic view of the meaning of intellectual effort, for it involves a critic's acceptance of his own failure. But it is in such recognition and acceptance that a critic (or any man) discovers

234 THE CRISIS IN CRITICISM

the limitations of human understanding and the transitoriness of human effort. As I. A. Richards says of an arrogant critic: "With him are many Professors to prove that years of endeavor may lead to nothing very remarkable in the end." (P. 37)

Maybe I. A. Richards bears some of the blame for encouraging Webster, but Webster alone is responsible for the breezy phrasing ("in a sense") and funereal inclusion of the "critic" with "any man." He closes this sermonette with a quotation from R. P. Blackmur's moving essay on Henry Adams in *The Lion and the Honeycomb*, and this has the effect of illuminating Webster's own bathos.

On and on it goes. There are bizarre comparisons between schools of literary critics and the Trobriand Islanders studied by Malinowski (p. 15); other occasions when banality edges into hip chatter about critics doing "their own thing" (p. 37); weird analogies, as when the "history of criticism" is said to resemble "a geological time table, with the critics of the older schools about to retire and the younger ones piled on top of them" (p. 43); and one statement after another of points that no one has ever questioned or seriously worried about. The final two pages of part one (pp. 58-59), in which Webster refers to his model as "a critical Baedeker, as it were," speaks of "ideological temperature" and other troubles, and advises us to "cultivate the virtue of humility," are breath-taking.

After concluding his theoretical labors, Webster turns to the New Critics. Here he is tackling a subject that has been studied often but rarely well. Richard Foster, Walter Sutton, and others have written useful books about the rise of the New Criticism, but they do not go much beyond rehearsals of Ransom's, Brooks's, Tate's, and the others' positions. For a variety of reasons, the New Critics have become the focus for vigorous debates about literary theory. As I have argued in part two, their influence, especially in the classroom, remains strong, and both teachers and critics still feel the anti-historical burden of formalism. Webster, however, does not advance the discussion in lively and interesting ways. He sets out the positions one more time, summarizing New Critical views on authorial intention, poetic language, and regionalism, and his account is uninspired. Again he tells us what we already know, and gives us reminders—we "should not forget the effect of the incredible bloodletting of World War I on postwar England" (p. 71)—we do not need. Webster singles out T. S. Eliot as the most influential "Tory Formalist"—the term Webster prefers to New Critic— yet then reviews Eliot's work and career in a numbing manner. When the analysis is not basic (see p. 91 on Eliot's "championing of the Metaphysicals"), it is facile (see p. 91 on the "obsolescence of Eliot's tradition and the creation of yet another critical revolution") or drearily dependent on others (see p. 133 on Eliot's early critical style, which reruns Hugh Kenner's remarks in *The Invisible Poet*). Elsewhere in this part of the book, we find the announcement of obvious distinctions— we should place "Eliot's criticism against the background of his life and times rather than in the context of the ultimate truth" (pp. 135-36); grab-bags of ideas and trends, as when Webster tries to evoke the "revolutionary fervor of the sixties in America" (p. 137); self-assured recitals of the real meaning of texts by Samuel Johnson and Jane Austen (pp. 199-200); and attempts to be clever that are vulgar and tasteless (p. 202).

Webster's analyses, like Wayne Booth's and Frank Lentricchia's, are not always appropriate to the subject. Kenneth Burke receives barely three pages, whereas Murray Krieger (who is judged to be "the classic case of a man born too late," p. 201) gets eleven. The few pages on Burke are narrow-minded and shortsighted, and in response to Webster's description of this critic as "an old-time American crank inventor who might have been Edison except that his work lacks any relation to reality outside his own mind" (p. 175), I can only say that Webster must be reading with blinders on. To dismiss in a sentence such a critical career, whatever its flaws and failings, is intolerable; and if this is where Webster's revolutionary "historical science of criticism" leads him, then I urge major revisions.

Webster's chapter on Yvor Winters, garishly titled "The Critic as Puritan Narcissist," is also regrettable. Though he reproaches Allen Tate for being careless about "facts and distinctions" (p. 145), Webster is guilty of the same faults. His linking of Winters and F. R. Leavis is sensible but is conducted in a petty way (p. 164); it is a small masterpiece of misleading and ill-considered argument. For all his piety, Webster is also not above slightly rerouting a quotation from *Forms of Discovery* to make Winters appear to be directly grouping Yeats with Mussolini, Father Coughlin, and Adolph Hitler (p. 169). Webster also states that Winters's "historical accomplishment has been to give evaluation in our age a bad name" (p. 172). Not quite. What Winters has done is to propose judgments that reorder the literary canon and tradition in ways that disturb our habitual responses and jar against our interests. As John Fraser has stated, "To admire the works that Winters celebrates, in the contexts that he furnishes for them, is to feel oneself being edged toward a perception of the world that is at times almost overpowering in its absence of reassuring solidities and unquestionable 'natural' données."[9] Like Webster, I am not captivated by the writings of T. Sturge Moore, Elizabeth Daryrush, and Winters's other favorite modern poets. But Winters's work on the sixteenth- and seventeenth-century lyric, particularly his recovery of Fulke Greville and Gascoigne, is stimulating and important, and his studies of Emerson, Stevens, Hart Crane, and other American writers are as shrewd as they are sharp-edged. Winters's judgments are often perverse, but a real analysis of his criticism will consider what lies behind the judgments, what motivates them and gives them their disturbing power. Such an analysis requires care and sensitivity, and emphatically not the lashing out at easy targets that Webster indulges in. For his "revolution of the history of criticism" to succeed, he will have to do much better in the subsequent volume he promises us (pp. x, 11, 21, 35). But then not all revolutions are fated to succeed.

Ihab Hassan. *The Right Promethean Fire: Imagination, Science, and Cultural Change*. Champaign: University of Illinois Press, 1980.

Like many contemporary critics and theorists of literature, Ihab Hassan believes that criticism should be creative and playful. And like others, he challenges assumptions about the difference between primary and secondary texts, as well as our insistence on keeping the academic disciplines separate. But Hassan differs from most others in practicing what he preaches. In this book, as in *Paracriticisms: Seven Speculations of the Times* (1975), he takes many risks, moving freely among many disciplines, disordering the page with flashy typography, surprising us with juxtapositions of ideas and images. Precisely because of its interdisciplinary range and verbal flair, *The Right Promethean Fire* will alienate and offend many readers. Its manner and means of approach, its focus on issues and themes rather than specific texts, and its typographic tricks and maneuvers will strike some as foolish or ill-considered. Hassan, one senses, knows that he will meet resistance and even mockery. His tone is sometimes bitter, for he recognizes that while readers celebrate imaginative play and invention, they do not want these kinds of creative style to violate the decorum of critical writing. There are failings in Hassan's ambitious enterprise, and I have my own reservations about his ways of working. But Hassan is a thoughtful writer, and he deserves a more serious response than he has been getting from readers and reviewers. He merits a response that neither gives in to ridicule nor offers tidy (and too often uncomprehending) praise for this critic's willingness to experiment.

The Right Promethean Fire is forthright and speculative, aiming to unsettle boundaries and test the limits of criticism, the form of the essay, and the belief that criticism should not be personal. The book consists of five chapters, whose major concerns are "imagination, science, and cultural change in our time," and four "interchapters," patched together from a journal that Hassan kept during a research trip abroad. It is hard to say more precisely what the book is "about," since it eschews "linear discourse" and lacks a sustained argument. But it is possible to isolate themes, the most notable of which is the place of the "imagination." The "old humanist vision," Hassan states, with its "intricacies of remorse, its pinched piety and riskless chatter," does not suit the present and will be hopelessly out of touch with the future (p. xix). If humanists persist in echoing Matthew Arnold and refuse to confront the changes that science has wrought in our world, they will merely testify to their own irrelevance.

"Humanism" is under attack on many fronts today, as the writings of Derrida, Foucault, Barthes, and their American followers bear abundant witness. But Hassan is suspicious of post-structuralism and deconstruction, remarking that it is all too simple to imitate fashionable "mannerisms" and repeat "sesquipedalian cant." Hassan rightly wonders about the "institution" of criticism, which is able to neutralize even the most feverish of radical theories and has already domesticated the new kinds of critical discourse that were supposed to contest it. Though he celebrates the imagination, and hopes for continuity and wholeness, Hassan recognizes how difficult it is to be an "original" critic and to locate a proper "critical" position. Neither the old humanism nor the fierce anti-humanist rhetorics compel assent, and the "new" appears effortlessly to become the faddish. We need to retain faith in the power of criticism, Hassan maintains, but we must expand our notion of what this power encompasses. "Our search" is for "a new liveliness, a new capaciousness, a new potency in criticism" (p. 25). This desire is an admirable one, especially when so many critics seem content to surrender to doomsaying and despair. Hassan affirms the power of the imagination and honors the function of criticism. He is admittedly uncertain about the "future" that science and technology are shaping for us, yet he is guardedly optimistic that the imagination, if freed from piety and defeatism, can take its measure. "Humanists," he pointedly concludes, "once prided themselves on taking the entire human universe, with all its wonder, cruelty, and crankiness, as province to their imagination. How many still do or can?" (p. 124).

Hassan's intellectual ambition and his claims for criticism are exemplary. But his over-zealous commitment to certain styles and "experimental" forms limits his effectiveness and allows his detractors to dismiss him without seriously engaging his work. Hassan is an adventurous yet modest critic, so there is much to be said for his glancing style that ranges widely but always tentatively, quick to inquire but not to assert. But the problem is that such a style often frustrates the reader, and this helps to explain why Hassan's writing is frequently unsatisfying. In his intriguing first chapter, for instance, Hassan refers to R. P. Blackmur, commenting on the "dark, original, poetic" style that "betrays" the artist in this brilliant critic. And in a shrewd and imaginative move, Hassan links Blackmur with Benjamin and Barthes, who similiarly reflect the "perversity of critical genius." This is so good that the reader expects and deserves more. But the relations briefly noted here are not developed; they are alluded to and supplemented with other points, but the main conjunction is not explicated in adequate ways. It is Hassan's right to forego "linear discourse" and argument, but perhaps he is wrong to put so much trust in his formal means of opposing them. He may disagree, but anyone can play with typography or gather odd assemblages of quotations. Not many critics, however, can neatly perceive the affinities and differences among Blackmur, Benjamin, and Barthes and then develop a coherent argument based upon these observations. Hassan provides us with the sharp perceptions but not the argument.

Possibly I am looking for what this critic is not interested in providing; and his refusal to make clear connections may, in fairness to him, be part of his strategy for involving the reader in imaginative work and requiring him or her to participate in the critic's playful enactments. But I cannot fail to register my disappointment that so many paths are suggested yet not followed. Hassan says that he is not a strict formalist (p. 48), but to my mind he does rely too much on formal experimentation. As his earlier books, particularly *The Dismemberment of Orpheus: Toward a Postmodern Literature* (1971; rev. ed. 1982), demonstrate, Hassan can give us an economical critical writing that is at the same time speculative and imaginatively risky. One wishes he would continue to see sustained argument as an opportunity, *enabling* the development of idea and imagination, and not merely as a cumbersome constraint. In *The Dismemberment of Orpheus*, Hassan states that "criticism is very seldom inevitable." He may feel that this ought to confound my desire for sustained argument, but it instead indicts his own present form of critical writing, writing that is indecorous and unsettling but unable to do full justice to his fine imagination. More than ever before, we need critics who affirm and can argue persuasively for the act of criticism. And since this need is central and pressing, I am obliged to counter Hassan's determination to place himself on the margins of the current scene. To challenge the complacencies of most criticism written today, Hassan might do well to adopt traditional forms and show that these still have force for the "future" of the "imagination."[10]

Christopher Norris. *Deconstruction: Theory and Practice*. New York: Methuen, 1982.

Christopher Norris's *Deconstruction: Theory and Practice* is an excellent guide to an important movement in literary theory. Norris deals well with the philosophical contexts of "deconstruction" and is particularly helpful in his commentary on Husserl and Nietzsche. He also provides good summaries of the major writings of Jacques Derrida and the American critics, including Paul De Man, J. Hillis Miller, and Geoffrey Hartman, who have drawn upon, revised, and extended Derridean insights. Norris also examines the "politics of deconstruction," noting the challenge that Derrida's arguments pose to Marxism. Derrida, explains Norris, teaches us to perceive that Marxism, like all doctrines and systems, is founded on the unstable ground of metaphor, figure, and trope, and thus it cannot claim to occupy a privileged position "outside language." Norris also considers Harold Bloom, Gerald Graff, and others who have sought to resist deconstruction and limit its totalizing power. Bloom, Norris points out, admires the analytical rigor of deconstruction but preserves the poet's "will-to-expression" and ability to clear "imaginative space." Graff, less sympathetic to deconstruction, attacks Derrida and his American followers, but finally seems unable to do much more than eloquently invoke "common sense" and "moral imperatives."

Deconstruction: Theory and Practice will displease many readers. Derrida's supporters will find many of Norris's formulations to be reductive, while Derrida's foes will doubtless see this handbook as confirming William Empson's recent verdict that "literary criticism is getting steadily more absurd."[11] Norris himself, in his introduction and elsewhere, is concerned about the risks of outlining and explaining deconstruction. He warns his readers not to expect a "handy and objective survey" of the deconstructive method, but rather to understand *Deconstruction: Theory and Practice* as a sustained "involvement" with knotted and difficult texts. But this disclaimer aside, Norris has indeed given us a reliable guide to deconstruction, and readers who wish to familiarize themselves with the movement and the controversies that it has provoked, or who need a summary statement or narrative line to aid them in negotiating Derrida's and De Man's complicated arguments, will benefit from this book.[12]

Norris writes lucidly and presents complex material in a cogent fashion. But at times his phrasing is irritating, as when he asserts that "the New Critics mostly followed Eliot in using the 'problem' of Milton's style as a cover for their deep dislike of his radicalism in politics and religion" (p. 16). This is simple-minded and jaundiced; when Eliot, Leavis, Ransom, and others criticize Milton's style, they mean what they say and are not merely employing arguments about "style" as a "cover" for their real convictions. They are disturbed by Milton's radical politics and religion, but they are equally disturbed by his poetic diction and techniques. The New Critics' engagement with Milton is more integrated—and also more vexed—than Norris realizes, and it is both slapdash and inappropriate to suggest that the New Critics stand guilty of a kind of insincerity.

What happens here and in other sections of *Deconstruction: Theory and Practice* is a failure of proportion. Derrida, De Man, and the deconstructionists loom so hugely in Norris's eyes that he sometimes exaggerates their importance or else ignores and over-simplifies the achievements of other writers, critics, and theorists. In an early section of his book, for instance, Norris celebrates Barthes's autobiography, offering high-spirited praise for Barthes's play with the reader and third-person style. The autobiography is clearly a subtle text, one that foregrounds Barthes's own "deconstructive" expertise, but Norris's praise sounds somewhat lame to any reader who knows *The Education of Henry Adams*, an autobiography whose third-person style and elaborate commerce with the reader achieve a depth and eloquence that Barthes's work does not approach. Norris has read widely, especially in literary theory and philosophy, but perhaps has not read widely enough; his focus on a certain group of texts—texts that owe much of their status to the winds of current doctrine—is too narrow, too limited, and it distorts his judgment.

Norris's over-valuation of Derrida, Barthes, and the others that he studies is understandable but still unfortunate; as Coleridge once remarked, "An inquisitiveness into the minutest circumstances and casual sayings of eminent contemporaries is indeed quite natural, but so are all our follies." Like others who revere deconstruction and portray it as something without precedent in literary and critical history, Norris reveals an odd lack of perspective. Derrida, De Man, Hartman, and Miller are stimulating theorists; all of us are indebted to them for their investigations of figurative language and inter-textuality. But when these theorists are viewed within the context of American literature, situated in a group that includes Emerson, Henry Adams, Henry and William James, Frost, and Stevens, they appear less original and less subversive. As Richard Poirier and Margery Sabin have argued, deconstruction does not mark a wholly new stage in literature and criticism; and it is a mistake to assume that nowhere else can we discover writings of comparable insight and profundity.[13] Rather than seeing the deconstructionists, as does Norris, as courageous innovators whose texts are "an affront to every normal and comfortable habit of thought" (p. xi), we might instead perceive them as belatedly catching up with the illuminating discoveries of our great creative writers.

The danger of endorsing deconstructive terms and attitudes emerges in Norris's chapter on "the politics of deconstruction." There is crisply-stated analysis in these pages, but also a damaging absence of political vision. Norris argues that it is difficult to connect Nietzschean/Derridean deconstruction and Marxism. "To deconstruct a text in Nietzschean/Derridean terms is to arrive at a limit-point or deadlocked *aporia* of meaning which offers no hold for Marxist-historical understanding" (p.

80). "The Marxist model of representation," Norris adds, "however refined in theory, is caught up in a rhetoric of tropes and images that entirely controls its logic" (p. 83). Norris properly calls attention to the *language* of Marxism, but he does not see that he is also ruling out human agency and the possibility of committing oneself to change. For Norris, Marxism, like any political program or party, is based on "a rhetoric," and in his view, this rhetoric is dominant and fully controlling. But if politics always boils down at last to rhetoric, then is there any real justification for political reform? What are the grounds for discrimination, choice, and action?

Armed with Derridean methods, Norris feels equipped to demystify Marxist political claims and to insist that linkages between deconstruction and Marxism are doomed to failure. But he does not grasp that it is precisely the demystifying power of "deconstruction" that has prompted Gayatri Spivak, Michael Ryan, and others to relate it to Marxism. Deconstruction, in its own right, possesses a certain political force; it resists totalization, opposes efforts to establish closure, and exposes the complicity between rhetoric, power, and authority. In this respect, deconstruction indeed gives us a political instrument whose insights are fortifying and revelatory. But one then wishes to progress beyond deconstruction, or else to supplement it with a concrete politics, in order to provide positive terms for one's work. Deconstruction promotes analysis, skepticism, and constant inquiry, all of which are essential, to be sure. But one labors *for* something, *on behalf of* something, and deconstruction cannot tell us why we should do so or justify a commitment once it is made.

"Once criticism enters the labyrinth of deconstruction," Norris contends, "it is committed to a skeptical epistemology that leads back to Nietzsche, rather than Marx, as the end-point of its quest for method. Nietzschean 'method' is no more perhaps than a lesson in perpetual self-defeat, but a lesson more rigorous and searching than the compromise assurances of post-structuralist Marxism" (pp. 84-85). This is perverse: the deconstructive critic goes nowhere, spinning in "self-defeat" like a perpetual-motion machine, but enjoys the satisfaction of knowing that his methods are "rigorous and searching." This passage makes clear why many Marxist critics regard deconstructionists with contempt; as Terry Eagleton observes in his study of Walter Benjamin, deconstruction "provides you with all the risks of a radical politics while cancelling the subject who might be summoned to become an agent of them."[14]

At one point Norris praises Said's *Orientalism*, describing it as "a very practical example of how deconstruction can engage cultural history on its own textual ground and contest its claims to objectivity" (p. 88). Said has certainly put to use the discoveries of Nietzsche, Derrida, and, above all, Foucault, but it is incorrect to enlist him in the ranks of those who undertake "deconstructive" projects. *Orientalism*, Norris maintains, "is an act of challenge which situates itself on rhetorical ground the better to meet and turn back the claims of a spurious objectivity" (p. 88). I do not believe that Said would agree that he locates his work on "rhetorical ground." On the contrary: he writes books like *Orientalism*, *The Question of Palestine*, and *Covering Islam* because he believes in the *reality* of poverty, exploitation, and political injustice and is convinced that these are *not* "rhetorical." In his account of Said, Norris is trying to rescue a political dimension for deconstruction, but his denial of human agency, stress on the controlling power of metaphor and trope, and insistence on the primacy of "rhetoric" make it impossible for him to deal with politics coherently.

Near the end of *Deconstruction: Theory and Practice*, Norris concedes that "the truth is that deconstructionist theory can only be as useful and enlightening as the mind that puts it to work" (p. 133). This sounds sensible enough, but it is in fact a startling admission. In its willingness to grant privilege to individual minds and allow for the distinctive work of human agents, it conflicts with everything that Norris has argued in his preceding chapters. Here, one might say, we catch Norris with his guard down. Deconstruction is, he implies, a provocative theory and makes available to us new tools for criticism, but the bottom line is that success or failure in the application of critical method depends on "the mind that puts it to work." This may well be the case, but one wonders how this point accords with Norris's major claim, reiterated throughout his book, that "deconstruction is the active antithesis of everything that criticism ought to be if one accepts its traditional values and concepts" (p. xii). Nothing is more "traditional" than the belief that the quality and flexibility of "the mind" produces the caliber of the criticism. Norris's master may be Derrida, but one suspects that he harbors a secret allegiance to T. S. Eliot and the assumptions that this critic sanctioned. "There is no method," Eliot reflects in *The Sacred Wood*, "except to be very intelligent."[15]

Deconstruction: Theory and Practice is thus very up-to-date yet also bears the signs of familiar beliefs and traditions. Norris adopts the fashionable, "deconstructive," stance that politics finally reduces to rhetoric, and that human agents, caught in the web of words, can only bear witness to their own "self-defeat." But he also clings to the notion that there is something beyond or outside language that is the true standard for appraising criticism. We measure criticism by responding to displays of "mind": what counts is not the dazzling, innovative method or the pervasive power of metaphor but the essential flair or genius of the critic. Norris attempts to embrace two positions—one that insists that language is controlling, all-encompassing, and domi-

nant, and another that says men and women can skillfully control
language and practice method—and he seems unaware of the gap
between them.

Success and Failure in Literary Theory

The books I have re-viewed in this chapter teach us much about the
problematical state of contemporary theory and criticism. What one
notices, first of all, is a willingness on the part of some theorists to
make daring statements without weighing the consequences. Norris
and White both emphasize the "groundlessness" of interpretive work;
Norris stresses the pervasive power of "rhetoric," while White calls
attention to the force of "figurative language." These insights are potent
when directed against certain naive or ill-considered referential views
of language, but they seem inadequate when inspected in their own
right. Such statements prevent the theorist from speaking intelligently
about politics, and they make any reference to significant reform or
change feel empty, the voicing of an illusion. Can Norris truly be
content with the political—actually, the anti-political—sentiments he
expresses? Can someone who possesses White's learning believe that
social, historical, and literary claims are all equally "fictive," based on
the shaky ground of figurative language? Why are these theorists pleased
with themselves for articulating notions that disable their own enterprise?

It is always bracing to encounter a boldly stated thesis; it unsettles
and reorients us, provokes and clarifies new thought. But theorists
today are too prone to wield global theories and explanations like a
club, and thus they end up simplifying complicated issues—the relation
between language and politics, for example—and putting themselves
in untenable positions. There is further evidence for this in Girard's
exaggerated esteem for the explanatory power of his "hypothesis" about
mimetic rivalry, and also in Webster's attempt to interpret critical history
by way of Thomas Kuhn. Critics and theorists are extremely self-conscious, but not in proper ways; they are so immersed in the formulation
of their theories, or else so taken by the effrontery of their discoveries,
that they fail to reflect on the impact of what they are saying.

A similar failure occurs—again the deconstructionist Norris is a good
case in point—when theorists grow too obsessed with the writings of
a master-figure. Derrida is, as I have already noted, now less the name
of a person than the title of an extensive body of texts and critiques;
there is so much material by and about him that a reader could easily
devote himself to nothing else. Obviously I am not implying here that
we should not read Derrida carefully; his theoretical and exegetical

labors demand scrutiny. What I am objecting to instead is the tendency to accept Derrida's (or some other master's) texts as though they are gospel and should control our response to all other kinds of texts. This leads to failures in critical judgment, to a shrinking of one's perspective on the central concerns of literature, criticism, and the discipline as a whole.

Another kind of distortion occurs when theorists do not situate their inquiries within an academic and professional context. Wayne Booth, as I have argued, misapplies his skills in *Critical Understanding*. He does not grasp that theoretical problems need to be framed in institutional terms, and thus he never manages to tackle the true dynamics of critical disagreement and debate. I am aware that there are dangers in urging Booth and others to acknowledge the formative influence of "professional" and "institutional" facts on the shape of "theory." One senses even now that theorists may go too far in this direction, and grow fond of discussing theory as if it were exclusively the product of careerism, one-upmanship, and marketability. But we should be able to distinguish between serious work and work that is sometimes serious and more often simply self-serving. For an intelligent understanding of theory, it is necessary to consider the institutional practices that Thorstein Veblen famously (and ironically) labeled "the higher learning in America" and elucidate how these interact with theoretical arguments.

I have said that we need to avoid the glamor of global theories such as those that Norris, Girard, and Webster propose. I think that we should also avoid another seductive idol, and that is the critic as "creator" or "experimental stylist." The act of writing is of course a crucial part of the critical performance, as I indicated in an earlier chapter. But this is not the same thing as saying that critics should give us new "creations" in their prose. "Creative" criticism is nearly always an excuse for the failure to prosecute arguments with clarity and rigor. No one who is familiar with the history of modernism in the arts can feel wholly comfortable about arguing against formal experimentation, re-orderings of the page, extravagant punning and word-play, and allusive gestures. The verdict lies, however, in the results that "creative" critics have produced so far—mostly cant and obscurity. What one witnesses is a refusal to bear down critically on the mind's desire to accept its private fascinations and reveries at face value.

In concluding this chapter, I want to comment more explicitly on the positive and negative lessons that the best of these books—*Orientalism*, *Literature against Itself* and *After the New Criticism*—teach us. Said's *Orientalism* shows us, first of all, the value of studying a "discourse," a range of both literary and non-literary texts that exhibits the workings of cultural and political power. Said analyzes a number of specific texts, but his concern is not primarily to provide a new set of explications. He is instead interested in tracing the linkages and patterns among texts, and in examining the build-up of ideological assumptions over time. What this book also illustrates is how much can be gained from making English studies include more than "English and American literature." It may seem odd—even perverse—to suggest that English studies should extend beyond the natural grouping of literary texts that it has taken as its province. But the truth is that this grouping is far less natural than we habitually assume. We select, order, and arrange the canon; it is not a given, something that has always been in place for each generation of critics and teachers to serve and service. For those in English studies to do their job honestly and responsibly, they need to acknowledge the impact of their *exclusions*—the texts judged to be non-literary, dismissed as not fit for serious analysis, or ignored because these appear better (i.e., more naturally) suited to history, black studies, women's studies, or some other department.

Like *Orientalism*, Graff's *Literature against Itself* and Lentricchia's *After the New Criticism* seek to transform critical practice. Graff strives to restore social and historical contexts for literary study, while Lentricchia draws upon Derrida and especially Foucault to demonstrate the new kinds of literary history we are now equipped to write. But like Said, Graff and Lentricchia flounder when they speak of "the real." To their credit, all three of these theorists wish to avoid the smug satisfactions of a certain brand of inter-textuality, one that sees reality as nothing but another name for a text or tissue of conventions. But none of them is able to reconcile this desire to express and affirm the real with the demystifying insights that post-structuralism offers and that each draws upon. To put the matter somewhat simply, these theorists want something they cannot have, something that their acceptance of key tenets in Derrida's and, to a lesser extent, Foucault's post-structuralist venture disallows. Said, Graff, and Lentricchia, in their different ways, acknowledge that a referential view of texts is extremely difficult, perhaps even impossible, to hold in the face of the challenge that deconstruction poses. They then want nevertheless to claim that texts do indeed refer to and instruct us about the real. In a word, they want such a connection to the real—how else can they sustain a case for the social, political, and historical bearing of literary study?—but cannot argue convincingly for it.

My answer to this dilemma is not so much an argument as an appeal. It is time to shift the focus of the discussion away from the deconstructive assault on categories such as reality and reference. This may look like an admission that deconstruction has triumphed, and in a sense it is. But I think that it might be more constructive simply to say that we do not seem to be making much progress in our efforts to unite the discoveries of post-structuralism with our determination to address "the

real." Deconstruction has taught us much, but it has assumed an un-
natural prominence in current debates in theory and criticism and
threatens to exclude the asking of other questions, questions that testify
to a less anxious attitude towards the real and the possibility of invoking
and making reference to it. As both Said and Lentricchia have shown,
deconstruction provides us with a superb means of opposing and overturning the natural, the given, the taken-for-granted. But it does not
take us beyond negation and demystification, and hence any theorist
who foregrounds a deconstructive vocabulary is going to upset the very
arguments he might propose on behalf of urgently "real" concerns.

Post-structuralism, particularly in its deconstructive branches, has
introduced a powerful critical spirit into literary study, and for this we
can only be grateful. But it would be foolish to exempt post-structuralism itself from the critical scrutiny that it has encouraged us to direct
towards everything else. The most apt criticism we can mount against
the questions that deconstruction has enabled us to ask is to say that
they have grown tiresome and unproductive and have caused too many
members of the profession to dwell endlessly on a single philosophical
crux. We should not grow self-satisfied about the "given" quality of
traditional procedures—here deconstruction can always prove useful
and cogent. But neither should we let ourselves become content with
our capacity to demystify: we should be willing to deconstruct even
the privilege accorded deconstruction.

We should be willing to do even more. "Theory" cannot cease; we
need always to study the assumptions that lie behind criticism and
teaching and must strive to make both of these more supple and historically sound. But contemporary theory is very much in need of a
dramatic reorientation, precisely because it no longer bears much relation to the critical and pedagogical practices of the discipline. At the
present time theorists are too content to write for one another, dispute
one another's positions, and provide occasions for further re-statements
of familiar platforms and debates. They are not seeking a means to
renovate and reaffirm the discipline, but rather are speaking in a privileged discourse to other members of a highly visible coterie. The "theory" game is a profitable one, and the quantity of books and articles
on the subject is astonishing. But whom does this work affect? Whose
interests does it serve? Has theory altered literary study in substantive
ways, or has it become a powerful distraction that keeps us from attending to recalcitrant facts that have changed very little in recent years?
As I argue in what follows, the Conclusion to a "theory" book should
be geared towards scholarly and pedagogical reforms. Such a Conclusion should even be—all the more so in view of current trends—"anti-
theoretical" in its effort to curb misuses and misapplications of theory
and in its concern that significant revisions in practice do indeed occur.

Conclusion

As scholars we have matured; as teachers we—the same people—are still children in our ignorance or innocence, still fumbling and faddish and lacking well-defined goals.

William Riley Parker, "Where Do English Departments Come From?"

In certain respects English studies is more prosperous than ever before. Valuable work is being done; many new journals have appeared; conferences and symposia abound; and literary theory continues to make new terms and tools available for critical reflection. But if English is thriving, then why does the state of the discipline disturb and anger many people? If important research is being undertaken, and if new areas in scholarship and theory are being explored, what generates the widespread feeling of decline, discontent, and "crisis"? Obviously part of the explanation is economic. The downturn of the economy has made both teachers and students fearful; teachers have lost (or else are worried about losing) their jobs, and students feel intensely concerned about securing a career in an era of diminishing opportunities. Many teachers and students do not see any pay-off in English, and members of both groups are strongly inclined to pursue work where the rewards are more tangible.

The "crisis," however, is more than the by-product of an economic recession, more than the consequence of forces that impinge on English from the outside. There are confusions and inequalities at the center of the discipline, a good many of them produced from within. No one can fail to notice, for instance, the degree of privilege accorded to a very small number of people in the profession, nearly all of whom are literary theorists. These are the men and women who speak at the major conferences, inaugurate journals, and publish in the most noteworthy places. "Privilege" is one of the facts of institutional life, and people who make significant contributions deserve to be rewarded. But privilege in our discipline often manifests itself in depressing ways, as the highly-regarded theorists grow increasingly isolated within their own profitable discourse and emerge only to address one another. Literary theory is intense and invigorating, but only within its own boundaries; it affects few people and exerts little influence on the daily practice of English.

Many of the major theorists began by calling attention to failures in practice, unexamined assumptions in criticism, and misunderstandings that warp pedagogy. But these theorists have allowed their studies to acquire a momentum that has taken them away from pedagogical and critical realities. Theory has become a game of its own, one whose compensation in status and professional visibility is all too apparent. And as theory has turned into a self-contained field, its proponents have left behind those who do the basic teaching in composition, introduction to literature, and survey courses, and who do not instruct bright graduate students in seminars on Nietzsche and Marx or Derrida and Foucault.

I see no way of ignoring the disparity between theory and practice, particularly "classroom" practice: the two rarely make contact and are basically separate domains. Some theorists agree, but imply that this split is inevitable and propose that we should not worry excessively about it. Fredric Jameson says that in his undergraduate teaching he provides the students with "content," whereas in his graduate seminars (and in his writing as well) he can be experimental and far more theoretically sophisticated.[1] Of course most members of our discipline do not have this option, and hence lack the exploratory freedom that Jameson is frequently able to relish. The real problem here, however, does not involve Jameson's greater opportunities, but is connected to the gap he perceives between pedagogy and research. One hopes for more enriching continuities and a more integrated approach, yet Jameson appears to feel destined to accept a compartmentalization of his labor. Eventually, and in some manner not spelled out, his and other theorists' discoveries will, he suggests, trickle down to the world of practice and cause changes in teaching, subject-matter, and undergraduate curriculum.

Unfortunately, theory will trickle down very slowly, if at all. If theory travels on its own course, it is likely to remain "theoretical," interesting and entertaining but dissociated from practical needs and successful only in amplifying the sense of disunity, disorder, and "crisis." Literary theory is so contentious and agitated an activity today, and so prominent in discussions of the discipline, that it conceals and distracts attention from the motley array of terms, ideas, and attitudes that characterize classroom teaching. Up to a point the debates about "theory" are enlightening; we cannot do without theoretical analysis and inquiry. But it is important to see one of the functions that theory now serves: it leads us into a field of discourse that prevents us from focusing on the banality, repetitiveness, and ahistorical nature of our teaching, which many are aware of and complain about but which no one seems able to alter. Theory ought to be slanted towards questions of pedagogy, education, social and cultural practice, and should be placed in dialectical relationship with research. But in most cases "theory" is directed towards nothing but itself and its advocates.

In his recent essay "Common Sense and Critical Practice: Teaching Literature," Tony Davies describes the limpness of the language we invoke in the classroom and contrasts it with the canny formulations of theoretical writing.

> Though the varied and competing criticisms —neo-formalist, post-structuralist, or whatever—have the greater clarity and glamor, it is in the humdrum, everyday and generally quite "untheoretical" activity of English teaching that the real effectivity of "Literature" as a practice is to be found; an activity within which those criticisms appear, if at all, as half-concealed traces, modal inflections of question and answer, a fluid and contradictory debris of discursive fragments.[2]

If theory is not related to the work of the classroom, then the depressed and dispirited condition of English will linger, as the chasm between theorists and the rank-and-file, between extreme sophistication and diluted New Criticism, widens. Theory and classroom practice are not identical; I am not contending that "theory" must always be equated with or reduced to the immediate needs of the teacher and student. But I do think that theory must have pedagogy as one of its focal points; we should employ theory to scrutinize teaching, speculate about its strengths and shortcomings, and inquire into plans for its improvement that will take us beyond the methods the New Critics devised. This does not imply—again I need to emphasize both what I am and am not saying—that theory ought to be imposed "from the outside" on the discipline as it is now constituted. We need to restructure English studies, mapping a new field for teaching and research. We should not view theory as giving us techniques that adjust and update methods of "close reading" of the masterpieces—this is the mistake J. Hillis Miller makes. Nor should we conceive of theory—here is where E. D. Hirsch errs—as providing us with "principles" that declare which interpretations of these texts are right and which are wrong.

We need bolder approaches to remaking English studies than we now possess. What happens at the present time is that one theory after another arrives on the scene, causes a momentary stir, and then dissolves into the background or turns into a new sub-industry, having failed to accomplish much of true significance or lasting effect. And this occurs because theorists generally are not radical or visionary enough; they take for granted that a stable canon exists, that our task is to craft critical essays ("readings") and to teach students to do the same, and that the goal of theory should be to assist us in this enterprise. Or else—this is the other side of the coin—theorists pay no heed at all to what occurs in the classroom, as though such humdrum pursuits were beneath their dignity. Some theorists thus supplement the pedagogical routines already in place, while others engage in "theorizing" that makes no contact with anything substantial or practical and that also leaves pedagogy unchanged. For theory to have a marked impact, it must first take aim on the constitution of the field, and this means charting a new curriculum. A call for curricular reform will neither awe nor inspire most readers. It sounds painfully familiar and evokes memories of department meetings that began vigorously and soon drifted into bickering and prattle. But the fact remains that the English curriculum is a mess, based, it appears, on little more than unexamined tradition and mere accumulation. Whitehead's words, spoken in 1917 about the curriculum as a whole, apply to English with particular force: "The best that can be said of it is, that it is a rapid table of contents which a deity might run over in his mind while he was thinking of creating a world, and had not yet determined how to put it together."[3]

When one reads through the bound volumes of *College English, English Journal*, and *PMLA*, as well as the many books and pamphlets that treat English, liberal arts education, and the humanities, one is startled by the discontent expressed about the structure of the discipline. Critics, teachers, educators, and administrators have been arguing for many years that disorder and disarray are the trademark of English studies. The curriculum is in chaos; teachers and critics lack understanding of their goals and principles; English is prone to accept any and all fashions—these and other complaints have been expressed with astonishing frequency since at least the early 1940s. The amount (and also the fervor) of this material is extraordinary, and what follows is just a small sampling:

1. The English major in most colleges has come to consist of a conglomerate of seven or eight courses in English, some in composition, some in criticism, but most in literature. These have seldom been related to one another; they are seldom directed toward any specific end; and of late years they have come more and more to be almost entirely courses that reach no further back than 1870. . . . Our English major has usually not been topped off by anything to indicate that it is a whole discipline; the degree is awarded for so many disparate fragments.

2. In spite of numerous experiments, innovations, and revisions in the college English program, it has proved to be almost impervious to change.

3. Often . . . a particular department of English is composed not so much of a group of men and women trying to teach English as of a group of

specialists in different fields of language and literature and education who happen that particular year to be teaching in that particular department.

4. Research, as reflected in scholarly publications, gives little help in learning the dimensions of the subject-matter; winds of doctrine and whims of individuals produce an unstable, ill-proportioned body of published research hardly confined to any stated purpose (largely, perhaps, because none exists), spilling over into other branches of knowledge, and neglecting many writers and writings that are commonly included in instruction. . . . In an acknowledged discipline, there is general consistency. English is prodigal, extravagant, inconsistent internally and externally.

5. Nobody, today, questions the place of literature in the curriculum. But few can give any reasoned justification for it. To the outsider the objectives seem undefined, the methods disorganized, the content in continual flux, and the results very difficult to evaluate. In short, there is no clear public image of the teaching of English literature. Its entrenchment in the curriculum is too often based wholly on tradition. . . . So these are the things that many would like to hold together in an English curriculum: a traditional bit of meaningless nonsense, a mere skill painfully taught but seldom acquired, and a nebulously vague subject-matter with an even vaguer method.

6. Anything that anyone thinks is good for youngsters can be dumped into the course because it involves some use of language. . . . Nothing is plainer than that the English curriculum should have some kind of continuous, cumulative development. . . . If one asks, however, what is the order of this continuity and what its guiding principle, one finds the usual state: a vast curricular disorder and no clear principle.

7. The time may come when we will work as a profession to define our discipline, and one might hope that the profession will come to include all who teach literature and language, not simply members of English departments. But for now, "English" can only be what the individual departments say it is. And the painful truth is that most of us "say," by our failure to provide adequately planned programs, that English is a loose collection of any of a dozen or so subjects, available for sampling in any conceivable order, to the end of accumulating a pile of credits of a given size.

8. Are we doing anything more than gathering facts and making random comments upon them? What philosophical end do we have in mind? What truth? . . . We explicate, we analyze structures, we examine genres—but we ask no questions about a work's role in anyone's life. Our methods create the mere illusion of critical procedure, for they are harmless; they affect no one. . . . The slavish adherence to traditions which have hardened into ideological masks allows us to ignore our students' most basic questions: Why is literature a good? Why is its study required?

9. Because there is so little agreement about what literary studies is and what it should be or should not be responsible for, the subject swells and contracts with the season. . . . Professors of English thus come to see the fuzziness on the border of their subject as if it were a gateway to power. Fiercely defensive in its nationalism, the profession is just as fiercely imperialistic, and the imperialism has taken the form of an inveterate trendiness.

10. A study has a territorial base when there is an area of human knowledge within which it can pronounce with little fear of rebuttal from outside itself. . . . Alone among the academic disciplines, English does not enjoy that confidence. It is a sorry uniqueness to have to boast of.

11. Since [the] curriculum is based on no principle, save possibly the attempt to "cover" a certain number of independent units, the philosophical contradictions it embodies need never obtrude on anybody's notice.[4]

This tradition of protest and complaint about the curriculum runs deep yet has never been confronted: no one has ever asked what it means and why it persists. The truth is that we are aware that the curriculum and methods of instruction are bad, but we prefer finally to stick to these bad habits. This ensures that the denunciations of "English" will win the assent of the profession—everyone will concede that the discipline is in crisis—yet never be acted upon. To put this point more precisely: everyone answers complaints about the curriculum in the same manner, and no one has considered whether this "answer" might be the source of the problem. Many theories have appeared on the scene during the past several decades, but all have either reinforced or ignored (and thereby let stand) customary procedures and have functioned to stabilize what is in place. And what is in place, in teaching and in most research, is a canon of texts that is challenged from time to time but that still establishes the center of our work, the work of "close reading."

As the essays by Rubin, Shattuck, Vendler, and Ellis that I cited in chapter six indicate, the legacy of humanistic close reading is powerful and pervasive. If the curriculum is distorted and in disarray, then, so these critics assert, we should restore the primacy of explicating the masterpieces. Trendiness should cease, and the "great books" and fundamental "human truths" they embody should be taught once again. But these truths have never been in jeopardy, despite the wave of theory and the seeming tumult of the curriculum. This is not to suggest that there have been no advances or innovations as a result of the recent boom in literary theory, but is rather to recognize that these have not profoundly affected the shape and structure of English. We should not take the writings of a handful of theorists and their followers to mean that the discipline is now undergoing wholesale change. There have indeed been changes, but one doubts that these indicate a *general* trend, a trend that reaches beyond a relatively small group of elite institutions. Precisely because the discipline is now under such severe economic, political, and institutional pressure, its members will tend all the more to return to what is known, familiar, conventional. Many departments are struggling to survive the combination of budget cutbacks, poorly prepared students (as well as students determinedly in pursuit of jobs), and declining enrollments; these departments are not likely to risk torpedoing themselves by opting for a revised curriculum and new programs. And this is the case even though, as I have contended, what *now* exists—and has existed for many years—as the standard definition of English studies has contributed enormously to the "crisis" that departments are trying to escape.

The best example of this practice of solving the discipline's problems by reinvoking them is James Knapton's and Bertrand Evans's *Teaching a Literature-Centered English Program*. This book is twenty-five years old, is geared more to the secondary school than the college, and my emphasis on it is somewhat unfair. But the book's assumptions have not dated, and because they are announced openly, they help to illuminate the ground for many proposals—such as the movement "back to basics" or to a "core" curriculum or to "general education"—that we have been hearing about in recent years as the discipline seeks to resolve its "crisis." Knapton and Evans begin by noting the problems that afflict English and underscoring the need for remedies. Teachers are in dire need of a revolution, and they have drawn upon one technique after another in the hope of providing true meaning and value for their labors. What Knapton and Evans champion is renewed concern for "the basic justifications for teaching English," and they devote their book to reviewing the most authoritative methods for grouping texts, presenting material, teaching literature, and improving student-writing.[5]

For my purposes, the most revealing section of *Teaching a Literature-Centered English Program* occurs in the early chapters that sketch plans for the curriculum. Knapton and Evans believe that "the best thing a work of literature, or any other work of art, can do is to provide the experience of itself as a work of art" (p. 6). The task that then confronts us is "choosing first-rate works" that contain the highest forms of this aesthetic experience (p. 10). Which works of literature should we select? "We can be sure," Knapton and Evans declare,

> about Homer and Virgil, Dante, Chaucer, Cervantes, Shakespeare, Milton. Among novelists, we can be sure of Fielding, Austen, the Brontes, Dick-

ens, Thackeray, Hardy, Conrad, Hawthorne, Melville, Twain, James. In drama we can be sure of the Greeks, Shakespeare, Goldsmith, Sheridan, Ibsen, Shaw. In the short story we can be sure of the best of Hawthorne and Poe, de Maupassant, Balzac, Tolstoy, Chekhov. (P. 11)

This list includes only three women writers and no third-world or minority writers, and in this respect is typical, even today, of most statements of the literary canon. It is also typical in its cultural isolation, its choices confined to the Western, Greco-Roman classics. But Knapton's and Evans's confident tone is as significant as the particular group of writers they nominate. They feel "sure" that these writers represent a classic tradition that no one would presume to question or quarrel with. This tradition, it is clear, is one that they judge to be beyond dispute and, even more, beyond history. History has rendered its judgment on these writers, and their place is secure.

One reply to such a "reformed" curriculum is to insist on the uncertain status of at least several of Knapton's and Evans's "canonical" writers. Fielding, Thackeray, and Sheridan, for example, would receive less wholehearted endorsement from other critics than they receive here. Even Milton, as the critical history of this century demonstrates, does not enjoy the kind of privilege that is assigned to him. But Knapton and Evans trust that the names on their list encompass aesthetic greatness, and they adhere to their choices steadfastly. And this entails the exclusion of history, society, and politics, as their references to *Uncle Tom's Cabin* show. "The prodigious social and political influence of *Uncle Tom's Cabin* in its own time made it seem a great novel." "It is in fact," they conclude, "a deplorable novel, artistically worthless." Stowe's novel is a "social document" and gives readers a "social," not an artistic, experience (p. 12). It bears witness to important facts about American life before the Civil War, but it is not "art" and hence does not belong in the canonical order of texts that defines the curriculum.

Knapton and Evans dismiss *Uncle Tom's Cabin* as "artistically worthless," however, only because their standards for good art, standards that feel natural and inescapable but that are deeply contestable, exclude it. Change the standards, value the revelation of historical myth-making and ideology more, and pay less heed to allegory and symbol (the key terms for Knapton and Evans), and a different canon will constitute itself.[6] Knapton and Evans are in fact not teaching "art" as much as they are encouraging students to view art ahistorically and to embrace an extremely limited—and provincial—canon. Their intentions are admirable; they are seeking to repair the damaged state of the discipline and restore order to a chaotic field. But their arguments—and they represent what has always been the majority opinion—are guaranteed to miseducate students, devalue history, and deform the "art" both men profess to serve. The move that these critics make is one that critics, teachers, and proponents of a "new" curriculum unfailingly perform whenever they strive to bring order and common sense back to center stage. They never see the historical, social, and political blind spots in their proposals, and they never grasp that their reforms give institutional sanction to problems they hope to rectify.

As someone who appreciates "the great tradition," I find it hard to say that we ought to center our teaching on something else. But until we do, English studies will remain confused, its practitioners disenchanted and dismayed, and students restless and bemused. Even if it is the case that *Uncle Tom's Cabin* is not "art" as we are accustomed to defining it, we should not assume that this novel should therefore be excluded from the curriculum. Furthermore, the question is not whether the canonical texts are "great" (though one could quarrel in particular cases) and should be "read" with care but is whether we should base our teaching on them and go on identifying English studies with their explication. The canonical books of poems, the plays, and the novels that we now teach, a dozen or more per course, weigh down and unbalance the curriculum. Teaching a large group of nineteenth-century "canonical" novels in a semester is something we almost surely cannot do well. We mostly rush through the texts, often at breakneck speed and with only the most superficial talk about the their place in history. We are addicted to a certain way of framing courses and designing a curriculum, and are so accustomed to this procedure that we cannot conceive of alternatives or even sense just why such a procedure is flawed.

It is difficult to imagine how the discipline can function without a canon that is taught year after year; we have always understood a select group of texts to be the nucleus of English, and it is an intimidating task to explain what might serve as a substitute. Where should we begin? What kinds of courses, projects, textual groupings should we recommend and sponsor? What should be the vocabulary through which we express our aims and values?

We need first to articulate strategy and goals, what we wish to teach and have students realize. We rarely do this, since it seems to smack of bad faith or bad form, and since all of us intuitively "know" (so we tell ourselves) the ends of English studies. Our intention *should* be to teach students how to undertake and accomplish "intellectual work." This means the mastery of detail, the ability to generalize, and the aptitude for making judgments. It also means the power to structure areas of knowledge and discourse, the capacity to respect counter-traditions and counter-statements, and proficiency in interpreting "against the grain" of current thought and valuation. "Intellectual work" in-

volves productive questioning and committed thinking, a willingness
to be skeptical but not a refusal to affirm the truth of one's position.
All of us, teachers and students alike, will be experts in particular fields,
languages, and theories. But if we envision our labor as "intellectual
work," we can share something in common and not suffer the fragmentation that results when we emphasize the canon, with each person
committed to its integrity and responsible for explicating one element
of it. All of us are already doing (or at least we should be doing)
intellectual work. What I am suggesting is that we should foreground
this as our conception of ourselves—we are intellectual workers—and
as our purpose both in research and in teaching.

For guidance and inspiration, we can look to Michel Foucault, a
theorist who speaks provocatively about historical understanding and
intellectual rigor, and whose writings will help to elaborate what I mean
by "intellectual work." Foucault does not extend an exact method or
system, nor does he offer us—contrary to some of his uncritical admirers—penetrating forms of political insight. Rather, he provides us
with a vocabulary, a "language" for research and pedagogy, from which
we can learn, and which we can adapt, fine-tune, adjust. To make a
distinction that is possibly too fine: Foucault is not a model, but his
descriptions of his identity as scholar, historian, and teacher are exemplary. From him we can start to discover a means to define our
intellectual role and describe our practice in the classroom.

My endorsement of Foucault is enthusiastic but needs to be qualified.
On certain issues he is misleading and simplistic. He assigns too much
prominence to "power" and does not always allow for finer discriminations of his ideas. He so totalizes power that on occasion his work
lapses into a kind of allegorical drama that is electrifying to read but
too grandiose (and too rigid) for truly productive inquiry. In *Discipline
and Punish* and *The History of Sexuality*, Foucault tells awesome stories
of power, but stories that at times feel too neatly plotted and intent
upon closure. While these books are rewarding, they are less valuable
for me than are the interviews and lectures in *Language, Counter-Memory,
Practice* and *Power/Knowledge*. And even in these texts, Foucault must
be read, as Emerson advises us to read in his "American Scholar" essay,
"creatively," "strongly," "for the ore."[7]

In Foucault we can discover a type of research that is not founded
on single texts or on an accepted canon, but that concentrates instead
on "systems of thought" and "discursive practices." "Discursive practices," Foucault explains,

> are characterized by the delimitation of a field of objects, the definition of
> a legitimate perspective for the agent of knowledge, and the fixing of
> norms for the elaboration of concepts and theories. Thus, each discursive

practice implies a play of prescriptions that designate its exclusions and choices. . . . These sets of regularities do not coincide with individual works; even if these "regularities" are manifested through individual works or announce their presence for the first time through one of them, they are more extensive and often serve to regroup a large number of individual works.[8]

Foucault is not denying the existence of discrete texts, but is emphasizing that the single text ought not to be taken as the basic unit in historical investigation. Foucault seeks to identify the "practices" that group texts together, weave them into relationships, and enable them to be arrayed as a corpus or canon. Rather than being interested in a canon that is a stable object of knowledge, Foucault focuses on the historical process of canon-formation. He recognizes, as literary critics often do not, that ideological choices and exclusions are part of the business of building and arguing for a set of canonical works. What is excluded, Foucault asks, when a canon is formed? What norms and standards are invoked to justify it? Why are we so determined to possess a canon as the center for the discipline? Whose interests does it minister to? What does it conceal or prevent from rising into visibility?

Not only do these questions move us beyond an attachment to "individual works," but they also oblige us to cut across disciplinary boundaries. The "regularities" that we investigate do not coincide

with what we ordinarily call a science or a discipline even if their boundaries provisionally coincide on certain occasions; it is usually the case that a discursive practice assembles a number of diverse disciplines or sciences or that it crosses a certain number among them and regroups many of their individual characteristics into a new and occasionally unexpected unity. (*Language, Counter-Memory, Practice,* pp. 199-200)

The "disciplines" produce certain forms of knowledge but also block the emergence of others, Foucault suggests. To discover what has been hidden, ignored, displaced, or set aside, we need to proceed *through* the disciplines, capitalizing on them yet not restricting ourselves to the knowledge that each of them sanctions. We cannot assume that some texts "belong" to one discipline and not to others, nor can we assign to each discipline a single kind of analytical task. Foucault urges us to be more ambitious, to combine and integrate the texts and procedures that are usually confined to separate fields and departments. This coordinated endeavor must reflect a deep immersion in the facts, details, and textures of history.

"History," Foucault explains, "is the concrete body of a development, with its moments of intensity, its lapses, its extended periods of feverish agitation, its fainting spells," and it is the job of the intellectual historian to trace "history" in all its complex unfolding and interwoven density.[9] "Genealogy" is the name that Foucault assigns to the analytical work we should undertake, and he is careful to spell out what this signifies. "Genealogy"

> does not pretend to go back in time to restore an unbroken continuity that operates beyond the dispersion of forgotten things; its duty is not to demonstrate that the past actively exists in the present, that it continues secretly to animate the present, having imposed a predetermined form to all its vicissitudes. Genealogy does not resemble the evolution of a species and does not map the destiny of a people. On the contrary, to follow the complex course of descent is to maintain passing events in their proper dispersion; it is to identify the accidents, the minute deviations—or conversely, the complete reversals—the errors, the false appraisals, and the faulty calculations that gave birth to those things that continue to exist and have value for us; it is to discover that truth or being do not lie at the root of what we know and what we are, but the exteriority of accidents. (*Language, Counter-Memory, Practice*, p. 146)

What makes "genealogy" powerful is that it is not merely history, but history-as-critique-of-history. Foucault examines the history of what we know and value, and then tries to unsettle it by revealing both what it comprehends and omits. He seeks to scatter and disperse history, breaking up its unity and disturbing its complacencies. This demands a rigorous, wide-ranging, and capacious research that thrives on "relentless erudition." It is also a kind of research, as Foucault has made increasingly clear, that is tactical, sharply focused, minutely detailed. The genealogist does not labor to supplement what is already known, but overturns and disfigures the "known" through the discovery of "subjugated knowledge," "those blocks of historical knowledge which were present but disguised within the body of functionalist and systematizing theory and which criticism—which obviously draws upon scholarship—has been able to reveal."[10] Such a knowledge is "a particular, local, regional knowledge, a differential knowledge incapable of unanimity and which owes its force only to the harshness with which it is opposed by everything surrounding it. . . . It is through the reappearance of this knowledge, of these local popular knowledges, these disqualified knowledges, that criticism performs its work." The "genealogical project," Foucault concludes, "entertains"

> the claims to attention of local, discontinuous, disqualified, illegitimate knowledges against the claims of a unitary body of theory which would filter, hierarchize and order them in the name of some true knowledge and some arbitrary idea of what constitutes a science and its objects. . . .
> By comparison, then, and in contrast to the various projects which aim to inscribe knowledges in the hierarchical order of power associated with sci-

ence, a genealogy should be seen as a kind of attempt to emancipate historical knowledges from that subjection, to render them, that is, capable
of opposition and of struggle against the coercion of a theoretical, unitary,
formal and scientific discourse.[11]

"Genealogy" is *critical*, intent on liberating "subjugated knowledge"
and analyzing the "practices" that have prevented it from being addressed. What is known, powerful, and apparently secure can be "resisted"; indeed, power and resistance-to-power are inextricably linked
to each other. We are always "inside power," working within disciplines and institutions.

> But this does not entail the necessity of accepting an inescapable form of
> domination or an absolute privilege on the side of the law. To say that
> one can never be "outside" power does not mean that one is trapped and
> condemned to defeat no matter what. . . . Resistance to power does not
> have to come from elsewhere to be real, nor is it inexorably frustrated
> through being the compatriot of power. It exists all the more by being in
> the same place as power; hence, like power, resistance is multiple and
> can be integrated in global strategies.[12]

This stress on the "resistances" to power has not satisfied Foucault's
critics, however. Frank Lentricchia says that Foucault's "theory of power,
because it gives power to anyone, everywhere, at all times, provides a
means of resistance, but no real goal for resistance"; and Edward W.
Said, even more unsparingly, notes that Foucault encourages both himself and his readers "to justify political quietism with sophisticated
intellectualism."[13] These objections are telling, but it is wrong to judge
Foucault too severely. His theory of power is flawed, and his political
views are elusive; it is indeed absurd to see him as the ultimate source
of political wisdom. But we should not press this critique of Foucault
too hard, for it distracts us from the extremely useful descriptions of
intellectual work that we can then enlist in political acts of analysis. It
is important to be sensitive to the political questions that Foucault's
work raises, but also important not to condemn him for weakness and
inadequacy in one area when he is strong in others. As my quotations
are designed to show, there is in Foucault an incisive set of guidelines
for disciplinary reform that is based on historical research and teaching.
Foucault is a central figure here not for what he concludes about madness or sexuality, and not for what his oeuvre reveals about political
action or quietism, but for what he says about his methodology and
intellectual activity.

There is now a tendency in American literary theory to highlight
"politics" at all times, a practice that is necessary but that can become
lurid and unprofitable. In today's debates in the academy, if intellectual

work does not reveal an immediate political bearing and utility, then it is often damned as ignoble and unworldly. Clearly we must be "political," alert to political ends and implications, but our politics will be more effective if we devote ourselves to specific projects, historical research, cultural criticism, and purposeful teaching. I am not saying that this work must be divorced from politics—there is no escape from politics, nor should we desire one. But we should not rush to declare political points too quickly. This is what often happens in advanced academic discourse—it even enters at times into arguments as rigorous as those that Lentricchia and Said present—and it succeeds only in rendering our political vocabulary sloppy and incoherent, and in wasting energy that could have more meaningful impact elsewhere.[14] Foucault should be neither over-praised nor over-criticized. He is not the transcendent figure that certain of his admirers make him out to be, and he is not the political quietist that his critics condemn—or if he is, he is not any less relevant for the changes we require in disciplinary formulations.

"What the intellectual can do," Foucault states,

> is to provide instruments of analysis, and at present this is the historian's essential role. What's effectively needed is a ramified, penetrative perception of the present, one that makes it possible to locate lines of weakness, strong points, positions where the instances of power have secured and implanted themselves by a system of organization dating back over 150 years.[15]

Opportunities are always "there" to be seized, moments when we can take the initiative and construct a strategic knowledge. These opportunities arise when we are given the freedom to initiate a new program or reform an old one, when we see a "demand" among students for a type of course that no one else on the faculty can provide, when we are asked to make an introductory course or seminar more provocative (and hence more appealing to students). It would be foolish to underestimate the degree of opposition that one often encounters in response to new gestures. But it would also be a mistake to assume that we cannot seize an opportunity when it does offer itself; we can make an effective difference and can set an example that will in time change attitudes and assumptions. Through concrete intellectual work and theory deployed in practice, we can engage in action that will, in small but significant ways, create the beginnings of real reforms in social and communal life.

But more needs to be said. It is all well and good to cite Foucault, appeal for a new and vigorous practice, and call for innovative kinds of "intellectual work" to replace the current curriculum. But what, in more precise terms, might such a curriculum look like? What signs are there that we have the tools and techniques to set a new direction for English studies?

There are, I believe, many projects that indicate the shape that a new curriculum might take. Jane T. Tompkins and Eric J. Sundquist, for example, have done pioneering work on American literature of the nineteenth century; both are engaged in recovering lost or little-known texts—political documents, social and economic tracts, sentimental novels—that have not been studied because of the prominent place accorded to Hawthorne, Melville, and other writers of the American Renaissance. What Tompkins and Sundquist are teaching us is the constitution of a counter-tradition, the "building up" of "knowledge" that has in the past been subjugated and not allowed to emerge. One can in turn imagine the study (and teaching) of the "literary monuments" of the American Renaissance in ways that would not take the canonical status of these texts for granted, but would rather regard this as a topic for examination.

One might refer here to Malcolm Cowley's remark about *Moby Dick*:

> The principal creative work of the last three decades in this country [might not be] any novel or poem or drama of our time, not even Faulkner's Yoknapatawpha saga or Hemingway's *For Whom the Bell Tolls* or Hart Crane's *The Bridge*; perhaps it has been the critical rediscovery and reinterpretation of Melville's *Moby Dick* and its promotion, step by step, to the position of national epic.[16]

Cowley judges the elevation of Melville's text to its place as our "national epic" to be one of the major achievements of *twentieth-century* literature. What was the process that led to *Moby Dick*'s emergence into such a privileged position? What arguments were invoked to diminish other texts and spotlight Melville's? What interpretive strategies were devised in order to "discover" the richness and complexity of *Moby Dick*, and what groupings of texts did these strategies fail to illuminate? In answering these questions, one might consider a number of the influential early studies of Melville, including the chapters in D. H. Lawrence's *Studies in Classic American Literature* (1923), E. M. Forster's *Aspects of the Novel* (1927), Constance Rourke's *American Humor* (1931), Yvor Winters's *Maule's Curse* (1938), R. P. Blackmur's *The Expense of Greatness* (1940), and F. O. Matthiessen's *American Renaissance* (1941). This early work should be canvassed not in order to trace "the growth of Melville's reputation" but rather to perceive the critical terms, tactics, and values that made the growth of Melville's reputation possible. What did *Moby Dick* represent for these critics? What kinds of aesthetic value did they ascribe to the novel? What groups of texts did they dislodge in making their case for Melville's distinction? What institutional status did the novel acquire? When did it begin to appear on reading lists in colleges and universities? How was it taught? What position does it occupy in the canon today and what are the pedagogical practices now deployed upon it? Through critical reading and historical research, we can answer these questions. We will sometimes "explicate" *Moby Dick* in the customary manner, but there is no reason why this should be absolutely central in either teaching or scholarly publication.[17]

We need to return the canon to history, making texts such as *Moby Dick*, *Culture and Anarchy*, James's later novels, and Eliot's poetry into something other than objects for additional "readings." How have we come to perceive these texts as we do? What values do they embody? How did they serve the society within which they were written, and how is this history related to our own? There are many questions that we can ask about the canon that are much more fruitful than those we are asking now, and that give students far greater insight into the history of educational and critical choices. It is one thing to train discriminating, sensitive readers—who could ever be against this policy? But it is another thing altogether to exclude many non-canonical and non-literary texts from consideration, to define "reading" too narrowly, and to deny students the crucial skills—as well as the pleasures—that can be gained from the study of these texts. Viewed from this angle, the appeal to "close reading" of the canon is a refusal to consider change, a failure to acknowledge the limits of one's vision, and a barely concealed admission that the literature that seems strong and resilient is actually defenseless, in need of our constant attention and protection.

The truly rewarding scholarship written during the 1970s and 1980s relies on skills we associate with "close reading" yet neither limits itself to canonical texts nor judges its goal to be the interpretation of a single work. Here I have in mind books such as Richard Slotkin's *Regeneration through Violence: The Mythology of the American Frontier, 1600-1860* (1973), Paul Fussell's *The Great War and Modern Memory* (1975), John Seelye's *Prophetic Waters: The River in Early American Life and Literature* (1977), Elaine Showalter's *A Literature of Their Own: From Brontë to Lessing* (1977), Sandra M. Gilbert and Susan Gubar's *The Madwoman in the Attic: The Woman Writer and the Nineteenth-Century Literary Imagination* (1979), and Sacvan Bercovitch's *The American Jeremiad* (1978). What these books share is an interest in a vast range of texts—pamphlets, letters, diaries, travel narratives, and so on—that the critic "reads" in order to advance cultural and historical arguments. These writers do not provide one more "reading" of an already over-explicated text, nor do they merely put on display a new terminology. Tompkins and Sundquist, in their different ways, are following similar paths in their research, and one can only hope that their investigations signal a trend towards an ambitious and adventurous critical enterprise, one that will eventually help to reorient the shape of the curriculum as well as enrich scholarship.

Whether we are studying the canonical texts, counter-traditions, children's novels, translations of the Bible, or some other grouping, we should direct discussion towards history, society, and culture. Despite the advances in recent literary theory and exceptions to the rule I have noted, we mostly continue to focus in teaching (and in much published work) on symbol, imagery, ambiguity, contradiction, linguistic difference, verbal pattern and complexity, self-dismantling and deconstructive moments, and other "intrinsic" concerns, and persist in keying this inquiry to the single "great" text. We might much more wisely teach different texts in a different manner. In addition, we might attempt to move beyond teaching single texts altogether; at least we can try to devise a curriculum that enables us to do something besides dwell on a single literary text or author. Obviously the usual kind of concentration teaches the student valuable skills, but there are other skills, as I have insisted, that the student should acquire. Whatever its errors and over-statements, Richard Ohmann's *English in America* exemplifies, in its study of advanced placement programs, freshman composition manuals, and the "writing" produced by "futurists" and foreign-policy experts, the type of ideological critique that teachers and students ought to feel empowered to initiate. What could be more instructive than exploring the instruments and systems through which education occurs and public policy is formed?

Taking Ohmann's book as our lead, we might also greatly extend and correct his account of the growth of English studies. The disquieting truth, as James J. Murphy has stressed, is that members of English departments judge their discipline to be "a final product of some natural evolution, a sort of divine, immutable origin of the species as we now know it."[18] We understand little about the discipline's history—where, when, and how it emerged; what it specified as its object of knowledge; what it saw as its essential claims; how it defined itself in relation to other disciplines. Most members of the profession in fact resist the very notion that English studies has a "history" that can be opened up for investigation and that can enable us to situate and criticize what we now do. Such a "history" involves work in other disciplines—sociology, political science, philosophy, history—and serves as a fertile site for integrating pedagogy and research. The projects that would result from the critique of English studies would startle us—and might teach us how to go about our business more intelligently and responsibly. These same projects would also display to students how intellectual work proceeds, critical thought functions, and "co-ordinating consciousness" forms itself.

What I am seeking to envision here is a new curriculum that is forthright and confident about the wide range of intellectual work that "English" might undertake. My suggestions in this Conclusion will no doubt prove controversial and will disturb colleagues in the profession. But I offer them in the hope that English studies can finally remedy the afflictions that have been ailing it. Teachers of English will then not be fearful of commerce with the world, because they will take their entanglement in history and worldliness as the basis for their pedagogical labor.

This is the natural place for me to conclude, but I do not wish to rest my Conclusion here. I have indicated certain projects to which those in English studies might dedicate themselves—the formation of counter-traditions, the critique of literary and cultural monuments, the study of educational practices and techniques, and the historical investigation of the discipline's origins. But I feel I should close with a more detailed illustration of the historical study I am recommending as a project for research and topic for pedagogy. I cannot do full justice to this matter in this book—that is the subject for the book that follows this one. But I do want to suggest the general direction that my inquiry has taken in order that others will be able to learn from, criticize, adapt, and revise it.

This project takes as its point of departure Booker T. Washington's *Up from Slavery* (1901), one of the best known and least analyzed American autobiographies. This text serves as an "opening" into the study of black life, culture, and history from Reconstruction to the First World War, a period often treated in English studies but not from the angle of approach I advocate. Washington (1856-1915) is one of the most controversial and enigmatic figures in American history; by the turn of the century, he had reached an unparalleled position of power and prominence as spokesman for his race, friend of financiers, and adviser to presidents. But he acquired and solidified power at a high cost, as his famous speech at the Atlanta Exposition (1895) makes painfully evident. Washington encouraged blacks to make progress in the industrial trades and thereby "lift themselves up" from poverty and degradation; whether a man be black or white, his merit will always be recognized and rewarded, Washington believed. But he also believed that blacks should set aside (at least temporarily) their aspirations for social and political equality; he did not openly contest segregation or restrictions on Negro suffrage. The historical scholarship on this "Atlanta Compromise" and the "age of Washington" is extensive, and much of it is superb. Louis R. Harlan, C. Vann Woodward, August Meier, Elliott Rudwick, and others have detailed Washington's rise to power, inspected the ambiguities in his educational program, mapped the elaborate network through which he sought to control Negro and white opinion, and explored the criticisms that W. E. B. DuBois, Monroe Trotter, and other contemporary black leaders advanced. Every student of the period is indebted to this impressive body of research and will incorporate it in his writing and teaching. But my aim here is not to review or recapitulate the historical scholarship. It is instead to suggest how the person trained in literary theory and criticism can take possession of Washington's text in a distinctive way, using it as a "ground" upon which to construct his own kind of historical inquiry.

Up from Slavery exists for historians as a source of information about Washington's life, and literary critics have paid almost no attention to it. It is, admittedly, a very unpromising text for those who seek "literary" complexity and stylistic flair. *Up from Slavery* is written in a flat, prosaic style; it is rough-hewn, awkward, rambling, anecdotal, and loosely organized. For precisely these reasons, critics have not seen fit to discuss it, even though it has been reprinted numerous times, translated into dozens of languages, and very widely read. The many recent books on "autobiography" rarely refer to it, and if they refer to it at all do so only in passing. Even the more specialized studies of "black autobiography," with the exception of those by Houston Baker, Sidonie Smith, and Robert B. Stepto, omit any serious consideration of *Up from Slavery*. In a word, the book is an embarrassment, unsound and backward in its politics and banal in its attempt at art.

Compared to the American autobiographies with which we are familiar and which we write about and teach, *Up from Slavery* does seem meager and unchallenging. Unlike Whitman and Thoreau, Washington does not undertake experiments in form, and he does not display any profound inner exploration as his text unfolds. He is not, unlike Henry Adams, conscious of his competitive relation to the autobiographical writings that have preceded his own; and he does not manifest, unlike either Adams or Henry James, a high degree of self-reflective awareness about the act of telling the "story" of his life. There is no need to go further with these kinds of comparisons: our critical categories show the superiority of these other texts to Washington's. And our political categories make clear the highly problematic nature of Washington's social and educational platform. When his ideas—which are few and limited to begin with—are set against DuBois's, Wright's, or Malcolm X's, they appear narrow, dubious, even exploitative. It is hard not to shudder when Washington celebrates the education that blacks received in the "school of American slavery," brushes aside the activities of the Ku Klux Klan during Reconstruction as "unpleasant," and commends Southern whites for their responsiveness to Negro progress and prosperity.

These may seem to constitute good grounds for indicting or ignoring *Up from Slavery*, but such a view would be mistaken. It would prevent us from attending seriously to this very strange text, the fascinating man who wrote it (Washington's intimates, in awe of his power, called him "the Wizard"), and the extraordinary command he exercised over black people in America. Washington is the most important and influential black leader in our history; though Frederick Douglass, DuBois, and Malcolm X are more admirable and compelling, they never dominated their era as Washington did, never held the centralized power he possessed. As Ellison's thinly-veiled account of Tuskegee Institute in *Invisible Man* (1952) testifies, Washington not only wielded great "power" but also dramatizes in his life and career a dilemma that blacks in America have never resolved—separation from or absorption into American life? Activist opposition to racism on all fronts or strategic compromise in the hope of making greater gains in "the long run"?

One of the obvious advantages of this emphasis on Washington's *Up from Slavery* is the *range* of texts and topics that it encompasses. Again I want to stress that my aim is not to provide a "reading" of Washington's book but to use it to make connections with other texts, some of which are literary and others that are not. These texts fall into a number of groupings that the researcher can examine and that the teacher can read and discuss with students:

1. Black autobiography. *Up from Slavery* has affinities with the slave narrative, but even more striking are the ways in which it contrasts with and bears upon the autobiographies that Douglass and DuBois wrote. Here one needs to speak of a curious plurality of autobiographical ventures. Washington, Douglass, and DuBois all wrote their life-story several times. Washington's "autobiography" is not just *Up From Slavery* but also *The Story of My Life and Work* (1900), *Working with the Hands* (1904), and *My Larger Education* (1911), just as Douglass's autobiography consists of the short *Narrative of the Life of Frederick Douglass* (1845), *My Bondage and My Freedom* (1855), *The Life and Times of Frederick Douglass* (1881), and the revised edition of *The Life and Times* (1892), and just as DuBois's autobiography includes *Souls of Black Folk* (1903), *Dark-water* (1920), *Dusk of Dawn* (1940), and his posthumous *Autobiography* (1968). These texts form a rich and complicated structure and display powerful inter-textual relations, as when Washington reflects in *Up from Slavery* on Douglass's assertions of personal dignity in the face of "Jim Crow" policy, or when DuBois returns in each of his texts to his vexing encounters with his great rival, Washington. Matters become even more inter-twined when one recalls that Douglass knew Washington and spoke at a Tuskegee commencement, when one considers the many articles and reviews that DuBois wrote about Washington's program,

and when one remembers that Washington wrote one of the earliest biographies of Douglass (1906), the man he succeeded as leader of the race and whose militant rhetoric he compromised.

2. Black leadership. The first grouping of texts naturally is bound to the many letters, lectures, addresses, speeches, and essays that these black leaders produced. Much of their most forceful and self-revealing writing occurs in these occasional pieces; one thinks, for instance, of Douglass's "The Meaning of July Fourth for the Negro" (July 5, 1852); Washington's speech at the dedication of the Boston monument to Colonel Robert Gould Shaw (May 31, 1897), his "Letter to the Louisiana State Constitutional Convention" (February 19, 1898), and his "View of the Segregation Laws" (December 4, 1915); and DuBois's "Declaration of Principles" and "Resolutions" of the Niagara Movement (1905-1906). These texts and many others, as well as the abundant material included in The Booker T. Washington Papers (1972-) and The Life and Writings of Frederick Douglass (1950-1975), render the history of black struggle, leadership, and racial oppression. In Washington's case they also pose provocative questions about authority and authorship, since many of his "papers" were written or revised by secretaries and assistants. Whether they were the work of Washington himself or his aides, all of these papers personify the values of the Atlanta Compromise and the doctrines of Tuskegee, and they therefore testify to what one might describe as "institutional" authorship, the writing of a collectivity.

3. The literature of "uplift" and "self-help." This group includes a range of texts that we rarely read today but that were enormously influential during the late nineteenth and early twentieth centuries. Here I have in mind the Horatio Alger books, Andrew Carnegie's books and essays, books and speeches by Charles W. Eliot and other prominent college and university presidents, and the many scholarly and popular articles that preached the "social gospel," the "survival of the fittest," the rise of "the self-made man." All of these texts pay homage to the "American success" who lifts himself up from poverty to wealth through hard work, determination, energy, and inventiveness. This is the story that Washington translates for his black and white audiences (Harlan has characterized Washington as "the black Horatio Alger") and whose reality—and availability for all Americans—he repeatedly affirms.

This grouping also includes the many books and articles on black education that were published after the Civil War and that became especially numerous during Washington's era. How should the freedman be educated? How "educable" is he? In what ways—many white writers asked—does the education of blacks endanger the social order?

What is the relation between educational "uplift" and political and social equality? There is in particular here a formidable body of both primary and secondary materials that deal with the emergence of "industrial education" for blacks, the pioneering efforts of General Samuel C. Armstrong (the founder of Hampton Institute in 1868 and Washington's "great white father"), and the consolidation of the "Tuskegee Machine" (as DuBois bitterly described it) as the central power in dictating the course of black education.

4. The literature of white racism. At the turn of the century, there was an explosion of racist writing, much of it astonishingly brutal and vicious. These texts include Charles Carroll's *'The Negro a Beast'; or 'In The Image of God'* (1900), William P. Calhoun's *The Caucasian and the Negro in the United States* (1902), William B. Smith's *The Color-Line: A Brief in Behalf of the Unborn* (1905), and R. W. Shufeldt's *The Negro, A Menace to American Civilization* (1907).

One of the most disturbing figures in this category is Thomas Dixon (1864-1946), author of *The Leopard's Spots: A Romance of the White Man's Burden, 1865-1900* (1902), and *The Clansman: An Historical Romance of the Ku Klux Klan* (1905), both of which were best-sellers. *The Clansman* was the basis for D. W. Griffith's 1915 film "The Birth of a Nation," which was screened at the White House for President Wilson—Dixon's classmate at Johns Hopkins and friend—and which Washington at one time planned to rebut by producing a film version of *Up from Slavery*. Dixon wrote a scathing indictment of Washington's ideas on black progress for *The Saturday Evening Post* (August 19, 1905) and made plans for a book (which he never completed) on "the fall of Tuskegee."

As a basis for comparison with these aggressively racist texts, one needs also to examine the writings of moderate and liberal Southerners, including G. W. Cable's *The Negro Question* (1888), Lewis H. Blair's *A Southern Prophecy: The Prosperity of the South Dependent upon the Elevation of the Negro* (1889), Edgar Gardner Murphy's *Problems of the Present South* (1904) and *The Basis for Ascendancy* (1909), and Thomas Pearce Bailey's *Race Orthodoxy in the South* (1914). When we measure these texts against the ravings of the demagogues and racists, they obviously strike us as informed and enlightened. Yet even these writers—Murphy is a notable case in point—fall victim to racist assumptions and tone down their sympathy for the Negro with doubts about his or her capacity for real progress. In reading these texts, we need to admire the perceptions that differentiate the writers from their racist counterparts, yet must also be able to see the bias that finally conditions and shapes their proposals.

What all of these texts help us to perceive is the rhetorical feat that Washington performs in *Up from Slavery* and his other writings. In the

teeth of white racism, he managed to create and secure Tuskegee Institute and promote a policy for black education. But even as one
acknowledges Washington's achievement, one is forced to inquire whether
it occurred *because of*—as much as in spite of—the intensity of racist
ideology. What is the true nature of Washington's "compromise"? Is
this the sign of his realism (he knew the limits of what he could argue
for) or his moral cowardice (he refused to confront racism directly and
advance a case for full equality)?

5. Historical scholarship. This grouping refers not to current work
but to the so-called "anti-radical" accounts of Reconstruction that historians crafted at the turn of the century and after, and that remained
very influential until Kenneth Stampp, John Hope Franklin, and others
revised them in the 1960s. These accounts vividly portray the horrors
of Reconstruction, decrying the power (such as it was) that Congress
extended to Southern blacks and emphasizing the tragic collapse of
white rule. Of the many relevant books and essays, I will take note
here of James Ford Rhodes's *History of the United States from the Compromise of 1850 to the Final Restoration of Home Rule in the South in 1877* (7
volumes, 1893-1906), J. W. Burgess's *Reconstruction and the Constitution,
1866-1876* (1902), William A. Dunning's *Reconstruction, Political and Economic, 1865-1877* (1907), Walter L. Fleming's *The Sequel of Appomatox*
(1919), and Claude G. Bowers's *The Tragic Era* (1929). For the critic these
texts raise disturbing questions about the narratives that historians devise, and they undercut the belief in "neutral" scholarship. All lay claim
to objectivity, assemble much evidence, and set out detailed arguments,
yet all embody—*build into* their analyses—suspicions about black potential, justify the currents of reaction that overcame Reconstruction,
and function to entrench white rule.

Obviously I can only present these groupings in an abbreviated
fashion, and I have omitted others such as protest thought and black
nationalism; depictions of Negroes in popular culture; fictional works
that deal with blacks and mulattoes written by Twain, Cable, Chesnutt,
James Weldon Johnson, and others; accounts of blacks in America that
appeared in *Atlantic Monthly, North American Review,* the *Nation,* and
other influential magazines and journals. But I hope what I have said
registers the extensive field of texts and issues to which *Up from Slavery*
connects. The project I am describing clearly demands a major commitment to historical inquiry and research; some might even contend
that this project is too massive in scope, too formidable in its ever-
proliferating materials. But the inter-textual layering and density of
these writings is one of the things that the literary critic, teacher, and
student should seek to engage. The task of co-ordinating and integrating

all of this material is one of its intellectual challenges, and it is also very much open to (and benefits from) the cooperative and communal labors of students working together in the classroom and library.

I am not recommending simply that the literary critic and teacher become more "historical" in attitude and orientation. Nor am I proposing (as might be suspected) that critics should transform themselves into historians. The literary critic—and in this I follow F. R. Leavis—possesses skills that the historian does not, is able, for instance, to grasp the workings of figurative language in texts as his colleague in this other discipline cannot. In my view those of us in English studies can "read" texts—literary and non-literary—and can trace affiliations among them in ways that are distinctive, *different* from those those the historian offers. This is why I retain the idea of a specific discipline called "English studies" even though I seek to enlarge and alter it. We have much to learn from the historian's practice: the appreciation of fact and detail, the emphasis on evidence and documentation, the flexible use of source materials. But it is also true that the historian still tends to under-read the materials he gathers and does not reflect adequately on elements of "interpretation" in his arguments. It is the "interpretive" caliber of the literary critic's analysis, his capacity to elucidate texts and probe inter-textual configurations, that distinguishes him from the historian. And I say this even though I greatly respect the skills in discrimination, judgment, and generalization that George M. Frederickson, C. Vann Woodward, Louis R. Harlan, Winthrop Jordan, and others have demonstrated in their studies of white racism and the Washington era.

How should one explicate the "language" of *Up from Slavery*? What purpose is served by focusing on a text whose prose is so homely and unsophisticated? Here I might point by way of illustration to one of the key chapters of *Up from Slavery*, "The Secret of Success in Public Speaking," in which Washington comments on the "torture" he is forced to suffer when he has to "sit through a fourteen-course dinner" before delivering his speech. "I rarely take part in one of these long dinners," he explains,

> that I do not wish I could put myself back in the little cabin where I was a slave boy, and again go through the experience there—one that I shall never forget—of getting molasses to eat once a week from the "big house." Our usual diet on the plantation was corn bread and pork, but on Sunday morning my mother was permitted to bring down a little molasses from the "big house" for her three children, and when it was received how I did wish that every day was Sunday! I would get my tin plate and hold it up for the sweet morsel, but I would always shut my eyes while the molasses was being poured out into the plate, with the hope that when I opened them I would be surprised to see how much I

had got. When I opened my eyes I would tip the plate in one direction and another, so as to make the molasses spread all over it, in the full belief that there would be more of it and that it would last longer if spread out in this way. So strong are my childish impressions of those Sunday morning feasts that it would be pretty hard for any one to convince me that there is not more molasses on a plate when it occupies a little corner—if there is a corner in a plate. At any rate, I have never believed in "cornering" syrup. My share of the syrup was usually about two tablespoonfuls, and those two spoonfuls of molasses were much more enjoyable to me than is a fourteen-course dinner after which I am to speak.[19]

In one sense this passage seems very straightforward: the successful public man remembers the simple life of his youth. But Washington's plodding style and dreamy recollection of his childhood may prevent us from seeing the strangely self-degrading aspect of his statement. This is not just the successful man longing to return to his boyhood but the free black who desires to go back to slavery. His preferred state, he implies, is slavery and subjugation. The issues here, once one acknowledges them, are terribly charged, yet Washington leaves them buried in awkward, flat phrasing. How seriously does he mean what he says about the bliss of those Sunday pleasures? Is he aware of the larger implications of his "wish"? Does he grasp the significance of his emphasis on dream, delusion, and self-deception? As the paragraph closes, it dwindles into hackneyed observation ("if there is a corner in a plate"), and Washington then lumbers forward to something else in his next paragraph. He does not take explicit note of his anxieties and fears—why they are present, what they reveal about the limits of his success, how they disfigure his thought and evoke pleasing yet self-crippling dreams. Washington simply tells the story and advances onward and is, it seems, unwilling to elaborate and analyze his meanings, whatever these might truly be.

Everything we know about Washington suggests that he used language with extreme care. He knew that a single ill-considered phrase could jeopardize his entire program, and in his chapter on "public speaking" he highlights his intention to "master" his audience, "control" their response, appeal to and manage their sympathies. He is in fact so attentive to his persuasive strategies and sensitive to rhetorical effects that one cannot help but wonder what he aims to accomplish—means for us to think and believe—when he records his longing for the simple pleasures of slavery. The more intensively one reads this passage (and there are many others like it), the more one becomes keenly conscious of what Washington is *not* saying, not calling attention to or remarking upon. At the moment the reader first encounters the passage, its meaning appears obvious, unsurprising, and inoffensive if somewhat maudlin. Yet its artlessness, the more one ponders it, comes to feel perplexing. Does Washington himself seek the life of a slave boy, or does he instead seek to convey the impression to the white audience he hopes to "master" that "the Negro", even when free and prosperous, still desires to return to slavery and become a child anxious to get molasses from the "big house"? Does Washington testify here to his slavish respect for white authority, or does he, more deftly and shrewdly, want to reinforce white authority in order to capitalize more adroitly upon it? This avowedly "plain" book sometimes feels to be a protracted magic-act that uses artless language artfully, seeming to tell the truth but all the while engaging in peculiar concealments and deceptions. The "big house" to which Washington refers, and which he evokes as if it were the mansion of a Southern aristocrat, was in fact a five-room farmhouse; it had neither white columns nor even a front porch.

Up from Slavery is a text whose clear meanings quickly become ambiguous and elusive once one applies even a slight amount of interpretive pressure to them. Washington appears candid, modest, unassuming, yet he is very withholding, evasive, and unwilling to address the troubling questions that his text gestures towards. Like Washington, Douglass in *My Bondage and My Freedom* refers to the "pleasures" that the slave sometimes enjoys, but his account stresses that these are part of the brutalizing "system." "Slaveholders," he observes, "try to disgust their slaves with what they do not want them to have, or to enjoy. A slave, for instance, likes molasses; he steals some; to cure him of the taste for it, his master, in many cases, will go away to town, and buy a large quantity of the *poorest* quality, and set it before his slave, and with whip in hand, compel him to eat it, until the poor fellow is made to sicken at the very thought of molasses."[20]

I cannot state that Washington means for us to have this passage in mind as he tells us his story of the boy who hungers for molasses. But it is hard not to feel that Douglass's sentiments filter into Washington's unadorned prose. *My Bondage and My Freedom* is a text that Washington knew well and admired, and one wonders about his response to its incisive verdict on racist practice. Its critique of the slaveholding "system" underscores the unreality of Washington's dreamy fondness for the benefits passed down from the "big house." Surely Washington cannot intend simply to re-write Douglass and tell happier truths; he experienced slavery and racism, and he could not have been wholly blind to their scarring effect. Washington claims that slavery had its rewards and that its simplicities beckon to him still, and this is in certain respects what he does believe. But he is much too astute to feel that Douglass was simply "wrong" about the awful facts of slavery, and this is why I think *My Bondage and Freedom* informs, enters into, exists as an essential part of *Up from Slavery*. Washington is not so much overcoming and substituting himself for Douglass as he is incorporating him, and letting us re-collect him as a significant presence.

One knows that Washington seeks to give the impression of sincerity, plain-spoken honesty, diligence, and humility. And as his very successful career testifies, he converted whites and many blacks to his cause. But he is queerly inaccessible once one reflects for a moment on what he is saying; his plain language grows ambiguous, and his straightforward representation of himself begins to dissolve. Most of his first audiences did not perceive this canny and unfathomable quality in Washington; he counted on the willingness of whites to accept fictions, fictions of black docility, lack of interest in suffrage, loving admiration for whites, gratitude for whatever whites deigned to give the Negro. Whites believed in the language Washington offered them, whereas blacks such as DuBois and Trotter (who termed Washington "the Benedict Arnold of his race") spurned it. Neither white nor black audiences saw the ambiguities in Washington's proposals—each audience saw what it wanted to see, as Washington assumed it would. As Harlan rather eerily tells us, this openness—or is it emptiness?—in Washington, this ability to be what his audiences wished him to be, is even apparent in descriptions of his appearance. Newspaper reports of his speeches vary greatly, differing in their portrayals of Washington's height, his build, the shade of his skin-color, the tone and timbre of his voice.[21]

As my critique of this passage indicates, I believe the critic has skills that derive from his training in "English" that should be evident in his scholarship and that he should teach to students. But this is not to say that the critic will seek to make "literary" distinctions among the texts he explicates and orders. He will constantly be making judgments, forming and testing generalizations, combining and co-ordinating texts, developing their discursive patterns and arrangments. But he will not be concerned to decree that some of these texts are indeed "artistic" or "literary" in their qualities (and therefore deserving of truly serious scrutiny) whereas others are not. The purpose of studying *Up from Slavery* and the many texts that weave in, around, and through it is to disrupt and break down the barriers between literary texts and other kinds. It is to realize that texts "group" and belong together in a manner that our reverence for the traditional "canon" and "literary art" often falsifies. The project I am outlining of course depends on texts and takes a single text as its origin; but its goal is not to produce "readings" of texts or to devolve finally on a selection of texts that figure forth literary merit. At the present time we need, perhaps above all else, to articulate the continuities between "English" and the wider world, between literary expertise and social, political, and cultural analysis and understanding. As Leavis memorably states in *Education and the University*, we must foster a "co-ordinating consciousness," recognizing that the "close reading of literature" is not sufficient in itself for the intellectual work we must be able to perform, and acknowledging that "criticism" must draw upon and engage other disciplines.

In this book I seek to disseminate explication, not do away with it. We should continue to apply and teach interpretive skills, but we should acquire and sustain skills in historical research as well, and extend the field of texts that we feel equipped and empowered to consider. And when we interpret texts, we should do so not in order to uncover and affirm literary value but rather to perceive inter-textual relationships, social and political problems that the language exposes, ideological gaps it helps to uncover. It is the rigorous pursuit of these matters that will enable us to make our practice worldly, defend the discipline with renewed confidence, and at last speak "the language of resistance," a critically trained and tempered resistance to exploitation, intolerance, and oppression that we have learned to express through work in English studies.

Epilogue

Literary theorists and critics have increasingly sought to contest the distinction between literary and non-literary, canonical and non-canonical, texts. And this development, one that has intensified since I completed my manuscript, strikes me as the most important revisionary activity currently underway in English studies. Much work, as I argue in my Conclusion, remains to be done: it would be naive to underestimate the antagonism to sustained departures from the traditional goals and practices of the discipline. But it would also be a mistake to downplay or undervalue the significant research now being undertaken, research that inquires into the history of the canon and the methods devised for its analysis, that demonstrates daunting range and displays "relentless erudition," and that challenges customary interpretive procedures and norms for evaluation.

It is true, of course, that part of the reason for this "opening up" of the canon is economic or "professional" in a rather dubious sense. The publication requirements for promotion and tenure are stiff, and many scholars eagerly labor to discover little-known texts that others have not explicated many times before. But the full explanation for the innovative work that is emerging in English studies is more interesting than this crude, if partially true, account implies. Literary theory, whatever its excesses and self-indulgent sprees, has taught us to probe the taken-for-granted business of the discipline; feminist criticism has sharpened our awareness of politics and the need for "counter-traditions" in criticism and pedagogy; and the writings of Michel Foucault have led—and, as I contend in my Conclusion, should lead even more vigorously and expansively—to new forms of historical critique.

Many in English studies do continue to "resist" theory and wish that the whole thing would simply disappear, but even this is, in certain respects, a positive sign. The fact that steadfast opposition exists suggests that "opposition" is still perceived to be necessary, and indicates that the guardians of the familiar ways dare not let down their defenses. Those who resist theory on principle (and there are indeed many who do so) realize, I believe, that once they allow themselves to confront the kind and quality of the work they now perform, they will see just how fragile and ill-considered are the arguments invoked to support it. If they were truly confident about their enterprise, they would not, in my opinion, be so hesitant to describe the tenets, goals, and values that it embodies. It remains a revealing truth about many members of literature departments that they profess themselves to be politically liberal, tolerant, and open-minded; yet they are profoundly conservative in matters of academic policy and committed to scholarly and disciplinary points of view that are extraordinarily narrow. They seem suspicious of change and declare themselves "against" theory despite never having engaged it.

But as my arguments in this book make clear, I also do not think that literary theorists should assume that they are doing a wholly effective (or even an admirable) job. True, literary theory has had good effects on the profession, but it also tends to be self-congratulatory and self-absorbed, unable to focus on practical concerns and quick to commend its own intensities. We need not only to initiate new research projects and promote revisions of the canon, but to strive to make certain that these studies bear on teaching, curriculum planning, departmental organization and design. For theory to have deep and lasting influence, it has to make its way into pedagogy and administration and contest the "ground" that traditional modes and customs have occupied. If theory does not do so, it will likely either fade away before too long or—as often seems to be the case at present—grow impressively sophisticated and at the same time marginal, at the center of attention yet incapable of inaugurating changes in the daily labors of the discipline. Opposition to theory will then no longer be needed, because departmental rituals, habits, arrangements of courses, and pedagogical routines will have weakened and eroded the vital, provocative results of theoretical exploration and research.

In part the New Critics succeeded in revolutionizing English studies because their methods were teachable, but even more because they devoted themselves as much to pedagogy as to criticism and scholarship. They wrote textbooks, handbooks, and rhetorics; they secured their techniques (and stabilized their revisions of the canon) not only in monographs and professional journals but in the classroom as well. Today the situation is different: the major theorists and critics and the writers of textbooks and pedagogical materials often seem to form two distinct populations who rarely come into contact with each other. Whatever their errors and misplaced emphases, the New Critics can still teach us certain lessons, the most important of which is the need to incorporate theory and practice, criticism and pedagogy. They saw, in a word, the urgency of an *integrated* approach to the reform of English studies.

My effort to orient literary theory towards "practice"—the practice of English studies as a discipline—has certain limitations, which by now are perhaps all too obvious. Perhaps the most notable of these is that I preserve departmental structure: I focus on "English studies" and do not call for the abolition of "departments" and "disciplines" as such. This may signal a failure of vision, but I believe that it does acknowledge the facts of academic life today. We might wish that departments would dissolve or waste away; we might sometimes judge that they impede, rather than stimulate, real progress in the formation of social, cultural, and historical thought. But to call for the end of departments and disciplines is to indulge in an unreal and irrelevant gesture. Before we leap to the conclusion that we can get along without the institutional structures now in place and in force, we should first seek to remake and revitalize them. Surely this task will require as much energy and endurance as we can muster.

Notes

Preface

1. F. R. Leavis, "Reply to Martin Jarrett-Kerr," *Essays in Criticism*, 3 (July, 1953), 364-65.

2. F. R. Leavis, *For Continuity* (Cambridge, England: Minority Press, 1933), p. 161.

3. This quotation, as well as my epigraph, are taken from an interview with Michel Foucault published in *Boston Globe*, November 25, 1982, section A, p. 64.

Introduction

1. Gerald Graff, "Who Killed Criticism?" *American Scholar*, 49 (Summer, 1980), 340.

2. See Ronald Lora, "Education: Schools as Crucible in Cold War America," in *Reshaping America: Society and Institutions, 1945–1960*, ed. Robert W. Bremner and Gary W. Reichard (Columbus: Ohio State University Press, 1982), pp. 223-60; and Alan Trachtenberg, "Intellectual Background," in *Harvard Guide to Contemporary American Writing*, ed. Daniel Hoffman (Cambridge: Harvard University Press, 1979), pp. 1-50.

3. Cleanth Brooks, "The Quick and the Dead: A Comment on Humanistic Studies," in *The Humanities: An Appraisal*, ed. Julien Harris (Madison: University of Wisconsin Press, 1950), pp. 20-21. This remains Brooks's position; see "Sounding the Past: A Discussion with Cleanth Brooks," *Missouri Review*, 6 (Fall, 1982), 139-60, esp. pp. 150-52.

4. Mary Pratt, "Art without Critics and Critics without Readers, or Pantagruel versus the Incredible Hulk," in *What is Criticism?* ed. Paul Hernadi (Bloomington: Indiana University Press, 1981), p. 183.

5. Alvin B. Kernan, *The Imaginary Library: An Essay on Literature and Society* (Princeton, N.J.: Princeton University Press, 1982), pp. 96-97.

6. I take this phrase from Whitman's 1855 preface to *Leaves of Grass*.

7. Edward W. Said, "Travelling Theory," *Raritan*, 1 (Winter, 1982), 59.

8. Randolph Bourne, "The War and the Intellectuals," 1917, in *The World of Randolph Bourne*, ed. Lillian Schlissel (New York: E. P. Dutton and Co., 1965), pp. 156, 158.

9. Peter L. Berger and Thomas Luckmann, *The Social Construction of Reality: A Treatise in the Sociology of Knowledge* (1966; rpt. New York: Anchor Books, 1967), p. 117.

Chapter One

1. *Validity in Interpretation* (1967; rpt. New Haven, Conn.: Yale University Press, 1974); *The Aims of Interpretation* (Chicago: University of Chicago Press, 1976). Hereafter cited as *Validity* and *Aims*. For a helpful collection of essays on *Validity*, see "A Symposium on E. D. Hirsch's *Validity in Interpretation*," *Genre*, 1, no. 3 (1968). Recent discussions of Hirsch's work include David Hoy, *The Critical Circle: Literature, History, and Philosophical Hermeneutics* (Berkeley and Los Angeles: University of California Press, 1978), pp. 11-40;

and P. D. Juhl, *Interpretation: An Essay in the Philosophy of Literary Criticism* (Princeton, N.J.: Princeton University Press, 1980), pp. 16-44. See also Richard E. Palmer, *Hermeneutics: Interpretation Theory in Schleiermacher, Dilthey, and Gadamer* (Evanston, Ill.: Northwestern University Press, 1969); Josef Bleicher, *Contemporary Hermeneutics: Hermeneutics as Method, Philosophy, and Critique* (London: Routledge and Kegan Paul, 1980); and Michael Ermarth, "The Transformation of Hermeneutics: Nineteenth-Century Ancients and Twentieth-Century Moderns," *Monist*, 64 (April, 1981), 175-94.

The sharpest critiques of Hirsch's theory are John M. Ellis's review of *Aims*, in *Comparative Literature*, 31 (Fall, 1979), 417-20; and Frank Lentricchia's "E. D. Hirsch: The Hermeneutics of Innocence," in *After the New Criticism* (Chicago: University of Chicago Press, 1980), pp. 256-80. Lentricchia is especially good in dealing with Hirsch's misunderstandings of Heidegger, Gadamer, and Derrida.

Hirsch has also written *The Philosophy of Composition* (Chicago: University of Chicago Press, 1977). This book has been examined in detail in two essays: Wallace W. Douglas, review of *The Philosophy of Composition*, *College English*, 40 (September, 1978), 90-99; and Patricia Bizzell and Bruce Herzberg, "'Inherent' Ideology, 'Universal' History, 'Empirical' Evidence, and 'Context-Free' Writing: Some Problems in E. D. Hirsch's *The Philosophy of Composition*," *Modern Language Notes*, 95 (December, 1980), 1181-1202.

2. Stephen Toulmin, "The Construal of Reality: Criticism in Modern and Postmodern Science," *Critical Inquiry*, 9 (September, 1982), 104.

3. For discussion of this point, see Susan Suleiman, "Interpreting Ironies," a review of Wayne Booth's *Rhetoric of Irony*, *Diacritics*, 6 (1976), 15-21. For general discussion of the problem of "intention" in modern criticism, see *The Critic's Notebook*, ed. R. W. Stallman (Minneapolis: University of Minnesota Press, 1950), and *On Literary Intention: Critical Essays*, ed. David Newton-De Molina (Edinburgh: Edinburgh University Press, 1976).

4. Jacques Derrida, "Positions," 1967, trans. in the Winter, 1972, issue of *Diacritics*, pp. 35-43. A somewhat different translation of this text is given in Derrida's *Positions* (Chicago: University of Chicago Press, 1981).

5. Jacques Derrida, "Structure, Sign, and Play in the Discourse of the Human Sciences," in *The Structuralist Controversy: The Languages of Criticism and the Sciences of Man*, ed. Richard Macksey and Eugenio Donato (1970; rpt. Baltimore: Johns Hopkins University Press, 1972), pp. 247-72 (includes a "discussion" of the essay), at p. 250. This text is also available, in a different translation, in Derrida's *Writing and Difference*, 1967, trans. Alan Bass (Chicago: University of Chicago Press, 1978), pp. 278-93.

6. Jonathan Culler, *Structuralist Poetics: Structuralism, Linguistics, and the Study of Literature* (Ithaca, N.Y.: Cornell University Press, 1975), pp. 250-51. Cf. Michel Foucault, *The Discourse on Language*, 1971, trans. Rupert Sawyer (New York: Harper and Row, 1976): "We know perfectly well that we are not free to say just anything, that we cannot simply speak of anything, when we like or where we like; not just anyone, finally, may speak of just anything" (p. 216). See also Frank Kermode's two essays: "Can We Say Absolutely Anything We Like?" in *Art, Politics, and Will: Essays in Honor of Lionel Trilling*, ed. Quentin Anderson, Stephen Donadio, and Steven Marcus (New York: Basic Books, 1977), pp. 159-72; and "Institutional Control of Interpretation," *Salmagundi*, 43 (Winter, 1979), 72-86.

Chapter Two

1. "Ariachne's Broken Woof," *Georgia Review*, 31 (1977), 44-60. This essay deals primarily with Shakespeare's *Troilus and Cressida*.

2. All of these books were published by Harvard University Press. Miller has also

written *The Form of Victorian Fiction* (Notre Dame, Ind.: Notre Dame University Press, 1968), and *Thomas Hardy: Distance and Desire* (Cambridge: Harvard University Press, 1970).

3. See "The Literary Criticism of Georges Poulet," *Modern Language Notes*, 78 (1963), 471-88; and "Geneva or Paris: The Recent Work of Georges Poulet," *University of Toronto Quarterly*, 39 (1969-70), 212-28. These two essays are combined in a slightly revised form in "Georges Poulet's Criticism of Identification," in *The Quest for Imagination: Essays in Twentieth Century Aesthetic Criticism*, ed. O. B. Hardison, Jr. (Cleveland, Ohio: Press of Case Western Reserve University, 1971), pp. 191-224. My quotations will refer to this essay. See also J. Hillis Miller, "The Geneva School: The Criticism of Marcel Raymond, Albert Béguin, Georges Poulet, Jean Rossuet, Jean-Pierre Richard, and Jean Starobinski," in *Modern French Criticism: From Proust and Valéry to Structuralism*, ed. John K. Simon (Chicago: University of Chicago Press, 1972), pp. 277-310; and Miller's brief remarks on Poulet in "Hommage à Georges Poulet," *Modern Language Notes*, 97 (December, 1982), n.p.

4. "Ariadne's Thread: Repetition and the Narrative Line," *Critical Inquiry*, 3 (1976), 73.

5. "Walter Pater: A Partial Portrait," *Daedalus*, 105 (1976), 104.

6. See similiar formulations in Miller's two essays on Wallace Stevens: "Stevens' Rock and Criticism as Cure," *Georgia Review*, 30 (1976), 5-31, 330-48: "The self is a linguistic construction rather than being the given, the rock, a solid point de départ" (p. 345).

7. "Three Problems of Fictional Form: First-Person Narration in *David Copperfield* and *Huckleberry Finn*," in *Experience in the Novel: Selected Papers from the English Institute*, ed. Roy Harvey Pearce (New York: Columbia University Press, 1968), pp. 21-48.

8. "The Fiction of Realism: *Sketches by Boz, Oliver Twist*, and Cruikshank's Illustrations," in *Charles Dickens and George Cruikshank* (Los Angeles: William Andrews Clark Memorial Library, University of California, 1971), pp. 1-69.

9. "Narrative and History," *ELH*, 41 (1974), 455-73.

10. See also on this issue "Optic and Semiotic in *Middlemarch*," in *The Worlds of Victorian Fiction*, ed. J. H. Buckley (Cambridge: Harvard University Press, 1975), pp. 125-45.

11. "The Interpretation of *Lord Jim*," in *The Interpretation of Narrative: Theory and Practice*, *Harvard English Studies*, vol. 1, ed. Morton W. Bloomfield (Cambridge: Harvard University Press, 1970), pp. 211-28.

12. Miller may also be too cavalier (or else too overwrought) in some of his references to the reading process. See, for instance, his essay on *Troilus and Cressida*: the "resonances" of Shakespeare's text "reduce the reader to the same state of exasperated dialogical madness of discourse that tears Troilus in two, makes him both be and not be himself" ("Ariachne's Broken Woof," p. 58).

13. "The Antitheses of Criticism: Reflections on the Yale Colloquium," in *Velocities of Change: Critical Essays from MLN*, ed. Richard Macksey (Baltimore: Johns Hopkins University Press, 1974), p. 149.

14. "The Still Heart: Poetic Form in Wordsworth," *New Literary History*, 2 (1970-71), 299.

15. "The Critic as Host," *Critical Inquiry*, 3 (1977), 443.

16. Joseph Riddel, "A Miller's Tale," *Diacritics*, 5 (Fall, 1975), 56-65.

17. "Fiction and Repetition: *Tess of the d'Urbervilles*," in *Forms of British Fiction*, ed. Alan Warren Friedman (Austin: University of Texas Press, 1975), p. 58.

18. "Beginning with a Text," review of Edward W. Said's *Beginnings: Intention and Method*, *Diacritics*, 6 (Fall, 1976), 3.

19. Miller's work appears less "radical" when it is compared to the criticism turned out by critical mavericks such as F. R. Leavis and Yvor Winters. Their tone, manner, and attitude towards scholarship and the academic profession are far more severe than Miller's.

20. In his essay Miller reiterates the point: "Any literary text, with more or less explicitness or clarity, already misreads itself" (p. 333). He seems unaware of how much hangs on the distinction he makes and fails to comment on later in the same essay: "In fact the moment when logic fails in their work [i.e., De Man's, Bloom's, Hartman's, and Derrida's] is the moment of their deepest penetration into the actual nature of literary language, or of language as such" (p. 338).

21. Miller's recent writings include *Fiction and Repetition: Seven English Novels* (Cambridge: Harvard University Press, 1982); "On Edge: The Crossways of Contemporary Criticism," *Bulletin of the American Academy of Arts and Sciences*, 32 (January, 1979), 13-32; "The Critic as Host," in *Deconstruction and Criticism* (New York: Seabury Press, 1979), 217-53; "A 'Buchstabliches' Reading of *The Elective Affinities*," *Glyph 4: Johns Hopkins Textual Studies* (Baltimore: Johns Hopkins University Press, 1979), pp. 1-23; "*Wuthering Heights* and the Ellipses of Interpretation," *Notre Dame English Journal*, 12 (1980), 85-100; "The Figure in the Carpet," *Poetics Today*, 1 (1980), 107-18; "Theoretical and Atheoretical in Stevens," in *Wallace Stevens: A Celebration*, ed. Frank Doggett and Robert Buttel (Princeton, N.J.: Princeton University Press, 1980), 274-85; and "Dismembering and Disremembering in Nietzsche's 'On Truth and Lies in a Nonmoral Sense'," *Boundary 2*, nos. 9-10 (Spring/Fall, 1981), 41-54.

In the commentary that follows, I will focus on "Theory and Practice: Response to Vincent Leitch," *Critical Inquiry*, 6 (Summer, 1980), 609-14; "The Function of Rhetorical Study at the Present Time," *ADE Bulletin*, 62 (September-November, 1979), 10-18; "The Ethics of Reading: Vast Gaps and Parting Hours," in *American Criticism in the Post-Structuralist Age*, ed. Ira Konigsberg (Ann Arbor: University of Michigan Press, 1981), pp. 19-41; and "Interview," conducted by Robert Moynihan, *Criticism*, 24 (Spring, 1982), 99-125.

22. Robert Langbaum, "Mysteries and Meaning," *New York Times Book Review*, April 4, 1982.

Chapter Three

1. René Wellek and Austin Warren, *Theory of Literature*, 3d ed. (New York: Harcourt, Brace, and World, 1956), p. 146. See also Wellek, "The Revolt against Positivism in European Literary Scholarship," 1946, in *Concepts of Criticism*, ed. Stephen G. Nichols, Jr. (1963; rpt. New Haven, Conn.: Yale University Press, 1973): "Every theory which puts the onus on the effects in the individual mind of the reader is bound to lead to a complete anarchy of values and ultimately to barren skepticism" (p. 265).

2. Essays that deal with Fish's work include Leslie Brisman, "Critical Priorities," *Diacritics*, 4 (Summer, 1974), 24-27; Ralph Rader, "Fact, Theory, and Literary Explanation," *Critical Inquiry*, 1 (1974), 245-72; Jonathan Culler, "Stanley Fish and the Righting of the Reader," *Diacritics*, 5 (Spring, 1975), 26-31; and Edward Regis, Jr., "Literature by the Reader: The 'Affective' Theory of Stanley Fish," *College English*, 38 (1976), 263-80. Other essays that deal with Fish and reader-response criticism are included in special issues of *College English*, 36 (1975), and *Genre*, 10 (Fall, 1977).

See also John Reichert, *Making Sense of Literature* (Chicago: University of Chicago Press, 1977), pp. 80-84; Catherine Belsey, *Critical Practice* (New York: Methuen, 1980), pp. 32-34; William Ray, "Supersession and the Subject: A Reconsideration of Stanley Fish's 'Affective Stylistics'," *Diacritics*, 8 (Fall, 1978), 60-71; Frank Lentricchia, *After the New Criticism* (Chicago: University of Chicago Press, 1980), pp. 146-48; and Suresh Raval, *Metacriticism* (Athens: University of Georgia Press, 1981), pp. 123-36.

For historical background and additional bibliography, see Robert DeMaria, Jr., "The Ideal Reader: A Critical Fiction," *PMLA*, 93 (1978), 463-74, and W. Daniel Wilson, "Readers in Texts," *PMLA*, 96 (1981), 848-63. For general discussions of reader-response criticism, see Steven Mailloux, "Reading in Critical Theory," *Modern Language Notes*, 96 (1981), 1149-59; Homer Obed Brown, "Ordinary Readers, Extraordinary Texts, and Ludmilla," *Criticism*, 23 (Fall, 1981), 335-48; and William W. Stowe, "Satisfying Readers: A Review-Essay," *Texas Studies in Literature and Language*, 24 (Spring, 1982), 102-19.

Fish's theoretical essays have been collected in *Is There a Text in This Class? The Authority of Interpretive Communities* (Cambridge: Harvard University Press, 1980). I examine this book in detail in a later chapter.

3. An exception is Steven Mailloux, whose essays on "reader criticism" deal perceptively with the differences between Fish's accounts of his theory. See his "Evaluation and Reader Response Criticism: Values Implicit in Affective Stylistics," *Style*, 10 (1976), 329-43; "Stanley Fish's 'Interpreting the *Variorum*': Advance or Retreat?" *Critical Inquiry*, 3 (1976), 183-90; and "Reader-Response Criticism?" *Genre*, 10 (Fall, 1977), 413-31. See also Mailloux, *Interpretive Conventions: The Reader in the Study of American Fiction* (Ithaca, N.Y.: Cornell University Press, 1982), especially pp. 19-65. One of the best discussions of the changes in Fish's work, a discussion that situates Fish in the context of the reader-response movement as a whole, occurs in Jane P. Tompkins's introduction to *Reader-Response Criticism: From Formalism to Post-Structuralism* (Baltimore: Johns Hopkins University Press, 1980), pp. ix-xxiv.

4. "What Is Stylistics and Why Are They Saying Such Terrible Things about It?" in *Approaches to Poetics*, ed. Seymour Chatman (New York: Columbia University Press, 1973), pp. 109-52.

5. "Literature in the Reader: Affective Stylistics," *New Literary History*, 2 (1970), 123-62, at p. 146. This essay is reprinted in *Self-Consuming Artifacts: The Experience of Seventeenth-Century Literature* (Berkeley and Los Angeles: University of California Press, 1972), pp. 383-427.

6. I should add here that in "Literature in the Reader" Fish claims to be arguing against W. K. Wimsatt's and Monroe Beardsley's famous essay "The Affective Fallacy," 1949, reprinted in Wimsatt's *The Verbal Icon: Studies in the Meaning of Poetry* (1954; rpt. London: Methuen, 1970), pp. 21-39. But he is not strictly accurate when he says that he "affirms" and "embraces" (see p. 123) the very arguments they use against the reader. Wimsatt and Beardsley mostly treat emotional responses and "feelings," such as fear, mystery, or delight. Fish rarely talks about the reader's emotional response to a passage, or asks whether a text strikes the reader as "beautiful," "mysterious," and the like. His method is a rational and cognitive one that stresses the making and revising of decisions.

7. See Morton W. Bloomfield, "Stylistics and the Theory of Literature," *New Literary History*, 7 (1976), 271-311, at p. 277.

8. "Interpreting the *Variorum*," *Critical Inquiry*, 2 (Spring, 1976), 465-85.

9. "Interpreting 'Interpreting the *Variorum*'," *Critical Inquiry*, 3 (1976), 191-96, at p. 196.

10. Edward W. Said, "Opponents, Audiences, Constituencies, and Community," *Critical Inquiry*, 9 (September, 1982), 9.

11. "How to Do Things with Austin and Searle: Speech Act Theory and Literary Criticism," *Modern Language Notes*, 91 (1976), 983-1025.

12. Michel Foucault, "Nietzsche, Genealogy, History," 1971, reprinted in *Language, Counter-Memory, Practice: Selected Essays and Interviews*, ed. Donald F. Bouchard, trans. Donald F. Bouchard and Sherry Simon (Ithaca, N.Y.: Cornell University Press, 1977), pp. 139-64, at pp. 151-52.

13. Michel Foucault, "The Subject and Power," *Critical Inquiry*, 8 (Summer, 1982), 777-95.

14. Fish makes this same point in a different context in "Normal Circumstances, Literal Language, Direct Speech Acts, the Ordinary, the Everyday, the Obvious, What

Goes without Saying, and Other Special Cases," *Critical Inquiry*, 4 (Summer, 1978), 625-44, at pp. 643-44.

15. Fish is akin to Derrida in his insistence that "authority" does not dissolve simply because we have come to perceive its conventional status. But there is an important difference between these theorists. Derrida acknowledges the limits of our criticisms of authority but sees our task lying in the effort to unsettle and dislocate it. Fish, on the other hand, appears to attribute so much power to authority that, even as he exposes and criticizes established authority, he concedes the futility, even the impossibility, of truly resisting and recasting it.

Chapter Four

1. Edward W. Said, "Roads Taken and Not Taken in Contemporary Criticism," *Contemporary Literature*, 17 (Summer, 1976), 338.

2. See the Higher Education Panel Report Number 54, June, 1982, "Undergraduate Student Credit Hours in Science, Engineering, and the Humanities, Fall 1980." This is the most recent year for which figures are available.

3. I. A. Richards, *Principles of Literary Criticism*, 1925 (New York: Harcourt, Brace, and World, n.d.), p. 227.

4. I. A. Richards, *Practical Criticism: A Study of Literary Judgment*, 1929 (New York: Harcourt, Brace, and World, n.d.), p. 291.

5. I. A. Richards, "Responsibilities in the Teaching of English," 1949, in *Speculative Instruments* (Chicago: University of Chicago Press, 1955), p. 266.

6. I. A. Richards, "Interview," 1968, in *Complementarities: Uncollected Essays*, ed. John Paul Russo (Cambridge: Harvard University Press, 1976), p. 266. Good recent accounts of Richards's influence and importance include Christopher Butler, "I. A. Richards and the Fortunes of Critical Theory," *Essays in Criticism*, 30 (July, 1980), 191-204; Cyrus Hamlin, "I. A. Richards (1893-1979): Grand Master of Interpretations," *University of Toronto Quarterly*, 49 (Spring, 1980), 189-204; John Paul Russo, "I. A. Richards in Retrospect," *Critical Inquiry*, 8 (Summer, 1982), 743-60; and John Needham, *The Completest Mode: I. A. Richards and the Continuity of English Literary Criticism* (Edinburgh: Edinburgh University Press, 1982).

7. Northrop Frye, *Anatomy of Criticism: Four Essays*, 1957 (Princeton, N.J.: Princeton University Press, 1973), p. 14.

8. Ibid., p. 8. For a detailed account of Frye's career, see Robert D. Denham, *Northrop Frye and Critical Method* (University Park: Pennsylvania State University Press, 1978); and his introduction to *Northrop Frye on Culture and Literature: A Collection of Review Essays* (Chicago: University of Chicago Press, 1978).

9. Jonathan Culler, *Structuralist Poetics: Structuralism, Linguistics, and the Study of Literature* (Ithaca, N.Y.: Cornell University Press, 1975), p. vii.

10. Wallace Martin, "The Epoch of Critical Theory," *Comparative Literature*, 31 (Fall, 1979), 321, 323.

11. John Passmore, *The Philosophy of Teaching* (Cambridge: Harvard University Press, 1980), p. 215.

12. Joseph Gibaldi, in his preface to *Introduction to Scholarship in Modern Languages and Literatures* (New York: Modern Language Association of America, 1981), reports that "the present state of scholarship in modern languages and literatures" is "at once far more complex and wide-ranging and far more lacking in unity of purpose than was evident in the decades prior to 1970" (p. vi).

13. See Walter Benn Michaels and Steven Knapp, "Against Theory," *Critical Inquiry*, 8 (Summer, 1982), 723-42. "Our thesis," they conclude, is that "no one can reach a

position outside practice, that theorists should stop trying, and that the theoretical enterprise should therefore come to an end" (p. 742). Cf. Iain McGilchrist, *Against Criticism* (London: Faber and Faber, 1982): "The only genuine critical theory is that of no-theory" (pp. 13-14).

14. John Crowe Ransom, "The Cathartic Principle," in *The World's Body* (1938; rpt. Baton Rouge: Louisiana State University Press, 1968), p. 174. Cf. R. S. Crane, "History versus Criticism in the Study of Literature," 1935, in *The Idea of the Humanities and Other Essays Critical and Historical*, vol. 2 (Chicago: University of Chicago Press, 1967), pp. 3-24: "Theory, however much it may be denied or neglected, is inescapable" (p. 13). For further discussion of this point, see Elizabeth W. Bruss, *Beautiful Theories: The Spectacle of Discourse in Contemporary Criticism* (Baltimore: Johns Hopkins University Press, 1982), pp. 3-79.

15. See my "Authors and Authority in Interpretation," *Georgia Review*, 34 (1980), 617-34.

16. Roland Barthes, "The Death of the Author," 1968, in *Image, Music, Text* (New York: Hill and Wang, 1977), p. 147.

17. Jonathan Culler, *Structuralist Poetics*, p. 258.

18. Stanley Fish, "Interpreting the *Variorum*," *Critical Inquiry*, 2 (Spring, 1976), 482.

19. Stanley Fish, "Interpreting 'Interpreting the *Variorum*'," *Critical Inquiry*, 3 (Autumn, 1976), 195-96. Fish has since repudiated this position; see *Is There a Text in This Class? The Authority of Interpretive Communities* (Cambridge: Harvard University Press, 1980), p. 174.

20. M. H. Abrams, "How to Do Things with Texts," *Partisan Review*, 49 (1979), 566. See also idem, "Rationality and Imagination in Cultural History: A Reply to Wayne Booth," *Critical Inquiry*, 2 (Spring, 1976), 447-64, and "The Deconstructive Angel," *Critical Inquiry*, 3 (Spring, 1977), 425-38.

21. Norman Rabkin, *Shakespeare and the Problem of Meaning* (Chicago: University of Chicago Press, 1981), p. 1.

22. E. D. Hirsch, *The Aims of Interpretation* (Chicago: University of Chicago Press, 1976), p. 13.

23. Roland Barthes, *S/Z*, 1970, trans. Richard Miller (New York: Hill and Wang, 1974), p. 140. See Edward W. Said's summary of this tenet of structuralist thought in *Beginnings: Intention and Method* (New York: Basic Books, 1975): "In structuralism no real distance exists between language and any of its articulations, since none of the latter is under any more than token obligation to a thinking subject. There can be no tone, in Richards's sense of the word, in any statement, no sense of an individual voice that is its own final authority, since for the structuralists the whole world is contained within a gigantic set of quotation marks" (p. 338). See also Barthes, *The Pleasure of the Text*, 1973, trans. Richard Miller (New York: Hill and Wang, 1975), p. 64.

24. Richard Levin, *New Readings vs. Old Plays: Recent Trends in the Reinterpretation of English Renaissance Drama* (Chicago: University of Chicago Press, 1979), p. 207.

25. John Bayley, review of Christopher Norris's *William Empson and the Philosophy of Literary Criticism*, in *New Review*, 5 (Autumn, 1978), 51.

26. Leslie Fiedler, "Against Literature as an Institution," *Boston Review*, 7 (October, 1982), 7. See also Fiedler, *What Was Literature? Class Culture and Mass Society* (New York: Simon and Schuster, 1982).

· 27. E. D. Hirsch, "What Isn't Literature?" in *What Is Literature?* ed. Paul Hernadi (Bloomington: Indiana University Press, 1978), p. 26.

28. Alastair Fowler, "Intention Floreat," in *On Literary Intention*, ed. David Newton-De Molina (Edinburgh: Edinburgh University Press, 1976), p. 255.

29. G. S. Fraser, *Vision and Rhetoric: Studies in Modern Poetry* (London: Faber and Faber, 1959), p. 83; Lionel Trilling, "On the Teaching of Modern Literature," 1961, in *Beyond*

Culture: Essays on Literature and Learning (New York: Viking, 1965), p. 9; William Arrowsmith, "The Shame of the Graduate Schools: A Plea for a New American Scholar," *Harper's*, 232 (March, 1966), 56; O. B. Hardison, Jr., *Toward Freedom and Dignity: The Humanities and the Idea of Humanity* (Baltimore: Johns Hopkins University Press, 1972), p. 23; Stanley Fish, "What Is Stylistics and Why Are They Saying Such Terrible Things about It?" in *Approaches to Poetics*, ed. Seymour Chatman (New York: Columbia University Press, 1973), p. 152; and Christopher Norris, *Deconstruction: Theory and Practice* (New York: Methuen, 1982), p. 133.

30. See George Watson, *The Discipline of English: A Guide to Critical Theory and Practice* (New York: Barnes and Noble, 1978): "If literary subjectivism were true, then it would be doubtful if English could rightly be called a study or a 'discipline' at all. To study something can only mean to study 'some thing,' a body of knowledge yet to be acquired. If no perception in literary studies is false, then the word 'knowledge' can hardly apply to it" (p. 35).

31. My emphasis in this chapter is literary/critical, not philosophical, but I do want to note here certain of the relevant philosophical studies that have influenced my thinking on the problem of "subjectivity" and its implications for English studies. See James Brown, *Subject and Object in Modern Theology* (New York: Macmillan, 1955); Wallace Martin, "The Hermeneutic Circle and the Art of Interpretation," *Comparative Literature*, 24 (Spring, 1972), 97-117; Joseph Margolis, "Robust Relativism," *Journal of Aesthetics and Art Criticism*, 35 (Fall, 1976), 37-46; David Bleich, "The Subjective Paradigm in Science, Psychology, and Criticism," *New Literary History*, 7 (Winter, 1976), 313-34; Walter Benn Michaels, "The Interpreter's Self: Peirce on the Cartesian 'Subject'," *Georgia Review*, 31 (Summer, 1977), 383-402; Joachim Israel, "Remarks Concerning Epistemological Problems of Objectivity in the Social Sciences," *Research in Sociology of Knowledge, Sciences, and Art*, 1 (1978), 63-80; and Stephen Toulmin, "The Construal of Reality: Criticism in Modern and Postmodern Science," *Critical Inquiry*, 9 (September, 1982), 93-111. I have also profited from the many books and essays written by Toulmin, Stanley Cavell, Hilary Putnam, and Richard Rorty. Within the American philosophical tradition, key texts that address the problem of "subjectivity" are Josiah Royce, "Doubting and Working," 1881, in *Fugitive Essays* (Cambridge: Harvard University Press, 1920), pp. 322-44; William James, "The Dilemma of Determinism," 1884, in *The Will to Believe and Other Essays on Popular Philosophy* (New York: Dover Books, 1956), pp. 145-83; George Santayana, "The Intellectual Temper of the Age," in *The Winds of Doctrine* (New York: Charles Scribner's Sons, 1913), pp. 1-24; idem, *Scepticism and Animal Faith*, 1923 (New York: Dover Books, 1955); and Alfred North Whitehead, *Science and the Modern World*, 1925 (New York: New American Library, 1956), especially pp. 90-92.

32. Richard Poirier, *The Performing Self: Composition and Decomposition in the Languages of Contemporary Life* (New York: Oxford University Press, 1971), pp. 86-87.

Chapter Five

1. Lionel Trilling, "The Two Environments: Reflections on the Study of English," 1965, in *Beyond Culture: Essays on Literature and Learning* (New York: Viking Press, 1965), p. 212.

2. George Steiner, "Critic/Reader," *New Literary History*, 10 (Spring, 1979), 437.

3. Ibid. See also Steiner's similar remarks in the symposium, "Modern Literary Theory: Its Place in Teaching," *Times Literary Supplement*, February 6, 1981, p. 135.

4. See Gerald Graff, "Do It Yourself," a review of Frank Kermode's *The Classic*, *American Scholar*, 45 (Spring, 1976), 309.

5. Thomas Roche, "Recent Studies in the English Renaissance," *Studies in English Literature (SEL)*, 16 (1976), 157.

6. Thomas McFarland, "Recent Studies in the Nineteenth Century," *Studies in English Literature (SEL)*, 16 (1976), 693, 694. An essay might be written on the genre that McFarland's review article exemplifies. Cf. Stephen C. Moore, "Contemporary Criticism and the End of a Literary Revolution," *Centennial Review*, 15 (Spring, 1971), 144-61: "America has been in the last one hundred years a staggeringly prolific nation. And now, along with our output of automobiles, planes, tanks, guns, artillery shells, razor blades, cigarettes, plastics, chemicals, steel, we can claim that we lead the world in the production of literary criticism. Production seems to be nearly the exact word. . . . Attitudes towards criticism have made corrosive imbalances in our culture" (p. 147).

7. Henry James, "Criticism," 1891, excerpted in *Theory of Fiction: Henry James*, ed. James E. Miller (Lincoln: University of Nebraska Press, 1972), pp. 329, 330. Cf. a less gifted use of similar language in Francis Whiting Halsey, *Our Literary Deluge, and Some of Its Deeper Waters* (New York: Doubleday, Page, and Co., 1902).

8. See René Wellek, "The New Criticism: Pro and Contra," *Critical Inquiry*, 4 (Summer, 1978), 615; and Douglas Day, "The Background of the New Criticism," *Journal of Aesthetics and Art Criticism*, 24 (Spring, 1966), 429-40.

9. "A College Professor," "The Pedagogue in Revolt," *Atlantic Monthly*, 142 (1928), 353.

10. *Anniversary Papers: By Colleagues and Pupils of George Lyman Kittredge* (Boston: Ginn and Co., 1913).

11. W. K. Wimsatt and Cleanth Brooks make a similar point in their *Literary History: A Short History*, 1957 (New York: Random House, 1967), pp. 542-43. Cf. René Wellek, "The Revolt against Positivism in Recent European Literary Scholarship," 1946, in *Concepts of Criticism*, ed. Stephen G. Nichols, Jr. (1963; rpt. New Haven, Conn.: Yale University Press, 1973), pp. 256-81; idem, "The Fall of Literary History," in *New Perspectives in German Literary Criticism*, ed. Richard E. Amacher and Victor Lange (Princeton, N.J.: Princeton University Press, 1979), pp. 418-31; Don Cameron Allen, "The Graduate Study of Modern Literature," *Graduate Journal*, 8 (1971), 429-37, especially p. 435; and Jost Hermand and Evelyn Torton Beck, *Interpretive Synthesis: The Task of Literary Scholarship* (New York: Ungar, 1975), pp. 11-24. More generally, see William Riley Parker, "Where Do English Departments Come From?" *College English*, 28 (February, 1967), 339-51.

12. Stuart Sherman, "Professor Kittredge and the Teaching of Literature," *Nation*, September 8, 1913, in *Shaping Men and Women: Essays on Literature and Life by Stuart Sherman*, ed. Jacob Zeitlin (Garden City, N.Y.: Doubleday, Doran, and Co., 1928), pp. 81, 85-86.

13. Stuart Sherman, "Graduate Schools and Literature," 1908, in *Shaping Men and Women*, pp. 36-37. Cf. J. E. Spingarn's "The New Criticism" and other of his essays published during this period, which are collected in *Creative Criticism and Other Essays*, new and enlarged edition (New York: Harcourt, Brace, and Co., 1931).

14. Randolph Bourne, "The History of a Literary Radical," 1919, in *The World of Randolph Bourne*, ed. Lillian Schlissel (New York: E. P. Dutton and Co., 1965), p. 233.

15. Edwin Greenlaw, *The Province of Literary History* (Baltimore: Johns Hopkins University Press, 1931). Cf. André Morize, *Problems and Methods of Literary History* (Boston: Ginn and Co., 1922).

16. Albert Feuillerat, "Scholarship and Literary Criticism," *Yale Review*, 14 (1924-25), 314.

17. See Elmer Edgar Stoll, "Certain Fallacies and Irrelevancies in the Literary Scholarship of the Day," *Studies in Philology*, 24 (October, 1927), 485-508. Cf. the New Humanist Norman Foerster's important monograph, *The American Scholar: A Study in Litterae Inhumaniores* (Chapel Hill: University of North Carolina Press, 1929). For a sampling of views

and set of reforms, see *The Teaching of College English,* compiled by Oscar James Campbell, English monograph no. 3, National Council of Teachers of English, 1934, especially pp. 130-60 on "the Ph.D. degree in English."

18. René Wellek, "The New Criticism: Pro and Contra": "I remember that when I first came to study English literature in the Princeton graduate school in 1927, fifty years ago, no course in American literature, none in modern literature, and none in criticism was offered. Of all my learned teachers only Morris W. Croll had any interest in aesthetics or even ideas" (p. 614). Cf. idem, "Prospect and Retrospect," 1978, in *The Attack on Literature and Other Essays* (Chapel Hill: University of North Carolina Press, 1982), pp. 146-58. See also Douglas Bush, "Memories of Harvard's English Department," *Sewanee Review,* 89 (1981), 595-603; and Winters's account of his early years as a member of the English department at Stanford, in "Problems for the Modern Critic of Literature," *The Function of Criticism: Problems and Exercises* (Chicago: Swallow Press, 1957), pp. 11-78.

19. See Cleanth Brooks, "A Conversation," conducted with Robert Penn Warren, *The Possibilities for Order: Cleanth Brooks and His Work,* ed. Lewis Simpson (Baton Rouge: Louisiana State University Press, 1976), pp. 4-5; and idem, "I. A. Richards and *Practical Criticism,*" *Sewanee Review,* 89 (1981), 586-95.

20. John Crowe Ransom, "Strategy for English Studies," *Southern Review,* 6 (1940-41), 235. See also Ransom's "Criticism, Inc.," in *The World's Body* (1938; rpt. Baton Rouge: Louisiana State University Press, 1968), pp. 327-50.

21. *Humanism and America: Essays on the Outlook of Modern Civilization,* ed. Norman Foerster (New York: Farrar and Rinehart, 1930), and *The Critique of Humanism: A Symposium,* ed. C. Hartley Grattan (New York: Brewer and Warren, 1930).

22. See, as a representative pairing, Stuart Browne, "A Professor Quits the Communist Party," *Harper's Monthly Magazine,* 175 (July, 1937), 133-42, and anonymous, "A Professor Joins the Communist Party," *New Masses,* October 5, 1937, pp. 2-7. In *The American College and University: A History* (New York: Random House, 1962), Frederick Rudolph observes that "change and uncertainty were the order of the day" on college and university campuses during the 1930s. But he adds that these social protests were not part of a coherent national movement, and certainly did not reflect any widespread support of the Communist party (pp. 465-68).

23. Daniel Aaron, *Writers on the Left: Episodes in American Literary Communism* (New York: Harcourt, Brace, and World, 1961); James Burkhart Gilbert, *Writers and Partisans: A History of Literary Radicalism in America* (New York: John Wiley and Sons, 1968); Marcus Klein, *Foreigners: The Making of American Literature, 1900-1940* (Chicago: University of Chicago Press, 1981), pp. 39-86; Richard H. Pells, *Radical Visions and American Dreams: Culture and Social Thought in the Depression Years* (New York: Harper and Row, 1973); Milton Cantor, *The Divided Left: American Radicalism, 1900-1975* (New York: Hill and Wang, 1978); Bernard K. Johnpoll and Lillian Johnpoll, *The Impossible Dream: The Rise and Demise of the American Left* (Westport, Conn.: Greenwood Press, 1981); and Leslie Fishbein, *Rebels in Bohemia: The Radicals of the Masses, 1911-1917* (Chapel Hill: University of North Carolina Press, 1982). See also David McLellan, *Marxism after Marx: An Introduction* (New York: Harper and Row, 1979), pp. 312-31, and the discussions in William Barrett, *The Truants: Adventures among the Intellectuals* (New York: Anchor/Doubleday, 1982), pp. 76ff., and Irving Howe, *A Margin of Hope: An Intellectual Biography* (New York: Harcourt Brace Jovanovich, 1982).

I do not deal here with the relation between the Agrarian movement and the New Criticism, a subject that has been treated in great detail in recent years. See John M. Bradbury, *The Fugitives: A Critical Account* (Chapel Hill: University of North Carolina Press, 1958); John L. Stewart, *The Burden of Time: The Fugitives and the Agrarians* (Princeton, N.J.: Princeton University Press, 1965); Alexander Karanikas, *Tillers of a Myth: Southern Agrarians as Social and Literary Critics* (1966; rpt. Madison: University of Wisconsin Press,

1969); Richard Gray, *The Literature of Memory: Modern Writers of the American South* (Baltimore: Johns Hopkins University Press, 1977); Michael O'Brien, *The Idea of the American South, 1920-1941* (Baltimore: Johns Hopkins University Press, 1979); Richard H. King, *A Southern Renaissance: The Cultural Awakening of the American South, 1930-1955* (New York: Oxford University Press, 1980); Anthony Dunbar, *Against the Grain: Southern Radicals and Prophets, 1929-1959* (Charlottesville: University of Virginia Press, 1981); and Daniel Joseph Singal, *The War Within: From Victorian to Modernist Thought in the South, 1919-1945* (Chapel Hill: University of North Carolina Press, 1982).

I have profited from the following historical studies: Robert H. Wiebe, *The Search for Order, 1877-1920* (New York: Hill and Wang, 1967); George E. Mowry and Blaine A. Brownell, *The Urban Nation, 1920-1980*, rev. ed. (New York: Hill and Wang, 1981); Roderick Nash, *The Nervous Generation: American Thought, 1917-1930* (Chicago: Rand-McNally, 1970); Ernest Earnest, *The Single Vision: The Alienation of American Intellectuals* (New York: New York University Press, 1970); Henry F. May, *The End of American Innocence: A Study of the First Years of Our Own Time* (1959; rpt. Chicago: Quadrangle Books, 1964); Alfred Kazin, *On Native Grounds: An Interpretation of Modern American Prose Literature* (1942; rpt. New York: Harcourt Brace Jovanovich, 1970), especially pp. 265-311, 400-452; Frederick J. Hoffman, *The Twenties: American Writing in the Postwar Decade* (New York: Viking Press, 1955); Richard Hofstadter, *Anti-Intellectualism in American Life* (New York: Random House, 1965); Henry Steele Commager, *The American Mind: An Interpretation of American Thought and Character Since the 1880's* (New Haven, Conn.: Yale University Press, 1950); and Morton White, *Social Thought in America: The Revolt against Formalism* (Boston: Beacon Press, 1957).

At the expense of making this note even longer, I want also to cite here a number of anthologies that gather critical essays written during the first three decades or so of this century. See *A Modern Book of Criticism*, ed. Ludwig Lewisohn (New York: Modern Library, 1919); *Criticism in America: Its Function and Status* (New York: Harcourt, Brace, and Co., 1924); *Contemporary American Criticism*, ed. James Cloyd Bowman (New York: Henry Holt and Co., 1926); *American Criticism, 1926*, ed. William A. Drake (1926; rpt. Freeport, N.Y.: Books for Libraries Press, 1967); *The New Criticism: An Anthology of Modern Aesthetics and Literary Criticism*, ed. Edwin Berry Burgum (New York: Prentice Hall, 1930); *Critiques and Essays in Criticism, 1920-1948*, ed. R. W. Stallman (New York: Ronald Press, 1948); *Literary Opinion in America*, rev. ed., ed. Morton Dauwen Zabel (New York: Harper and Brothers, 1951); *American Literary Criticism, 1900-1950*, ed. Charles I. Glicksberg (New York: Hendricks House, 1952); and *Essays in Modern Literary Criticism*, ed. Ray. B. West, Jr. (New York: Rinehart and Co., 1952).

24. Kazin, *On Native Grounds*, p. 410.

25. Allen Tate, "The Present Function of Criticism," 1940, in *Collected Essays* (Denver: Alan Swallow, 1959), pp. 4, 7.

26. Tate, "Miss Emily and the Bibliographer," 1940, in *Collected Essays*, p. 57.

27. Tate, "Preface to Reactionary Essays on Poetry and Ideas," 1936, in *Collected Essays*, pp. xiv-xv. See also "The Present Function of Criticism," pp. 3-8. Cf. Ransom, "Criticism, Inc.," pp. 346-47, which describes the poem's "fictions, or inventions, by which it secures 'aesthetic distance' and removes itself from history." See also Zabel, foreword to *Literary Opinion in America*, p. v.

28. See also Tate's two essays in the *New Republic*: "A Note on Elizabethan Satire," March 15, 1933, pp. 128-30; and "Poetry and Politics," August 2, 1933, pp. 308-11.

29. I owe this point to my colleague at Wellesley College, Patrick F. Quinn.

30. Leo Spitzer, "History of Ideas versus Reading of Poetry," *Southern Review*, 6 (1940-41), 593.

31. Ibid., pp. 595-96. As Spitzer's title indicates, one of his main targets is the "history of ideas" approach that became popular during the 1930s. The leader of this movement was A. O. Lovejoy, whose *The Great Chain of Being* appeared in 1936. Other books

published during this period, books that either drew from Lovejoy or treated "ideas" in a somewhat different fashion, include J. W. Beach's *The Concept of Nature in Nineteenth Century Poetry* (1936), Hardin Craig's *The Enchanted Glass: The Elizabethan Mind in Literature* (1936), and Perry Miller's *The New England Mind* (1939). The "history of ideas" was never a candidate for primary status in the field of literary criticism. This approach required too much erudition for it to gain acceptance as a pedagogical technique; and it was not tailored to encourage discrimination and judgment in the analysis of *literary* texts.

32. John Crowe Ransom, "Criticism, Inc.," p. 335.

33. W. K. Wimsatt, "The Domain of Criticism," 1950, in *The Verbal Icon: Studies in the Meaning of Poetry* (1954; rpt. London: Methuen, 1970), p. 232; and René Wellek and Austin Warren, *Theory of Literature*, 3d ed. (New York: Harcourt, Brace, and World, 1956), p. 147. See also Wimsatt, "What to Say about a Poem," 1962, in *Hateful Contraries: Studies in Literature and Criticism* (Lexington: University of Kentucky Press, 1966), pp. 215-44, and Wimsatt, "Battering the Object," 1968, in *Day of the Leopards: Essays in Defense of Poems* (New Haven, Conn.: Yale University Press, 1976), pp. 183-204.

34. See René Wellek in "The New Criticism: Pro and Contra": "The New Criticism surely argues from a sound premise, that no coherent body of knowledge can be established unless it defines its object, which to the New Critic will be the individual work of art clearly set off from its antecedents in the mind of the author or in the social situation, as well as from its effect in society" (p. 620).

35. William Van O'Connor, "A Short View of the New Criticism," *College English*, 11 (November, 1949), 63, 64.

36. See George Core, "Agrarianism, Criticism, and the Academy," in *A Band of Prophets: The Vanderbilt Agrarians after Fifty Years*, ed. William C. Havard and Walter Sullivan (Baton Rouge: Louisiana State University Press, 1982), pp. 131-32; and John Holloway, "The New Establishment in Criticism," 1956, in *The Charted Mirror: Literary and Critical Essays* (New York: Horizon Press, 1962), pp. 204-26. For statements of the New Criticism's effect on the *teaching* of literature, see John H. Fisher, "Prospect," in *The College Teaching of English*, ed. John C. Gerber (New York: Appleton-Century-Crofts, 1965), p. 9; Charles Child Walcutt and J. Edwin Whitesell, *The Explicator Encyclopedia*, vol. 1, Modern Poetry (Chicago: Quadrangle Books, 1966), pp. ix-xviii; and Bernard Bergonzi, "Critical Situations: From the Fifties to the Seventies," *Critical Quarterly*, 15 (1973), 65-66. On the influence that the New Criticism exerted in shaping curricula and the advanced placement program, see Alan C. Purves, "Literature in the Secondary Schools," in *The Encyclopedia of Education*, vol. 6 (New York: Macmillan Co. and the Free Press, 1971), p. 18. Cf. *Freedom and Discipline in English*, by the Commission of the College Entrance Examination Board (Princeton, N.J., 1965), and Michael F. Shuegrue, "New Materials for the Teaching of English: The English Program of the USOE," *PMLA*, 81 (1966), 3-38.

Chapter Six

1. Morris Dickstein, "The State of Criticism," *Partisan Review*, 48 (1981), 11.

2. Murray Krieger, "Remarks," *Approaches to the Study of Twentieth-Century Literature*, Michigan State University, May 2-4, 1961, p. 107. See also Krieger's preface to the 1963 edition of *The New Apologists for Poetry* (Bloomington: Indiana University Press), p. vii.

3. John Crowe Ransom, "The New Criticism," *Kenyon Review*, 10 (Autumn, 1948), 682. See also Ransom's more detailed account, "Poetry I and II," *Kenyon Review*, 9 (1947), 436-56, 640-58.

4. Cleanth Brooks, foreword to *Critiques and Essays in Criticism*, 1920-1948, ed. Robert Wooster Stallman (New York: Ronald Press Co., 1949), pp. xv, xvi.

5. Austin Warren, "The Achievement of Some Recent Critics," *Poetry*, 77 (1951), 239.

As Ransom remarks in "Poets and Flatworms," *Kenyon Review*, 14 (Winter, 1952), the New Critical "innovation was real, it was momentous; but it was not complete, and now it has bogged down at a most embarrassing point" (p. 159).

6. On this point, see Richard Levin, *New Readings vs. Old Plays: Recent Trends in the Reinterpretation of English Renaissance Drama* (Chicago: University of Chicago Press, 1979), p. 1.

7. Malcolm Bradbury, "The State of Criticism Today," in *Contemporary Criticism*, ed. Malcolm Bradbury and David Palmer (London: Edward Arnold, 1970), p. 15. See also A. Walton Litz, "Literary Criticism," *The Harvard Guide to Contemporary American Writing*, ed. Daniel Hoffman (Cambridge: Harvard University Press, 1979): "At the center of this 'practical' New Criticism lay the act of explication or close reading, the detailed analysis of language and structure" (p. 53).

8. Jonathan Culler, "Beyond Interpretation," *Contemporary Literature*, 28 (1976), 244–56; my quotation is taken from the revised version of this essay included in *The Pursuit of Signs: Linguistics, Literature, and Deconstruction* (Ithaca, N.Y.: Cornell University Press, 1981), p. 5. For a detailed account of what it means to "explicate" a text in the New Critical mode, see George Arms, "Poetry," in *Contemporary Literary Scholarship: A Critical Review*, ed. Lewis Leary (New York: Appleton-Century-Crofts, 1958), 235-57. Comparisons between this New Critical style and Continental forms of "explication" are given in Edgar Lohner, "The Intrinsic Method: Some Reconsiderations," in *The Disciplines of Criticism: Essays in Literary Theory, Interpretation, and History*, ed. Peter Demetz, Thomas Greene, and Lowry Nelson, Jr. (New Haven, Conn: Yale University Press, 1968), pp. 147-72. See also W. D. Howarth and C. L. Walton, *Explications: The Technique of French Literary Appreciation* (London: Oxford University Press, 1971); and Edward Wasiolek, introduction to Serge Doubrovsky, *The New Criticism in France* (Chicago: University of Chicago Press, 1973), pp. 1-34.

9. Louis D. Rubin, Jr., "Tory Formalists, New York Intellectuals, and the New Historical Science of Criticism," *Sewanee Review*, 88 (Fall, 1980), 683.

10. Ibid. See also Cleanth Brooks, "Literary Criticism: Poet, Poem, and Reader," 1962, reprinted in *Perspectives in Contemporary Criticism*, ed. Sheldon Norman Grebstein (New York: Harper and Row, 1968). The critic considers "the structure of the poem as poem. With this kind of examination the so-called 'new criticism' is concerned. I should be happy to drop the adjective 'new' and simply say: with this kind of judgment, literary criticism is concerned" (p. 103). Cf. René Wellek, "The New Criticism: Pro and Contra," *Critical Inquiry*, 4 (Summer, 1978): "Much of what the New Criticism taught is valid and will be valid as long as people think about the nature and function of literature and poetry" (p. 611).

11. Gerald Graff, *Poetic Statement and Critical Dogma* (Evanston, Ill.: Northwestern University Press, 1970); idem, *Literature against Itself: Literary Ideas in Modern Society* (Chicago: University of Chicago Press, 1979); and Richard Strier, "The Poetics of Surrender: An Exposition and Critique of New Critical Poetics," *Critical Inquiry*, 2 (Autumn, 1975), 171-89.

12. Roger Shattuck, "How to Rescue Literature," *New York Review of Books*, April 17, 1980, p. 31.

13. In his opposition to "theories" of literature, Shattuck is more severe than the New Critics themselves. In *The World's Body* (1938; rpt. Baton Rouge: Louisiana State University Press, 1968), for example, Ransom stresses that "the reputed condition of no-theory in the critic's mind is illusory, and a dangerous thing in this occupation, which demands the utmost general intelligence, including perfect self-consciousness" (pp. 173-74).

14. Nothing is more New Critical than Shattuck's insistence that critics focus on the text and not engage in extra-literary forms of analysis. See, for instance, Ransom's contention, in "Criticism as Pure Speculation," in *The Intent of the Critic*, ed. Donald

Stauffer (Princeton, N.J.: Princeton University Press, 1941), that, "in strictness, the business of the literary critic is exclusively with an esthetic criticism" (p. 102). Cleanth Brooks makes a similar point in "The Formalist Critic," *Kenyon Review*, 13 (Winter, 1951), when he states that "the formalist critic is concerned primarily with the work itself" (p. 74). This is, of course, the informing principle of Brooks's *Modern Poetry and the Tradition* (1939; rpt. Chapel Hill: University of North Carolina Press, 1967) and *The Well-Wrought Urn: Studies in the Structure of Poetry* (New York: Harcourt, Brace, and World, 1947). And it reiterates what Brooks and Robert Penn Warren assert in the first paragraph of their "Letter to the Teacher" in *Understanding Poetry: An Anthology for College Students* (1938; rpt. New York: Henry Holt and Co., 1950): "The poem in itself, if literature is to be studied as literature, remains finally the object for study" (p. xi). For the New Critics, "a work of art is autonomous," says Robert Wooster Stallman in "The New Critics," in *Critiques and Essays*; "it is a construct having a life of its own, and it is limited by its own technique and intention. The New Critics isolate the meaning of a poem only in terms of form" (p. 503).

15. Helen Vendler, "The Presidential Address, 1980," *PMLA*, 96 (May, 1981), 344.

16. I owe this point to John L. Stewart, *The Burden of Time: The Fugitives and Agrarians* (Princeton, N.J.: Princeton University Press, 1965), pp. 188-89.

17. I am indebted for this quotation to Thomas Daniel Young, *Gentleman in a Dustcoat: A Biography of John Crowe Ransom* (Baton Rouge: Louisiana State University Press, 1976), pp. 298-99.

18. See on this point Daniel Joseph Singal, *The War Within: From Victorian to Modernist Thought in the South, 1919-1945* (Chapel Hill: University of North Carolina Press, 1982), pp. 218-19. For further discussion, see Louis D. Rubin, *The Wary Fugitives: Four Poets and the South* (Baton Rouge: Louisiana State University Press, 1978), and Thomas Daniel Young, *Waking Their Neighbors Up: The Nashville Agrarians Reconsidered* (Athens: University of Georgia Press, 1982).

19. John M. Ellis, "The Logic of the Question, 'What is Criticism?'" in *What is Criticism?* ed. Paul Hernadi (Bloomington: Indiana University Press, 1981), p. 25.

20. The reader who wishes to study the origins of the New Criticism should consult R. S. Crane's "History versus Criticism in the Study of Literature," 1935, reprinted in *The Idea of the Humanities and Other Essays Critical and Historical*, vol. 2 (Chicago: University of Chicago Press, 1967), pp. 3-24, and should then proceed to Ransom's "Criticism, Inc.," *The World's Body*, pp. 327-50. See also Ransom's "Strategy for English Studies," *Southern Review*, 6 (1940-41), 226-35, and *The New Criticism* (Norfolk, Conn.: New Directions, 1941). These should be compared with Allen Tate's "Miss Emily and the Bibliographer," 1940, and "Understanding Modern Poetry," 1940, both of which are included in *Collected Essays* (Denver: Alan Swallow, 1959), pp. 49-61, 115-28. As I note in my previous chapter, commentators on the New Criticism agree that the movement had secured power by the early to mid-1950s.

21. J. Hillis Miller, "The Critic as Host," in *Deconstruction and Criticism* (New York: Seabury Press, 1979), p. 252.

22. Edward W. Said, "Interview," *Diacritics*, 6 (Fall, 1976), 32, 35. Said amplifies this argument in "Reflections on Recent American 'Left' Literary Criticism," *Boundary 2*, no. 8 (Fall, 1979), 11-30, especially p. 13. For related critiques of deconstruction, see Henry Sussman, "The Deconstructor as Politician: Melville's *Confidence-Man*," *Glyph 4: Johns Hopkins Textual Studies* (Baltimore: Johns Hopkins University Press, 1978), pp. 32-56, especially p. 53; Rodolph Gasché, "Deconstruction as Criticism," *Glyph 6: Textual Studies* (Baltimore: Johns Hopkins University Press, 1979), pp. 177-215; and T. K. Seung, *Structuralism and Hermeneutics* (New York: Columbia University Press, 1982), especially p. 271.

23. F. R. Leavis, *The Common Pursuit*, 1952 (London: Chatto and Windus, 1972), p. 287.

24. F. R. Leavis, *Education and the University: A Sketch for an "English School"* (1943; rpt. London: Chatto and Windus, 1972). See also the updated version of Leavis's argument, "The Literary Discipline and Liberal Education," *Sewanee Review*, 55 (Autumn, 1947), 586-609.

25. William Barrett, "A Present Tendency in American Criticism," *Kenyon Review*, 11 (Winter, 1949), 3, 5; Richard Chase, "New vs. Ordealist," *Kenyon Review*, 11 (Winter, 1949), 12; Leslie Fiedler, "Toward an Amateur Criticism," *Kenyon Review*, 12 (Autumn, 1950), 564.

26. Richard Foster, *The New Romantics: A Reappraisal of the New Criticism* (Bloomington: Indiana University Press, 1962), pp. 13-14. Compare Maxwell Geismar, "Higher and Higher Criticism," 1956, in *American Moderns: From Rebellion to Conformity* (New York: Hill and Wang, 1958), pp. 28-33: "[The New Criticism] could be called a literary monopoly" (p. 28); and John Henry Raleigh, "The New Criticism as an Historical Phenomenon," *Comparative Literature*, 11 (Winter, 1959), 21-28: "The era of the New Criticism, everyone agrees, is over" (p. 21).

To be sure, one can find statements in the writings of the New Critics similar to those made by Barrett, Chase, and the others. See, for instance, Tate's "The Function of the Critical Quarterly," 1936, and "The Man of Letters in the Modern World," 1952, both of which can be found in *Collected Essays*, pp. 62-72, 379-93. But these are the exceptions that prove the rule; in general, the New Critics strive to make "English Studies" into a self-contained discipline. Criticism, for them, means the close reading of particular literary texts, and they regard other procedures, methods, and concerns as posing a danger to this basic emphasis. See Cleanth Brooks, "The Quick and the Dead: A Comment on Humanistic Studies," in *The Humanities: An Appraisal*, ed. Julien Harris (Madison: University of Wisconsin Press, 1950), pp. 1-21: "The critic's concern is finally with the poem as a poem. The critic's concern is not inimical to the historian's, but it goes beyond it, and properly so" (p. 18).

27. John Crowe Ransom, "Humanism at Chicago," 1952, reprinted in *Poems and Essays* (New York: Vintage Books, 1955), p. 101. Compare his earlier, more detailed discussion in *The World's Body*, pp. 29-54, especially pp. 44-45. See also Allen Tate's claim, in "The Present Function of Criticism," *Southern Review*, 6 (1940-41), that "the high forms of literature offer us the only complete, and thus the most responsible, versions of our experience" (p. 236).

28. In her stimulating essay, "The Reader in History: The Changing Shape of Literary Response," Jane P. Tompkins presents an argument that reaches conclusions similar to my own. This essay is included in her anthology, *Reader-Response Criticism: From Formalism to Post-Structuralism* (Baltimore: Johns Hopkins University Press, 1980), pp. 201-32.

The following passage, taken from David Hirsch's "Penelope's Web," *Sewanee Review*, 90 (Winter, 1982), might serve as a coda to my essay: "The king is dead. Long live the king! Reports that the New Criticism is dead, though they have been circulating for a long time, are nevertheless exaggerated" (p. 126).

Chapter Seven

1. Roger Sale, "Lionel Trilling," *Hudson Review*, 26 (1973-74), 241-47. The secondary literature on Trilling is extensive. The reader should consult Marianne Gilbert Barnaby, "Lionel Trilling: A Bibliography, 1926-1972," *Bulletin of Bibliography*, 31 (1974), 37-44; and Jeffrey Cane Robinson, "Lionel Trilling: A Bibliographical Essay," *Resources for American Literary Study*, 8 (Autumn, 1978), 131-56. Two book-length studies are William M. Chace, *Lionel Trilling: Criticism and Politics* (Stanford, Calif.: Stanford University Press, 1980), and Edward Joseph Shoben, *Lionel Trilling* (New York: Ungar, 1981). Of the many recent

essays and reviews, the most helpful are Tom Samet, "The Modulated Vision: Lionel Trilling's 'Larger Naturalism'," *Critical Inquiry*, 4 (Spring, 1978), 539-57; Denis Donoghue, "Trilling, Mind, and Society," *Sewanee Review*, 86 (1978), 161-86; Tom Samet, "Lionel Trilling and the Social Imagination," *Centennial Review*, 23 (Spring, 1979), 159-84; Jeffrey Cane Robinson, "Lionel Trilling and the Romantic Tradition," *Massachusetts Review*, 20 (Summer, 1979), 211-36; René Wellek, "The Literary Criticism of Lionel Trilling," *New England Review*, 2 (Autumn, 1979), 26-49; Mark Krupnick, "Lionel Trilling, Freud, and the Fifties," *Humanities in Society*, 3 (Summer, 1980), 265-81; and William Barrett, "The Authentic Lionel Trilling," *Commentary*, 73 (February, 1982), 36-47. See also *Salmagundi*, 41 (Spring, 1978), which is devoted to Trilling and includes a number of good articles about his work and career, and the discussion of Trilling in *Three Honest Men*, ed. Philip French (Manchester, England: Carcanet New Press, 1980).

2. See Lionel Trilling, *Beyond Culture: Essays on Literature and Learning* (New York: Viking Press, 1965), p. 179.

3. Lionel Trilling, *The Opposing Self: Nine Essays in Criticism* (New York: Viking Press, 1959), p. 46.

4. Ibid., pp. 17, 19ff.

1959), p. 46.

Brown, and Co., 1976).

6. Trilling, *Beyond Culture*, p. 118.

7. Trilling, *The Opposing Self*, p. 156.

8. *D. H. Lawrence: Novelist* (1955; rpt. New York: Simon and Schuster, 1969), pp. 13, 15.

9. See my essay "Lawrence's 'Purely Destructive' Art in *Women in Love*," *South Carolina Review*, Fall, 1980.

10. In addition to the Mulhern and Bilan books, see Ronald Hayman, *Leavis* (London: Heinemann, 1976); Garry Watson, *The Leavises, the "Social" and the Left* (Swansea, England: Brynmill, 1977); Edward Greenwood, *F. R. Leavis* (New York: Longman, 1978); Robert Boyers, *F. R. Leavis: Judgment and the Discipline of Thought* (Columbia: University of Missouri Press, 1978); William Walsh, *F. R. Leavis* (Bloomington: Indiana University Press, 1980); and P. J. M. Robertson, *The Leavises on Fiction: An Historic Partnership* (New York: St. Martin's Press, 1981). William Baker is now completing a two-volume bibliography for Garland Press.

For a survey of Leavis's career, see René Wellek's two essays: "The Literary Criticism of Frank Raymond Leavis," in *Literary Views: Critical and Historical Essays*, ed. Carroll Camden (Chicago: University of Chicago Press, 1964), pp. 175-93, and "The Later Leavis," *Southern Review*, 17 (July, 1981), 490-500. See also the discussion of Leavis in *Three Honest Men*, ed. Philip French, and in G. Singh, "Remembering F. R. Leavis," *World Literature Today*, 54 (Spring, 1980), 230-34. The best introduction to Leavis is still George Steiner, "F. R. Leavis," 1962, in *Language and Silence: Essays on Language, Literature, and the Inhuman* (New York: Atheneum, 1967), pp. 221-38. For an analysis of Leavis's relation to Continental criticism, see Glenn W. Most, "Principled Reading," *Diacritics*, 9 (Summer, 1979), 53-64.

11. See the symposium on *Scrutiny*, in *Essays in Criticism*, 14 (January, 1964), 1-42.

12. "T. S. Eliot as Critic," 1958, in *Anna Karenina and Other Essays* (New York: Simon and Schuster, 1969), pp. 177-96. For useful studies of the relations between Eliot's and Arnold, T. S. Eliot, and F. R. Leavis (London: Chatto and Windus, 1968); Lesley Johnson, Leavis's work, see Vincent Buckley, *Poetry and Morality: Studies on the Criticism of Matthew Arnold, T. S. Eliot, and F. R. Leavis* (London: Chatto and Windus, 1968); Lesley Johnson, *of English Literary Criticism* (Edinburgh: Edinburgh University Press, 1982); and Pamela Kegan Paul, 1979); John Needham, *The Completest Mode: I. A. Richards and the Continuity Leavis* (Atlantic Highlands, N.J.: Humanities Press, 1982).

13. Robert Garis, "Too Much in the Sun," *Hudson Review*, 21 (Winter, 1968-69), 748.

14. Wayne Booth, "Kenneth Burke's Way of Knowing," *Critical Inquiry*, 1 (September, 1974), 1.

15. Grant Webster, *The Republic of Letters: A History of Postwar American Literary Opinion* (Baltimore: Johns Hopkins University Press, 1979), p. 175.

16. Marius Bewley, *The Complex Fate: Hawthorne, Henry James, and Some Other American Writers* (London: Chatto and Windus, 1952), p. 222. For a full account and examples of criticism on Burke, see *Critical Responses to Kenneth Burke, 1924-1966*, ed. William H. Rueckert (Minneapolis: University of Minnesota Press, 1969); and Hayden White and Margaret Brose, eds., *Representing Kenneth Burke* (Baltimore: Johns Hopkins University Press, 1982). Rueckert's volume includes a bibliography of writings by and about Burke. Useful introductions to Burke's work include Stanley Edgar Hyman's *The Armed Vision: A Study in the Methods of Modern Literary Criticism* (1947; rev. ed. New York: Vintage Books, 1955), pp. 327-85, and René Wellek's "Kenneth Burke and Literary Criticism," *Sewanee Review*, 79 (Spring, 1971), 171-88. More detailed studies are George Knox's *Kenneth Burke's Categories and Critiques* (Seattle: University of Washington Press, 1957), and William H. Rueckert's *Kenneth Burke and the Drama of Human Relations* (Minneapolis: University of Minnesota Press, 1963). Both books are informative, but they are too deeply inside Burke's system to be satisfactory. Neither achieves a critical perspective on its subject. Burke himself has discussed his work and career in interviews in *Michigan Quarterly Review*, 11 (Winter, 1972), 9-27, and *Sewanee Review*, 85 (Fall, 1977), 704-18.

17. Armin Paul Frank, *Kenneth Burke* (New York: Twayne, 1969), p. 11.

18. See Timothy C. Murray, "Kenneth Burke's Logology: A Mock Logomachy," *Glyph 2: Johns Hopkins Textual Studies* (Baltimore: Johns Hopkins University Press, 1977), p. 151.

19. Merle E. Brown, *Kenneth Burke* (Minneapolis: University of Minnesota Press, 1969), p. 14.

20. Burke's own words about William Empson are apt: "Empson is still, unfortunately, inclined to self-indulgence, as he permits himself wide vagaries. But presumably that is his method—so the reader, eager to get good things where he can, will not stickle at it. He will permit Empson his latitude, particularly since it seems to be a necessary condition for his writing" (The *Philosophy of Literary Form*, p. 422).

21. Fredric Jameson, "The Symbolic Inference; or Kenneth Burke and Ideological Analysis," *Critical Inquiry*, 4 (Spring, 1978), 509.

22. Benjamin DeMott, "The Little Red Discount House," *Hudson Review*, 15 (1962-63), 551-64; reprinted in *Critical Responses to Kenneth Burke*, p. 362. In his *Philosophy*, Burke refers on several occasions to a forthcoming monograph on Coleridge. This publication has never appeared, and Burke's inability or unwillingness to integrate his thoughts about that difficult poet has kept him from having much effect on Coleridge studies. In the important books by J. R. de J. Jackson (1969), Owen Barfield (1971), Paul Magnuson (1974), Lawrence S. Lockridge (1977), Katherine Cook (1979), and Edward Kessler (1979), he is not even cited. An exception to the rule is Reeve Parker's *Coleridge's Meditative Art* (Ithaca, N.Y.: Cornell University Press, 1975), where Burke is praised as "a critic of signal importance for the understanding of Coleridge" (p. 79).

23. See Russell Fraser, "R. P. Blackmur and Henry Adams," *Southern Review*, 17 (January, 1981), 69-96. Cf. Fraser's biography, *A Mingled Yarn: The Life of R. P. Blackmur* (New York: Harcourt Brace Jovanovich, 1981); and Denis Donoghue's review, "In Search of the Sublime," *Times Literary Supplement*, October 22, 1982, pp. 1147-48. The reader should consult Gerald Pannick's "R. P. Blackmur: A Bibliography," *Bulletin of Bibliography*, 31 (October-November, 1974), 165-69, which is useful but incomplete and inaccurate in places. Helpful discussions of Blackmur's criticism include: Stanley Edgar Hyman, *The Armed Vision: A Study in the Methods of Modern Literary Criticism* (1947; rev. ed. New York: Vintage Books, 1955), pp. 197-236; Richard Foster, *The New Romantics: A Reappraisal of the*

New Criticism (Bloomington: Indiana University Press, 1962), pp. 83-106; Joseph Frank, "R. P. Blackmur: The Later Phase," 1963, reprinted in *The Widening Gyre: Crisis and Mastery in Modern Literature* (Bloomington: Indiana University Press, 1968), pp. 229-51; René Wellek, "R. P. Blackmur Re-Examined," *Southern Review*, 7 (July, 1971), 825-45; and Grant Webster, *The Republic of Letters*, pp. 149-61.

24. Russell Fraser, "R. P. Blackmur: The Politics of a New Critic," *Sewanee Review*, 87 (Fall, 1979), 564.

25. See *American Issues*, vol. 2, ed. Willard Thorp, Merle Curti, and Carlos Baker (Chicago: J. B. Lippincott Co., 1941), p. 869.

26. B. L. Reid, "The View From the Side," *Sewanee Review*, 88 (Spring, 1980), 229.

27. William Dusinberre, *Henry Adams: The Myth of Failure* (Charlottesville: University of Virginia Press, 1980).

28. *The Education of Henry Adams*, edited with an introduction and notes by Ernest Samuels (Boston: Houghton-Mifflin Co., 1973), p. 66.

29. Ibid., pp. 288-89.

30. Tony Tanner, "Henry James and Henry Adams," *TriQuarterly*, 11 (Winter, 1968), 99.

31. See Quentin Anderson's complaint, in *The Imperial Self: An Essay in American Literary and Cultural History* (1971; rpt. New York: Vintage Books, 1972), that Blackmur is too often "where no critic ought to be, between the writer's pen and his page, or at least acting as a passionate acolyte at the altar, watching the consummation of the sacred mystery" (p. 195). See also Foster, *The New Romantics*, pp. 176-81.

32. R. P. Blackmur, "The Chain of Our Own Needles: Criticism and Our Culture," in *Modern Literary Criticism, 1900-1970*, ed. Lawrence L. Lipking and A. Walton Litz (New York: Atheneum, 1972), pp. 345-51.

33. Laurence B. Holland, "A Grammar of Assent," *Sewanee Review*, 88 (Spring, 1980), 260; A. Walton Litz, in *Modern Literary Criticism, 1900-1970*, p. 256; and Russell Fraser, "The Politics of a New Critic," p. 566.

34. R. P. Blackmur, *The New Criticism in the United States* (1959; rpt. The Folcroft Press, 1970), p. 1.

35. Both essays are included in *The Lion and the Honeycomb: Essays in Solicitude and Critique* (New York: Harcourt, Brace, and Co., 1955), pp. 176-98, 199-212. See also *The New Criticism in the United States*, pp. 1-16.

36. Robert Boyers, *R. P. Blackmur: Poet-Critic, Toward a View of Poetic Objects* (Columbia: University of Missouri Press, 1980).

37. Ibid., pp. 7-8.

38. Geoffrey Hartman, *Criticism in the Wilderness: The Study of Literature Today* (New Haven, Conn.: Yale University Press, 1980), p. 176.

39. Edward W. Said, "Interview," *Diacritics*, 6 (Fall, 1976), 32.

Chapter Eight

1. R. P. Blackmur, *The Lion and the Honeycomb: Essays in Solicitude and Critique* (New York: Harcourt, Brace, and Co., 1955), p. 178.

2. A. Bartlett Giamatti, "On Behalf of the Humanities," *Profession 79*, Modern Language Association, 1979, p. 14; Peter Shaw, "Degenerate Criticism," *Harper's*, October, 1979, p. 99; and Leonard Kriegel, "The New Schooling of America," *Nation*, October 6, 1979, p. 309.

In *Explanation and Power: The Control of Human Behavior* (New York: Seabury Press, 1979), Morse Peckham looks at these problems differently and comes up with a novel remedy. "In the academic world," he explains, much of the verbal behavior of the faculty is devoted to inflaming each other's resentments against the administration, or against "society" for not providing them with what they judge to be appropriate economic rewards, or for not giving them sufficient respect for their superior culture and intellect—and all this in spite of the fact that higher education faculties form one of the most pampered groups in the country. That this interferes with faculty competence is, from my observations, irrefutable, if only in the amount of useful time such behavior wastes. Consequently, happiness and competence in the academic world depend principally on avoiding one's colleagues. (P. 204)

3. Patricia Meyer Spacks, review of *English in America*, in the *Yearbook of English Studies*, 8 (1978), 202. Other reviews include C. L. Barber, "Is There Hope for English?" *New York Review of Books*, May 27, 1976, pp. 29-32; Steven Marcus, "A Syllabus for Radicals," *Times Literary Supplement*, August 27, 1976, pp. 1042-43; William Kerrigan, "English in the Death House," *Virginia Quarterly Review*, 53 (Winter, 1977), 179-92. See also Gerald Graff, *Literature against Itself: Literary Ideas in Modern Society* (Chicago: University of Chicago Press, 1979), pp. 103-27.

4. For an overview of Kermode's career, see Jonathan Arac, "History and Mystery: On Frank Kermode," *Salmagundi*, 55 (Winter, 1982), 135-55.

5. See, for example, Warwick Gould, "A Misreading of Harold Bloom," *English*, 26 (1977), 40-54.

6. Roger Sale notes the decline of Trilling's reputation in the 1960s and early 1970s in "Lionel Trilling," *Hudson Review*, 26 (1973-74), 241-47. See note one to chapter seven herein for books and essays that deal with Trilling.

7. See the listings in note eighteen to chapter seven herein.

8. As Philip Rahv notes in *Literature and the Sixth Sense* (Boston: Houghton-Mifflin, 1970), Leavis increasingly tends "to circumscribe the literary medium by setting up preconceived and obligatory values for it" (p. 299).

9. See the cogent statement of this point by Maria Ruegg, "The End(s) of French Style: Structuralism and Post-Structuralism in the American Context," *Criticism*, 21 (1979), 216. Cf. Evan Watkins, "Conflict and Consensus in the History of Recent Criticism," *New Literary History*, 12 (Winter, 1981), 345-65.

10. A. J. A. Waldock, *Paradise Lost and Its Critics* (Cambridge: Cambridge University Press, 1947), p. 24.

11. Stanley Fish, *Surprised by Sin: The Reader in Paradise Lost* (New York: St. Martin's Press, 1967), p. 207.

12. Stanley Fish, "Literature in the Reader: Affective Stylistics," *New Literary History*, 2 (1970), 123-62.

13. Lawrence Hyman, *The Quarrel Within: Art and Morality in Milton's Poetry* (Port Washington, N.Y.: Kennikat Press, 1972).

14. Joseph Wittreich, "The New Milton Criticism," *Review*, 1 (1979), 123-64. For discussions of the current state of scholarship in Renaissance literature, see Gary F. Waller, "Author, Text, Reading, Ideology: Towards a Revisionist Literary History of the Renaissance," *Dalhousie Review*, 61 (1981), 405-25; idem, "Acts of Reading: The Production of Meaning in *Astrophil and Stella*," *Studies in the Literary Imagination*, 15 (1982), 23-35; and Jonathan Goldberg, "The Politics of Renaissance Literature: A Review Essay," *English Literary History*, 49 (Summer, 1982), 514-42.

15. A. S. P. Woodhouse, "The Historical Criticism of Milton," *PMLA*, 66 (1951), 1033.

16. Harold Bloom, *A Map of Misreading* (New York: Oxford University Press, 1975), p. 125.

17. Northrop Frye, "Agon and Logos: Revolution and Revelation," in *The Prison and the Pinnacle* (Toronto: University of Toronto Press, 1973), pp. 157-58.

298 NOTES TO PAGES 189–213

18. Barbara Lewalski, "Innocence and Experience in Milton's Eden," in *New Essays on Paradise Lost*, ed. Thomas Kranidas (Berkeley and Los Angeles: University of California Press, 1969), pp. 86-117; and Boyd Berry, *Process of Speech: Puritan Religious Writing and Paradise Lost* (Baltimore: Johns Hopkins University Press, 1976), pp. 242-67.

19. For discussions of Hartman's work, see Gerald Graff, review of *Criticism in the Wilderness*, in *New Republic*, November 1, 1980, pp. 34-37; Denis Donoghue, "Reading about Writing," *New York Times Book Review*, November 9, 1980, pp. 11, 32-33; Michael Sprinker, "Hermeneutic Hesitation: The Stuttering Text," *Boundary 2*, no. 9 (Fall, 1980), 217-32; and Daniel Hughes, "Geoffrey Hartman, Geoffrey Hartman," *Modern Language Notes*, 96 (December, 1981), 1134-48. See also the interview with Hartman, conducted by Robert Moynihan, *Boundary 2*, no. 9 (Fall, 1980), 191-215.

For studies of Fish, see the listings in note two to chapter three herein. See also R. P. Bilan, "We Interpreters," *University of Toronto Quarterly*, 51 (Fall, 1981), 102-12.

20. See Edward W. Said, "The Text, the World, the Critic," in *Textual Strategies: Perspectives in Post-Structuralist Criticism*, ed. Josué V. Harari (Ithaca, N.Y.: Cornell University Press, 1979), pp. 161-88.

21. Richard Ohmann, *English in America: A Radical View of the Profession* (New York: Oxford University Press, 1976), p. 335; and Fredric Jameson, *The Political Unconscious: Narrative as a Socially Symbolic Act* (Ithaca, N.Y.: Cornell University Press, 1981), p. 17. See also my listings for Said, note one to chapter nine herein.

See also Michael Ryan, *Marxism and Deconstruction: A Critical Articulation* (Baltimore: Johns Hopkins University Press, 1982); Gayatri Chakravorty Spivak and Michael Ryan, "Anarchism Revisited: A New Philosophy," *Diacritics*, 8 (Summer, 1978), 66-79; Michael Ryan, "Self-Evidence," *Diacritics*, 10 (Summer, 1980), 2-16; Gayatri Chakravorty Spivak, "Revolutions That As Yet Have No Model: Derrida's *Limited Inc.*," *Diacritics*, 10 (Winter, 1980), 29-49; and idem, "Reading the World: Literary Studies in the 1980's," *College English*, 43 (November, 1981), 671-79. See also the special issues of *Contemporary Literature*, 22 (Fall, 1981); *Humanities in Society*, 4 (Fall, 1981); *Critical Inquiry*, 9 (September, 1982); *Diacritics*, 12 (Fall, 1982); and *Social Text*, 2 (Spring, 1982).

For discussions of Bennett's work, see Graham Pechey, "Formalism and Marxism," *Oxford Literary Review*, 4 (1980), 72-81; and Anne Reilly and Prospero Saiz, "Volosinov, Bennett, and the Politics of Writing," *Contemporary Literature*, 22 (Fall, 1981), 510-42.

22. See Gerald Graff, "Politics, Language, Deconstruction, Lies, and the Reflexive Fallacy: A Rejoinder to W. J. T. Mitchell," *Salmagundi*, 47-48 (Winter-Spring, 1980), 78-94, and idem, "Textual Leftism," *Partisan Review*, 49 (1982), 558-75.

23. Michel Foucault, "The History of Sexuality," 1977, in *Power/Knowledge: Selected Interviews and Other Writings, 1972-1977*, ed. Colin Gordon (New York: Pantheon Books, 1980), p. 189.

Chapter Nine

1. See "An Ethics of Language," *Diacritics*, 4 (Summer, 1974), 28-37; *Beginnings: Intention and Method* (New York: Basic Books, 1975), chapter five; and "The Problem of Textuality: Two Exemplary Positions," *Critical Inquiry*, 4 (1978), 673-714. Said's most recent analysis of Foucault occurs in "Travelling Theory," *Raritan*, 1 (Winter, 1982), 41-67, especially pp. 60-67. See also his important studies of the politics of interpretation: "Roads Taken and Not Taken in Contemporary Criticism," *Contemporary Literature*, 17 (1976), 326-48; "Reflections on Recent American 'Left' Criticism," *Boundary 2*, no. 8 (Fall, 1979), 11-30; and "Opponents, Audiences, Constituencies, and Community," *Critical Inquiry*, 9 (September, 1982), 1-26. See also the interview with Said in the Fall, 1976, issue of *Diacritics*, and his further discussion of Orientalism, "Raymond Schwab and the Romance of Ideas," *Daedalus*, Winter, 1976, pp. 151-67.

Orientalism has been widely reviewed. One of the most detailed reviews is James Clifford's piece in *History and Theory*, 2 (1980), 204-23. The book has also been severely criticized by members of the "Orientalist" establishment. See, for example, Bernard Lewis, "The Question of Orientalism," *New York Review of Books*, June 24, 1982, pp. 49-56; see also the exchange between Said and Lewis in the August 12th issue, pp. 44-48. Cf. also Fabiola Jara and Edmundo Magana, "Rules of Imperialist Method," *Dialectical Anthropology*, 7 (November, 1982), 115-36.

2. Eugene Goodheart, *The Failure of Criticism* (Cambridge: Harvard University Press, 1978), p. 8.

3. Graff's other essays on these issues include: "Yvor Winters of Stanford," *American Scholar*, 44 (1975), 291-98; "Do It Yourself" (a review of Frank Kermode's *The Classic*), *American Scholar*, 45 (1976), 306-10; "Fear and Trembling at Yale," *American Scholar*, 46 (1977), 467-78; a review of Frank Kermode's *The Genesis of Secrecy*, in *New Republic*, June 9, 1979, pp. 27-32; "New Criticism Once More," *Critical Inquiry*, 5 (1979), 569-75; "Deconstruction as Dogma, or, 'Come Back to the Raft Ag'in Strether Honey'," *Georgia Review*, 34 (1980), 404-21; "Politics, Language, Deconstruction, Lies, and the Reflexive Fallacy: A Rejoinder to W. J. T. Mitchell," *Salmagundi*, 47-48 (Winter-Spring, 1980), 78-94; and "Textual Leftism," *Partisan Review*, 49 (1982), 558-75.

For discussions of Graff's work, see Michael Fischer, "Defending the Humanities," *Georgia Review*, 33 (Summer, 1979), 433-37; Daniel T. O'Hara, "'The Freedom of the Master'," *Contemporary Literature*, 21 (Autumn, 1980), 648-61; Christopher Norris, "Wrestling with Deconstructors," *Critical Quarterly*, 22 (Summer, 1980), 57-62; Michael Sprinker, "Criticism as Reaction," *Diacritics*, 10 (Fall, 1980), 2-14; Donald Marshall, "Truth or Consequences," *Diacritics*, 10 (Winter, 1980), 75-85; John Fekete, "On Interpretation," *Telos*, 48 (Summer, 1981), 3-25; Rudolph Gasché, "Unscrambling Positions: On Gerald Graff's Critique of Deconstruction," *Modern Language Notes*, 96 (December, 1981), 1015-34; Jane P. Tompkins, "Graff against Himself," *Modern Language Notes*, 96 (December, 1981), 1091-96; and Thomas De Pietro, "The Socialist Imagination: Gerald Graff's Defense of Reason," *Centennial Review*, 26 (Fall, 1982), 375-87.

4. For a fuller statement of this position, see Frank Kermode, "Can We Say Absolutely Anything We Like?" in *Art, Politics, and Will: Essays in Honor of Lionel Trilling*, ed. Quentin Anderson, Stephen Donadio, and Steven Marcus (New York: Basic Books, 1977), pp. 159-72; idem, "Institutional Control of Interpretation," *Salmagundi*, 43 (1979), 72-87; Stanley Fish, *Is There a Text in This Class? The Authority of Interpretive Communities* (Cambridge: Harvard University Press, 1980); Michel Foucault, *Power/Knowledge: Selected Interviews and Other Writings, 1972-1977*, ed. Colin Gordon (New York: Pantheon Books, 1980); and Jonathan Culler, *Structuralist Poetics: Structuralism, Linguistics, and the Study of Literature* (Ithaca, N.Y.: Cornell University Press, 1975).

5. For detailed critiques of Lentricchia, see Gregory S. Jay, "Going after New Critics: Literature, History, Deconstruction," *New Orleans Review*, 8 (Fall, 1981), 251-64; and Andrew Parker, "'Taking Sides' (On History): Derrida Re-Marx," *Diacritics*, 11 (Fall, 1981), 57-73.

6. On Girard and Freud, see Sarah Kofman, "The Narcissistic Woman," *Diacritics*, 10 (Fall, 1980), 36-45. See also the special issue of *Diacritics* (Spring, 1978) devoted to Girard, and Eric Gans, "Scandal to the Jews, Folly to the Pagans," *Diacritics*, 9 (Fall, 1979), 43-53. For further discussion of Girard, see the several review essays in *Modern Language Notes*, 93 (December, 1978), 1007-26, and the special issue of *Esprit*, "Sur René Girard," April, 1979.

7. For a suggestive account of White's view of history, see Fredric Jameson, "Figural Relativism, or, The Poetics of Historiography," *Diacritics*, 6 (Spring, 1976), 2-9; and David Carroll, "On Tropology: The Forms of History," *Diacritics*, 6 (Fall, 1976), 58-64. For additional treatment of White's work, see *History and Theory*, Bieheft #19, "Metahistory:

Six Critiques"; and Dominick LaCapra, review of *Tropics of Discourse*, in *Modern Language Notes*, 93 (December, 1978), 1037-43.

8. Hayden White, "Ethnological 'Lie' and Mythical 'Truth'," *Diacritics*, 8 (Spring, 1978),

9. Both White's and Girard's books are important examples of "interdisciplinary" studies. For discussion of this trend, see Michael W. Messmer, "The Vogue of the Interdisciplinary," *Centennial Review*, 22 (Fall, 1978), 467-78. Cf. Ray Holland, *Self and Social Context* (New York: St. Martin's Press, 1977), especially pp. 16-19, 258-88; Michel Grimaud, "Delusion and Dream in Literary Semiotics," *Semiotica*, 38, nos. 1-2 (1982), 177-90, and idem, "Frameworks for a Science of Texts: The Compleat Semiotician," *Semiotica*, 38, nos. 3-4 (1982), 193-241.

10. John Fraser, "Leavis, Winters, and 'Tradition'," *Southern Review*, 7 (1971), 967.

10. For a lengthy treatment of Hassan's work, see Hayden White, "Fiery Numbers and Strange Productions: A Cento of Thoughts on Ihab Hassan," *Diacritics*, 10 (Winter, 1980), 50-59.

11. William Empson, "There Is No Penance Due to Innocence," review of John Carey's *John Donne: A Life*, in *New York Review of Books*, December 3, 1981, p. 42.

12. Other recent books on deconstruction include Michael Ryan, *Marxism and Deconstruction: A Critical Articulation* (Baltimore: Johns Hopkins University Press, 1982); Jonathan Culler, *On Deconstruction: Theory and Criticism after Structuralism* (Ithaca, N.Y.: Cornell University Press, 1982); and Vincent B. Leitch, *Deconstructive Criticism: An Advanced Introduction* (New York: Columbia University Press, 1982).

13. See, for example, Richard Poirier, "Writing Off the Self," *Raritan*, 1 (Summer, 1981), 106-33; Margery Sabin, "The Life of English Idiom, The Laws of French Cliché," part one, *Raritan*, 1 (Fall, 1981), 54-72, and part two, *Raritan*, 1 (Winter, 1982), 70-89.

14. Terry Eagleton, *Walter Benjamin, or towards a Revolutionary Criticism* (New York: Schocken Books, 1981), p. 139.

15. T. S. Eliot, *The Sacred Wood: Essays on Poetry and Criticism*, (1920; London: Methuen, 1972), p. 11.

Conclusion

1. Fredric Jameson, "Interview," *Diacritics*, 12 (Fall, 1982), 72-73.

2. Tony Davies, "Common Sense and Critical Practice: Teaching Literature," in *Re-Reading English*, ed. Peter Widdowson (London: Methuen, 1982), p. 34.

3. A. N. Whitehead, "The Aims of Education," 1917, in *The Aims of Education and Other Essays* (London: Williams and Norgate, Ltd., 1932), pp. 10-11.

4. William Clyde DeVane, "The English Major," *College English*, 3 (October, 1941), 49; Roy P. Basler, "The College English Program," *College English*, 7 (March, 1946), 345; Thomas Clark Pollock, "Should the English Major Be a Cafeteria?" *College English*, 15 (March, 1954), 328; William Randel, "English as a Discipline," *College English*, 19 (April, 1958), 360; H. A. Gleason, Jr., "What Is English?" *College Composition and Communication*, 13 (1962), 3; Herbert J. Muller, *The Uses of English* (New York: Holt, Rinehart, and Winston, 1967), pp. 4, 18, 39; Wayne Booth, "The Undergraduate Program," in *The College Teaching of English*, ed. John C. Gerber (New York: Appleton-Century-Crofts, 1965), pp. 200-201; Louis Kampf, "The Scandal of Literary Scholarship," in *The Dissenting Academy*, ed. Theodore Rozak (New York: Pantheon, 1968), pp. 52-53, 55; Richard Poirier, "A Case of Mistaken Identity: Literature and the Humanities," *Partisan Review*, 41 (1974), 527, 529-30; George Watson, "Literary Research: Thoughts for an Agenda," *Times Literary Supplement*, February 25, 1977, pp. 213-14; and Gerald Graff, "Who Killed Criticism?" *American Scholar*, 49 (Summer, 1980), 343-44.

The complaints are evident before the 1940s. Indeed, as I noted in chapters four and five, complaint and protest seem ingrained in the discipline. But from my own survey, I conclude that these feelings intensified during the 1940s, largely, I suspect, because the New Criticism was rising to power and prominence during this period. The New Critics engineered reforms that many valued but that many others detested and fought against.

5. James Knapton and Bertrand Evans, *Teaching a Literature-Centered English Program* (New York: Random House, 1967), p. vii.

6. See Jane T. Tompkins, "Sentimental Power: *Uncle Tom's Cabin* and the Politics of Literary History," *Glyph 8: Textual Studies* (Baltimore: Johns Hopkins University Press, 1981), pp. 79-102; and Eric J. Sundquist, "From Revolution to Renaissance: The Question of Slavery," forthcoming. Cf. Leslie A. Fiedler, *The Inadvertent Epic: From "Uncle Tom's Cabin" to "Roots"* (New York: Simon and Schuster, 1979).

7. Foucault's own words about Nietzsche are apt: "I am tired of people studying him only to produce the same kind of commentaries that are written on Hegel or Mallarmé. For myself, I prefer to utilize the writers I like. The only valid tribute to thought such as Nietzsche's is precisely to use it, to deform it, to make it groan and protest. And if commentators then say that I am being faithful or unfaithful to Nietzsche, that is of absolutely no interest." See *Power/Knowledge: Selected Interviews and Other Writings, 1972-1977*, ed. Colin Gordon (New York: Pantheon Books, 1980), pp. 53-54.

8. Michel Foucault, *Language, Counter-Memory, Practice: Selected Essays and Interviews*, ed. Donald F. Bouchard, trans. Donald F. Bouchard and Sherry Simon (Ithaca, N.Y.: Cornell University Press, 1977), pp. 199-200.

9. Ibid., p. 145.

10. Foucault, *Power/Knowledge*, p. 82.

11. Ibid., pp. 83, 85.

12. Ibid, pp. 141, 142. For more detailed accounts of "power" and "resistance," see *The History of Sexuality*, 1976, trans. Robert Hurley (New York: Pantheon Books, 1978), pp. 92-97; and "The Subject and Power," *Critical Inquiry*, 8 (Summer, 1982), 777-95, especially pp. 791-95.

13. Frank Lentricchia, "Reading Foucault," part two, *Raritan*, 2 (Summer, 1982), 51; and Edward W. Said, "Travelling Theory," *Raritan*, 1 (Winter, 1982), 64.

14. See Jameson, "Interview," p. 75.

15. Foucault, *Power/Knowledge*, p. 62.

16. Malcolm Cowley, *The Literary Situation* (New York: Viking, 1954), pp. 14-15.

17. As evidence for the insecure place of *Moby Dick* in the "canon" as it stood as late as the 1930s, see Robert G. Berkelman, "*Moby Dick:* Curiosity or Classic?" *English Journal*, 27 (1938), 742-55. Cf. Leslie Fiedler's comments on the novel in *An End to Innocence* (Boston: Beacon Press, 1955): "There is a Melville whom one scarcely knows whether to call the discovery or invention of our time, our truest contemporary, who has revealed to us the traditional theme of the deepest American mind, the ambiguity of innocence, 'the mystery of iniquity', which we had traded for the progressive melodrama of a good outcast (artist, rebel, whore, proletarian) against an evil bourgeoisie" (p. 197).

18. James. J. Murphy, "Rhetorical History as a Guide to the Salvation of American Reading and Writing: A Plea for Curricular Courage," in *The Rhetorical Tradition and Modern Writing*, ed. James J. Murphy (New York: MLA Publications, 1982).

19. *Up from Slavery*, 1901, In *The Booker T. Washington Papers*, vol. 1, ed. Louis R. Harlan (Urbana: University of Illinois Press, 1972), p. 345.

20. Frederick Douglass, *My Bondage and My Freedom*, 1855 (New York: Dover Press, 1969), p. 256.

21. Louis R. Harlan, *Booker T. Washington: The Making of a Black Leader, 1856-1901* (New York: Oxford University Press, 1975), p. 233.

Index

Abrams, M. H., 35, 38–39, 40, 42, 46–47, 49, 74–75, 196, 197, 208, 218, 229
Adams, Henry, 90, 146–58, 234, 240, 265
Aeschylus, 209
Alger, Horatio, 267
Althusser, Louis, 176, 201
Armstrong, Samuel C., 268
Arnold, Matthew, 24, 126, 127, 138, 151, 168, 169, 237
Ashbery, John, 168
Auden, W. H., 138, 173, 229
Austen, Jane, 171, 235
Author: in Barthes's criticism, 73, 75–76; in Belsey's criticism, 201–2; in Fish's criticism, 57–58; in Miller's criticism, 35–37; in Said's criticism, 213–15

Babbitt, Irving, 88, 95
Baker, Houston, 265
Balfour, Arthur James, 210
Barrès, Maurice, 211
Barthes, Roland, xii, 73, 128, 176, 182, 201, 216, 219, 220, 221, 223, 230, 237–38, 240
Bataille, Georges, 228
Bayley, John, 77, 80
Beardsley, Monroe, 73, 82
Béguin, Albert, 34
Belsey, Catherine, 200–202, 206
Benjamin, Walter, 42, 161, 189, 237–38, 241
Bennett, Tony, 202–5, 206
Bercovitch, Sacvan, 262
Berger, Peter L., 11
Berry, Boyd, 186
Bersani, Leo, 128, 170
Bewley, Marius, 136
Bilan, R. P., 135–39
Blackmur, R. P., xiii, 2, 83, 94, 104, 121, 164, 190–91, 234, 237–38, 261; literary criticism of, 146–58; and the academy, 159–61
Blake, William, 138, 188

Bleich, David, 51
Bloom, Harold, xiv, 33, 45, 63, 167, 168–69, 174, 181, 184, 190, 221, 231, 239
Bloomfield, Morton W., 56
Booth, Wayne, 42, 46, 139, 218, 228, 229–32, 235. See also Pluralism
Bourne, Randolph, 1, 8, 10, 92, 94, 95, 101
Bové, Paul, 222
Boyers, Robert, 125–29, 157–58
Bradbury, Malcolm, 106
Brooks, Cleanth, xvii, 2, 70, 72, 85, 94, 95, 98, 100, 101, 105, 113, 115, 142, 143, 156, 234; on the role of the humanities, 4–6. See also Close reading; New Criticism
Brown, Merle E., 140
Brown, Norman O., 171
Burke, Kenneth, 94, 121, 161–62, 190, 195, 229, 230, 235; literary criticism of, 139–46
Burton, Richard, 211
Bush, Douglas, 94, 188

Camus, Albert, 224, 227
Canon, in literature and criticism, xvii, 24, 43–44, 48, 174, 252–56, 275
Carlyle, Thomas, 169, 189
Carnegie, Andrew, 267
Chaucer, Geoffrey, 45
Close reading, xi–xii, xviii, 2, 49, 72, 102, 105–6, 169. See also Brooks, Cleanth; New Criticism
Coleridge, Samuel Taylor, 143–44, 184
Conrad, Joseph, 37, 137
Cowley, Malcolm, 4, 142, 261
Crane, R. S., 72, 100, 228, 229, 230, 235
Creative style, in criticism, xiv, 244. See also Hartman, Geoffrey
Critical consciousness, 9–10
Croce, Benedetto, 226
Cromer, Lord, 210
Crosman, Robert, 178–80

About the author

William E. Cain is associate professor of English at Wellesley College.
He has edited *Literature and Philosophy: New Essays on Nineteenth- and
Twentieth-Century Texts* and is general editor of the Garland Press
Bibliography Series on Modern Critics and Critical Schools.